Carl Rogers' Person-Centered Approach

Toward an understanding of
its implications

John K. Wood

PCCS BOOKS
Ross-on-Wye

First published in 2008

PCCS Books Ltd
2 Cropper Row
Alton Rd
Ross-on-Wye
Herefordshire
HR9 5LA
UK
Tel +44 (0)1989 763 900
www.pccs-books.co.uk

© John Keith Wood, 2008

All rights reserved.
No part of this publication may be reproduced, stored in a retrieval system, transmitted or utilized in any form by any means, electronic, mechanical, photocopying or recording or otherwise without permission in writing from the publishers.
The authors have asserted their rights to be identified as the authors of this work in accordance with the Copyright, Designs and Patents Act 1988.

**Carl Rogers' Person-Centered Approach
Toward an understanding of its implications**

A CIP catalogue record for this book is available from the British Library

ISBN 978 1 906254 05 6

Cover image by John K. Wood and Lucila Machado Assumpçao
Cover design by Old Dog Graphics
Printed by Cpod, Trowbridge, UK

CONTENTS

i
Abstracts

iii
Forewords
Maureen O'Hara

Brian Thorne

Vera Engler Cury

Jaime Roy Doxsey, Lucila Machado Assumpção,
Márcia Alves Tassinari and Raquel Wrona

13
Chapter One
Approaching the Approach
An introduction

22
Chapter Two
The Person-Centered Approach to Psychotherapy
The principles of client-centered therapy

35
Chapter Three
The Person-Centered Approach to Small Groups
More than psychotherapy

68
Chapter Four
**Applying the Person-Centered Approach vs.
Applying the Principles of Client-Centered Therapy**

79
Chapter Five
**An Example of the Pitfalls in 'Giving People an Experience of
the Person-Centered Approach' instead of Applying the Approach**

90
Chapter Six
The Person-Centered Approach to Large Group Workshops
Communities for learning

141
Chapter Seven
A Rehearsal for Understanding the Phenomenon of Group

157
Chapter Eight
Learning about Learning
The person-centered approach applied to education

169
Chapter Nine
Effect of Group

196
Chapter Ten
On Becoming a Culture

223
Chapter Eleven
What's Wrong with the Psychology of Client-Centered Therapy

255
Chapter Twelve
Toward a Psychology for Applications of the Person-Centered Approach

261
References

275
Index

Abstracts

Chapter One   Approaching the Approach: An introduction
Rogers always had an *approach*: a *stance*, a set of attitudes and intentions, *a way of being* for his work. Around 1940, his approach to psychotherapy began to congeal. For some thirty years, he referred to it as the client-centered approach. For the last 30 years or so, he called it the person-centered approach. Its most elucidated application to date is client-centered therapy. This first chapter discusses, 'What is the person-centered approach?' The difference between 'client-centered therapy' and 'the person-centered approach' is also clarified.

Chapter Two   The Person-Centered Approach to Psychotherapy: The principles of client-centered therapy
Six of Rogers's seminal papers on the development of client-centered therapy are discussed. The person-centered approach is evident in the principles of the therapy. The principles are summarized.

Chapter Three   The Person-Centered Approach to Small Groups: More than psychotherapy
A brief history of the development of small group therapy suggests that all groups are one. More relevant for an understanding of the person-centered approach, it shows that groups are not merely client-centered therapy with additional people present. The small group from the person-centered approach is a *different* phenomenon. The principles of client-centered therapy are even at times non-facilitative when applied to the group phenomenon. It must be understood on its own.

Chapter Four   Applying the Person-Centered Approach vs. Applying the Principles of Client-Centered Therapy
Examples of *applications of the person-centered approach* are compared to examples of *the principles of client-centered therapy applied to non-therapy situations*. The differences between the two, as well as the dangers in confusing them, are discussed.

Chapter Five   An Example of the Pitfalls in 'Giving People an Experience of the Person-Centered Approach' instead of Applying the Approach
A critical analysis of a conference convened to resolve complex conflicts in Central America using the person-centered approach. This conference demonstrated more 'how no' than 'know how.' For this reason, it is perhaps an extremely valuable example of not only the destructive possibilites in blindly applying 'principles,' but also in the constructive potential of applying the approach itself.

Chapter Six   The Person-Centered Approach to Large Group Workshops: Communities for learning
Large group workshops were originally conceived in an attempt to understand the person-centered approach's possible relevance in social situations.

Although these workshops were therapeutic for some participants, they were not effective as psychotherapy (nor were they meant to be). However, they were often effective in provoking insights into not only how to facilitate transnational communications or how to resolve intergroup conflicts but also how culture itself is formed and transformed. On reflection, indications for how to improve individual psychotherapy are also apparent.

This chapter presents a sample workshop—beginning to end—with comments on its development in key aspects of social 'dynamics' and with relevant material from adjacent studies.

Chapter Seven   A Rehearsal for Understanding the Phenomenon of Group
A phenomenological research of a low-structured, leaderless, transnational, transcultural, large group workshop from the person-centered approach is reported. This chapter provides examples of the personal, interpersonal and transpersonal dimensions of the phenomenon of group suggested in the previous chapter.

Chapter Eight   Learning About Learning: The person-centered approach applied to education
Rogers' 'passionate statement' on American education was warmly welcomed in the United States in the 1960s. It was a revolutionary corrective that was badly needed in schooling at that time.

Now, some thirty years have passed. Much of Rogers' view remains relevant. However, it needs to be understood and revised in the context of the complexity that time has inevitably brought.

Chapter Nine   Effect of Group
A lengthy discussion of various hypotheses concludes with one that proposes (what everyone should suspect, but often doesn't) that the mind functions differently when one participates in a group and when one thinks in solitary.

To understand both the weaknesses and the strengths of the 'exceptional states of consciousness' provoked in individuals gathered together, an analysis is made of 'traditional groups.' It is possible to see that modern groups continue to express many of the same tribal impulses—both wise and foolish—as traditional societies. Constructive trends are noted.

Chapter Ten   On Becoming a Culture
Reflections on the client-centered therapy culture. With no self-reflective consciousness, systems of personality change and continuing groups may become cultures in themselves. An analysis of some twenty years of 'cross-cultural communication workshops' in Europe reveals this tendency. Although little is evident regarding 'cross-cultural communications,' much may be noted about the creation of a portable group culture.

Chapter Eleven   What's Wrong with the Psychology of Client-Centered Therapy
A reflection on the various applications of the person-centered approach reveals that the psychology of client-centered therapy is unable to explain these phenomena. Furthermore, in spite of the therapy's evident continued effectiveness, its psychology does not offer a comprehensive explanation of its workings.

Chapter Twelve   Toward a Psychology for Applications of the Person-Centered Approach
A direction for the construction of a psychology for applications of the person-centered approach (which would naturally include client-centered therapy) is suggested.

Forewords

Maureen O'Hara

When Lucila asked me to write a foreword to this new compilation of work by my friend John K. Wood I agreed without hesitation. I was honored by the privilege and looked forward to it, but as it turned out, I was oblivious to the emotional challenge it would be. The book covers what were surely the most formative times of my life. The exquisitely observed descriptions of workshops and training programs evoke memories of the years John and I worked together—often with our friend and teacher Carl R. Rogers—and rekindle the joy, fury, terror, pleasure, and pain of experiences that are part of the core of who I am today and of how I understand my reality and what I hope for the future. On my bookshelf still lies the reed flute John gave me at the end of the second person-centered approach workshop at Mills College, in 1975. As we wandered along the tree-shaded path back to the dining room after a group session, he handed it to me without much comment, but wrapped in a copy of the first few lines of *The Reed*, a poem by the great Sufi poet Rumi.

> Listen to the reed as it tells its tale;
> it complains of separation.
> Since they cut me from the reed-bed,
> men and women have been crying over my lament.
> I wish for someone with a bosom torn apart by separation,
> so that I can tell them the meaning of the pain of longing.
> Everyone who stays far away from his own origin
> seeks to get back to the day he was together with it.

From time to time, I blow into it even now—I can't call it playing—and as the breathy notes float out I imagine John's essence carried out on the sound. The tone hints of melancholy, at a sweet longing for a fulfillment that may never come, at a paradise imagined but yet to be gained, at anticipations of the Divine glimpsed yet still beyond the grasp. An eloquent wordless telling of the story of the work he committed his life to and of the yearning for reconnection with something beyond himself, that is the undertone of so many of the stories in this book. So like John.

I met John in 1973. I had traveled from Ohio, where I was a professor at a small college, to meet with Carl Rogers, who had just agreed to be a member of my

PhD dissertation committee. Rogers had also suggested that while I was in La Jolla I meet John K. Wood who, he promised, was 'quite brilliant' and who 'shared many of the same interests in expanding client-centered thinking into a wider and more evolutionary perspective.' I took his advice. We agreed to meet the next day at two o'clock at Center for Studies of the Person, 'for an hour.' Our meeting lasted until nine—seven hours of exhilarating exploration of his thinking about consciousness and how it overlapped and intertwined with my own. I don't remember that we even talked about Rogers' work at all. That day began a wondrous journey as co-explorers of human consciousness—its mysteries and its manifestations—that took us to many countries and continues even now as I read his words.

John and I worked together in over 30 person-centered approach workshops and training programs in the United States, United Kingdom, Italy, Mexico, Hawaii, and especially Brazil, and many of these workshops provide the raw material for this book. John's exquisite talent for catching the meaning of significant moments in odd and often challenging ways, comes through in these raw and untempered stories. The poetic language evokes events that are part of my own life-long search to understand love and the relationship between individual and group consciousness. Reading these stories reminds me of countless hours spent in conversation with him as he applied his unique and quirky sensibility to whatever captured his interest. The Brazilian *macumba* ceremony, the workshop in the redwoods of Santa Cruz, scuffling on the streets of London with R.D. Laing, debriefing a psychotic episode in a community meeting, watching him beat the pants off players half his age on basketball courts in every location we worked, watching retired nuns lift their skirts to go paddling in the moonlight in Bahia, jammed in with pilgrims in St. Peter's Square, trying to understand 'charisma' as Pope John Paul passed us in his Popemobile, rushing to Carl's São Paulo hotel room at two in the morning to help Carl work through a sudden loss of nerve about the apparent chaos in an 800 person encounter then underway, drinking *cerveja* on the beach in Pernambuco, reading dervish tales on Natalie Rogers' houseboat in Sausilito, California preparing for the Ashland, Oregon workshop, now forms the storyboard of my own life's narrative. I recognize in my bones what he describes, because I was there. And yet reading about these events and many more as they are unpacked, rethought, turned on their head and seasoned with John's penetrating wit, to become re-spun into a vision of a person-centered approach that is uniquely John's, is both comforting and unsettling.

These chapters thrust me back to this life-transforming work as if it were yesterday.

Both John and I were trained as scientists. We were in the world as open-minded explorers, and we were also in the world as skeptics. Despite the fact that he was often considered to be in line to inherit Carl's mantel as the theoretical leader within the person-centered community, John's abhorrence of bandwagons and orthodoxy and his habit of popping self-congratulatory bubbles meant that he actually occupied a somewhat marginal role, patrolling the periphery of the community with a critical eye and all the time yearning for deeper more truthful understanding that is often hard to see from the center. Both iconoclastic and yet profoundly wise, he believed that the greatest threat to PCA was its true believers, and those who saw it as a change technology or an intervention, and not an approach to life or a way of being. A strong theme in all our conversations, much in evidence in this volume, was our shared desire to expand the horizons of awareness at the same time as we avoided falling into the manifold conceptual traps and self-deceptions that were ever present, and that often seemed to be overtaking some of our colleagues—including Rogers. John had a strong aversion to any attempts to turn the subtle implicate reality of the person-centered approach into locked down, rule-bound methods or finished theories. He believed the true potential of the person-centered approach was missed this way, and instead of taking humanity forward into an expanded capacity to deal with what faces us as individuals and as a species, it often results in ritualized behavior and pseudo-enlightenment. His way was the way of inquiry. This childlike willingness to point out a naked emperor if he saw one often antagonized those who felt that they had found truth with a capital 'T' and more than once it resulted in John being uninvited to events that would have been strengthened by his presence. It was no surprise to us that when Rogers was taken to visit a Brazilian medium that claimed she could 'help Carl Jung get a message to him from the other side,' John and I were somehow 'disinvited' from the visit. But it was precisely because we both felt that something extraordinary had been glimpsed in these large person-centered group processes, that maybe we were witnessing some manifestation of consciousness that went beyond what we yet imagined, that we were committed to trying to understand it without illusion. We tried to keep each other honest because we understood, as John would point out, that 'fool's gold is only attractive because real gold exists.' We were in search of the real thing.

John was a truth practitioner. He would never settle for easy answers—preferring no answers at all. He lived in the questions and in search of an ever expanding experience of reality. But with every new experience we shared, John and I would sift through it, looking for learning, new insights, for false consciousness, for self-deception and for disillusionment. He would challenge me, I would challenge him; we encouraged each other to get way out onto the edge of what we knew and we picked each other up when we fell—and believe me, there were times when we each had profound doubts about whether any of it was any use at all. Yet from within the crucible of a dialogue that lasted years emerged a person-centered theory of large groups that held out for the possibility that human beings might have the capacity to emancipate their spirit even further, and to tap into the vast potentialities of a still expanding universe.

Over the decade from 1974 to 1984 our multiple observations of the groups in which we were involved suggested that the large group process could potentially provide a more powerful (although much scarier) path to consciousness development than either the small group or individual therapy. More startlingly, we observed that sometimes a group could arrive at a state of consciousness in which the collective wisdom of the community—the group's mind—could be both accessed and fed by any individual. I became convinced that the next stage in human evolution will be a collective process, where we learn how to harness the power of the minds of communities without subordinating the individual subjectivities of their members. The search for such a process has been at the center of my work ever since.

There are many who had such conversations with John while he was with us. The essays that have been collected here provide an opportunity to engage in dialogue with him once more, to participate in his creative process, to experience his intellectual courage and poetic imagination. His keen observations of person-centered processes and practitioners are a gift to anyone who is interested to delving deeper. They are both loving and fierce. Some of the essays are highly critical in a way that only a true friend has any right to be; none more so than the essay on the workshop Rogers and colleagues organized with Central American government officials in Rust, Austria. Offering a divergent perspective from the one published by Rogers, John lays bare the ways in which Rogers' consummate naïve American optimism and simplistic ideas about the nature of conflict, resulted in underestimating the scope of the long-standing antagonisms among those present to the point of hubris, and misjudging how difficult it would be to make any real progress towards reconciliation in such a short time. John considered the event a failure, not because of any flaw in the principles of the person-centered approach per se, but in flawed application. In particular, he considers that the difficulties faced were self-inflicted because organizers strayed from what John considered to be the essence of a person-centered approach—honoring the subjective experience of the participants and trusting in the self-organizing wisdom of the group—and in their anxiety, opting instead for an over-facilitated process and setting up expectations which bordered on cultural insensitivity. What John could not know when he wrote his critique is that participant Oscar Arias, President of Nicaragua at that time and again now, recently sent a message to one of the organizers stating that he keeps a photograph of Carl Rogers in his office and that the experiences of the meeting at Rust are with him still.

The scathing discussion of Charles Devonshire's cross-cultural workshops is also sure to make people uncomfortable as John questions to what extent they were 'cross-cultural' at all, and exposes what he considers to be the cult-like characteristics of these events like the use of insider jargon, repetitive rituals, the presence of attendee 'regulars,' and facilitator-contrived agendas. In John's view presented here these workshops mimicked the form of the person-centered approach workshops but missed its essence.

Not all the essays as are critical as these two, but as any conversation with him inevitably would, these works prod, provoke, poke fun, dispute, undermine, and frequently debunk much of what these days is taught as person-centered psychotherapy. Like the shamanic trickster, John's dissident interpretations and wildly unconventional framing should force person-centered practitioners, especially those who convene large groups, to think again about what they are doing, and what they believe, and to radically re-examine the assumptions undergirding their views. These accounts reveal, I think, the deep philosophical differences that gradually opened up between client-centered orthodoxy and a smaller heretical group that was involved in large group encounters and in a sense a wider mission. For some of us, who had experienced many person-centered approach workshops in diverse locations, there had emerged a shared intuition that if faith in the basic relational principles central to the person-centered approach (though by no means exclusive to it) could be sustained long enough, and the darker existential moments faced without denying them or trying to suppress them, something far more valuable and more transformative than a better psychotherapeutic method was at stake. Somewhere along the way a shift in our consciousness took place and we began to understand what we doing less in the terms of an instrumental and causal phenomenon and more as an emergent process by which a vast implicate wisdom might be apprehended and brought to the service of a suffering world, and ultimately to the evolution of consciousness. In these pages you participate in John's thought process as he explores these ideas through the years, for his own understanding and for the benefit of anyone interested in the question of humanity's future. He sought people as friends and colleagues who would engage with him in the difficult questions. Here in the chapters that follow is an opportunity for the conversation with him to continue. In one of the essays John says something we discussed many times that the 'person-centered approach may not be as much as people believe, but it might be far more than they imagine.' If readers allow themselves to enter this dialogue with John, they will inevitably become part of the evolution of the person-centered approach, and perhaps much more than they imagine.

Readers should not look for the academic form of scholarship in these pages. John was a voracious reader, mining for the deep meanings of what his authors are saying. Provocateur, master storyteller and hugely original thinker—but he is not an academic. Like accomplished creators of parables of any age, he casts a wide net for his supporting evidence, quoting poets as often as neuroscientists, and works from centuries ago along with contemporary research, and his reasoning is that of the alchemist as much as the scholar. Most significantly for any students who read this, he makes no attempt to follow scholarly conventions such as a balanced treatment, a comprehensive literature review, the most contemporary sources, or evidence that might counter his arguments. What readers will find however, is a quicksilver mind at play with the material of a lifetime of closely observed experience. If readers allow themselves to be carried along on his rigorous and unsentimental examination of the many weaknesses and unrealized potential of the person-centered approach they might find the gold. John had more faith in conversation as a path to wisdom than almost anything else. He sought people who would engage with him anywhere he went. Here in the chapters that follow is an opportunity for his conversation to continue.

Professor and Chair of Psychology, National University, La Jolla, California
President Emerita, Saybrook Graduate School, San Francisco

Brian Thorne

John K. Wood was a deeply reflective man. He also allowed himself to submit to experience without the fear that he would somehow lose himself in a bewildering confusion of emotions. Perhaps the word that fits him best is 'solid' but without the implication that he somehow lacked imagination or creativity. On the contrary, it was his very solidity that often permitted him to explore further, to take risks and sometimes to think almost unthinkable thoughts.

In his book, which is in many ways his legacy to his colleagues throughout the world, John is bold enough to express thoughts and feelings which are the outcome of a life lived in depth and of a fidelity to an approach which he believed could be transformative and whose potential had only been partly glimpsed. The emphasis throughout is indeed on an *approach* as John is quick to castigate those who, in his opinion, have become needlessly caught up in attempts to differentiate the person-centred approach from client-centred therapy or to categorise it as a psychology, a philosophy, a school or movement. The final chapter concludes with a breathtakingly simple summary of the quintessence of this approach which Carl Rogers spent a lifetime embodying and implementing. 'The most important thing Rogers had to say', John writes, 'was simply "yes" to personal improvement, to real learning, to constructive behavior, to nourishing relationships, to honest thinking, to life'.

Such an apparently uncomplicated summary should not be taken as a sign that this book is in any way anti-intellectual. Quite the opposite is the case. John did not suffer fools gladly and his many years of deep involvement with Carl Rogers and of experience of both small and large groups had shown him that there were those who were only too ready to view uncritically the processes that had occurred. The book is rich in John's analysis of group experiences, in many of which he had himself shared. He does not deny that there were occasions when remarkable things occurred and when individuals underwent profound changes. There were also times when, given the opportunity to create a community characterised by honesty, compassion and hopefulness, the participants proved capable of reaching a level of interpersonal trust which was inspirational. At the same time, with searing clarity, he does not hesitate to recall processes which were destructively chaotic and when the staff facilitators were culpably ill-prepared to respond to the primitive forces which were unleashed. He also draws attention to the tendency—even of Rogers himself—to turn a blind eye to negative outcomes or to desert the very principles of the approach out of panic or mistaken reliance on past experience.

These criticisms, real and well-founded as they are, are not made in a spirit of hostility or condemnation. On the contrary, they are made by a man who saw in the approach a powerful force for good in the evolution of humankind. As a result, this book, because of its refusal to deny shortcomings and mistakes and, even more, by its brilliant analysis of how these could be remedied, leaves the reader with realistic hope rather than idealistic yearning. What is more, John K. Wood demonstrates time and again that he lives in a world infinitely larger than that of psychotherapy and counselling. The American who chose to live in the Brazilian countryside and who was respectful of the culture of Europe inspires confidence as one who speaks with authority because he has tasted the liberty of the global citizen. Goethe, Buber, Freud, Rogers, William James, De Quincey, Einstein and many others appear in the dramatis personae of this remarkable book. John K. Wood is thoroughly at home in such a community.

Emeritus Professor of Counselling
University of East Anglia, Norwich, UK
Co-founder, The Norwich Centre

Vera Engler Cury

John Wood loved to be left alone, with his thoughts and his projects, but he was also very fond of being together with people, especially honest, transparent, intelligent and creative ones. He was not a theoretical scholar, but searched for the meaning of psychological processes, as much as he was interested in learning about the secrets of his farm, from the seeds to winds and worms. He was a courageous person, strong and stubborn, yet a lovely and comprehensive friend. He maintained his loyalty to Carl Rogers' legacy and humbly worked to keep PCA principles from being distorted and mystified. When he decided to move to Brazil in order to join the woman he loved he did not ask for his American friends' permission and was blamed for that; still he never betrayed the ideals of the La Jolla PCA Group. It was not easy for him to become a Brazilian citizen; there were many cultural differences to be faced, but he always kept a good-humored posture about that.

In his last years John read many books on evolutionary biology and wrote about the applications of the PCA from the perspective of evolutionary psychology. It may go against some PCA orthodoxy, but he was not afraid of criticism; what he really feared was ignorance and prejudice. In my opinion he made a route back to where Rogers started and brought some insights on the environmental and cultural aspects of human psychological experiences. He also reinforced the importance of phenomenology as a way to comprehend subjective life, and argued strongly against those who tried to change Rogers' hypothesis and principles into religious dogmas. He stressed that applying person-centered attitudes was effective enough to prove its force, but he was very aware of the need for revision on some of Rogers' theoretical statements, due to the new developments in relevant fields. John was especially interested in human groups; latterly he applied PCA principles in meetings held with his neighborhood farmers in order to build a local cooperative way of growing and distributing agricultural products.

John wanted to be buried on the farm where he and Lucila lived for more than two decades, where they had preserved a green area as their heritage for future generations. Unfortunately it was not possible, but he rests nearby in a flowery, rural cemetery. Lucila came up with a way that his wish to be buried at home could in part be met: she invited us to bring some writings, photos, memos, objects that each one of us, his closest Brazilian friends, believed to be part of our friendship with him. We put all of our gifts inside a bottle and buried it under a large tree near the swimming pool. For us it was a spiritual ritual, and we all believed John was there participating and saying goodbye for a while. I still miss John a lot, but progressively, as time goes by, have learned to make him part of my classes, my papers, my history. As Lucila whispered to him in his last moments: 'It is always learning, John.' My dearest friend, I now thank you for so much learning which you generously shared with us.

Campinas, São Paulo, Brazil

Jaime Roy Doxsey, Lucila Machado Assumpção, Márcia Alves Tassinari and Raquel Wrona

John Wood first visited Brazil in 1977 and again in 1978 as a member of Carl Rogers' La Jolla staff, invited by Eduardo Bandeira for two important events: the Brazilian Encounters, held at the Aldeia de Arcozelo, Rio de Janeiro. These large community encounters had enormous national repercussions, representing an important point in the development of the person-centered approach in Brazil, as well as contributing to Rogers' reflections about large group or community encounters. During these years, John Wood, Maureen O'Hara, and another a visiting staff member, influenced many Brazilian professionals through training, reflection groups and short courses offered in several major Brazilian cities: Rio de Janeiro, São Paulo, Recife, Brasília and João Pessoa.

At the First International Forum of the Person-Centered Approach in 1982, in Oaxtapec, México, Dr. Rachel Lea Rosenberg, full professor of psychology at the University of São Paulo, negotiated with John the possibility of an advanced course in the person-centered approach to be held in Brazil. Dr. Rosenberg invited 30 participants from Brazil, Uruguay and Argentina, with PCA experience, to attend the course.

From 1983 to 1985 this course promoted learning experiences with group process as well as personal growth opportunities for all participants. Many of them produced academic papers, research proposals, essays and diverse personal contributions shared within the community. John was especially significant as a mentor to participants and group processes.

John's facilitations of groups focused on how complex events occurred. His way of being demonstrated the importance of understanding these complexities, as well as the relevance of their social and cultural contexts, opposing tendencies by many to seek rapid explications of 'why' things were as they were. This process orientation led us to new levels of perception of the possibilities in our work and personal life. His partnership with Lucila gave many of us with histories of broken relationships new hope and meaning for incorporating love and creativity as energy for life.

John influenced directly and indirectly the destinies of numerous Brazilian professionals. He taught for five years at the Catholic University in Campinas, São Paulo. He revised all of Rogers' writings and organized the 'Jaguariúna group,' a group composed of professionals from a variety of backgrounds (psychologists, professors, a sociologist, and a plastic artist), who after four years of bimonthly meetings, selected and translated six seminal papers of Rogers, which for John as well as the group, represented the evolution of Carl Rogers' thinking. John's thoughts and reflections were presented in a second section, as he explained the implications and relevance of a person-centered approach for a client-centered psychotherapy. This became the book *Abordagem Centrada na Pessoa,* printed in Portuguese.

John never stopped working and refining his vision, and this book, now in his mother tongue, distills the core of his thinking. He saw the person-centered approach as much more encompassing than a psychotherapy centered in the client. He saw it as a way of seeing and being—a collection of attitudes, beliefs and intentions. Psychotherapy is presented as just one of applications of this way of being.

This clarification opens the possibility for advancing our understanding of other applications of the person-centered approach, especially in regard to group work—an important dimension which has been pursued in Brazil, and still requires refinement and understanding of its potential. In this sense this book offers a stimulus to the thinking of professionals and students interested in the advancement of knowledge and practice of the paradigm of belief in the human being and in the formative tendency of the universe.

For the last twenty years, John directed a project of interdisciplinary studies and action at the Estância Jatobá, a 200-acre wetland site in the interior of São Paulo. The property became an ecological reserve, officially recognized by the federal environmental protection agency. As well as protecting and cultivating the natural forests, preserving the biodiversity and integrity of the ecosystem, the project involved sustainable agriculture, agro-ecology, community development and environmental education. John was President of the Rural Council, dedicated to preserving agrarian values and promoting regional economies in the municipality of Holambra, São Paulo.

John's death left us with a profound emptiness filled previously by his deep knowledge of the human condition, great capacity for listening and compassion, his warm and tender outlook and sharp sense of humor. He was gifted with a privileged mind, curious and disciplined, capable of a precise observation, be it of a person, animal or plant, and at the same time able to discern the overall pattern of a group, an ecosystem or a thought system. John was an avid reader and constant learner until his last breath—he held degrees in mathematics, engineering and a PhD in psychology and his work with the land and studies of ecology allowed him to apply his ideas to more diverse areas of study.

Also gifted with an excellent memory, his erudition permeated his texts, making frequent quotes in the middle of his often poetic writing style. An eternal seeker of the truth, John read spiritual books with depth and intent—these were always his sources of inspiration and integrity. A great teacher who lived according to his beliefs, influencing others through his attitudes and behavior, neither intrusive, nor seeking to convince. John discovered in Brazil, his home, his soul mate, and a great wealth of knowledge and reflection.

Jaguariúna, São Paulo, Brazil

CHAPTER ONE

Approaching the Approach
An introduction

The state of 'being known' is a further evolutionary stage of the phenomenon itself.
J.W. von Goethe

Rogers always had an approach: a *stance*, a set of attitudes and intentions, *a way of being* for his work. Around 1940, his approach to psychotherapy began to congeal; for some thirty years he had referred to it as the *client-centered approach* but for the last thirty years or so he called it the *person-centered approach* (PCA). Its most elucidated application to date is client-centered therapy. This first chapter discusses, 'What is the person-centered approach?' The difference between 'client-centered therapy' and 'the person-centered approach' is also clarified.

A professor friend of mine said, 'To discuss the term "person-centered approach" is a moot point because it has already appeared in many books.' I agree. I am not interested in discussing whether or not the term should be used. I am interested in what it *means*.

And from what one hears these days it is *everything and nothing.* By people who claim to be its representatives, it has been referred to as 'a major school of thought in American psychotherapy', 'an influential concept,' a 'framework,' 'a model for human relations training,' 'a family of scholars and practitioners,' 'a source of status and influence,' (amazingly) a 'tradition' and, as expected (though just as inaccurate as the rest), a 'therapeutic response.' The person-centered approach is also thought of as a 'means of communication' and 'offering skills in helping us talk with each other.' It is also held to be a 'philosophy' and 'set of values' which include 'really respecting the dignity, autonomy and capacity for change of people' and a belief that 'people move in the direction of self-actualization' if a 'growth-promoting atmosphere' is provided.

Rogers (1986a) has described what he considered a friendly contradiction associated with the person-centered approach:

> It emphasizes shared values, yet encourages uniqueness. It is rooted in a profound regard for the wisdom and constructive capacity inherent in the human organism. At the same time, it encourages those who incorporate these

values to develop their own special and unique way of being, their own ways of implementing this shared philosophy. (pp. 3–4)

Sometimes the person-centered approach has been promoted as a 'set of attitudes'. In addition to the well-known facilitative attitudes of client-centered therapy, it has been suggested that 'what is essential to any real person-centered awareness is a sense of wonder and hope and humility as we stand before the mystery of persons'[1] (Land, 1987). Frequently, it is pictured as like-minded dissidents marching to 'questions around social power, influence and continuity in the person-centered movement'; if not a social movement, a utopian way of life. Some followers do not hide their concept of an ideal world of 'empathy, truth, unconditional love, openness' providing 'mutual support,' in which each one would facilitate the emotional well-being of the other. This could be achieved, they believe (as do most missionaries), if only everyone were devoted to being *more* 'person-centered.' It is not only within the light-aired confines of California or the privileged European centers that such enthusiasm is evident: '*Estamos viviendo una experiencia nueva y de gran movilidad*' echoes an announcement for a 'person-centered' encounter in South America.

Themes and Scholastic Rituals

It is also popular to think of the person-centered approach as a 'theme' capable of being amalgamated with other philosophies or techniques; it seems that the more unlikely the pair, the better. A university professor, for example, suggests joining 'the person-centered approach theme' and Tai Chi Chuan. Recently, I came across proposals for wedding the person-centered approach with Taoism's technique of the 'microcosmic orbit,' and perhaps more astonishing though no less serious, the person-centered approach coupled with a French physician's philosophy of human development based on the architecture of the human inner ear. Believe it or not, there is a psychiatrist who says he gives 'person-centered electroconvulsive shock treatments.'

To confuse matters more, even some of those who contributed to the development of client-centered therapy have violated what have come to be considered its 'basic principles.'[2] Eugene Gendlin, for example, says of his practice of therapy:

> I will respond client-centeredly for a while and maybe if I see that [the client] is prepared to tell me a whole history ... then I will interrupt and say, 'Let's just be quiet and kind of scan inside.' (Monteiro dos Santos, 1985)

University 'researchers,' as usual, have been busy analyzing what seems like the bones of an archeological dig, comparing what they find to similar specimens. So far, they have paired Rogers' ideas with those of the psychoanalysts Sigmund Freud,

Carl Jung and Heinz Kohut; the psychiatrist, Milton Erickson; the anthropologist, Gregory Bateson; the communitarian, H.C. Boyte; the pedagogue, Paulo Freire; and the philosopher, Martin Buber. Carl Rogers' practice of psychotherapy has been likened, if you can believe it, to Mr Rogers, the well-known host of a North American television show for children. Carl Rogers' thought has also been linked with Taoism, Zen Buddhism, the Bach flower remedies, the Christian doctrine of original sin, and the New Testament virtues. His professional struggle against orthodox psychiatry has reminded a graduate student of Martin Luther's stand against the Catholic Church.

The range of activities that are labeled (both erroneously and correctly) 'the person-centered approach' is so great and so diverse as to justify the psychiatrist Robert Lifton's (1983) observation about modern innovation in general that within the atmosphere of 'chaotic eclecticism' it becomes 'difficult indeed to distinguish narrow dogma and intensified cultism from sustained commitment, superficiality from bold experiment, and excessive claim from genuine accomplishment (p. 21).'

Diversity

More and more frequently, its diversity has become a description of the person-centered approach. Even Rogers (1986a), in his eagerness to make its merits more widely known, ignored the confusion of labeling to announce that:

> The attitudes and philosophy underlying client-centered/person-centered therapy have ... infiltrated education, where their revolutionary implications stir controversy. They have influenced marriages and partnerships. They have affected parenting. They have reached into industry and schools of management. ... Medical education and medical practice have felt a change. Even the legal profession is not untouched. Pastoral counseling has been deeply changed. Workers in community development operate differently. People in many occupations and in all walks of life have found themselves empowered, have discovered a deeper understanding of self, have learned intimacy. (p. 4)

To many clinical psychologists, particularly those associated with Rogers at the University of Chicago, the person-centered approach is essentially a method of one-to-one psychotherapy backed by a precise theory and an impressive body of research. Those in the business of forming counselors, tout it as a foundation of counselor training programs, though they differ as to whether its value is realized by grafting on behavioral techniques to the 'core conditions' or preserving its purity by cultivating special attitudes (Bozarth & Temaner, 1984). 'Person-centered' institutes in Europe offer 'facilitator development' to ease people into the psychotherapy profession or dabble in 'cross-cultural communications' while in the United States the best efforts try to 'empower the person.'

Marching for the PCA

When novices become lost in all this confusion, some old-timers shrug their shoulders, turn their palms heavenwards and smile, 'That's the ol' PCA. Great, isn't it?' In reality, the veterans are divided. Some rally beneath the person-centered approach flag and reject client-centered therapy (its most coherent application to date) as indolent, ineffective or simply irrelevant. One seasoned person-centered approacher, for example, imperiously dismisses client-centered therapy and brags that he has not bothered to read any of Carl Rogers' books. There is also the adept who flaunts the 'person-centered approach (not client-centered therapy)' as 'one of the two linguistic frames that most approximate my understanding.'

This group has been joined by a worldwide collection of what often seem to be crackpots (to use a precise, if not scientific, word) who are convinced they are 'person-centered'(as if this were a race or nationality) because they share beliefs about democracy or self-respect. Although they are frequently schooled in the latest politically correct speech, they often know little about Rogers' work. This does not prevent them from eagerly spreading the word in order 'to make our approach better known.' There is even a so-called 'person-centered' dentist whose calling cards urge people to *Discover Carl Rogers*. And what is one to think of the European university professors who organized an international conference on the person-centered approach and, without further explanation, requested participants to 'bring teddy bears' for a 'teddy bear session' they had programmed. For those who did not take to stuffed animals, the organizers promised they would be able to sing along with someone who 'does person-centered approach in vocal training.' Nobody could blame intelligent people if they shunned such events.

Backlash: More of the same

Under an opposing banner (as in politics, economics, and religion) there are fundamentalists who are turning with 'conviction' back to client-centered therapy. Some are occupied priggishly nitpicking the 'purity' of practice, and hairsplitting the finer points of client-centered therapy's rapidly fossilizing theory. They turn up their noses at more complex phenomena (such as large group activities) leaving the field open to opportunists who can, consciously or not, cash in on emotionalism. To these 'purists,' the person-centered approach is nothing less than another heresy that destroys families, schools and the moral fiber of America. Client-centered therapy is promoted as the only true representative of the person-centered approach, and all the other professional activities Rogers engaged in could be dismissed as having been under the psychedelic influence of California.

On the positive side, good-willed people in this latter group are trying to keep the person-centered approach in focus, to preserve the genuine fundamentals that have developed from it for an effective psychotherapy, to prevent the approach from becoming meaningless. Likewise, good-willed people in the first group want to see the approach applied constructively in areas other than psychotherapy. Why not dentistry (with teddy bears or whatever)? They are no less serious but do not wish to overly limit possibilities or to suffocate promising social experiments. Some, not so sure how to deal with the relationship between client-centered therapy and the person-centered approach, are declaring, 'client-centered therapy or the person-centered approach': just different labels for the same thing. Whatever feels good. It's a free country. The more informed respect that similarities and differences may exist. They write 'client-centered therapy *and* the person-centered approach.' The diplomatic (or merely opportunistic) cast aesthetics to the wind and program their word-processors to produce 'client-centered/person-centered approach.' Though tasteless, this symbol at least has the advantage of appealing to those who think the two concepts are the same, those who think they are different and those who don't care. The person-centered approach? Its fate is not so different from Hamlet's father: 'Tis here, 'tis here, 'tis gone. Alas, poor ghost.'

Is This Confusion Necessary?

Some things are confusing because they are complex, more than most minds can master. Trying to make sense out of the literature on what is effective psychotherapy is an example. Some confusion exists because of mistranslation, misunderstanding. And some things are confusing because people prefer them that way. For example, those who wish to align with a 'movement' and all that this implies will try to maintain the concept of the person-centered approach as vague, like the term 'democracy' that has lost any concrete sense in many places and now merely denotes 'those who are in the right.' They will prefer slogans and stirring emotions. Their desires are satisfied, as Fromm observed about the fanatics in psychoanalysis, by

> dogma, a ritual, a leader, a hierarchy, the feeling of possessing the truth, of being superior to the uninitiated, yet without great effort, without deeper comprehension of the problems of human existence, without insight into and criticism of their own society and its crippling effects on man, without having to change one's character in those aspects which matter, namely, to get rid of one's greed, anger and selfishness; basically without even escaping one's isolation. (Bettleheim, 1989: 55–6)

The Person-Centered Approach is an *Approach*

The person-centered approach is neither a *psychotherapy* nor a *psychology*. It is not a *school* as in 'the behaviorist school.' Itself, it is not a *movement*. However, that does not mean that a movement may not attach itself to its name. As William James (1907) observed of the philosophy pragmatism:

> A number of tendencies that have always existed in philosophy have all at once become conscious of themselves collectively, and of their combined mission; and this has occurred in many countries, and from so many different points of view, that much unconcerted statement has resulted. (p. 5)

Likewise, people who have nothing more in common than that they share a dislike for psychoanalysis or whatever, at times gather in conferences or workshops in the name of the person-centered approach. In this setting they quickly fall to bickering as it becomes obvious that they are linked by only a *word*, not a reality. Although many have noted 'existential' positions in its attitudes and others have referred to 'phenomenologic' perspectives in its intentions, the person-centered approach is also not a *philosophy*. Nor is it most of the other things previously mentioned.

Difference between Client-Centered Therapy and the Person-Centered Approach

Client-centered therapy and the person-centered approach belong to different categories. Client-centered therapy is a *psychotherapy*; the person-centered approach is an *approach*: to psychotherapy, to education, to encounter groups, to large group workshops. Client-centered therapy has a specific and coherent *theory* (Rogers, 1959). The person-centered approach has no theory. There is a *method* for conducting client-centered therapy; it has not been as well specified as the theory and varies substantially between therapists, however, Rogers' own technique has been extensively documented (including many films and audio recordings) and can be precisely described. (Analyses are plentiful; for recent ones see Brodley, 1994 and Ellis and Zimring, 1994). On the other hand, the *approach* has no specific method: methods are developed according to the demands of each application. For example, facilitative behavior in groups is somewhat different, and at times may even be contradictory, to therapist behavior in individual therapy intended to facilitate personality change. Nevertheless, they are derived from the same *approach*. We will return later to the subject of method in applying the approach.

For client-centered therapy, a substantial body of *research* has accumulated that has tested hypotheses proposed from studying its theory and practice. Although the research has in general been unable to convince the majority of psychologists of the theory's validity, what has been most convincing and has improved psychotherapy on the whole has been client-centered therapy's success in the clinic. The person-centered approach has not been researched as such.

An Approach by Any Other Name

The person-centered approach is the same approach that was used to develop client-centered therapy and other activities. Of course, the approach has only recently been called 'person-centered.' In the beginning, it was merely *an* approach.

As a young psychologist in Rochester, Rogers already spoke in terms of 'approach': he was 'moving away from any *approach* which was coercive or pushing'. At the 1937 meeting of the National Council of Social Work in Indianapolis, the paper he presented was titled 'The Clinical Psychologist's *Approach* to Personality Problems' [my italics]. In his first major book, *The Clinical Treatment of the Problem Child* (Rogers, 1939), Rogers sketched the *approach* he admired, gleaned from what he regarded as commonalities between all successful therapies. Then, as his distinctive method for practicing psychotherapy began to be better formulated, the *approach* became known by the subsequent developments: the *non-directive approach* (Rogers, 1942) and then the *client-centered approach* (Rogers, 1946). Until the early 1970s, it continued to be called the 'client-centered approach,' then, as applications of the approach began to be further developed in fields other than psychotherapy, it became known as the *person-centered approach* (Rogers, 1977).

The first 30-year *client-centered approach* period was largely concerned with the development of a system of personality change which concentrated on the individual's subjective world. The following 30 years of the *person-centered approach* period has been concerned as well with social interactions and has concentrated on learning from doing.

The following schematic may help visualize this history.

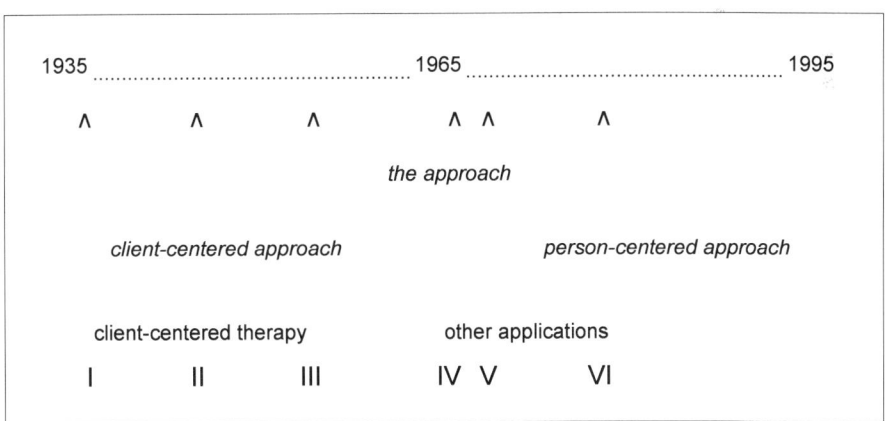

I. Attitudes of the therapist: Characterized by Rogers' book *Counseling and Psychotherapy*, published in 1942.

II. Methods of therapy: Identified by the publication *Client-Centered Therapy* (1951).

III. Internal process or experience: Corresponds with the best-seller *On Becoming a Person* (1961a).
IV. The facilitation of learning: *Freedom to Learn* (1969).
V. Interpersonal relationships: *On Encounter Groups* (1970b).
VI. Social processes and cultural transformation: *On Personal Power* (1977) and *A Way of Being* (1980).

Rogers' View

Although, client-centered therapy and the person-centered approach are different, Rogers (1987) made it clear that the *approach* itself, by whatever name, was the same. He insisted:

> To speak of a 'client-centered approach' and a 'person-centered approach' as though they were entities opposed to each other is, in my estimation, a sure road to futile wrangling and chaos ... I hope I may be allowed to be one whole person, whether I am called upon for help in a relationship deemed to be client-centered or in one that is labeled person-centered. I work in the same way in each. (p. 13)

What did Rogers mean when he said that he worked 'in the same way' in each situation? Did the same empathy exist in his sympathetic and caring gestures towards the woman who sobbed in an individual therapy interview; in his cool brashness toward the young 'hippy' who pointed his finger in a small group, accusing Rogers of betraying 'the revolution'; in his suppressed yawning while a smug university professor droned on about Sartre and philosophies of liberty in a large group meeting?

Although his apparent reaction, his manner of expression, his feelings and the circumstances may have been different in each of these situations, I believe that Rogers *approached* them in the very same way. He approached each situation with the same desire to understand, the same good humor, the same humility, the same honesty, the same non-judgmental acceptance of the individual or the group, the same curiosity and openness to learning, the same will to facilitate a constructive outcome for the individual and the group. He improvised from his knowledge and abilities in each specific case.

The development of effective client-centered therapy has resulted in the formulation of certain principles. Some have become part of the theory, some part of the belief system of practitioners, some part of the folklore that inevitably surrounds the activities of a group of people involved in the same endeavor. For the *approach,* there are no principles as such.

What Follows

Sixty years ago, the person-centered approach was a reality without a consistent name. Today, due to widespread applications (some mere dabbling, some well-intentioned though ineffective, some significant), it is in danger of becoming a mere name with no relevant reality. The accomplishments of its applications have not always been as good as believed. On the other hand, the approach is better than imagined. In large part, its potential has yet to be realized.

The chapters that follow will discuss applications of the person-centered approach to psychotherapy, small groups and large groups. Some of the strengths and weaknesses of these applications will be discussed. In the final chapter, a definition of the approach will be proposed and the relevance of the approach suggested.

Whenever a student or colleague worried that some new research finding or idea might make the person-centered approach look bad, Rogers remained unconcerned, and his response has become legendary: 'Don't you see? Facts are always friendly.' This book is intended as an exposition of 'facts' which are hoped to be 'friendly'– to enlarge, illuminate and render more useful an understanding of not only this subject but also help in pursuing the question behind the questions: How do we help each other to become complete human beings?

Notes

1. Rogers (1959:194), in stating the theory of client-centered therapy in its most comprehensive form, stressed that it was 'basically a group enterprise' and that he had 'drawn upon specific written contributions to theory made by Victor Raimy, Richard Hogan, Stanley Standal, John Butler and Thomas Gordon.' Also, he acknowledged 'the valuable influence' of Oliver Bown, Desmond Cartwright, Arthur Combs, Eugene Gendlin, Abraham Maslow, Julius Seeman, John Shlien and Donald Snygg on the theory he presented.

2. I am not against innovation. Although I feel that innovation for the sake of novelty has no place outside the entertainment business or advertising, as will be evident in the rest of the text, I *am* in favor of an innovative attitude.

CHAPTER TWO

The Person-Centered Approach to Psychotherapy
The principles of client-centered therapy

Uma pessoa sonhando é apenas um sonho; duas já é realidade.[1]

Six of Rogers' seminal papers on the development of client-centered therapy are discussed in this chapter. The person-centered approach is evident in the principles of the therapy and these principles are summarized.

Known as a dreamy youngster with few friends, he always kept pretty much to himself; he had a lively curiosity but was shy and never found it easy to join social groups, however, having certain religious inclinations, which were doubtless related to the traditions followed at home, he enrolled in a Sunday morning YMCA group. In the beginning, it was a frustrating experience for him and the others. The 'Y' group was unlike school, where the teacher lectured and the class followed a well-planned curriculum of readings, recitations and examinations. It was also unlike his family, where father enforced (lovingly) strict rules of behavior and schedules for his activities. In the Y group the leader followed no apparent system, gave no instructions, and established no rules or programs for the young man or his classmates. The group was left completely to its own devices.

The group leader presented a real puzzle to this young participant. Clearly a well-intentioned person, friendly, always attentive, curious, the leader seemed to be learning along with the others, enjoying shared discoveries. He seemed to genuinely like the class and its participants. Yet, thought the youngster, he was obviously weak. Why, the young man frequently wondered, does he not tell us what to do, what he wants us to learn, and how? Surely, he must not know.

Left completely free to engage in any kind of activity, the students overcame the 'vacuum' in leadership and quickly became involved in many different types of projects. Since they made their own decisions and choices, they easily learned, and set up a parliamentary method of self-governance. They established their own curriculum and organized all kinds of social and educational programs. As the group followed its learning impulses, going deeply into discussion topics, it became very well-informed and close-knit. The participants came to know and to trust each other profoundly. For the first time, outside his family, the shy youngster found intimacy with others. Impressed by this powerful experience, he reflected on it often. A suspicion, which took years to mature, grew within him: perhaps the group leader was not completely incompetent; perhaps there was wisdom in those clumsy and seemingly foolish ways of his; could the group leader have known what he was doing after all? If he did, he really understood learning: he seemed to be saying through his actions, 'I'm not what's important; what's important is what is being offered you: the actual experience of learning.' Though the students clamored for what they were accustomed to receive, he seemed to be saying, 'Don't look for how you think things should be, see how they actually are.'

A situation had evolved which fell short of the participants' expectations, yet this new experience was far more diverse and creative than they could have imagined possible. What tremendous power was released by this simple acknowledgment and respect for learning potential; and the friendships which developed in this group of twenty-five young men became a crucial element in their future lives. When the youngster himself had reached a ripe age, he wrote a notable book on the facilitation of learning. He revealed:

> When I have been able to transform a group—and here I mean all the members of a group, myself included—into a community of *learners*, then the excitement has been almost beyond belief. To free curiosity; to permit individuals to go charging off in new directions dictated by their own interests; to unleash the sense of inquiry; to open everything to questioning and exploration; to recognize that everything is in process of change—here is an experience I can never forget. I cannot always achieve it in groups with which I am associated, but when it is partially or largely achieved, then it becomes a never-to-be-forgotten group experience.

Yet, such is the mystery of profound learning that even after he wrote these words, near the end of his own life, the participant still was not certain whether the YMCA group leader was truly wise or merely foolish and lucky.

> The Group Leader: Professor George Humphrey
> The Participant: Carl R. Rogers
> Place and Time: Madison, Wisconsin; 1919

Rogers had had an important personal experience of learning. It profoundly changed him. As a group member, he was conscious of the value of the *participant*'s individual initiative, curiosity, intelligence and willpower in significant learning but not so sure of the group leader's contribution. Later, Rogers, as *professor* or psychotherapist or group facilitator, was aware of his conscious intention to create 'psychological conditions of growth' for participants. Ironically, members of his classes, therapy sessions and groups sometimes viewed him in the same way as he had viewed Professor Humphrey! This illustrates the futility, at times, of trying to understand an approach with the preconceptions of a limited point of view.

On Becoming a Therapy

Rogers began his career as a psychotherapist in the 1930s, working with individuals at the Institute for Child Guidance in New York. He had been educated in the theories of the day and dominated by their methods: writing lengthy case histories in which he interpreted the parent's behavior as being implicated in the behavioral problems of their children. One of his first turning points came when Alfred Adler visited the clinic. Freud's former patient and chief rival for control of the Vienna psychoanalytical group suggested that case histories were not necessary for successful treatment. Rogers took his advice and began to listen to what his patients were saying about their lives and what meaning their feelings had for them, instead of what their 'case histories' said.

As he began to practice psychotherapy, Rogers was also influenced by the ideas of Otto Rank. As with Adler, the contact with Rank was brief and Rogers did not really take to his formal theory, however, it is in the practice of psychotherapy that one can see many similarities in their outlooks and approaches. It could be said that, with the introduction of their 1924 book, *The Development of Psychoanalysis*, the Austrian, Otto Rank, and the Hungarian, Sandor Ferenczi, invented *psychotherapy* (Ferenczi & Rank, 1956/1924). Freud's favorite students and colleagues, they were less concerned with analyzing than with helping patients. They advocated a brief, active, intensive therapy focusing on the present rather than the past, and actual emotion rather than intellectual understanding. They recommended setting a termination date for therapy sessions; introduced the notion that there may be reactions to the analyst in his own right, not merely those transferred from the patient's past; and suggested the therapist's true feelings should not be concealed from the patient.

The two great streams of psychology, after World War I, were psychoanalysis and behaviorism. One credited causation to internal conflicts, the other to conditioning by the external environment. To this day, they continue to cohabit, as Lieberman (1985) suggests in his biography of Rank, because of their common 'focus on the past, and a contempt for the will.' Rank insisted that:

> in order to pretend that control and prediction are possible, one had to deny the individual's own will, his emotional instability, and the large part chance plays in the sphere of our psychical life even more than in our cosmic life. (Taft, 1958)

By insisting that choice is *also* a factor in human development, he was contributing to the foundation of humanistic psychology. The will that Rank promoted was optimistic. He believed in the worthiness of his patients and toiled not with the idea of finding out new things about human behavior from a patient, but just helping to put him on his own feet (Lieberman, 1985).[2] A patient related that 'With Rank, there was no dogma ... nothing was imposed on you. Rank was not looking for disease, he was not trying to eradicate anything. He wanted you to open up and be as you might want to be but didn't dare to.' A student in 1938 noticed that 'the actual therapeutic relationship is the curative factor' in Rank's approach (Lieberman, 1985).'To each particular case,' Rank (1966) explained, 'I apply no general therapy or theory. I let the patient work out his own psychology, as it were.' Anais Nin, herself a patient of Rank, affirmed this view: 'He was not practicing mental surgery. He was relying on his intuition, intent on discovering a woman neither one of us knew. A new specimen. He improvised' (Nin, 1966).

Commenting on Jessie Taft's legendary permissiveness, Rank said 'The therapist may do whatever he [or she] believes is pertinent to the process and *moment of therapy* with a particular individual as long as he takes responsibility for and deals helpfully with what he precipitates in the patient' (Lieberman, 1985).

Eventually, Rank gave up producing in favor of merely living. Abandoning writing for a time, he observed 'there is already too much truth in the world—an overproduction which apparently cannot be consumed' (Taft, 1958). James Lieberman (1985) summarizes Rank's career: 'Freeing the trapped or downtrodden human will was Rank's special mission. He felt it could only be done with honesty, humor, humility, and a will of one's own.' Otto Rank's life and work gave an answer to the Shakesperean epigram to his first book, *Art and Artist:* 'Is it possible, he should know what he is, and be that he is?' (Rank, 1989/1932).

Something Which Came From Me

It was in December, 1940, when Rogers gave a talk at the University of Minnesota, that he began to feel that his way of working and thinking was not merely an extension or revision of someone else's. Although he had been influenced by others, his approach began to be 'regarded as new, controversial, radical, and threatening.' Rogers began to realize 'that I was saying something which came from *me*, that I was not simply summarizing a general trend, and that I was developing a viewpoint which was my *own*' (Rogers, 1970a).The title of his talk was 'Newer Concepts in Psychotherapy.' This new approach, Rogers stated 'relies much more heavily on the individual drive toward growth, health, and adjustment. [Therapy] is a matter of freeing [the client] for normal growth and adjustment.' Furthermore, 'this therapy places greater stress upon ... the feeling aspects of the situation than upon the intellectual aspects' and 'this newer therapy places greater stress upon the immediate situation than upon the individual's past.' Finally, 'this approach lays stress upon the therapeutic relationship itself as a growth experience.'

Thirty years later, in the introduction to a book on client-centered therapy, Rogers (1974) stated that this characterization still described the essence of his therapy. He also mentioned four other elements that he believed had been implicit from the beginning. First, 'The willingness to change, the openness to experiential and research data has been one of the most distinctive features of client-centered therapy.' Second, 'Another implicit feature is that the client-centered therapist has seen the unique, subjective, inner person as the honored and valued core of human life.' A third element 'is the recognition that the affluent person of today is literally crying out with hunger for a human relationship which is deep, real, non-defensive—a truly person-to-person relation. This, I believe we have helped to provide from the first.' Finally, an implicit assumption is that 'training for a person who desires to engage in a helping relationship cannot be cognitive only, but, in fact, must be primarily *experiential*.' This final aspect, Rogers felt, had implications for public education.

Can I be of help?

In a poll of his working colleagues, North American clinical psychologists and counselors, who were asked to judge the 'ten most influential therapists,' Rogers' name appeared on the top of the list. (Smith, 1982).[3] Nevertheless, even more impressive than popularity (which television personalities, movie actors and athletes easily achieve) were his real achievements. In 1947, after many years of dedicated work developing a truly humanistic psychotherapy, Rogers was elected president of the American Psychological Association. This event marked a point of no return for the American society's recognition of the role of clinical psychologist as counselor or psychotherapist. The APA also conferred its first Distinguished Scientific Contribution Award and later its Distinguished Professional Contribution Award on Rogers. He was also the first president of the Association of American Psychotherapists (1956–1958). Rogers wrote more than 250 articles and published some twenty books. A dozen or so films were made of him at work in individual therapy sessions and group encounters. It is difficult to estimate the enormous number of hours of recorded audio and videotapes made of his psychotherapeutic interviews.

Questions He Asked by Applying the Approach to Therapy

Reviewing the production, particularly material between 1940 and 1970 when his ideas were most precisely formulated, one may easily be impressed by the range and depth of the questions he posed and tried to answer. Even for one with such a long and distinguished professional career, the list is astonishing: Who am I? Can I help? How? What should I not do? How does a person change? What is the starting point? What might be the end-point? What might an ideal person be like? How do I approach the task of facilitating personality change? What do I intend? What are my attitudes, my values? What do I think and feel? What are the facts? What really works? Is listening enough? What is the effect of honesty? of congruence? How do I relate to the client? Do I really care about him or her? What is the goal of therapy? What is the client's perception of me, of the relationship, of the activity? What is the world of the client like? What is a person? What is the nature of man? What does our relationship mean? What are the wider implications of our discoveries? What is education? Can I facilitate learning? How? Can I be a facilitative person in a group? Can I help improve communications between antagonists? Are there implications in my way of working to the critical problems of the day?

Seminal Thoughts on the Nature and Practice of Psychotherapy

Six of Carl Rogers' original articles may serve as an excellent review of not only the development of the principles of client-centered therapy but also of Rogers' thought. This selection does not pretend to represent a complete panorama of his writings. It is a sample of his tasting of experience, his learning, his wisdom, if you wish. It expresses his 'way of being.' Therefore, these papers are also central to an understanding of the person-centered approach and its application not only to psychotherapy but to education, encounter groups and large-group workshops. The reader is urged to study these writings in their entirety.

These articles appeared between 1946 and 1963, some having been written many years before publication. Although his first coherent proposal of a 'new psychotherapy' appeared in 1940 (in a lecture at the University of Minnesota) and he continued to publish on this subject until his death in 1987, these six articles forcefully present his essential thought on psychotherapy. After all this time, they still retain a peculiar strength; perhaps because of his quest for truth, evident in the searching with which he records his thoughts. In later years some of the same articles have appeared more diluted by the context of 'What the great man thought about psychotherapy, etc.' These original, perhaps less ambitious, articles retain a vigor, transmitting, perhaps more than anything, Rogers' childlike pleasure in discovering a truth and finding the precise words to express it.

Significant Aspects of Client-Centered Therapy

This article was published in 1946 in *The American Psychologist* (Rogers, 1946), having been carefully written for presentation to a skeptical audience at the Menninger Clinic. It is a good candidate for a seminal statement, being neither one of his early experimental versions nor his later polished ones. By this time, the bugs in non-directivity have been pretty well worked out and the therapist's woodenness and subtle manipulativeness have given way to a more natural warmth and acceptance. Rogers does not appear defensive about other doctrines and, although not fully elaborated, client-centered therapy has emerged whole, a thing in itself. Rogers and his colleagues had found 'both clinically and statistically, that a predictable pattern of therapeutic development takes place [in client-centered therapy].' This is because 'there exist in individuals growth forces, tendencies toward self-actualization, that may act as the sole motivation for therapy.' This experience, which 'releases the growth forces within the individual will come about in most cases if the following elements are present':

- If the counselor operates on the principle that the individual is basically responsible for himself and is willing for the individual to keep that responsibility.
- If the counselor operates on the principle that the client has a strong drive to become mature, socially adjusted, independent, productive, and relies on this force, not on his own powers, for therapeutic change.
- If the counselor creates a warm and permissive atmosphere in which the individual is free to bring out any attitudes and feelings which he may have, no matter how unconventional, absurd or contradictory these attitudes may be. The client is as free to withhold expression as he is to give expression to his feelings.
- If the limits which are set are simple, based on behavior not attitudes.
- If the therapist uses only those procedures and techniques in the interview which convey his deep understanding of the emotionalized attitudes expressed and his acceptance of them. This understanding is perhaps best conveyed by a sensitive reflection and clarification of the client's attitudes. The counselor's acceptance involves neither approval nor disapproval.
- If the counselor refrains from any expression or action which is contrary to the preceding principles. This means refraining from questioning, probing, blame, interpretation, advice, suggestion, persuasion or reassurance.

If these conditions are met, then it may be said with assurance that in the great majority of cases the following results will take place:

- The client will express deep and motivating attitudes.
- The client will explore his own attitudes and reactions more fully and will become aware of aspects previously denied.
- He will arrive at a clearer and more conscious realization of his motivating attitudes and will accept himself more completely. This realization and this acceptance will include attitudes previously denied. He may or may not verbalize this clearer conscious understanding of himself and his behavior.
- In the light of his clearer perception of himself he will choose, on his own initiative and on his own responsibility, new goals which are more satisfying than his maladjusted goals.
- He will choose to behave differently in order to reach these goals and this new behavior will be in the direction of greater psychological growth and maturity; it will also be more spontaneous, less tense, more in harmony with the social needs of others, and will represent a more realistic and comfortable adjustment to life.

In addition to stating the principles of the *psychotherapy*, the implications of the underlying *approach* are also laid out, anticipating the trends of Rogers' future work. He suggests that the approach might yield:

- a greater understanding of the process of psychotherapy and the improvement of its practice,
- applications to education,
- a greater respect for the philosophy of self-determination,
- applications to social and group conflict resolution.

The following statement made by a beginning client-centered therapist illustrates in personal terms the inner dialogue of a counselor as he applies the person-centered approach. One can note how a method of counseling may be derived.

> The technique seems deceptively easy to master. Then you begin to practice. A word wrong here or there. You don't quite reflect the feeling, but reflect content instead. It is difficult to handle questions. You are tempted to interpret. Nothing seems so serious that further practice won't correct it ... Only gradually does it dawn that if the technique is true it demands a feeling of warmth. You begin to feel that the attitude is the thing. Every little word is not so important if you have the correct accepting and permissive attitude toward the client ... But you still have those troublesome questions from the client. He simply doesn't know that next step. He asks you to give him a hint, some possibilities; after all you are expected to know something, else why is he here? ... Then you begin to wonder. The technique is good, but ... does it go *far* enough? Does it really work on clients? Is it *right* to leave a person helpless, when you might show him the way out? ... For here is demanded of you what no other person can do or point out—and that is to rigorously scrutinize yourself and your attitudes toward others. Do you believe that all people truly have a creative potential in them? That each person is a unique individual and that he alone can work out his own individuality? Or do you really believe that some persons are of 'negative value' and others are weak and must be led and taught to be 'wiser,' 'stronger' people? You begin to see that there is nothing compartmentalized about this method of counseling. It is not just counseling, because it demands the most exhaustive, penetrating, and comprehensive consistency ... When genuine acceptance and permissiveness are your tools it requires nothing less than the whole complete personality. And to grow yourself is the most demanding of all. Instead of demanding less of the counselor's personality in the situation, client-centered therapy demands more. It demands discipline, not restraint. It calls for the utmost in sensitivity, appreciative awareness, channeled and disciplined. It demands that the counselor put all he has of these precious qualities into the situation, but in a disciplined, refined manner. It is restraint only in the sense that the

counselor does not express himself in certain areas that he may use himself in others. Even this is deceptive, however. It is not so much restraint in any area as it is focusing, sensitizing one's energies and personality in the direction of an appreciative and understanding attitude.

Some Observations on the Organization of Personality

In 1947, this article was published in *The American Psychologist* (Rogers, 1947) and had been prepared as the outgoing president's address before the American Psychological Association. Electrical recordings of therapy sessions had by now revealed that 'changes that occur in the perception of self and in the perception of reality' result in changes in behavior. The 'I' becomes reorganized to something more appropriate to the realities of the time and place; that is, to the culture of therapy, a culture that mediates between the inconsistencies of a person's social values and the sensations of his or her organism. In this paper, Rogers shows some of the client's side of the relationship with the therapist. A client writes to her counselor:

> It's almost impersonal. I like you—of course I don't know why I should like you or why I shouldn't like you. It's a peculiar thing. I've never had that relationship with anybody before and I've often thought about it ... A lot of times I walk out with a feeling of elation that you think highly of me, and of course at the same time I have the feeling that 'Gee, he must think I'm an awful jerk' or something like that. But it doesn't really—those feelings aren't so deep that I can form an opinion one way or the other about you.

From the observational material from interviews it is also possible to view changes in self-concept over the course of therapy. For example, at the onset of counseling, a client says:

> I feel disorganized, muddled; I've lost all direction; my personal life has disintegrated ... I don't care about my personal appearance. I don't know anything anymore. I feel guilty about the things I have left undone. I don't think I could ever assume responsibility for anything.

After a little over a month in therapy, after some eight interviews, the client has this to say:

> I'm feeling much better; I'm taking more interest in myself. I do have some individuality, some interests. I seem to be getting a newer understanding of myself ... I've been making plans about school and about a job; I've been working hard on a term paper; I've been going to the library to trace down a

topic of special interest and finding it exciting ... I'm getting out and mixing with people; I am reacting sensibly to a fellow who is interested in me seeing both his good and bad points. I will work toward my degree; I'll start looking for a job this week.

From observations such as these, a principle began to form:

> The observed phenomena of change seem most adequately explained by the hypothesis that *given certain psychological conditions, the individual has the capacity to reorganize his field of perception, including the way he perceives himself, and that a concomitant or a resultant of this perceptual reorganization is an appropriate alteration of behavior.*

The Process Equation of Psychotherapy

When Rogers received the Distinguished Scientific Contribution Award from the American Psychological Association in 1957, he wrote this article. It was published in 1961 in the *American Journal of Psychotherapy* (Rogers, 1961c). This paper was an attempt to describe precisely from scientific observations 'the process by which change in personality and behavior is achieved in psychotherapy.' The process can be represented by this equation:

> The more the client perceives the therapist as real or genuine, as empathic, as having an unconditional regard for him, the more the client will move away from a static, unfeeling, fixed, impersonal type of functioning and the more he will move toward a way of functioning which is marked by a fluid, changing, acceptant experiencing of differentiated personal feelings.

The Concept of the Fully Functioning Person

This article has been substantially controversial. Later versions, largely due to the more ambitious context in which they appeared, have given the impression of elitism, at worst, and naïveté, at best. Nevertheless, the original (circa 1952, published 1963) is one of Rogers' most influential writings. Initially it simply tried to answer the perfectly reasonable and appropriate question: 'If we were as successful as therapists as we would wish to be, what sort of persons would have developed in our therapy? What is the hypothetical end-point, the ultimate of the therapeutic process?' Rogers concludes thus:

> Here then is my theoretical model of the person who emerges from therapy— a person functioning freely in all the fullness of his organismic potentialities;

a person who is dependable in being realistic, self-enhancing, socialized and appropriate in his behavior; a creative person, whose specific formings of behavior are not easily predictable; a person who is ever-changing, ever developing, always discovering himself and the newness in himself in each succeeding moment of time. This is a person who in an imperfect way actually emerges from the experience of safety and freedom in a therapeutic experience, and this is the person whom I have tried to describe for you in 'pure' form.

Between this article and the previous 'Process Equation of Psychotherapy' there is substantial overlap. However, attempts to simplify, to study one of these articles and not the other, leave out essential ideas and perspectives. It may be noted that these two articles are complementary and must be considered together. The 'process equation' is written primarily in the mode of consciousness that might be called 'analytical,' 'linear,' 'logical' or 'scientific.' While the 'fully functioning person' article adopts primarily an holistic mode of consciousness. This complementariness of different modes of consciousness is important to understand in studying Rogers' work. The following article makes this insight explicit.

Persons or Science? A philosophical question

In this article, published in 1955 in *The American Psychologist* (Rogers, 1953), Rogers proposes a dialogue between the two different, but complementary, modes of consciousness. The paper is the result of a feeling he describes this way: 'I have felt an increasing discomfort at the distance between the *rigorous objectivity* of myself as scientist and the *almost mystical subjectivity* of myself as therapist" [italics added]. After a long debate on the equally meritorious qualities of each position, Rogers proposes an 'integration' between the 'experientialist' and the 'scientist.' Although he never followed up with a formal description of the integration, it is clear that his best work incorporates an intimate interaction of these two modes: objective/subjective, scientific/experiential, intellectual/intuitive. This is a thread that runs through all effective applications of the person-centered approach and may provide part of the basis for understanding the approach. Incidentally, in this article Rogers uses, perhaps for the first time in print, the phrase 'person-centeredness.'

The Necessary and Sufficient Conditions of Therapeutic Personality Change

In 1957, in this statement in the *Journal of Counseling Psychology* (Rogers, 1957), Rogers reviews the background, theory and research of his system of client-centered therapy, whose principles he suggests are valid for psychotherapy in general. This piece is perhaps his most famous and much more accessible than the more elaborate and formal treatment prepared for Koch's 1959 publication (Rogers, 1959). The polished theoretical statement for constructive personality change is the following:

1. Two persons are in psychological contact.
2. The first, whom we shall term the client, is in a state of incongruence, being vulnerable or anxious.
3. The second person, whom we shall term the therapist, is congruent or integrated in the relationship.
4. The therapist experiences unconditional positive regard for the client.
5. The therapist experiences an empathic understanding of the client's internal frame of reference and endeavors to communicate this experience to the client.
6. The communication to the client of the therapist's empathic understanding and unconditional positive regard is to a minimal degree achieved.

No other conditions are necessary. If these six conditions exist, and continue over a period of time, this is sufficient. The process of constructive personality change will follow.

Summary

The contents of these articles contain the *principles* of client-centered therapy that were derived from the application of the person-centered approach. Many have confused these principles of therapy with the approach itself.

From these articles one can also perceive the *motivation* of Rogers to do what he did; his *intention*, what he hoped to realize; his values that gave meaning to his sentiments; his *thoughts* and *observations*; his *posture*, physical and mental, as he put himself into the therapeutic relationship; his *attitude*, trying to understand what the client was communicating at a deep level, continually attempting to improve the effectiveness of his psychotherapy; his *alertness* to detect what was unexpected, surprising, what challenged his own experiences; his *mental openness* to let the phenomena speak for itself and to formulate theories based on learnings earned in practice. That is, one may perceive the person-centered approach being applied to the phenomenon of psychotherapy.

In the case of client-centered therapy, the person-centered approach was characteristically expressed with an intense *empathic understanding*, within a *genuine* person-to-person relationship, where the therapist, due to the particular state of consciousness provoked by empathy, *accepted* without question or judgment the client's thoughts and feelings.

Notes

1. 'One person dreaming is merely a dream; two, becomes reality.' A phrase spray-painted on a wall on Coronel Silva Teles Street in Campinas, Brazil.

2. Freud, on the other hand, appeared pessimistic: 'Only a few patients are worth the trouble we spend on them so that we are not allowed to have a therapeutic attitude,' he complained, 'but we must be glad to have learned something in every case' (Weiss, 1970: 37). If not positive, Freud was at least practical. He advised Jung, 'Just give up wanting to cure; learn and make money, those are the most plausible conscious aims' (Lieberman, 1985: 106).

3. Several such surveys have been made to determine eminence among psychologists. Smith (1982) asked psychologists and counselors to rate the ten most influential therapists. In another survey (Korn, Davis & Davis, 1991) historians of psychology were asked to rank the ten most important contemporary psychologists. These rankings were compared to those obtained from graduate psychology department chairpersons. Both historians and chairpersons ranked B.F. Skinner first.

CHAPTER THREE

The Person-Centered Approach to Small Groups
More than psychotherapy

Der Mensch Wird am Du zum Ich.[1]
  Martin Buber

The first North American occurrence of small group meetings for psychotherapy is thought to have been the 1905 'classes' conducted by Reverend Elwood Worcester, PhD, and an internist, Joseph Henry Pratt, MD, with tuberculosis patients in Boston. Loneliness, pessimism, depression, desperation and other psychological effects of their disease were relieved through the emotional support as well as the challenge of a stable group of people with similar concerns and experiences.

Worcester, an associate of William James, described the group leaders' attitude toward their innovative work: 'As we are attempting to establish no new dogma, and as our motives are entirely disinterested, our single desire is to give each patient the best opportunity of life and health which our means allow' (Pinney, 1978: 111). From their statement, their approach was consistent with the person-centered approach.

In Vienna, about this time, Sigmund Freud was convening his Wednesday Psychological Society study group. Sandor Ferenczi, Alfred Adler, Otto Rank and others who were to become notable psychologists were among the group's members. As an interest in oneself is so compelling, the meetings frequently drifted from case discussions and analysis of patients to the analysis of group participants. Emotional outbursts were not uncommon. Although the group was not organized as therapy or for 'encounter,' doubtless, it was not different in many respects.

Competition over the ownership of ideas, hostilities between members, challenges to the group's leadership and, of course, time's erosion of compatibilities, contributed to the abandonment of the initial activities. As frequently happens, reorganization to a broader institutionalized form ('international' psychoanalytic movement) was the solution to, one: the group's inability to deal with the complex feelings between involved human beings; and, two: the reluctance to call it quits and simply disband.

This is a revision of a chapter which first appeared in Gazda, GM (1982) *Basic Approaches to Group Psychotherapy and Group Counseling.* Springfield, IL: Charles Thomas.

Many groups face the problems of Freud's study group. That it could not resolve the various conflicts could be accounted for, in part, by the inexperience of group members in such a context and their inattention to interpersonal relations. This state of affairs would doubtless be due in part to an over-attention to the analysis of the subjective reality of individuals. Further, as any university professor who attends committee meetings with colleagues can attest, one should not underestimate the force of stubborn self-centeredness in sabotaging a group's effectiveness. Logan Pearsall Smith (1934), in one of his witty phrases, explained this phenomenon, 'It's an odd thing about the Universe that though we all disagree with each other, we are all of us always in the right.'

One of Freud's (1959) major contributions was the recognition that *all psychotherapy is a group phenomenon*. 'In the individual's mental life,' he observed, 'someone else is invariably involved, as a model, as an object, as helper, as an opponent; and so from the very first, individual psychology ... is at the same time social psychology as well.'

Also in Vienna, Jacob Moreno, the founder of the *psychodrama* approach, was conducting group therapy as theater as early as 1910. Moreno encouraged acting out a problem situation to increase a participant's awareness of his conflict and to suggest possible solutions. He introduced the terms *group therapy* and *group psychotherapy*. In fact, he claims, 'Modern group psychotherapy started in the sexual ghetto of Vienna, in a natural setting ... ' (Moreno, 1966).

Most of the various perspectives, theories and practices one is likely to hear about, formally or informally, in a modern small group for psychotherapy or encounter had been developed in the United States *before* the Second World War. Group treatments involved the use of music, dance and plastic arts, participants frankly and truthfully expressing their feelings and thoughts and their mutual encouragement and support, getting to know each other, becoming aware of each other's perceptions of themselves, lifting the façades each wears in social and professional life.

Group populations included schizophrenics, hospitalized mental patients, prison inmates as well as normal people with the ordinary problems of life. Doctors, nurses, social workers and other personnel had also been organized into the same discussion groups to enhance the group therapy programs in hospitals. Even 'therapeutic communities' had been organized where staff and participants lived and worked together. The idea that a group was like a family, with father, mother and siblings was put into practice. Actual family members were included in outpatient groups.

In such experiences participants learned that the thoughts and feelings they believed isolated them from society were actually what they had in common with others. In groups inspired by Alfred Adler, they learned the value of social equality. He observed, 'There is no principle more generally valid for all human relationships than 'on top of' and "underneath"' (Lieberman, 1985). In general, the dictum of one of the group therapy pioneers L.C. Marsh was followed. He liked to say, 'By the crowd they have been broken; by the crowd they shall be healed' (Gazda, 1982).

Group psychotherapy to this point was largely a medical treatment: persons suffering from an illness were treated by a physician and group therapy was an option. The medical model persists in psychotherapy, Strupp (1983) has observed, not merely because of the artifacts of language taken from medicine: 'patient,' 'therapist,' 'diagnosis,' 'etiology,' but because psychotherapy undeniably attempts to alleviate human suffering.

In the 1940s Kurt Lewin was developing an approach based on the viewpoint that the group is not a mere collection of individuals, but an entity in its own right, with characteristics that may differ from those of its members. Lewin introduced the term *group dynamics* for the study of group qualities. Individual consciousness and behavior, he held, must be understood within the social field in which the individual is embedded. *Group pressure* was also coined by Lewin to describe the influence of the group in altering or attempting to alter the behavior of a member (Lewin, 1951). Members, of course, also influence the behavior and character of the group as a whole.

Freud had characterized therapy as 're-education.' In 1947, the National Training Laboratories, employing this concept and following Lewin's ideas, elaborated the educational emphasis to small group work. Volunteers (not patients) joined T-groups (T, for training) to learn skills in leadership as well as group efficiency in problem-solving and cooperative tasks (Bradford, Gibb & Benne, 1964).

Personal growth groups and encounter groups in the 1960s expanded this educational concept, not just to industrial or academic leaders, but to ordinary citizens who wished to improve their personal relations and the quality of their life.

Wilfred Bion in England in the 1960s elaborated a theory of group dynamics based on the 'mental life' of the group as a whole. Bion formulated three aspects of group members' activity that can take place independently. They can be characterized roughly as follows: Members of the group are looking for a leader to sustain and protect them (dependency). When they realize no such savior exists, they turn to each other for salvation or diversion (pairing). When they realize no one can fulfill the impossible role they fantasize, they become disappointed and angry, fighting it out with each other or abandoning the group by leaving (fight or flight). Individuals taking responsibility for their decisions and behavior contribute to a mature level of group functioning (Bion, 1959).

S.H. Foulkes, who developed group analytic psychotherapy, attempted to intertwine the patient's past experiences with the here-and-now action of the group. Foulkes gave importance to the relation between group members and to the group as a therapeutic agent. He likened the group therapist to a conductor of music, following, not leading, the melody the group is trying to play (Grotjahn, 1978).

Group approaches tend to adopt many techniques, even including those from systems with opposing philosophies. The behavior therapy approach, for example, differs from the analytic therapy approach in its view of psychological disorders. It is not because of conflicts, inhibitions, resistances, psychological barriers that some people suffer, suggests Arnold Lazarus (1982). 'Many people,' he claims, 'suffer emotionally because their learning histories failed to provide them with the necessary coping skills' (p. 214). 'Modeling,' 'rehearsal,' 'coaching,' and 'feedback' are concepts from behavior therapy that have found their way into other approaches to group therapy.

It is worth emphasizing that proponents of a system may adapt a concept from another without realizing it. They may even come to regard the imported concept as essential to their own system, even when it is in fact contradictory. For example, McIlduff and Coghlan (1989) incorrectly assert that, 'One well-established dynamic of all person-centered groups is the function of the staff as a model of facilitative behavior.' This *modeling* they speak of is a tenet of behaviorism. It is an attempt to influence and manipulate a person's behavior by taking advantage of the natural human tendency of *mimicry*. Rogers (1970b) warned of the danger of participants mimicking the behavior of incompetent group facilitators. To 'model facilitative behavior'—that is, to encourage a group participant to mimic the behavior of someone in authority—is operant conditioning. It is diametrically opposite to the person-centered approach which would be more interested in participants discovering their own 'way of being.'

Although Rogers and his colleagues had been previously interested in group work (Peres, 1947; Gordon, 1951), it was not until the 1960s that he became seriously involved in groups.[2]

Rogers' interest, at that time, was in encounter groups. Following the method of process descriptions utilized in client-centered therapy, he also analyzed the group process. He also defined the role of the group leader as a 'facilitator' and emphasized the 'climate of psychological safety in which freedom of experience and reduction of differences gradually occur.'

According to Rogers, the facilitator helps to develop this 'climate' principally through 'facilitator attitudes' of genuineness, acceptance, and empathy. Although in practice he trusted, and at times was helpless to do more than merely admire, the 'wisdom of the group,' beyond proposing these facilitative qualities Rogers did not formulate the group factors which make up a facilitative 'psychological climate.'

His work demonstrated, however, that very little directiveness or technique is required of the facilitator for significant therapeutic progress to take place in both the experience of individual group members and in their collective functioning. Rogers confessed, 'I have a real "thing" about artificiality ... On rare occasions, when frustrated or when a group has seemed to reach a plateau, I have tried what I think of as devices, but they rarely work. Probably this is because I myself lack faith that they are really useful' (1970b: 56).

State of the Art

The history of approaches to group therapy is a record of innovations to deal with the necessities of participants by mobilizing the personal and collective resources of these very same participants. To resolve a personal problem, to reorganize one's life after the loss of a loved one, to relieve the distresses related to the mind or body, to discover a meaning for life, to realize untapped potentialities, are some of the reasons that may bring a person to a group.

The function of person-centered groups is not different from that of group therapy in general. That is, they are thought to instill hope, to provide an opportunity for experiencing and expressing feelings, for interpersonal learning, for altruism, for experiencing universality (we are not alone in our suffering), for existential encounters, as well as to provide information, conditions of the primary family group, opportunities for imitative behavior and development of social skills (Yalom, 1985).

Although the question of Parloff and Dies (1977): 'What kinds of changes are produced by what kinds of interventions provided by what kinds of therapists with what kinds of patients/problems under what kinds of conditions?' has yet to be answered, from a careful review of relatively well-designed studies of group therapy, Bednar and Kaul (1978) have concluded that, 'accumulated evidence indicates that group treatments have been more effective than no treatment, than placebo or non-specific treatments, or than other recognized psychological treatments, at least under the same circumstances.'

The Person-Centered Approach Applied to Small Groups

In brief: A facilitator with certain attitudes and intentions and, say, eight to twelve participants who are seeking change, engage in a ritual they believe they must enact for healing and personal growth to take place. Together they enter an exceptional state of consciousness in which personal insights may be realized and values may be reformulated. Meanings may be derived for the various feelings one experiences in this state and integrated into the person's perceptual framework. A new meaning for one's life and new directions for constructive action may also be formulated. The culture and the less noticed factors of the ambiance are influential. The form of the resulting ritual and the behaviors of facilitators and participants may differ from client-centered therapy and other applications of the person-centered approach.

Thus, *the person-centered small group is not merely a bigger version of client-centered therapy.* It possesses the same capacities for healing and self-knowing as the therapeutic relationship of client-centered therapy as well as the additional social therapeutic potential: a greater understanding of others and improving effective communications with others. Further, the group's functioning as a collective is likely to become more significant. The group offers an opportunity to become aware of the patterns and the consequences of conscious and unconscious collaborations between group members—that is, the group as a whole.

Understanding Others

Just as in client-centered therapy, the person-centered group experience tends to enhance the 'unique, subjective, inner person as the honored and valued core of human life' (Rogers, 1974: 9). Judging blind film segments of a 16-hour group, Meador (1971) has verified this outcome.

This research also verified that participants became more genuine in their personal relationships. Thus, the person-centered group experience appears to go a step further than client-centered therapy in possible constructive consequences. Client-centered therapy could not be shown to result in clients gaining more respect and acceptance for others (Gordon & Cartwright, 1954). However, the person-centered approach applied to small groups *is* likely to result in such changes. For example, six months following the completion of 49 person-centered groups (a total of 461 participants in all), 87% of the participants could say that they were able to understand people better (Tausch, 1983b). It appears that group therapy, in general, helps participants achieve 'more positive and perhaps more healthy evaluations of themselves and others' (Bednar & Kaul, 1978).

Encounter: Cultural innovation

With the advent of the encounter group, the distinction between 'therapy,' 'healing,' 'growth' and 'learning' has been further obscured. Although controversial for a time, the encounter group was surely a manifestation sanctioned by the culture. By 1977 it was estimated that 5,000,000 persons had participated in an 'encounter group' or 'personal growth' group in the United States alone.

There have been many explanations offered for the encounter group's widespread popularity. Doubtless, it enhanced certain North American values: equality, rugged individualism, straightforwardness, self-directiveness, improvement through willpower and idealism. In an introduction to an anthology on the subject, Rogers (1972) explained what he considered the attraction of such groups: 'For one thing,' he wrote, 'it appears to be a significant part of the cultural attempt to meet the isolation of contemporary life ... We would like somehow to find ourselves in real contact with other persons ... in a climate of freedom, group members move toward becoming more expressive, more spontaneous, more flexible, more closely related to their feelings, more open to their own experience and to that of others' (p. ix).

Transpersonal awareness cannot be ruled out as one of the attractions of encounter groups. Erich Fromm (1956) said of this phenomenon, 'If two people who have been strangers, as all of us are, suddenly let the wall between them break down, and feel close, feel one, this moment of oneness is one of the most exhilarating, most exciting experiences of life.'

With less stable communities and the decline of organized religion, the small group also could offer a congenial communal setting for the creation of a stabilizing mythology and inspirational ritual. Perhaps the encounter group served as a microcosm of American idealism where the defeat of loneliness, finding a sense of meaning, anti-intellectualism, and religiosity were all possible. The books of the time were filled with such ideas.

Though often therapeutic, the encounter group is *not* however psychotherapy. It concentrates on the here-and-now situation as opposed to relating historical problems or explanations for behavior and feelings or discussing events which occur outside of the group. It stresses personal responsibility as opposed to letting others decide one's opinions and direct one's behavior. It emphasizes the capacity for growing, for loving, for experiencing joy as well as pain. As a path to self-awareness, it demands honesty and confrontation between participants, and transparency—communicating one's private world to others in a language that they can clearly understand (Jourard, 1971).

The small group is a very complex phenomenon and provides the possibility for multiple changes. Doubtless, along certain dimensions of change, some people improve and others do not.[3] Any strong experience that revises a person's perspective of herself and her relations to others can be expected to influence other aspects of her life as well. Group experiences may have a positive or negative effect on character, may modify superficial aspects of the person or may provoke changes with deep value for the complete human being.

Simply discovering oneself to be not so different from others as one imagined—that others also may long for undeserved luxury, may have a weakness for some vice, may harbor vicious thoughts, may feel jealousy, may wish for revenge, may have unmentionable feelings even towards those closest to them, may wish to be wicked at times—is one of the immediate benefits of the group. If it were to end here, humankind would likely be not much better off. However, the group also does not ignore its members' constructive qualities. Through emotional support, comfort and encouragement, the person's positive traits and strengths are also revealed. Thus, the group participant no longer stands out in society by virtue of anti-social sentiments or because of a peculiar emotional problem, but by virtue of the special strength and constructive potential he possesses.

It should be remembered that all such groups are of limited value. Who am I? Where did I come from? Where am I going? What is my potential? are complex questions. This kind of group may not have the answers. As Friedman (1984) explains:

> We become ourselves through each particular action; we choose ourselves in each act of becoming. Actually, we cannot know our real potentialities in the abstract at all. All we can know are generalizations about ourselves from past situations in which we had other and different resources ... Potentiality is not in us as an already existing objective reality. We know it only as it becomes actualized in response to each new situation. (p. 61)

The facilitator and other group members constitute an environment in which such questions may be provoked. They may be explored within the capacities of the group. Although encounter groups or psychotherapy groups may not have the answers, they may nevertheless play a preliminary part in preparing persons for finding them.

Thrills

The group environment is not always friendly. At times, it may even be threatening. Furthermore, research suggests that the consensus of a group tends to reflect a more risky position than the average risk represented by individual proposals prior to the group discussion (Wallach, Kogan & Bem, 1962; Bateson, 1966). Thus, the group is likely to be less conservative than its members and tends to value risk-taking. Group members who take more risks, become, in one way or another, leaders in the group. Even extremists, who may be disliked personally, command a respect and substantially influence group decisions. Providing psychological risks is one of the encounter group's compelling features, at least it seems to be so for North Americans, whose culture favors more dangerous alternatives over the safer, longer approach.

Although in no way essential, attending an encounter group may frequently involve putting forth unpopular proposals, confronting people directly with uncomplimentary perceptions or even aggressive feelings, disclosing some intimate secrets or fears or personal inadequacies. Since the risk often brought respect and perhaps euphoric feelings for the successful initiates, some groups exaggerated this aspect into what Klein (1983) called, the 'equivalent of interpersonal sky-diving.'

This trend reached a horrifying extreme in India. In 1978 I interviewed participants (mostly Europeans) in 'encounter groups' at a guru's ashram. Often with black eyes or plaster casts on their arms or legs, they reported that leaders of the groups regularly encouraged nudity, sexual encounters, physical violence, including rape, and any activity that would confront the participant with an opportunity to risk 'totally.' It was thought that through this 'total encounter' enlightenment could be achieved. What occurred more often instead was a hepatitis infection.

In spite of the obvious limitations, each participant I spoke with considered his experience (no matter how torturous it might have been) to be positive and attributed to it some sense of benefit. Not a single person considered himself or herself a serious casualty. The look of proud suffering in the faces of these survivors reminded me of the expressions of army recruits who were completing a tough basic training. Doubtless, for the survivors, the positive effects they had experienced greatly outweighed the negative ones.[4]

Self-satisfaction is not limited to participation in an encounter group. The euphoria that accompanies risk may be achieved in an uncountable number of social actions. Observe, for example, the following description: 'I was feeling ... the sense of lightness, of release ... temporarily outside of things, I was somehow closer to their center ... the very same feelings of connection or belonging or being fully used and alive that we feel sometimes in solitude or sex ... a sense of being, for the moment, where we belong ... a stripping down of essentials, a rebellion against the trappings of fashion and cant, a sense of being nakedly exposed to, and therefore alive to, what really matters ... a life of conscience as completion rather than a duty, as a source of joy as well as obligation.' A description of an encounter group? LSD trip? Religious experience? It could be, but isn't. It is a description of a protester's feelings on being arrested for blocking the office of an American Congressman whose opinions differed from his own (Marin, 1985).

Rogers' Description of Encounter

According to Rogers' (1970b) concept of the encounter group, the facilitator organizes the physical surroundings, a schedule for meetings, meals and free time. Apart from this there is no predetermined structure. Thus, the group members become immersed in their own experience and must grapple with the illumination of its meaning.

Initially, they are confused. Awkward silences, squirming bodies, polite but pointless chatter characterizes the beginning. Several people may make suggestions which are frequently ignored or followed by unrelated statements. 'Let's introduce ourselves.' 'What does one do in such groups anyway?'

Sometimes, participants relate some experience from the past: a nasty divorce, grief, a grave health problem, an obstacle which has been overcome. Occasionally, someone attacks the person who has just spoken, denouncing his contribution as irrelevant or superficial.

The group facilitator is more often the target of this early aggressivity. 'Why can't you direct the group in a more productive manner?' In attacking the facilitator, and in coming to her defense, members of the group begin to speak more frankly. Eventually there is an expression of immediate feelings with a supportive exploration of their meanings to the person speaking—in the broad context of his life, both inside and outside the group. This marks the beginning of constructive encounter. The person-centered approach applied to small group encounter usually manages to integrate both aggressors and victims of aggression as well as other members who, for some reason, may have become as renegades.

In his conceptualization of the group culture, Rogers has emphasized the use of feedback and confrontation and the 'cracking of façades'—that is, the transformation of the public face a member presents to the group into the one he shows only to intimates.

Though it had been found that the more the person's own description of himself agrees with others' description of him, the less will be his perceptual defensiveness and the more adequate his personal adjustment (Chodorkhoff, 1954), the value of this knowledge may have been overrated, due to its novelty in the epoch in which it won popularity. Many petty and unjustified judgments can be expressed in the early moments of a group. They may be intended as 'helpful feedback,' to improve the person's 'self-esteem.' However, they may have negative consequences also.

Koch (1970) challenges this procedure, 'Are all so-called façades phony and psychically crippling accretions?' he asks. 'Are all surface traits façades? If there is a distinction between a surface trait and a façade, who is to make it? Is every individual or reference group equally competent to do so relative to a given case? Who is qualified to tell Proust to get rid of his fur coat and his hypochondria; Eliot to ditch his reserve; Mann his rather bourgeois surface rigidities; Gide his exhibitionistically asserted homosexuality; Joyce his propensity for occasional fugues of high living; Dylan Thomas his alcoholism and arrogant scrounging? Is the 'facilitator,' 'change agent,' 'therapist' to be the chap that shouts, 'come out from behind the lectern, Doc'? Is it to be Carl Rogers?' (p. 41).

Acceptance of diversity and a keen discernment are necessary for the facilitator and group members to avoid foolishness. When a person *is* hiding behind a social mask and *wants* to be free of such restraints, to have a choice in how she presents herself, perhaps there is a social wisdom in the group to help her uncover the 'real person.' On the other hand, for the one who does *not* wish to free herself of a social role, how is one to know that the social 'wisdom' of the group is preferable to the individual wisdom of the person? 'The person,' as Friedman (1984) observes, 'may have taken the true measure of this group and may know intuitively, if not consciously, that it does not have the resources to confirm his or her otherness, whatever its rules, aspirations, and stated intentions' (p. 69).

A broad outlook and a sensitivity to each person and his needs is required of the facilitator and group members to guard against the harmful application of any social pressure. Courage is also required in order to confront whatever thoughtless tendencies toward conformity may arise. And courage is required to, in fact, confront one's own ghosts.

Although he strictly opposed groups which permitted violence, sex, or bizarre behavior, especially under the direction of authoritarian and overbearing group leaders, Rogers did not hide his enthusiasm for the encounter group (as he knew it). He was widely quoted as saying, 'the encounter group may well be the most important social invention of the century' (Rogers, 1968).

Rogers also acknowledged aspects of Koch's concern, particularly the tendency of practiced participants to correct their colleague's behavior. If a person making an effort to be nice struck other group members as actually trying to hide bitterness, for example, they might try to provoke an expression of this 'hidden anger.' Trying to make *her* feel the anger they suspect, she may indeed become angry, but not for the reasons they imagine. With their aggressive probing they may even precipitate a serious psychological problem in a person unprepared for such hazing. Many bizarre events have followed this outrageous, though seemingly innocent, application of logic.

Rogers (1970b) calls this the 'old pro phenomenon.' He describes their behavior:

> They feel they have learned the 'rules of the game,' and subtly or openly try to impose these rules on newcomers. Thus, instead of promoting true expressiveness or spontaneity, they endeavor to substitute new rules for old—to make members feel guilty if they are not expressing feelings, or are reluctant to voice criticism or hostility, or are talking about situations outside the group relationship, or are fearful to reveal themselves. (p. 42)

The direct experience of emotion may be liberating and *may* lead to significant learning. Speaking about a feeling, however, can be quite another matter. James (1890) reminds:

> When I say, 'I feel tired,' [it] is not the direct state of tire; when I say 'I feel angry,' it is not the direct state of anger. It is the state of *saying-I-feel-angry*—entirely different, so different that the fatigue and anger apparently included in them are considerable modifications of the fatigue and anger directly felt the previous instant. The act of naming them has momentarily detracted from their force. (p. 190)

The effective facilitator tries to help group members avoid the pitfalls of every convention, even the expression of feelings or activities which a participant has retained from his previous successful group experience.

Directing attention only to one's inner self may contain such pitfalls. Rather than becoming more self-aware, the person may merely become more self-centered. It is not the purpose of person-centered groups to bring about a preoccupation with *me*. The climate intended for the group is to allow the participant to focus inwardly, not to the exclusion of effective life in the world, but solely to contact and unite the tendency toward personal integration. Obviously, this implies integration of the person in the world as well. Ideally, the group environment would allow the expression of, but not the provocation of, previously guarded feelings; would allow emotion, but not mere talking about emotions; would allow self-awareness, but not mere self-centeredness. In short, it would allow the genuine experience of, but not the falsification of, human feeling, creativity and interaction.

People Gathered Together

It should be evident by now that there is no *one* encounter group. This makes it difficult to assess research and to generalize the group's effects. On the other hand, it makes criticisms easy. For example, a magazine writer, ignoring the constructive achievements, called the encounter group, 'callous exploitation and sham group therapy' (Maliver, 1973).

Koch (1970), in a vehement yet valuable criticism, called the group movement, 'the most extreme excursion thus far of man's talent for reducing, distorting, evading, and vulgarizing his own reality.' Koch particularly objected to the vulgarization of noble human qualities through the attempt, 'to court spontaneity and authenticity by artifice; to combat instrumentalism instrumentally; to provide access to experience by reducing it to a packaged commodity; to engineer autonomy by group pressure; to liberate individuality by group shaping.' In this version of encounter, 'openness becomes transparency; love, caring, and sharing become a barter of "reinforcements" or perhaps mutual ego-titillation; aesthetic receptivity or immediacy becomes "sensory awareness."' He may have exaggerated by declaring it the 'most extreme' excursion of mankind vulgarizing its own reality. There are certainly many more likely candidates for the *most* extreme. Nevertheless, his list of vulgarizations that can occur in group activities is a priceless reminder of pitfalls to avoid.

In small group activities there is always the possibility of exploitation and the trivialization of human qualities. This possibility should be prevented. Just as it should be prevented in education, medicine, politics, religion, and other endeavors. It should be remembered that spontaneity, authenticity, autonomy, love, caring, joy, intimacy, are human qualities that *also* appear genuinely in small groups just as in other activities of life.

It also may be recognized that many aspects—both positive and negative—of encounter groups and therapy groups are not inherent to that activity but belong to the nature of people-gathered-together. Group pressure is an example.

A few winters ago my wife and I joined an Austrian ski school. We were assigned to two different groups, commensurate with our respective abilities (she was an excellent skier; I, a beginner). Through moments marked by fear, adventure, intense existential concentration, awe, competition, defeat and victory, each group quickly became cohesive. Inspired by the majesty and glacial beauty of the Alps, the exhilaration of brisk fresh air, the physical tests, while isolated from their normal patterns of living, group members challenged their human limits *and* possibilities and naturally grew to be closer emotionally.[5]

These were not people who subscribed to the habits of encounter groups. They came to ski. Nevertheless, they also did what people do under the influence of being together: become close and jealously guard their intimacy against invasion from outsiders. When my wife and I wanted to have lunch together, our respective groups of colleagues reacted to the separation like any encounter group. They were markedly opposed to anyone 'breaking up the group.' Though they did not confront us forcefully with their feelings of being abandoned, their disguised attempts to both threaten and seduce us into staying 'with the group' made them clear enough. Knowing that it is a characteristic of groups to insist on loyalty to them, helped us to enjoy our vacation.

Group Culture

In the small group, participants are strangers to each other. As they are more than visitors in this new setting, they may be closer to immigrants. They must establish themselves in the new culture. They must define who they are, not only to others but to themselves. They must realize what they want, what they see, what they feel, what they believe.

Without the past from which to draw information, each person must teach the others about herself. In the language of emotion and the customs that are being established together, she also learns who she is.

Outside the group, it may be of value to be strongly self-sufficient and not to reveal feelings. Within the group, the opposite may be true: you should 'really be yourself,' 'say what is on your mind.' On the outside, it may be of value to be able to chat and keep the conversation lively. In the group, this might be considered superficial behavior. Being informed, philosophizing, telling jokes may be of value or not, depending on the context, just as these activities are valued differently by regional cultures.

The tendency toward cohesion, cooperation, the physical arrangements and the various liaisons which take place are largely instinctive. People have, for example, a feel for what is the appropriate behavior for a place—for the capacity of the whole. In physical terms this is demonstrated by sociological studies of plazas and public gardens where a relatively constant density tends to be maintained. Even though there is space for more people, they do not sit.[6]

Each group is unique, and explicit and implicit rules vary widely. Generally speaking, in groups from the person-centered approach, physical violence is prohibited, policies are adopted around starting and ending times for the meetings, tardiness, the admittance of new members, and a procedure for terminating the group. In the United States, group members usually feel they owe each other an explanation for behavior outside the meetings which affects the group—liaisons between members, gossip in the corridors, and such. Though arrived at by frequently exhausting consideration of each member's wishes, the established policies are nevertheless frequently changed.

Often the group will insist that each member attend every meeting of the group from start to finish. This rule varies widely, depending on the location. In Brazil, for example, it is not uncommon for a person to join a group in the middle of a session, become intensely involved, and leave before the conclusion of the meeting. On the other hand, in most parts of North America and even more so in northern Europe, this behavior would seldom be acceptable to the group.

Members of the group, through their concepts, beliefs, feelings, perspectives, behavior, establish the group culture. At the same time they are creating the culture, they are being changed by what they are creating.

Facilitator Participants and Participant Facilitators

The behavior of participants in the group, the interpersonal interaction, the complex problems that arise, are likely to be less predictable than in client-centered therapy. With more people interacting, the level of emotional arousal is also often higher. Chaos, confusion and ambiguity are more likely in the group setting. The function of the facilitator is to do what is necessary to facilitate an effectively functioning group with a growth-promoting climate for its participants. To accomplish this, greater flexibility in his or her behavior may be required in the group than in client-centered therapy.

The egalitarian principle that forms a part of most manifestations of the person-centered approach also has an influence in the group. What is expected of group participants is also expected of the facilitator. He is expected to behave openly and spontaneously, expressing honestly his personal feelings and thoughts in the present moment. In this regard, *predictable* actions are less tolerated, both for facilitators and participants. This can be a problem for some client-centered therapists who are accustomed to controlling the therapeutic relationship—even though this control may be as unobtrusive as merely maintaining a certain receptive posture to allow the client the center stage. In the group, such behavior is rarely permitted. *In general,* more genuineness, as expressed through the attitudes, intentions and behaviors of the facilitator, will be expected in the group than in the client-centered therapy situation.

In a certain sense, transparency, that is so much the cornerstone of the success of the *client* in client-centered therapy, becomes more demanded of the *facilitator* in the small group. On the other hand, perhaps because interactions between *participants* are more likely than between facilitator and participant, the establishment of empathic understanding in the group becomes more the prerogative of the group participant.

In the group, the social and biological connections between members are more difficult to ignore. Although the attitude of non-judgmental acceptance is very similar as in client-centered therapy, it may be the facilitator's and participants' acceptance of the group (that is, their trust in the group itself) that is more essential to success. As participants become more aware of the group as a whole and the *pattern* of the sum of individual actions, they are more likely to develop a diffused, all-at-once, perception. An awareness that their individual feelings, intentions and actions have a consequence for the group—and thus, for their own futures—may facilitate a mature functioning of the group as well as the creation of an environment in which constructive personality change and personal growth are more likely.

Since the group is more likely to be convened in a beautiful and tranquil resort setting, the effect of place is doubtless more influential than in client-centered therapy. A receptive consciousness is not only facilitated by the effects of air and water and space but also by conviviality: group members taking meals together, participating in recreational activities and so forth.

Flexibility

Corey (1985) lists some procedures he considers should *not* be part of the person-centered facilitator's role. They include giving advice, using planned techniques, diagnosis, evaluation, giving homework assignments and intervening in a directive way. Under behaviors he feels characterize the person-centered facilitator, he lists: 'listening actively, reflecting, clarifying, summarizing, linking, demonstrating respect, affirming a client's capacity for self-determination, accepting and caring for a client' (p. 233).

This proposal for the facilitator applying the person-centered approach to the small group represents a logical extension of behavior noted in client-centered therapy. However, the group is not a logical extension of this phenomenon. The group is, in general, much more complex. It's ambiance may be one that encourages constructive insight and change, the fresh air of humor, growing in maturity, new ideas, joyful moments, hope. But it also may be one of chaotic interactions, frustration, confusion, boredom, fear, anguish, sadness, hopelessness. The facilitator and participants often live in a situation that they cannot predict, frequently do not like, and often do not understand.

The priority of the facilitator is not to follow an approved list of behaviors. It is to do what is necessary to facilitate the effective functioning of the group. It may be necessary not only to tolerate uncertainty but to react to an unexpected situation in an unexpected way. To be effective may even mean behaving in a 'disapproved' manner. (See examples of 'idiosyncratic empathy' cited by Bozarth, 1984.)

Corey (1985), in spite of his favorable disposition toward person-centered small group facilitation, doubtless would not approve of such flexibility. He has criticized what he feels is 'excessive floundering' in a 'totally loose' structure. This is a personal reaction. Some facilitators and participants will feel greater or lesser comfort within the group's structure—whether loose or rigid. Within reason, the justification for the degree of structure should not be based on the facilitator's comfort level, patience or impatience, but on its advantages in realizing the group's goals. Research studies suggest that groups which are more structured may perform better initially, but over time, their performance is no better than low-structured groups (Crews & Melnick, 1976). Greater structure doubtless gives advantages in certain situations; low structure, in others. The low-structured group that develops a situation-centered approach may be better prepared for unexpected problems, that so often arise, than the group that has relied on a pre-set pattern for its actions.

Just as the best structure is that which best suits the group and not necessarily the one outlined by textbook, the best facilitator is not necessarily the one with the most training or the most impressive credentials. In one encounter group project, for example, four out of five professionally trained therapists were *not* acceptable as group leaders (Bebout, 1976). The best facilitators are the ones who facilitate best.

Successful facilitators do not decide in advance to direct the person or the group in a particular way. They do not, likewise, decide in advance *not* to direct the group, to be non-directive or unstructured, as this does not come from the necessities of the actual moment either. The approach taken by the effective facilitator is not inactive, it may involve intense concentration even when she appears to be doing nothing.

Facilitating is not the same as motivating. Leaving people alone may be facilitative in a given situation. Sometimes a person, sitting silently, not directly involved in the interaction, is profoundly affected. In fact, both clinical practice and research findings challenge the common assumption that the more a group participant speaks, the more he benefits. For example, Smith, Bassin and Froehlich (1960) measured the length of speech and words spoken by members of a small group and could find no relationship between the extent of verbal participation and client improvement. Nevertheless, the group facilitator or participant, speaking or silent, is *communicating*. 'No matter how hard one tries, one cannot not communicate,' observed Watzlawick, Beavin and Jackson (1967), 'Activity or inactivity, words or silence, all have message value; they influence others and these others, in turn, cannot not respond to these communications and are themselves communicating' (pp. 218–19). When this communication is significant for the participant and she is participating in what is for her a meaningful way, her participation *is* related to therapeutic improvement (Sechrest & Barger, 1961).

In other words, group participants who express anger or other strong emotions, give and receive feedback, disclose secrets of their history or subjective world, do not necessarily learn more about themselves than those who do not do such things. Learning is associated with the integration of emotion, feedback and disclosure into the person's cognitive scheme, his self-concept, perception of the world, his reality (Lieberman, Yalom & Miles, 1973).

It does not hurt facilitators to be humble about their contributions. McCardel and Murray (1974), in comparing three different group experiences with the effect of a plausible attention situation and a no-contact control group, found that the effects of the three group experiences were virtually indistinguishable from, what they called, the 'placebo' group. These results were significantly different from the control group.

Coulson (1970) has gone as far as to propose that the 'critical group event is simply the process of time passing and our staying together ... the sole necessary and sufficient condition for an encounter group is that there be an occasion for it ... The encounter will happen if you give people sufficient time together without a distracting task and put somebody with them as a leader [facilitator] who will not do traditional leaderly things—who knows enough, that is, not to get people organized, not to tell them how to encounter, or to set an agenda' (pp. 6–11).

Because he does not do 'leaderly' things does not mean that the facilitator sits back and does nothing. Even when 'nothing is happening' he must be intensely involved. And at times he is in the center of the action. At such moments he may be able to do no better than to surrender to his own personal consciousness, to be open to unexpected emotions and behavior that is demanded by the situation.

For example, in an encounter group, a participant (let's call her Janet) suddenly announced that she was in love with the facilitator. This stunned him, as well as other participants. Some imagined a scandalous liaison. Others were merely embarrassed by a revelation of such intimacy, whether it was true or not.

It was not. The fact is that they had not even spoken to each other outside of the group meetings. Nevertheless, they were suddenly thrown into an unexpected complicity: they were the only ones in the group who knew the truth.

The facilitator was tempted to avoid any personal involvement. As a 'therapist,' he could help her explore her fantasies, so rich in transference, seduction and manipulation. At the same time, he respected her courage to try to reach beyond the ordinary constraints of convention—and even time and space.

Before analyzing all the alternatives, he instinctively entered the encounter as a person. He admitted that he did not love her but that he did respect her. 'Here we are, together in a completely unedited situation. What do we do now? Can anyone help us?'

Another participant in the group, a physician, happened to be very insightful and understanding. He made the right observations and asked the right questions to help them through the first awkward moments. They expressed how they felt toward each other, toward the situation, toward the other group members, and spoke about aspects of their personal life that related to this moment. Other participants described their own relationships, both within the group and back home. Members of the group expressed varied feelings. They recounted experiences of promiscuity, infidelity, devotion, marriage, love. The group session ended with participants feeling they had a very deeply engaging and fruitful encounter.

The next meeting, Janet admitted that she had always wished to be able to begin a sentence on an impulse, at best a half-truth, and just go ahead and see how it ended. She had done just this. Not working it out ahead of time, she launched her project. Then, once in motion, she became terrified that the facilitator might abandon her in that strange 'space.' Worse, he might even treat her like a patient, kindly helping a 'troubled person' deal with her foolishness. She was not only grateful that this did not happen, but also that the group had the resourcefulness to benefit from the episode.

This willingness, not obligation, on the part of the facilitator (or any participant) to face the 'pure reality' (Mente & Spittler, 1980), to be changed by the experience he is living in the group, characterizes the person-centered approach and perhaps distinguishes it from other approaches. It is an example of the attitude expressed by Buber (1966) when he reflected, 'I felt I have not the right to want to change another, if I am not open to be changed by him as far as it is legitimate.'

In this less predictable environment, the effective facilitator learns to trust immediate sensations, emotions, reasoning and intuitive faculties, to live in the moment. Other group participants come to know that the facilitator will be genuinely what she is feeling. She responds to the moment even if that means saying or doing something unpopular or even what might appear non-therapeutic. She may make mistakes. By avoiding the safety and also the artificiality of learned techniques, she tries to minimize saying or doing the wrong thing at the right time and even the right thing at the wrong time.

As regards the ideal attitude of the facilitator, it is difficult to improve on the sentiments of Reverend Worcester and Dr. Pratt that began this chapter: 'As we are attempting to establish no new dogma, and as our motives are entirely disinterested, our single desire is to give each patient the best opportunity of life and health which our means allow' (Pinney, 1978: 111).

Genuineness

'Attending' each person with 'empathic responses,' has become for many the customary method of client-centered therapy. This may be effective for some group participants. It may also be ineffective for some persons. It depends on time, place and people. Generally speaking, group participants will not at first tolerate such methods. Of course, for brief periods at the beginning of the group (or in the contrived structure of training or demonstration) it may be permitted. However, even in such cases, prolonged predictable responses from the facilitator, especially those practiced as a facilitative technique, will eventually be challenged by group members. 'What about you?' they may demand. 'Can you only repeat what we say? How do you feel? What do you think? Who are you?'

Participants in the group insist on frank and emotionally congruent expressions (verbal and non-verbal) from all participants, and particularly the designated facilitator. On this aspect, Rogers (1970b) comments, 'As time goes on the group finds it unbearable that any member should live behind a mask or front ... the smooth coin of tact and cover-up—amply satisfactory for interactions outside—are just not good enough ... Gently at times, almost savagely at others, the group *demands* that the individual be himself, that his current feelings not be hidden.' In the case of the facilitator, this mask (in the eyes of group members) could be her method of therapy, her technique of facilitating. It is artificiality they wish to abolish, but *not* the reality of facilitation. Thus, the facilitator must be 'herself' and be facilitative without using 'professional' devices.

Most of all, perhaps, a *pattern* of Rogerian reflective statements or 'focusing' advice is annoying. The following example illustrates this point. A participant, trained in 'communication skills,' made what she regarded as a 'facilitative response' to each person who spoke in the group. Following what each person said, she repeated the speaker's words, kindly offered some interpretation aimed at demonstrating empathy, and whenever possible, urged the speaker to 'focus on his feelings.' In spite of her apparent sincerity, the people she tried to 'facilitate' promptly ignored her. The gentler speakers would pause until she had exhausted the intervention, then continue. After several 'reflective responses,' group participants became visibly annoyed. One irritated speaker asked her to shut up and mind her own business so that he could complete his thoughts.

Later, at the lunch table, she turned to Carl Rogers and said, 'This group doesn't seem to appreciate being offered *accurate empathic responses*. Some say they like my effort to reflectively listen, but most of my interventions fall flat.' Rogers swallowed a bite of salad and, after a moment's thought, replied diplomatically, 'I think the group is challenging us to reach within ourselves for a *deeper empathy*.' In client-centered therapy, a reflective mode of empathy may become a permanent aspect of the dialogue between therapist and client. In the small group, a 'deeper empathy' is demanded.

How does one express a deeper empathy? In whatever way is appropriate at that moment. To genuinely understand another person is very different from possessing the genuine *need* to be *seen* as an understanding person. Group participants can easily tell the difference. 'We are all in this together,' is their point of view. After this becomes a reality, anyone can be empathic with whomever he pleases and in whatever way that works—even, perhaps, using reflective statements or 'focusing' devices, within reason.

Facilitator attitudes expressed in the group setting may take a form different from those same attitudes expressed in client-centered therapy. In fact, what was successful in the two-person situation may backfire in the group setting. For example, in a study of hospitalized mental patients, Truax, Carkhuff and Kodman (1965) found that participants, in groups in which facilitators were involved at high levels of accurate empathy and unconditional positive regard, made greater improvement than clients in groups with relatively lower levels. An expected result. However, a surprising finding that contrasted to previous studies of individual therapy (and that emphasizes that groups are not merely bigger versions of therapeutic dyads) was that *negative* relationships were obtained between the level of therapist genuineness and client change.

It is possible that, for example, within the hospital setting of this research, when a psychologist claims to be nobody special, denying that he is in fact a *professional* who participates in deciding the fate of the hospital's inmates, he becomes *inauthentic*. Ordinary people would certainly think so.

Congruence also depends on the context. Thus, a person who would be genuine might behave differently according to the demands of different settings. The facilitator who tries to be 'one of the boys' and decides to share something from his personal life that will make him *appear* 'real' (usually with the motive of 'modeling' correct behavior or of 'motivating' participants) is doubtless genuine, but a genuine phony. Why would disturbed clients in group therapy react differently to him than ordinary people?

The expression of personal feelings by the therapist may not even be appropriate in certain cases. Mente and Spittler (1980) from their research on group therapy in Germany, suggest that this practice may be counterproductive (at least in that culture). The importance of appropriate facilitator response is supported by research that suggests that premature sharing of personal material by the group facilitator may be disruptive, whereas more timely disclosures (sharing what is 'real' at the moment in harmony with what is happening or stimulated by strong personal emotions) could be constructive (Dies, 1973). There is evidence that suggests that facilitator genuineness in the context of the *group as a whole* tends to have more impact on the outcome for a given participant than the level of genuineness the *individual* may 'receive' from the facilitator (Truax, 1966; Truax et al, 1965).

Nobody's Perfect

It could be said that the person-centered facilitator's attempt at understanding also must be directed inward as well as outward: 'What do I feel in this moment?' The facilitator is asked to know himself and express this knowing—just as the participant is expected to do.

Spontaneity, simplified, is a knee-jerk reaction. It is an uncensored, automatic response to a stimulus. Genuineness has to do with honesty, purity. Put them together. A pure feeling is perceived from the complexity of sensations that makes up one's consciousness and expressed in a straightforward and honest way, without self-censoring but in a nevertheless appropriate way: congruence.

It may sound simple, but it is not always so easily accomplished. In the following example from the filmed encounter group, *Because That's My Way* (McGaw, 1971), Rogers (one of the facilitators) is not only receptive and sensitive to pain or tears, but he also angrily confronts a group participant. Thus, he engages fully in the same process all participants are living. But is it an example of congruence? Is it facilitative?

> *George:* I still have to get back to the fact that sure, right now this [the group experience] is real. Okay. That's all well and good. But yet we all do know that if we're going to take what this here and now gives us and go out into tomorrow's here and now, then for us to really apply this to our life and the future, we're going to have to be revolutionaries. We're going to have to tear down society. Aren't we?
>
> *Rogers:* Okay. I feel there are quiet revolutionaries and violent ones. I think most of my life I've been a quiet revolutionary.
>
> *George:* We don't all have channels open to us that you have open to yourself to be a quiet revolutionary. For the masses of kids, we tried to be, the hippie movement tried to be quiet revolutionaries. Now, these very same kids ... and it just makes me all the more bitter and cynical. We got our heads beat in after trying to get McCarthy elected. [George sobs] I'm really bitter about that, you know.
>
> *Rogers:* Just full of rage about that, really.

George: [bitterly] The only way I can deal with rage is to be violent! I can't be a quiet revolutionary. They won't let me. You can sit over there, sanctimonious, and say, 'I'm a quiet revolutionary.' They won't let me!

Rogers: [angrily] You're mad at me and call me a sanctimonious revolutionary. Okay. But by God, I am a revolutionary: but, I will not be a revolutionary in your way. And that's what you don't like!

George: Well, you see, I tend to feel that your way has been proven time and time again to be totally superficial, totally ineffectual, totally counterproductive. You're channeling off a lot of students' energies.

After this, George, unable to feel he belonged (in spite of pleas to stay from other participants, including the other facilitator, Tony Rose), left angry and frustrated.

His leaving the group would have to be considered a failure of the group. That is, in any evaluation that considered more than mere personal objectives as part of success. Of course, there are people who deliberately set out to destroy a group and easily succeed. This is not the group's fault. The group is after all a delicate entity and is easily sabotaged. However, George put himself into the group. He did not seem to *deliberately* sabotage the group. He was involved. He expressed deep feelings. He did not feel understood. As proof of this, he returned with his wife after this session. In one last ditch effort, he asked her, 'to help him explain his political concerns.' This did not appear in the film version of the group (Rose, 1986).

George expressed who he really was. And at the critical moment empathic understanding was not evident. There was a clash of values or at least of identities. George believed fervently in 'violent revolution.' Rogers was proud of being a 'quiet revolutionary.' George attacked Rogers' 'way of being.' Rogers lashed back. He was brash and confrontive (which sometimes passes for congruence). He was clearly angry, but was everything being said? Perhaps he was also fed up with George ruining the group. Perhaps he wished that George would just shut up and let the group 'progress' (and perhaps make a useful educational film?). Perhaps he was hurt. Much of this supposition is supported by the fact that, after George abandoned the group, Rogers expressed relief that he was gone, feeling the group was 'progressing much better without him' (Rose, 1986). Had Rogers managed to express more of the *complexity* of his immediate reality, who knows, perhaps George might have reacted differently. Even if he did not feel better understood, he might have been challenged to also be more genuine with his own feelings.

Thus, being congruent is not merely having sufficient *chutzpah* to blurt out whatever is on one's mind, or to lash back at what appears to be aggression, or to automatically repay what one perceives as kindness with a crushing hug. Congruence is extremely demanding. It requires not only honesty with oneself, but also self-knowledge, to know what one is feeling. An ability to communicate. An ability sufficiently refined to convey to others the complex and often contradictory feelings which make up what one calls 'experience' or 'reality,' is also necessary. As can be noted, even a facilitator as skilled as Carl Rogers did not always achieve congruence.

The group facilitator, though not expected to be perfect, is expected to be honest, authentic, good-willed, and courageous. She is expected to do what is implicitly required of any group participant. She is a human being in a group of human beings. As Doxsey (1986) has remarked, 'In most approaches, the facilitator intervenes; in the person-centered approach, he *interacts*.' The facilitator is a *participant* in the group, but not a *patient*. He may share his personal feelings and perhaps his difficulties in life, as appropriate in the moment.

Power

Although the facilitator quickly becomes another participant in terms of group interaction, she may continue to enjoy a special status in the group. This may be due to her personal qualities but is more likely to derive from the leadership role she played in convening the event, her previous experience in participating in similar activities and the fact that she symbolizes the commanding principles of the system under which the group is operating. (Although it may be noted that other participants may understand the system better and are often better spokespersons for it during the group experience.)

The inevitable dispute over whether the facilitator has more power than participants is resolved by merely noticing that she is part of the phenomenon she describes, what William James (1890) called the 'psychologist's fallacy' (p. 196). In the facilitator's view, she has no more power than anyone else and she proceeds to behave accordingly. However, the participant may view her as more powerful than himself. Thus, the phenomenon consists of her perception and his. Any realistic perception of the phenomenon must include both and must be dealt with by the group.

Personal attitudes of the facilitator may reveal what he is feeling, thinking and trying to accomplish as he goes about contributing to a complex phenomenon. Valuable information. However, the perspectives of participants may also be important for a more comprehensive understanding. To consider only the subjective perspective of the facilitator in attempting to understand the environment of a successful person-centered group would be the equivalent of considering the climate of a baseball park, for example, and all that contributes to the outcome of the game, as consisting of merely the hitter's attitudes and superstitious warm-up gestures that prepared him on one of his successful trips to the plate. Facilitators may have more effect on others for reasons they do not imagine and less effect for reasons they believe they have.

Acceptance

In spite of the demands for genuineness, there are moments when, as in client-centered therapy, the facilitator may be able to directly help a group participant formulate the truest expression possible of his inner experience at that moment. To do so, the facilitator listens sensitively. Rogers (1970b) says, 'I listen as carefully, accurately, as I am able, to each individual who expresses himself. Whether the utterance is superficial or significant, I *listen*' (p. 47). The words of Lao Tse suggest the power of profound and enlightened attention, 'It is as though he listened and such listening as this enfolds us in a silence in which at last we begin to hear what we are meant to do' (Buber, 1957).

In order to enter this personal world of the other, it may be necessary to temporarily surrender one's own version of *the* world. To appreciate and follow the other's experiencing, without interfering. The effective facilitator surrenders reliance on theories and opinions and, with more difficulty, beliefs of how things *should* be for the other, for how things really *are*. The goal of this listening is not just to 'get in touch with feelings,' it is to follow the personal exploration through the moment's rich labyrinth of experiencing and to facilitate the formulation of a whole 'it' into a present meaning.

This acceptance that allows insightful moments is neither inactive nor overlyactive. The facilitator is active *enough;* in order to provide the acceptance necessary. In their study of encounter groups, Lieberman, Yalom and Miles (1973) found that the leaders who could be characterized as *providers*, specializing in caring and meaning attribution—gave love as well as information and ideas on how to change—produced positive changes while minimizing the number of participants who had negative outcomes. (The poorest showings were made by a leader style that uses frequent structured exercises and extreme control over participants' interactions and, at the opposite extreme, by an inactive *laissez-faire* style.) 'The warmer and more positive the relationship,' state the researchers, 'among the group leader and members and the more the leader can help the members to increase their cognitive understanding of themselves and their relationships, the more benefits to members.'

Though the facilitator may be accepting and non-judgmental, may respect diversity in the individual and trust her capacity to know herself and find her own pace and direction for personal change, perhaps his most essential attitude is an acceptance of the group itself. Of this attitude, Rogers (1970b) says, 'I trust the group ... the group seems like an organism, having a sense of its own direction even though it could not define the direction intellectually' (p. 44).

After sufficient experiences of the group resolving seemingly hopeless problems and demonstrating a wisdom superior to the sum of its individual members, one 'trusts' the group. This means one does not panic so easily, but can tolerate the difficult process that may result in this 'wisdom.' It does not mean that one sits back and enjoys the ride, confident that the group will arrive at its destination safely. Each new crisis challenges all earlier justifications for faith. Surely *this* situation is beyond the group's capacity. Enormous energy on the part of facilitators and participants may be required to help bring about an outcome worthy of continuing 'trust.'

Rosenberg (1977) recounted such an experience from her years of clinical practice: 'I see a certain client, a 30-year-old failure in every aspect, brilliant and bitter, ill and heavily drinking, hating himself and the world, having wasted every opportunity to build a meaningful life for himself.' Although this client had been for some time in a therapeutic relationship with her, Dr. Rosenberg suggested group therapy because she felt he lacked genuine warm human contact. She records, 'We had the fifth weekly [group] session this morning, and the changes in him are dramatic. He told me today that for the *first* time in 12 years, he has spent a whole week without a drink, *and* has done the first things he has ever found meaningful. In two of those five sessions, he was dead drunk, could barely stand on his feet, was "impossible" and aggressive. I tried to send him home (when I found him sleeping on the floor at 7:30 in the morning in the waiting room, unable to stand or speak clearly). I am humbly grateful that he refused. In the group, he received support, inquiring challenge, confrontation, but neither pity nor rejection, which he was accustomed to receiving ... that's the group. '

Even Rogers, who frequently eulogized the 'wisdom of the group,' was confused by the group's ability. He was often struck by how group participants and *not* the facilitator most often turned a chaotic situation (one that he had given up on) into something constructive. On the other hand, he regarded the facilitator as the key to group success. Returning home from an experience where the 'group wisdom' prevailed, Rogers related his observations. His travel companion replied, 'Do you mean to tell me that this would have happened, if you were not there?' At a loss to explain how it could have happened without him, he began to emphasize his 'way of being' to explain his importance in a significant event that did not involve him centrally. He 'approached' the situation with a certain 'way of being.' In other words, he applied the person-centered approach. He was part of the phenomenon. His way of being influenced the outcome. So did the way of being of each participant. Each way of being and more contributes to an efficient and wisely functioning group.

Perry (1976) has observed, from his successful treatment of schizophrenia, that:

> Providing a protective sanctuary for persons in this state, with a firm subculture ... deviating from the generally accepted, prevailing cultural outlook, becomes the critical factor that releases these people from their turmoil so quickly. This sanctuary requires an accepting atmosphere, free from prejudicial judgments, thus removing that very negative, difficult and painful state of insanity that promises to be so unpredictably explosive ... Even more effective than acceptance, of course, is the general tenor that we can only call a loving

atmosphere. The word love must be qualified to avoid any sentimental implications that it may convey. Loving here means caring, being attentive, really wanting to understand, to reach the essential person behind the outer manifestations. (p. 15)

Group as a Whole

Experience is seriously diminished by concentrating only on *text*—the inner subjective world that can be verbalized—and not paying enough attention to what goes *with* text, that is *con*text, the rest of reality. Perceiving the general patterns of the group can be useful in the facilitation of an effectively functioning collective. What are we doing as individuals? as a group? Who is saying what to whom? for what reason? What is not being said? What is the movement of the group now? What is being avoided? Why this lull? Why is this participant being singled out just now? Something is always happening, not only within individuals but also between individuals as well as collectively. How these things are happening influences the outcome of the group. This is the environment of the group. The facilitator does not *create* this environment; he and the participants and the situation *are* the environment.

Besides cultivating a diffused all-at-once perception, becoming aware of the group as a whole helps to facilitate awkward moments when direct interaction may be impossible. For example, an angry confrontation between two participants that has not been resolved will likely paralyze the entire group. Factions that continue to oppose each other over petty differences in beliefs dilute interactions between all participants. A romantic alliance that generates jealousy in other group members may confuse interpersonal relationships between all participants. Those who avoid any emotional subject in the group meetings, but candidly express themselves in the corridors lower the level of trust for all participants. Making an observation that everyone is thinking and no one is saying may unblock an uncomfortable impasse. An active awareness of the obvious is the responsibility of every mature participant.

To be aware of the group as a whole is not merely an intellectual process. It involves a special perception, perhaps an artistic one. Cézanne, for example, said, 'The landscape thinks itself in me and I am its consciousness.' (Merleau-Ponty, 1964). Thus, it could be said that the group 'thinks itself' in the facilitator or participant, allowing for global understandings.

On the other hand, in being concerned with the patterns of the group, with the dangers of 'epidemic' emotions that may infect the group, with the group's efficiency, one cannot become overly fascinated with 'group' and lose sight of the individual. There is evidence to suggest that emphasizing the group-as-a-whole, *without* attention to individual members and without an ambiance which includes empathy and acceptance may not only be unhelpful but even harmful to participants (Colson & Horwitz, 1983).[7]

Thus, the effective facilitator's sensitivity is to individuals and interrelations in the *context* of the group-as-a-whole. The following example illustrates this attention and also the fact that another group member may be more central to a facilitative event than the designated facilitator.

At the beginning, the group progressed in the usual ways. There were personal explorations in which the facilitator encountered participants directly. There had been encounters between group members. Then, a woman began to speak. She told a passionate story. But, on being questioned by group members, she became very confused and began contradicting what she had said previously. Some people began to be annoyed with her rambling. Their irritation and impatient probing increased her confusion.

Others, sympathetic with her inner confusion and vulnerability, began to defend and comfort her. While these two sub-groups debated the nature of her 'problem,' she sank into desperation. Trembling and pale, she crouched in one corner of the room.

A cloud of gloom engulfed the group. Although everyone was deeply involved, none could make any real human contact with her. And, at the same time, none could initiate a new topic of conversation. The group became silent, paralyzed.

Looking around the room, the facilitator also experienced a feeling of hopelessness. He could read the despair in participants' faces. He considered acknowledging in words the state of the group. Perhaps through discussion they could discover a way out. Then he noticed Evelyn, an ordinary middle-aged housewife. While others squirmed nervously, Evelyn's posture suggested something of a concern for the suffering person *and* an urge to speak. He asked if there was something that she wished to say.

This was the impetus needed. 'Yes, there is something ...' she began. She formed her phrases carefully, but with such vividness, reflecting such a depth of feeling, that everyone's attention became riveted on her. Group members seemed stunned by her simple, honest, insightful observations of their dilemma. She was able to make sense out of this woman's suffering, the group's suffering. The confusion cleared. Somehow she captured what others could not put into words, but nevertheless could recognize as the truth.

There was an immediate transformation: from a collection of constricted, tense individuals, a relaxed and cohesive group began to form. Ann, the woman so withdrawn, recovered her name. She joined the discussion with a surprising clarity and enthusiasm. She was not crazy. She had needed some link of mutual understanding between her and the group. Evelyn supplied it. Ann became spontaneous and self-confident. Now that she had her feet on the ground, she could make sense out of her previous confusion.

Group members could not remember exactly what Evelyn had said. Although the facilitator's recognition of Evelyn at the critical moment was perhaps the most facilitative thing he did, it went unnoticed, and rightly so. What everyone did recall was the moment when Evelyn 'saved the group.'

A Broader Perspective

Speculations and explanations of the group process, theories of therapeutic change and observations of human nature may help one to appreciate the challenge, but can rarely help one to live fully in such an experience. To manage this kind of complexity, the effective facilitator relies both on the accumulation of facts and linear reasoning and on a more diffused all-at-once perception. In focusing attention on himself, on another member of the group, on an encounter between participants, on the 'mood,' or 'climate' of the group, the facilitator relinquishes analysis and evaluation in favor of this more holistic perception.

It is possible to sense the immediate feelings of each individual, to listen sensitively, even in that person's silence. 'What is he trying to say?' 'What meaning might this have for him?' Yet, not only, 'What does he feel right now?' may be asked, but also, 'How does this fit in his existence?' 'What significance does this have to others here? to society?' 'What effect will this experience have on his life (or mine) next week, next year?' 'Who am I? Who are we? here? now? *and* outside of this situation?'

It is possible (and perhaps necessary for effectiveness) to keep in awareness a sense of life before and after the group, of one's surroundings, one's family, of the lead story in the New York Times, the progress of the Boston Celtics, of how one's present actions compare to perennial values and the available learnings of wiser men and women.

It is a contradiction to *think* all this, but it can be present in the context of consciousness, even as the group is electrified with some strong emotion. When this occurs, the facilitator cannot avoid feeling the same emotion. Nevertheless, he tries to formulate, based on the awareness of the moment, an expression based on the broader context, a response to the person who is trying to find the truest expression of her present experience. That action, if it is harmonized with the person's own complex consciousness, would not embarrass either of them, were they to meet in the supermarket after the group glitter has worn off.

The following example illustrates how the facilitator may react, through a broader perspective, to a troubled group member. It also illustrates the good will, but sometimes ineffective efforts, of group participants giving what they imagine is 'support.'

Francisco, a young Latin American psychiatrist, speaks at length about his work and the distress he feels. 'I have received training in medicine, with a formation in psychiatry, studied abroad, and practiced for several years in my homeland. I have worked very hard to prepare myself, mastering all the leading theories and completing training in several specialties.' He looks up from the cigarette he has been rolling slowly between his fingers. His tone of voice lowers. 'In spite of the best training I could get and myself having a burning desire to help people … uh … I feel terribly … inadequate. There are hundreds of theories of psychotherapy; what is one to *believe*?'

'Oh, come on, Francisco,' Sally interrupts. 'I don't think theories are so important, really.'

'Sure,' Robert adds, 'I bet you are a splendid therapist.'

Members of the group try to reassure Francisco, but every piece of advice is met with stronger objections: 'But, my inadequacies exist, my training, my theoretical preparations.' This is a characteristic of such groups: A distressed person will sometimes find information helpful; patronizing reassurance or advice, however, is rarely appreciated.

'Is there anything,' Barbara asks, 'you would like us to give you, Francisco?'

'I would just like to know what is the right thing to do.'

'You want somebody to tell you what to do,' Michael says. 'You have to do that yourself, man.'

'No, it is not exactly that,' Francisco stammers, '... that I would like someone to tell me ... Well, I should like to *know*.'

'What would you do,' Sally inquires, 'if you had all the answers?'

'I would ... uh ...'

'I feel sucked in; then you run,' an exasperated Al interrupts Francisco, 'You aren't really giving us *you*. I feel I am being manipulated in some kind of question and answer game and I am getting irritated.'

'It is not my intention,' Francisco apologizes. 'Well, let's discuss something else, since everyone thinks I am monopolizing the attention.'

Francisco shuffles distressfully in his chair. The expression of despair on his face is now lined with pain. In reality, only one person has challenged Francisco; still, he feels the 'group' has turned against him. This is also common. Participants feel good or bad based on one or two comments. The facilitator points this out, then he continues:

'I would like to say something to you, Francisco.' He reviews Francisco's feelings, repeating in his own words what Francisco has said about his inadequacy, his desire to help, and wanting to be close to people. He has taken what Francisco said at face value. 'Have I gotten the meaning of what you have been trying to express?'

'Yes,' Francisco says. 'You have understood me correctly.'

'Francisco,' the facilitator replies, 'I would come to you for therapy ... and I would send a loved one to you for treatment.'

As his eyes grow moist, a smile flashes across his face. 'Yes, yes,' he says. 'Yes, now I understand.' The tension melts from Francisco's body.

A reasonable aspect of the facilitator's expression spoke to confusion in Francisco's mind (incapable of understanding the unreasonable question, 'What is the meaning of my life?'): 'Yes, of course, I believe you are confused, just as you say.' And at the same time, some instinct said: 'I trust you to help me. That's what matters in therapy.' The facilitator's expression was not merely kind, it was congruent with his feelings—he believed what he said. He used neither technique nor theory; his response was not designed; he spoke simply and honestly in the immediate moment *and* in the context of the long-range relationship that might develop with

Francisco. Francisco *lived* a vivid experience that the group could neither talk him out of nor pry out of him.

On the surface, the facilitator's comment might be taken as reassurance, but it was nothing like the reassurances Francisco had already received. The facilitator was not *trying* to reassure Francisco. The innocent truth in what he said became a powerful fact. The question behind the question, which was not formulated, was answered.

An effective facilitator (or group participant) is alert to follow *or* to lead *or* simply to wait for the right moment. She is willing to live unattached to a particular form of outcome, to be surprised by the unique creation of each group of persons.

Therapeutic Relationships

In spite of the importance of the facilitator, it is nevertheless the behavior of the group's participants, not merely the facilitator's, that may explain much of its effectiveness. After their heralded study of encounter groups, Lieberman, Yalom and Miles (1973) concluded, 'Change does not revolve around the solitary sun of the leader; the evidence is strong that psychosocial relations in the group play an exceedingly important role in the process of change' (p. 428). Yalom (1985) presents more recent evidence reinforcing this view. Patients who had successfully completed group therapy with him were asked about the 'turning point' in their therapy. They invariably recounted an 'incident that is highly laden emotionally and involves some other group member, rarely the therapist' (p. 27). Even in a demonstration of individual psychotherapy within a group, a client is often much more influenced by the group than by the therapist (Slack, 1985).

Additional evidence against the view that empathic understanding is something 'offered' by the therapist to the client comes from group therapy research in Germany. Results of studies suggest that empathic understanding generated between participants may be much more significant than between facilitator and group member. In fact, Mente and Spittler (1980) found that the group member's *own* capacity for empathic understanding may be a better predictor of success in psychotherapy than the facilitator's.

From his research in person-centered therapy groups with neurotic outpatients, lasting approximately 14 months, Mente suggests that one of the therapist's primary tasks (after carefully composing the group) is to facilitate the *client's* capacity for empathic understanding (Giesekus & Mente, 1986). That is, 'the client's experiencing of feelings and their meanings as they exist for and affect another group member (or person) in that person's "otherness"'. In these studies, it has been observed that group participants selected a 'significant person' in the group (and may replace this person with another later) without any help from the therapist (Mente & Spittler, 1980). Remember that even in client-centered therapy with some clients there may be more empathic understanding in the therapeutic relationship than with others— even with the very same therapist (Moos & MacIntosh, 1970).

Thus, the task of the facilitator (or any participant) in a person-centered group becomes not to 'offer' or 'provide' empathy, not even to express empathic understanding but, to *facilitate the phenomenon* of empathic understanding. For the person-centered approach, the crucial question becomes: 'When are participants experiencing empathic understanding?' Not, 'When is the therapist showing that she is attempting to understand the client's inner frame of reference?'

Composition

An underemphasized, but nevertheless important, factor in determining the success of a group is the composition of its members. The little research on group composition suggests that effective groups contain some participants who are warm and affectionate and those who have been successful in dealing with personal problems in the past (Bixenstine & Abascal, 1985). Some studies suggest that psychologically minded persons function better in insight therapy and persons with strong internal locus of control may function better in low-structured groups (Abramowitz & Abramowitz, 1974; Abramowitz et al., 1974; Kilmann et al., 1975).

The strength of the small group may be in its diversity and adapting its form to the composition of the participants. Nevertheless, a group probably cannot be everything to everyone. To realistically assess the possibilities with a prospective participant is an important beginning in forming a group for therapy or encounter. The congruence between the person's motives for attending the group and what the facilitator believes is possible to achieve is assessed by the prospective participant and facilitator. Together they decide. The person with realistic expectations, who believes he may benefit from the experience and will be able to contribute to the group process, is usually accepted. This initial contact, though simple, is by no means unimportant. The values participants bring to the group may be the most significant influence on the outcome (Lieberman, et al., 1973). Participants with less favorable expectations are less likely to benefit from the group experience and less likely to contribute to the group's capacity to help (Caine, Wijesinghe & Wood, 1973). The question is open and continues to be explored in the group. 'Is this the right experience for me? What am I learning? What will happen when I leave the group?'

Are Groups Dangerous?

A controversy persists over potential benefits and dangers from group participation. On the one hand, Lieberman, Yalom and Miles (1973) reported an alarming rate of negative outcomes in their study of encounter groups in a university setting. Despite suspicions of programmatic faults and persuasive criticism (Rowan, 1975; Schutz, 1975), this study remains one of the most extensive and influential on small groups.

Briefly, out of 206 students participating in the study, 16 were judged to be 'casualties' by the researchers. Unfavorable outcomes were attributed, in most instances, to unrealistic expectations and psychological problems which participants brought with them to the groups, coupled with aggressive, intrusive, rejecting behavior of group leaders and an unsupportive group environment (pp. 177–93).

Having worked as a psychotherapist in a university hospital, I can attest that there are considerable dropouts and 'casualties' from merely *attending* a university. One wonders how the casualty rate of the groups in this study compares to the overall casualty rate of the university (using the same criteria). In their report, the authors cite a study by Katz (1968) of changes in college students from their first year through their senior year. This research concludes that, when viewed as a *total activity* (which is how their most outspoken critics view them), 'the effects of encounter groups are not massive in number or substantially different in kind from those reported for collegiate experience as a *total* activity.'

Also in a university setting, Bebout and Gordon (1972) studied over 1,000 encounter group participants and their 100 non-professional leaders as part of a four-year investigation. The theories of Rogers and Jack Gibb were stressed as the foundation of the group approach. Findings suggest that groups generating the most positive change consist of active, self-initiating members and helpful, but not overly intrusive, leaders. 'The least positive effect,' conclude the researchers, 'can be expected from groups and leaders who are mutually inactive and insensitive.' Referring to most of the sample, they stated: 'We have found significant positive changes in members almost wherever we looked. Self-esteem increases, the self-concept changes in many positive directions, self-actualizing tendencies are greater …' (p. 117). In the first 28 months of the project there were four persons who had 'serious reactions.' In this study persons who entered the program 'positively motivated and with appropriate expectations' gained the most.

Two tape-led groups (leaderless groups) in the study by Lieberman and colleagues (1973) produced no casualties. Although liked less by members than groups with leaders, one of the tape-led groups produced one of the highest rates of positive change. Lieberman (1975) believes this is due to the fact that 'nonprofessional groups like tape groups are less leader- and more group- centered. The group as a unit can build up its own limits—its own level of tolerable intensity' (p. 54).[8] In the case of 'leaderless groups' and groups with 'weak leaders,' one must look elsewhere, besides to the facilitators, to explain the results.

Not poor facilitation, but the group's own remarkable ability to effect change may, paradoxically, represent its greatest danger. Group therapy could be used as a conditioning device for societies. It has not been uncommon for the governments of countries to require their citizens to join small groups so they will learn how to alter or support the society in a 'correct' direction (Whyte, 1974). In the Philippine Islands, in 1978, I was taken to tour a showcase government facility where Rogerian encounter groups were proudly claimed as part of the indoctrination process for high government officials.

The person-centered approach, because of its basis in essential life processes and its many applications, may also run the risk of developing 'true believers.' Frank (1961) presents a general review of systems of personality change and the aspect of control they may exert over group members: 'The means by which changes in the [trainee] are brought about include a particular type of relationship and some sort of systematic activity or ritual. The essence of the relationship is that the [trainer] invests great effort to bring about changes in the [trainee's] bodily state or attitudes that he regards as beneficial. The systematic activity characteristically involves means of emotional arousal, often to the point of exhaustion. This may be highly unpleasant, but it occurs in the context of hope and potential support from the [trainer] and the group ... The [trainee] may be required to review his past life in more or less detail, with emphasis on occasions when he may have fallen short of the behavior required by the world view, thus mobilizing guilt, which can only be expiated by confession and penance. This serves to detach him from his former patterns of behavior and social intercourse and facilitates his acceptance by the group representing the ideology to which he becomes converted.'

One can see how closely this description fits many group activities. This does not mean group activities should be abandoned. It means that the same methods and nonspecific factors of change are involved in a variety of activities with vastly different goals. It underlines the necessity for our understanding these factors and for the refinement of group therapy goals and practices. It also suggests the value of a group-centered approach instead of a facilitator-centered one.

A limitation of group therapy suggested by these examples is this: the preoccupation with the means of producing change may eclipse the realization of a truly creative experience for participants. There is the danger (even within the life of a group) that the system or technique or the group itself will come to be regarded as 'the truth.' When passed on to the next 'generation,' instead of cultivating a more complete person, the group experience could simply result in another form of 'religious' conditioning. Coulson (1980) was asked by a participant in a group, 'Why do we have to be 'person-centered,' can't we do what we want to do?' Coulson's advice, in this regard, is, 'Perhaps we can aim for an uncluttered experience of life which for some will turn out to match the definition of effective therapy in vogue, while for others the experience will yield benefits we may never be aware of.'

The facilitator and the group participants must have the willingness to destroy their own theories, to abandon—if necessary—even 'what worked last time,' to work within whatever form that allows them to follow a creative path as it unfolds. Living in a vast and mysterious universe is bound to continuously offend our meager notion of facilitation and effective group therapy. Assessments of group effectivity must be continuously revised to conform to the necessities of participants and the realities of the culture.

Notes

1. *A human being becomes I through the Thou* (Buber, 1979: 32).

2. See Raskin (1986) for a review of early group work in client-centered therapy. The only flaw in this article is that it does not merely acknowledge client-centered therapy's important role in the later development of group therapy and encounter, but also suggests that the encounter group is some kind of extension of client-centered therapy. The present chapter shows that this is not the case. The small group from the person-centered approach is a different phenomenon and must be understood from its own perspective.

3. The 'deterioration effect' is a term given to the following discovery: When treated and untreated groups of patients in individual therapy were compared, it was found that the treated group showed greater variability on the criteria for change than the untreated group; yet, the two groups (treated and untreated) showed similar overall change. The interpretation suggested is that some patients improve while others deteriorate as a result of psychotherapy treatment (Bergin, 1971).

4. However distasteful this tendency may be to one, it should not be underestimated. Witness the longevity of hazing rights in fraternities, despite their continued risks (Cialdini, 1985).

5. Research supports this observation: People who meet in a situation in which they are anxious or in danger are more likely to interpret the feelings of arousal they experience as attraction to the other persons (Dutton & Aron, 1974).

6. From a film documentary called *Nova* shown on public television in the United States, 29 November 1981.

7. W.R. Bion (1959), who pioneered the approach to group work studied in this research and whose groups *were* doubtless helpful, has written a realistic and extremely sensitive and insightful account of people in groups with a facilitator who does not organize the group activities. Applying Bion's theories without the proper sensitivities, apparently can result in contrary effects.

8. Although groups with leaders and groups without have both been shown to do well, alternate meetings of a group, with and without a facilitator, was shown to have a disruptive effect on some clients (Parloff & Dies, 1977). The *way* in which meetings are alternated could be decisive (Mente & Spittler, 1980).

CHAPTER FOUR

Applying the Person-Centered Approach
vs.
Applying the Principles of Client-Centered Therapy

Keep a cool head, for it is better not to understand something than to make such great sacrifices to understanding.
         Sigmund Freud [1]

Rogers' major descriptions of client-centered therapy (for example, 1946, 1951, 1961a, 1980) always included developments in education and groups. In his book, *Client-Centered Therapy*, these subjects were put under the heading of 'applications of therapy.' Thus, it is understandable that many (and even Rogers, at times) might confuse 'applying principles of therapy' with 'applying the person-centered approach.'

However, from a close reading of descriptions of 'student-centered teaching' and 'group-centered leadership' it is clear that these activities are substantially different from client-centered therapy. Nevertheless, the attitudes and orientation (that is, the *approach*) of the educator and the group leader is the same. So, what are more likely being presented are not applications of therapy, but applications of the approach itself. This is an extremely important distinction.

By the time he described, 'A Theory of Therapy, Personality, and Interpersonal Relationships,' for Koch's (1959) *Psychology: A Study of Science*, Rogers had already begun to distinguish between applications of therapy and applications of the underlying approach that the therapy was based on. In this case, he called the approach, 'the Client-Centered *Framework*.' In less formal contexts he refereed to it as the client-centered approach.

It is important not to confuse 'applying principles of therapy' and 'applying the approach upon which they have been based.' In applying the principles of therapy one is doing what one 'knows' how to do. In doing so, it may be difficult to avoid therapeutic goals. Thus, in trying to demonstrate the principles of empathic understanding, congruence and non-judgmental acceptance in the classroom, a teacher may turn a good opportunity for learning into a bad session of therapy. Education, not psychotherapy is the goal. (Obviously, education that was *also* therapeutic would be more desirable. But here we are speaking about *goals*.)

Applying principles instead of meeting the phenomenon on its own terms may not only be ineffective in achieving one's objectives, it may even be harmful. There is evidence that two large projects based on 'models' and principles derived from client-centered therapy may not have been as successful as they could have been. One project was the attempt to modify a private school system (Coulson, 1989). The other was an attempt to resolve conflict between groups (see following chapter).

Applying the Principles of Client-Centered Therapy is Not Always Effective Outside of Psychotherapy

The previous chapter on encounter groups offers several examples of how applying the principles of client-centered therapy in the group (as valuable as they are in one-to-one psychotherapy) may be ineffective and might even be harmful.

A good example is the woman in chapter three who is trying to give 'accurate empathic responses' and 'focusing' advice. Instead of facilitating the group's progress, she is perceived as extremely disruptive and is eventually rebuked by participants. According to Rogers, in this case, following the client-centered principle of conveying one's understanding through the reflection of the other's feelings and concentrating on those feelings is not sufficient. He suggests that the group is seeking a 'deeper empathy.'

How does one express a deeper empathy? In whatever way is appropriate at that moment. Perhaps even by 'focusing' on or by 'reflecting' the other's feelings. But not by applying principles of psychotherapy—or principles of mathematics or whatever.

In this same chapter on small groups there is a discussion of the therapeutic 'condition' called congruence. It is evident that the facilitator's congruence takes on a wider meaning in the group. Who he or she is and how the facilitator regards the group as a whole become important. The group is not merely a series of one-on-one encounters with the facilitator in which he or she can act like a psychotherapist. Being congruent with the group itself may be more important than with individual members. Certainly, beginning facilitators, attempting to be congruent, are instead brash and impatient. Instead of being accepting, they may be passive and inactive.

These facts of groups frequently surprise client-centered therapists who cannot believe that, with all their good intentions and conscious effort not to, they are nevertheless applying a method or playing a role. Even Rogers himself, who adopted the completely innocent posture of 'trying to understand every single thing the person was saying,' has been called to task for being so 'impassive' and not saying 'how you really feel' in a demonstration psychotherapy interview within a large group workshop.

The 'client' remarking on his impressions of the 'therapy' just concluded, related: I still feel that feeling of sort of a structured—I feel I'm being used. I think you follow your rule book, you know, and I'm sure that if you really let go, you'd sort of look at the heart of these things, you'd open up a bit more and wouldn't be so impassive' (Rogers, 1986b: 25).

One wonders if this would have happened in a consulting room with only Rogers and his client present. It may seem otherwise, but this was in a *group*, and part of the phenomenon of group. The 'client' verifies this effect-of-group and his disappointment when he remarks, 'as much as I would love this to be a real sort of encounter, I'm trying to ignore, you know, the invisible faces.'

In Confronting a New Situation, even 'Experience' May Not Be Reliable

Doubtless, many people trying to apply the person-centered approach will not ignore the persons and the phenomenon they are confronting in order to apply 'principles.' They will work in a way that they believe is effective, based on their experience and beliefs. They may apply 'principles' only that have proven to be effective in the past.

Nevertheless, care must be taken with this attitude. For, what does it matter if it is a 'principle' or a 'conviction based on experience' that prevents a group from realizing its creative potential?

For example, in 1977 I first came to Brazil with Carl Rogers, Maureen O'Hara and Jack and Maria Bowen, all of us members of the Center for Studies of the Person in La Jolla, to convene a large group workshop similar to those we had initiated in 1974. As a prelude to this workshop which would be held in the state of Rio de Janeiro with some 300 participants, we also convened even larger two-day workshops in three major Brazilian cities: Recife, São Paulo and Rio de Janeiro.

We began in Recife, with a meeting in a gigantic sport's complex. The area was arranged for a traditional academic presentation: rows of moveable chairs lined up in front of a stage with a long table at which the presenters sat before microphones. Other microphones on long extension cords had been provided for members of the audience to ask questions. There were said to be some 800 to 1,000 participants.

Rogers began to speak. Our plan was for each of us Americans to give a brief talk on our own interests and then to invite discussion from the audience.

After only a few minutes, the lecture became tedious. Members of the audience had difficulty in understanding what Rogers was saying. They complained that they did not wish to hear us lecture, but for everyone to speak together. So, we suggested that they form small groups: move their chairs into a small circle and get to know each other. We formed a similar circle on the stage. What they spoke about I don't know. What we spoke about was what to do in this situation. Some of us suggested that we had nothing to lose, why not just form a large group? At this point a woman came from the audience and said that she thought we did not really trust them, that they had not come here to talk to each other but to talk with us and that it was quite possible to speak together in a large group.

We suggested that the group form one large circle. We will converse. Microphones were passed hand-to-hand to whoever wished to speak. Sonia was the first to speak. She roundly criticized us, for what we had done, for speaking about the old and safe and not answering the important political questions.

The preachers next took the floor: A Christian padre from the interior, a syndicate boss, a marxist sociology professor.

Then I got the microphone and replied to Sonia. 'Sonia, I want you to know that at this moment I have no excuses or answers to offer, but I am *not* ignoring you. I am listening carefully. I *do* hear your disappointment, and it matters to me. And I know that you are angry, and your anger reaches and touches me.' (Sonia says later that she could have been satisfied with nothing less than this response.)

Then, a series of statements fix themselves in my memory: 'This is the first time I have stood up in public and said what I feel ... to criticize, to say what I really think.' Isabel speaks the last words I recall, 'I haven't said anything until now, but I just have to express my joy. ... I came here feeling so *lost*, like I was alone in my pain and my struggle. It's all just too big for me: the poverty of my people, the political realities of the world in which I live, the pain in my marriage, my family, my job. I couldn't do it alone ... and now I realize that I am not facing it alone. ... I feel strong, I feel nourished and now I can go on. Maybe this won't last, but in a way that doesn't really matter. What matters to me is that *I feel it today.*'

For us, this was a grand success: more than 800 persons could speak in one meaningful conversation and that this could be significant (we learned from later reports) to many participants.

Next, we went to São Paulo. A small group for public television went well. Then the large group meeting in a convention center—a high-tech auditorium with fixed seats in tiers. Nevermind, we thought. The space is not important (a principle from client-centered therapy where the space was rigidly controlled: two people in a closed room). The important thing is that people be able to speak personally (what we had learned from previous experience). We know how to do this work. Wasn't it effective in Recife? (Previous success, but under completely different conditions.) Our experience has taught us that all you have to do is provide 'space' for people to converse—that is, pass around microphones.

We Americans stationed ourselves in various parts of the auditorium facing the stage, which was empty. Microphones were available on long cords. Rogers stood up and invited people to speak. The outcome was a disaster. Everyone was disoriented, looking at the backs of others. People speaking as if from the clouds. Chaos. Many people walked out and apparently did not return the next day. The morning newspaper headline read something like: *Psicólogo Faz Nada: Provoca Caos* (Psychologist does nothing: provokes chaos). Our Brazilian friends began to refer to *Caos* Rogers, instead of Carl Rogers.

What went wrong? We applied 'principles' instead of the person-centered approach. Instead of respecting the culture and meeting people 'where they are,' we imposed our values/structure/will on them. Had we respected the culture, we would have favored the traditional fashion: on stage, short talks, questions and answers, breaking into small groups and finally a grand plenary conversation—

which is what we did the second day, when we regained our senses. This proved to be successful.

Second, we ignored the influence of the environment. Arrogantly, we thought we could overcome ambiential constraints with our 'principle' of person-to-person encounter. And most devastating, we did not face this new situation as *new,* but tried to apply our latest 'learnings' to an event that had still more to teach us.

Applying the Person-Centered Approach

One of its secrets (due to lack of understanding) is that the person-centered approach often functions best in situations where conventional methods (including applying the principles of client-centered therapy) have failed.

Unlike applying the principles of therapy, applying *the person-centered approach* means confronting a phenomenon (such as psychotherapy, classroom learning, encounter groups or large groups) with a certain 'way of being' described earlier and which may also include not only respecting others, but being able to deal with their hostility and skepticism. It may mean facing both the unknown and one's own fear and doubt. It may mean fighting for one's own ideas, but giving them up for better ones. It frequently requires an active patience: to allow various perspectives to become apparent before deciding, while, at the same time, not withholding one's vital participation while data is accumulating.

An example from a public mental health project

In the late 1960s in the United States many people underwent dramatic life transitions. Not only young people. Due to political decisions thousands of middle-aged scientists and engineers were unemployed and many were forced to make radical changes in their ways of living. Throughout the nation, some 100,000 scientists were unemployed. This example concerns some 250 of this group who lived in San Diego, California.

The crisis began with the government's cancellation of contracts for the construction of a supersonic aircraft. In one sense, it was a victory for the environment, as this vehicle was expected to cause certain ecological damage. On the other hand, it was a devastating defeat for those who lost their jobs.

Who were these people? The population consisted of technical workers, engineers and scientists, almost all men. A familiar story was the following. A young man joined the armed forces during World War II. He served his country honorably. With the war's end, he took advantage of veteran's benefits and enrolled in a university. After four years he had been awarded a degree in engineering. (For some, a couple of more years led to a master's degree. A few went on for a doctorate in physics, biology, or an engineering specialty.)

On graduating from the university, his services were in great demand. This was the time that the country was rebuilding and expanding. Job offers were abundant, especially in the growing 'aerospace industry.' He got a good job and began to advance within the organization. He bought a house in the suburbs, a boat, or a trailer for camping excursions, a new car every year. He made investments, provided insurance for his survivors, arranged for his children's teeth to be straightened, put away money for their university education, and, in general, became a valued and contented member of his community. Two decades or so later, around age 48, he lost his job.

When I arrived in San Diego (an ex-mathematician and engineer myself), there were some twenty or so engineers and scientists voluntarily organizing a 'job bank,' to help each other find employment. I joined them. At first, we thought perhaps people could find employment with other manufacturers of aircraft or aircraft components. All we had to do was to contact the companies, find out what openings they had, and put the right man in the right job.

What we quickly learned was that there were virtually no job openings in the aerospace industry.

So, we began to look into related activities: bio-medical engineering, pollution management, environmental specialties, technical marketing, small business management and so forth. Disappointingly, these industries wanted only young people trained in the technology that they dealt with.

Next, we petitioned local politicians such as the mayor and the board of supervisors of the region, the governor. We proposed that every level of community was in need of technical assistance to resolve various problems: control of air pollution, sewage disposal and treatment, crime and security. Why not hire an unemployed engineer? Yes, the problems exist. Yes, we need help. No, we do not have funds to employ your people.

Could the state give a grant for scientific research? Could the county pay for a study of its swamp lands and the ecological threat that housing developments were introducing into the area? Could scientists be hired as teachers in the city school system? We made proposals to every sector of the community: without success.

A 'demonstration' was even staged, a quiet march through the downtown streets to advertise our plight. The television journalists loved it, but nothing came from this effort. After a couple of weeks, the journalists were looking for what was new. Unemployed scientists quickly became an old story.

The telephone campaign continued. Engineers and scientists, themselves unemployed, worked on a voluntary basis in a small office the state loaned us. They tried to find jobs for their colleagues who came into the office to register for the meager unemployment insurance. Volunteers telephoned local businesses, factories, and other sources of employment on a regular basis asking for what openings existed and recommending that the enterprise consider our population.

The volunteers also listened to the stories of the recently unemployed who came to the office for help. They told their own stories as well. A common pattern was repeated: At first the unemployed person was not too concerned. He was receiving a few weeks of insurance payments. Also, most received a pretty good payment from funds their previous employer had put aside for their retirement. Thus, they had income for a few months.

At first, they concentrated on looking for a job as good or better than the one they had. They certainly would not consider working with less status. Without success, they began to apply for lower-level jobs. For example, managers of big engineering departments began applying for jobs as ordinary engineers. Still, with no success and time passing, they began to become worried and applied for jobs well beneath their training and ability. Many related that they had eventually become desperate and had even tried to get work in a gasoline filling station. They were turned down because they were 'over-qualified.' They were willing to work, but no matter how humble they became, nobody wanted them. This experience was not only humiliating, it often left the person depressed and hopeless.

While we tried everything we could think of to find work for people and to help them prepare themselves in the best possible way to present themselves in job interviews and while we listened to their stories in the volunteer office, we noticed an inexplicable but nevertheless constructive and encouraging phenomenon: Volunteers who came to the office, worked the telephones and talked to people coming in, quickly found employment: if not a formal job, nevertheless, a satisfying new direction for their lives.

Were they to have always found employment in their old line, we could suspect that they were merely privy to inside information about job openings and stepped in to claim the prize, instead of passing it on to one of their unemployed colleagues. However, this was not the case. As often as they found similar employment, they resolved their problem creatively: sometimes beginning a completely new career in a different line.

What was happening? What did this observation mean? Could it be that by merely sitting around the office and drinking coffee, trying to help another (and oneself), conversing with each other more honestly than one might converse with acquaintances, sharing one's life story and aspirations, a person's life transition could be facilitated?

If it were so, we could certainly take advantage of this discovery. To test the hypothesis, a small prototype project was proposed: we would invite unemployed scientists to a group meeting where they would have a chance to do what was taking place within our office spontaneously: that is, learn what they needed to know to look for work effectively, reflect on their common life situation, share informally their feelings regarding this crisis, explore with others practical solutions to their and other's problems. Although nobody could produce a theory to explain how this might be beneficial, the fact was that in spite of a Herculean effort, no other approach had offered the slightest hope of helping, let alone success on a significant scale.

The results of the small group we convened to test this hypothesis, confirmed its potential value. Participants in the group quickly resolved their problems. On the basis of the pilot group's success, the state government gave us a small grant to conduct a longer program that would also be researched to better understand what was going on. Unemployed people were given the opportunity to attend what were called 'job clinics.' There were some 20. Each consisted of a group of around 10 unemployed scientists, one or two counselors or supervisors from the state unemployment service (who, through their participation, were also receiving training which they could later use in their work), and two group facilitators (usually a male and a female—only a few facilitators and no participants took part in more than one group). The group met daily for a week which included a two-day intensive experience and afterwards, once a week for three hours in the evening for ten weeks.

For the purpose of research, this group was matched with an equal number of similar persons who did not participate in the 'job clinics' and did not participate in any government program of counseling or retraining. A third group was constituted from the official reports of people who received the authorized unemployment counseling from professionals who work for the government agencies.

Six months after a person had completed the 'job clinic,' he was asked to evaluate his transition. The results were significant. People who participated in the 'job clinic' had an 80 percent chance of being engaged in a satisfying occupation. Around half of these persons were trying out and were content with something they thought they would like which was different from their previous work. Almost one-third were engaged in an endeavor that they had always wanted to do. For example, one fellow became a veterinarian; another, who had invented a two-cycle gasoline engine as a hobby, was hired by a large motor manufacturer to supervise the design and fabrication of his engine; a metallurgist whose hobby was photography became a crime photographer for the police force; an aircraft stress analyst became a successful filmmaker, inventing several special effects techniques.

People who 'did nothing' had around an *even* chance (57 percent in San Diego and around 46 percent nationwide) of realizing these same options. Statistically, these findings are indisputable: the 'job clinic' definitely helped people reconstruct their lives in a positive and creative manner. The astonishing finding was that unemployed scientists and engineers who would have received conventional unemployment assistance through government counselors had a mere 30 percent chance of achieving what the other groups achieved. Thus, it may have been better to 'do nothing' then to receive certain kinds of help.

Reflections on this case from the perspective of the person-centered approach

Unwittingly, in developing these programs to help unemployed scientists, we had applied an approach indistinguishable from the person-centered approach.

What had we done?

After testing, to no avail, all the conventional wisdom, we applied no further theories. Without realizing it, we followed the advice of J.W. Von Goethe: 'Let the facts themselves speak for their theory. Don't look for anything behind the phenomenon; they themselves are the theory' (Bortoft, 1986). The unemployed person himself spoke for the 'theory' and we followed this lead.

It must be emphasized that we were extremely active. We tried everything we (or anyone else) thought of that might resolve the problems of the group or of an individual in the group. Almost every approach we tried was unsuccessful in facilitating the life transitions of a significant number of persons in the unemployed group.

By exhausting every recourse, trying to help the person in crisis formulate his own response to his situation, and observing the subtle realities that were taking place, we finally recognized that there were certain psychological factors that were active in helping people make a successful transition and that these factors could be promoted to be of real help to more people. In this case, we realized the truth in Martin Buber's (1958) insight: 'Only when every means has collapsed does the meeting come about' (p. 12).

Attempts at 'helping'

At first, because they asked, we tried to teach people how to look for work: how to write a curriculum vita, how to dress for interviews, how to present oneself. Then, when we discovered that there were psychological factors involved, we offered group experiences which were structured in a way to elicit participants to speak about and to reflect on their lives. Later, we discovered that the essential elements were already present in the *meeting*. Our task was to provide the moment and the place and the unencumbered time necessary for deep reflection to take place. This was not as difficult as it may seem because participants intuitively realized this and they themselves provided both the urgency and the creative vitality necessary.

The personal dimension

A promising psychology is beginning to develop around the basis of evolutionary biology. Neurological studies, brain researches, and advances in cognitive psychology are contributing to this development. One concept that is receiving substantial support from these fields is that consciousness is not the integrator of brain functions, but that the brain, instead, consists of various 'modules'—specialized functions that have developed during evolution and that now switch in and out to deal with particular necessities of the organism. Some of the difficulties an individual encounters may be the result of using a 'module' or a way of thinking, perfectly developed for one case, but that is not suitable for the problem at hand.

Whether this was the case or not, one could nevertheless notice a similar phenomenon among the population of unemployed scientists and engineers. For example, many thought like a twenty-three-year-old first beginning a career: 'I must find a good paying job. It must have room for advancement, so that my salary may increase to provide for my growing family: buy a good home, education, and so forth. I may wish to do something else, but I must not think of myself. My family must come first.'

However, a forty-eight-year-old man whose children were grown and whose house was paid for and who, for the first time in his life, had the opportunity to do what he *really wanted to do*, and thought like a twenty-three-year-old was surely using the wrong 'module.'

Often, beginning to think in a more realistic way about what one really wished to do for the rest of his life put him on the road to this new life.

The social dimension

Unemployed persons who shared their feelings, view of life, their hopes and fears with those who were facing similar problems—that is, with those who could understand at a deep level what they were experiencing—seemed to more quickly find the way out of their difficulties.

This was no mere catharsis. In addition to sharing feelings, they offered practical advice to each other. Not gratuitous advice, they offered suggestions which were synchronous with the person's desired direction. For example, an engineer whose lifetime desire was in art, who painted, but never showed his work, was put in touch with the brother-in-law of another group participant who had an art gallery. The contact resulted in the new artist selling several of his paintings and putting his new career on a solid basis.

There is also something to be said for the process of helping each other dream of how they wish to spend their life. This results not only in mutual support and encouragement but also in bringing the dreams more into focus, and somehow bringing them more within reach.

The ambiance

The location of the group meetings seemed to influence the initiation of a creative process in group participants. When meetings were conducted in a drab government warehouse where space had been allotted, participants were much more inhibited and much less likely to explore their feelings deeply. When meetings were held in the eucalyptus grove that surrounds the beautiful University of California campus, the process of self-discovery in participants seemed to be facilitated by the place alone.

Thus, the successful approach was not at all efficient, but it was *effective*. It was, as I have learned from farming, a bit like nature herself: preferring *potential* to productivity and rewarding *patience*, instead of enterprise. I used to think that the approach helped to develop personal potential. Now, I feel it preserves potential. That is, it allows one to be ready, not with stock responses to a situation, but with the inner resources to respond appropriately.

Therefore, in this case, the person-centered approach might be described, in part, as consisting of:

> A *belief* that something can be done and that those who have a problem also have the creative resources to overcome this problem.

- A *respect* for the dignity and autonomy of the person. He or she is the one to decide about his or her life.
- A *recognition* of the value of social interaction: one alone is nothing: two is a unity. The majority of persons, both in the 'experimental group' and those who 'did nothing,' said that they found their 'new direction in life' through personal relations with others.
- A *tolerance* for uncertainty. We tried things that we understood and they did not work. We did things that we did not understand and they did work.

It is clear that these observations should be added to the body of facts that would eventually make up a comprehensive definition of the person-centered approach. The essence of which remains: We turned the best part of ourselves toward the best part of our colleagues in order to accomplish something of lasting value that none could have done alone.

Based on this example, Rogers might have hypothesized, 'Given the appropriate environment and psychological conditions, people possess the capacity to reorganize their perceptions of themselves and their reality and to make creative and constructive life transitions.'

Notes

1. Freud's advice to Carl Jung. Cited by Lieberman (1985).

CHAPTER FIVE

An Example of the Pitfalls in 'Giving People an Experience of the Person-Centered Approach' instead of Applying the Approach

The frantic desire to reach a conclusion is the most disastrous and sterile of manias.
Jorge Luis Borges

Even as the then new and exciting client-centered psychotherapy was emerging and being formulated, Rogers glimpsed and proposed possible implications of the *approach* that was producing this extraordinary system. In one of his seminal papers, 'Significant Aspects of Client-Centered Therapy,' in 1946, he stated that he and his colleagues were learning an approach that had, 'deep implications for the handling of social and group conflicts' and, he felt, that, 'a significant clue to the constructive solution of interpersonal and intercultural frictions in the group may be in our hands' (Rogers, 1946). In addition, he suggested implications for psychotherapy itself, for group therapy and for education. What he could merely imagine in 1946 did, in fact, become substantially realized over the next forty-five years. For the most part the reality exceeded his imagination in terms of the constructive contribution the system he helped to develop made to the North American culture.

Applications of the person-centered approach burgeoned during the late 1960s and early 1970s in education and small encounter groups. In 1985, the Rust Workshop (Rogers, 1984, 1986c) was an attempt to apply the person-centered approach to conflict resolution. It presents a useful context in which to study some of the problems that may arise in applications of the person-centered approach. What early reports of the workshop, in spite of good intentions, demonstrate to me is that the person-centered approach is not as good as believed; but, it is better than imagined.

The workshop was held in the Seehotel in Rust, Austria, between the first and fifth of November. The theme of the event was, 'The Central American Challenge.' 'Among the fifty participants,' Rogers (1986c) relates, 'were high-level government officials, especially from Central America, and other leading political and professional figures, from seventeen countries in all.' Rogers goes on in his paper to describe and analyze the workshop and discuss 'errors and difficulties.'

This first appeared in *The Person-Centered Journal, 1* (3), 1994.

An analysis of this workshop reveals more weaknesses in the application than in the approach itself; some innocent, some grave. It uncovers nothing to suggest that the approach does not have potential for facilitating mutual understanding between conflicting groups and when possible the resolution of conflict. Personally, I believe that the person-centered approach has contributions to make that are yet beyond the imagination of those currently promoting or criticizing it.

I intend to examine some critical points and to suggest where I think the approach might have been applied more effectively. It seems to me:

1. The basic assumptions about the nature of conflicts were too simplistic

Rogers (1984) proposed, as he had repeatedly done (see also Rogers & Ryback, 1984), that the 'underlying pattern in any serious dispute' is that each side thinks, 'We are right and you are wrong. We are good and you are bad.' While this hypothesis may be logically indisputable, to take it as a guiding assumption for facilitating conflict resolution seems to me to provide an inadequate perspective (let alone values) for facilitators who are about to face an extremely difficult situation.

I am reminded of Edgar Friedenberg's review of Rogers' ideas on education (Kirschenbaum, 1979) where he observes, 'Like another American philosopher, Huckleberry Finn, Carl Rogers can get in almost anywhere because the draft of his vessel is so terribly shallow; it never gets hung up.' In one sense, this is actually an advantage. By making a straightforward simple hypothesis, he is able to quickly undertake a project that 'academics' might study for years and raise so many questions no action would be possible.

However, as Friedenberg continues, 'It is almost eerie to read a discussion of basic existential issues affecting human life by a man who, despite an enormous range of honestly assimilated experience, seems to have no sense of tragedy, and not as much as one might expect of the complexity of human conflict.' By not acknowledging the terribly complex nature of serious disputes, Rogers makes himself appear unprepared for facing this complexity and, worse, runs the risk of trivializing the subjective experiences of participants in trying to point out to them that they only *think* the other side is wrong and they are right.

Rogers' 'simple pattern' ignores complex and explosive attitudes, feelings and actions that make up conflicts. It seems to ignore (a cornerstone of client-centered therapy) the subjective experience. No one who has ever had the barrel of a loaded and cocked revolver pressed against his temple and told that he was about to die for whatever reason could swallow such simplicity. Conflicts may not decide necessarily who is right and who is wrong. They decide who lives and who dies.

Violent and tragic conflicts are emotional. And although it may help, 'to get to know the other,' this may not not always *resolve* the basic 'issues.' Encountering the murderers of her parents, no matter how good-willed the organizers of the encounter might be, may not, in itself, move a victim to forgive her enemies. Sometimes opponents know each other only too well. Conflicts are also not limited to mere emotions. Humans squabble and even kill each other over commercial advantages, for power over others, to possess territory or wealth (or even a man or woman), for greed, to spread an ideology, to preserve or enhance a race, to prove something: one's manhood, one's dedication to a cause, the power of one's superstitions.

Disputes in the Middle East and other areas where humans have lived for thousands of years might have existed for a good part of that history. Thus, the matter of *tradition* must be considered. The matter of *honor* is also involved in conflicts. *Revenge* should be respected as a strong motive. (Aren't the majority of North American films based on this theme?) Not only the common tit-for-tat variety, but also revenge that might involve a religious mission. A member of a family may have a sacred *duty* to revenge the death of his kin and thus correct an injustice.

All of these motives may surface in a serious conflict. A teenager on one side may murder a shopkeeper from the other, not merely because he thinks he is right and the other is wrong. His more urgent motive might be to accomplish his society's rite of passage, to gain the manly respect of his comrades. Or it might be driven by religious fervor, by a sense of justice. Or perhaps for revenge. Or just for the hell of it. Throughout history people have been slaughtered, not because the victim did anything (wrong or otherwise), perhaps not even because the assassin was righteously angry or filled with the love of God, but merely because he was doing his job.

That it is superficial is one of the most common criticisms leveled against client-centered therapy. It is said to be an 'easy' or 'safe' approach that the inexperienced may employ. In practicing this approach, critics imagine, one may not have to think critically nor go deeply into a subject. One is not required to do much. In therapy, it is not necessary to commit to a diagnosis, or an analysis of one's client. The impression is that one need not be involved, just be nice and listen.

I believe just the opposite. To practice client-centered therapy is one of the most involving activities one may engage in. It demands all that one has. It demands that one turn the best in oneself toward the best in an other in order to bring out the best that that relationship might offer.

Anyone who has tried to practice psychotherapy knows this. But the literature, overall, does not give this impression. It says the hypotheses are simple. And they are. But that does not mean the practice is easy, without complexity.

A simple hypothesis for a workshop in the person-centered approach may provide a starting point. But it may have to be discarded in light of the reality that emerges in the group discussions. There is no evidence in the reports of the workshop that suggests that this happened. There is evidence (some of which will be examined further on in this chapter) that:

- the facilitators remained aloof from the participants,
- because of ignorance, the facilitators sometimes offended members of other cultures,
- the facilitators tried to impose their own cultural values on participants,

- there was 'inadequate communication and inadequate understanding' between the facilitators and the Latin Americans who were more intensely involved in trying to resolve disputes in their region.

All of this suggests the possibility that a more realistic hypothesis and better preparation might have helped the facilitators work more constructively with the group.

2. The organizers did not sufficiently trust the 'wisdom of the group'

The central hypothesis of the person-centered approach applied to groups, according to Rogers (1984), is that, 'groups of individuals have within themselves vast resources for understanding and accepting their dynamics, for reduction and resolution of conflicts, and for constructive change in group goals and behavior.'

The major evidence that the organizers did not sufficiently trust this hypothesis is the following.

Facilitator overkill

For 50 participants (four of whom could attend 'only one or two sessions,' which leaves only 46), there were 10 facilitators, 11 if you count Rogers himself. If the translators, who were apparently skilled facilitators, would be included and some of the participants who were experienced in the person-centered approach, there may have been one 'facilitator' for every three 'participants' during the major part of the workshop.

Actions speak louder than words. The organizers apparently did not feel this group could be trusted to organize itself constructively.[1]

Restrictive structure

Organizing the time into small groups, big groups, lectures and so forth also suggests a distrust of the group being able to organize *itself* to deal with its own urgencies in a manner most conducive to it. Could not 'high level government officials' and 'leading political and professional figures' be expected to establish their own agenda and schedule?

3. The organizers misunderstood or at least misapplied past experience in this new situation

Rogers defends the organizers' choice of structure in his report on the workshop. He states, 'The reason for thinking that this was just the right amount of structure is that there was none of the arguing or bickering about schedule, assignments and format which so often accompanies a workshop. To our amazement, there was not even a discussion about smoking or non-smoking.'

Why were they amazed? In what kind of 'workshop' is there bickering about the schedule and discussions of smoking or non-smoking? It is true that such discussions have taken place in large group workshops which consisted largely of psychologists and educators who, with no agenda, met under very low-structured conditions and with a tenuous purpose. When there was something more interesting or urgent to engage the group, these discussions did not take place. I imagine that this would not have occured, whatever the preimposed structure, in a workshop with 'high-level government officials, especially from Central America' who were motivated to resolve painful conflicts in their region.

What I have observed over several years and have taken as a tentative hypothesis about the nature of group is that the group's 'wisdom' is likely to be proportional to the group's 'urgency.' A group with nothing better to do will discuss whether it should allow smoking or not or whether tape-recording or filming sessions should be permitted. However, if the group has a greater urgency, someone is sick, someone is threatening the life of another, there is a conflict to resolve, a problem that touches and involves the majority of participants, it will deal with that with the greatest efficiency and creativity that it can muster. The proverb, 'When the house is on fire, the toothache flies out the window,' is applicable in this case. Also, the most elegant solutions to knotty group problems, it seems to me, were arrived at in the most severe crises. The 'wisdom' is produced according to need.[2]

It is doubtful that this group of 'international participants' would have squandered their time discussing housekeeping rules regardless of how little structure had been imposed on them. They had more important things to do and very little time to do them. However, had they not been restricted by organizers, they may have been able to deal more effectively with the difficulties they faced and the grave issues that troubled them in their regions. Were they to have been trusted more and been less 'facilitated,' they might even have devised a more efficient and effective approach to dealing with their urgencies and realized an even more constructive outcome.[3]

Rogers also refers to the Heurigen celebration as 'good fortune.' Of course it is an ancient cultural event with considerable focus on interpersonal relations and it occured at 'the exactly right moment in the workshop.' This was indeed fortunate. From what Rogers suggests, what would the workshop have been without it? However, the fact that such an event was considered 'chance' by the organizers suggests that previous learnings had not been absorbed. If this were the first time such an emotional 'turning point' occured in a workshop, one might be obliged to give credit to the fact, as Rogers does, that, 'some mistrust was dissolved in alcohol.' This sort of experience is one of the most consistent occurences in workshops. That is, *the group frequently uses an unplanned activity to facilitate what is needed to be faciliated at that moment*. Such 'breakthroughs' are usually a surprise to organizers because they often find it difficult to imagine that such a constructive outcome could occur outside of their 'facilitated' activities.

This tendency to credit chance, rather than an ancient ritual itself, or, more relevant here, the creativity of the group, again suggests that, although attention has been paid to superficial patterns (such as establishing rules about smoking) which change with context, the essential patterns of group interaction had not been given enough attention by the organizers. The 'workshop' consists not merely of the planned time blocks and formalities, but as a total experience—a phenomenon—beginning to end.

4. The primary goal of the workshop was not even conflict resolution

Rogers (1984) in the workshop proposal states that, 'The purpose of this workshop will be threefold. [First], it will give the participants the opportunity to experience a person-centered approach to group facilitation to the reduction of whatever tensions exist or arise in the participant group.'

At that moment in his career, Rogers had not hidden his desire to 'have an impact,' to 'give others an experience of the person-centered approach.' And why not? It was quite understandable that he would want people to be able to use the person-centered approach for the betterment of humankind.

Nevertheless, to have as a *primary* goal, wanting to *give* people an experience of the person-centered approach, not only is contrary to the approach itself (which might more likely adopt an objective such as, 'to facilitate conflict exploration'), it nearly guarantees failure. We had learned years ago that such an attitude proved disasterous. It was exactly when the organizers of learning events believed they now had the answers and thus no longer needed to risk failure or embarrassment by entering into the unknown realms of experience with the participants, that those events could be easily judged as failures. This had been a central learning from client-centered therapy as well.

The person-centered approach is not static. Attitudes may be assumed (Oscar Wilde said, 'The first obligation in life is to assume a stance'), intentions may be measured, may be applied. However, an effective outcome may be realized only through adapting to the context as it changes moment-to-moment. (By not doing so, the second half of Wilde's quip is verified: 'The second obligation has still not been discovered.')

Furthermore, a proposal such as the one Rogers drafted seems aimed not at competent 'high level government officials' or insightful diplomats, but more toward bureaucrats or politicians who would be in need of expanding their perspective. Of course, in general, some diplomats may be ignorant, short-sighted, even corrupt, as a certain percentage of any profession may be, including psychologists and university professors. But no matter what their character, the central figures in any conflict are the ones who are most likely to be the best qualified to deal with that conflict and should be respected.

Outsiders, of course, always offer an 'objective' or at least 'different' perspective to local disputes, and therefore enrich provincial thinking. However, they are severely limited in their ability to generate creative solutions. For one thing, their stakes are not high. They don't have to live with the outcome. Of course, their values have a place in the phenomenon, as every other participant's values have. But this is a fine point: when facilitators try to force their provincial values on participants, they become a limiting force, instead of a facilitating influence, as the Fermeda Experiment also demonstrated (Doob, 1970).

In my opinion, Rogers' *second* purpose should have been his *first*. It was, 'for staff and participants alike to contribute their knowledge, experience and skill to the formulation of an approach, drawing on the wisdom of all present, an approach which might be used in dealing with antagonistic groups or nations.'

5. The staff also appears to have had as an implicit goal the teaching of their own cultural values to the participants

Dr. Larry Solomon, one of the facilitators, in his perceptive report on the workshop (Porter, 1986), states, 'Each small group had two facilitators, a man and a woman. That was intended to provide an opportunity for modeling gender interaction, which might differ significantly from the kind of gender interaction that occurs in some of the cultures that were represented there.' It appears that the tendency of citizens of the United States to impose their values onto Central America has not changed. Early on, it was businessmen (with government backing), introducing 'capitalism.' Then the United States government itself tried to introduce 'democracy' in various ways. Now psychologists themselves are trying their hand, introducing political correctness: 'gender-interaction.'

Each of these colonizing efforts were doubtless imposed for the Latin American culture's own good. I do not suppose here that any were intrinsically good or bad. I do wonder when citizens of the world might be expected to meet each other on an equal basis and lay aside the desire to change others before even knowing very much about what might be changed and whether or not it would really be constructive or not.

6. The organizers allowed the event, and what it meant to North Americans and Austrian bankers and other 'third parties,' to take precedence over both the goal of the organizers and the goal that could be legitimately assumed for the participants: the interests of Central America, in particular and, conflict resolution, in general

Even the 'group process,' so sacred to group psychologists, was set aside as outside interests interfered. In the final moments of the workshop, significant members of the group had to leave to attend to the selfish interests of an Austrian bank who, because it helped to fund the workshop, doubtless felt it had a right to interfere. This serious distraction, according to Rogers, occured at the 'peak' of the program and 'damaged the group process.' Why did he allow this?

7. The staff seems to have given an unnecessary amount of attention to itself

Rogers says that it met in the mornings and at the end of the day as a 'support group for each other in a new and challenging situation.' Were not the participants also in a new and challenging situation? Did the staff require more 'support' than the participants because they were 'supporting the group'? This Herculean image may be convincing for other approaches, but not for the person-centered approach. The notion that, as Rogers states, 'It was essential that the staff keep in solid communication so that our unity would help the unity of the group,' is a somewhat mystical idea from the person-centered approach workshops of the 1970s. This way of thinking was discarded when it was realized that although the principles which determine the workshop's process may indeed be hidden, but nevertheless real (that is, mystical), they apply to the group as a whole, not merely to an elect staff group that would be an intermediary for the hidden projections (as is the case in many religions).

Thus, whatever the staff needs, do the participants not also need? Is everyone in this boat together, as the facilitators imply, or not? To the justifiable criticisms to the contrary from the participants, Rogers replies weakly, 'We must have seemed aloof because of this. At the time we could not see any way of remedying this deficiency.' The obvious remedy would have been to trust the group.

8. Factions (that had little to do with the 'Central American Challenge') were built into the group, even before the first meeting, due to the manner in which the event was organized

This concern with 'unity' in the staff group would have been better to have been applied to the workshop's origins. It began with a serious schism in the community. Solomon (Porter, 1986) reports that there was no common theme that communicated the workshop's purposes to participants who would be forming the group. 'CSP' (the Center for Studies of the Person, the institute to which Rogers and many of the facilitating team belonged), he states, 'recruited people with the expectation that this was going to be an application of the person-centered approach.' Whereas, Solomon continues, 'the University for Peace in Costa Rica recruited the Latin American participants. In doing so, they set up expectations that this was going to be a diplomatic conference at which opposing positions could be presented, with the idea that those positions might be better understood by those in opposition once the full presentation had been made ... We just started out with *our* expectations and they had *their* expectations and the two never completely got together.'

The facilitators' post-workshop evaluation suggests the experience may have been more positive than negative for small group participants. However, there is evidence that one of the most important Latin American dignitaries, influential in organizing the event from Central America, left the workshop 'feeling hurt and somewhat unrecognized.'

That participants have different expectations, even opposing expectations, is not uncommon in person-centered workshops. If a common thread unites them, there is the possibility to use these differences, even differences in values, to find creative solutions to conflicts. A workshop that cannot even resolve these basic differences cannot boast much for resolving international tensions.

A Final Note

Until now, the person-centered approach's accomplishments in the area of conflict resolution are somewhat meager. A group of residents in Northern Ireland was assembled in Pittsburgh in 1972. Carl Rogers and Pat Rice facilitated an encounter that was filmed by Bill McGaw. This group was perhaps Rogers's most legitimate attempt at conflict resolution. Little may have occured when participants returned home. But it is difficult to believe that the group experience did not affect the lives of the participants and therefore the conflict between them. Perhaps, had the group been realized in the *context* of the conflict, instead of the context of documenting an encounter group, there might be more to report. The workshop Rogers convened in El Escorial, Spain, which he mentions briefly as an example of 'conflicting groups making progress in understanding each other,' seems to have resolved nothing whatsoever. It merely proved, for the *nth* time, that people from 22 different countries could survive ten days together in a resort setting. Of course, all the benefits of a large group encounter were doubtless possible—both constructive and destructive. All of this was hardly a new learning. Rogers' so-called black/white encounters in South Africa were not aimed at resolving any specific conflict, though they apparently helped to stimulate clearer communication on both sides. The context for his meetings was a conference to meet an internationally known psychologist. Doubtless, even in this somewhat superficial setting important learnings were realized and perhaps even significant changes in perspective between representatives of conflicting groups who may have attended the conference. However, this can scarcely be regarded as an example of conflict resolution.

From these criticisms, it might seem that the Rust Workshop was just that: rust in the mechanism of the person-centered approach. However, I believe that it was a valuable example of how difficult it is to work from a person-centered approach. Good intentions are not sufficient. When the organizers *give an experience*, instead of *participate in*, the person-centered approach, just as when they *use* the Tavistock approach, or any other approach, with an attitude, conscious or not, of having predetermined answers for a group, or wanting to 'model values to them,' the group is doubtless hindered in achieving its self-governing and innovative potential. By respecting the inherent creative potential in any group and beginning with the attitude, 'Let's see what we can accomplish together, applying all our will and resources,' and genuinely being willing to be changed by what occurs, facilitators may be able to legitimately count themselves part of an evolutionary step forward in consciousness.

Notes

1. It is also possible that the staff did not trust itself. Although Rogers eulogizes it as a very experienced staff, tempered by working together, to my knowledge this particular selection had never been tested as *a unit* under actual stressful conditions. Nobody can blame the staff for not knowing exactly what to do at every moment. No one really knows what will actually happen in these unedited situations. In retrospect, most of the serious mistakes I have witnessed (and contributed to) were made by not trusting sufficiently the approach. (And this applies to Rogers as well.)

2. I don't mean to suggest (as Rogers does) that discussions about details of 'format, assignments, schedules and smoking rules' may not be important or even urgent to the group. Discussions of housekeeping rules may still establish many of the cultural principles on which the group will base its future behavior. These may be as readily determined through discussing smoking as more exciting issues.

    What I wish to emphasize is that it is the group that establishes what is urgent for it. Thus, I suspect that the 'Central American question' would be more likely to be more interesting to *this group* then establishing smoking regulations, no matter what structure would have been established by the organizers.

3. Again, it seems that preparation was lacking. Rogers and his staff seem not to have benefited from the mistakes of, and seem to have unwittingly repeated many of the *faux pas* of, the organizers of the Fermeda Experiment (Doob, 1970).

    Sixteen years earlier, in 1969, a workshop was convened in the Italian alps for the purpose of applying behavioral science approaches to the peaceful resolution of conflicts. The organizers' excellent detailed report illustrates many of the pitfalls to which convenors of such events may become victim.

    Representatives who possessed ability and influence were invited from the countries of Somalia, Ethiopia, and Kenya—three neighboring nations involved in a border dispute. The participants were organized into a large group which operated in a 'Tavistock model' and several small groups which followed the 'NTL or Bethal approach.' Thus, like the Rust Workshop, there were small 'encounter group' meetings with facilitators and a 'large group' meeting of the entire population.

    Participants in the Fermeda workshop described the staff as acting evasive at times, holding themselves aloof for most of the workshop, and treating participants as though they were guinea pigs in an experiment. By their own admission, the staff 'did not always appreciate the nuances of what participants told [them]. The [facilitators] occasionally gave unintentional offense through their interventions.' As a comparison: in Rust, participants also noted the aloofness of the staff. Also, Rogers reports that the facilitators, due to cultural ignorance, offended some participants. How many times must this be learned?

    A Fermeda participant offers the following observation about the effect of the assumptions that guided the staff's perceptions: 'The [facilitators], who gave a highly psychological interpretation to self knowledge, regarded ideology as something that was not of deep concern and hence distracted attention away from the real intentions of individuals. Given these limitations, the activities of the participants can only be described as acquiescence or mere playing along with the activity of the group and the method under which it was guided. ... Both the arrangement of the discussion and the manner in which the participants entered the arrangement precluded any serious engagement' (Doob, Foltz & Stevens, 1970).

By enforcing their own values, and regarding ideology as unimportant, and not allowing the group to formulate appropriate responses for their deep concerns, such as ideology, the Fermeda organizers contributed to blocking the group from confronting and resolving its conflict. The group had no genuine opportunity to develop its own structure and methods to deal with the regional conflict of values, the cultural differences, the historical disputes and the other factors that made up the actual context of the conflicts. In the final phases of the workshop, the group could only resort to disappointing political recourses.

In the Rust Workshop there is evidence of a similar situation. One of the staff members relates, 'They were talking about life and death issues—very real life and death issues. Our focus, as facilitators, was on the process. We were struggling with the question: "Is the process more important than the content here?"' (Porter, 1986). Based on the experience this team would be expected to have and on information available in the literature on the subject, shouldn't this struggle have been resolved before the workshop?

CHAPTER SIX

The Person-Centered Approach to Large Group Workshops
Communities for learning

So that men should not be burdened with too many things, we gave them succession, issue, the plural day and the singular night. We also bestowed upon them the gift of experimenting with certain variations.
   Jorge Luis Borges, attributed to a Japanese divinity

During the late summer of 1973, an application of the person-centered approach—a large group workshop (community for learning)—was casually conceived.[1] Scores of similar events followed. Participants in the large group meetings of the workshops considered here have ranged in number from 40 to 2000. They have included persons from a wide range of endeavors, but most were psychologists, educators and helper-oriented persons. The meetings, usually residential, have been held on a rambling and dilapidated coffee plantation in South America, in a European monastery, in ivy-covered university courtyards and college dormitory halls in North America, in retreat centers, a hunting lodge, in front of television and film cameras and in many other settings. These minimally structured events have lasted from one to twenty days, but most often around ten days.

The workshop organizers' initial proposal was merely to convene a large group of interested people who would examine *together*, through direct experience, the relevance of using the approach, from which client-centered therapy had evolved, in social situations. The aim of these workshops was to explore those forms of social interaction based on respect for the individual that might yield the wisest collective action in a given predicament. An early theme was: 'How can one function specifically, locally, and privately in a way that the individual is enhanced at the same time he or she contributes to the welfare of humanity?'

It was quickly realized that although the *principles* of client-centered therapy were rarely directly relevant, applying the person-centered approach did have enormous potential. The large group workshops that resulted from this experiment were called 'person-centered,' a term which rapidly spread to identify all such endeavors of what, until then, was called the client-centered approach.

Portions of this chapter have previously been published in R Levant & J Shlien (Eds) (1984) *Client-Centered Therapy and the Person-Centered Approach*. New York: Praeger.

Large Groups

Since 1967 the La Jolla Program (Rogers, 1970b) had been training encounter group leaders. To supplement the structured program of small group encounters, brief plenary sessions were held. These meetings demonstrated that it was possible for over 100 persons to speak in one significant and intelligible conversation. Also, for several years the psychologist Jack Gibb had been working with large groups that did not rely, as the La Jolla Program, on structured small groups but, on non-verbal relationships between participants to establish temporary 'communities.'

Departing from these experiments, the person-centered large group workshops not only established the gathering together of the entire 'community' as the core of activities, but also provided conditions for the workshops to be designed largely by participants themselves. They formulated the activities, scheduled events and even established their own tuition fees, commensurate with their individual income levels, to pay for the costs of the program (Rogers, Wood, Nelson, Fuchs & Meador, 1986).

The early workshops were organized from a sense of inquisitiveness and adventure. Participants were invited to be colleagues in a mutual exploration, not as customers, not as subjects in an experiment, not as students in training, nor as an audience for a congress, but as equals with the organizers in a spirit of discovery. Staff members did not hold themselves apart from the group, but joined in as full-time participants. This beginning doubtless facilitated participatory problem-solving and the group's ability to confront and resolve crises after the workshop was underway. In theory and practice these workshops explored the question, 'What could applying the person-centered approach to a large group teach us about community?'[2]

Convenors of the Large Group Workshop: Staff

The primary function of the organizers of these large group workshops was to arrange the time and place, to state the initial purpose of the meeting, and to invite participants. Since it was not conceived primarily as a psychological event, the staff (the term Rogers most often used for the group of organizers) sought diversity in the participation of persons from a wide range of age, profession, economic class, race, and 'life experience.' One familiar with all the factors that effect the outcome of such workshops may note that the choice of place was probably the most significant decision the staff made. Most often, a quiet private setting was selected for a workshop to be held during the summer months (Rogers, 1977).

Prospective participants were asked to make a written application for admittance to the workshop. Each member of the staff, including Rogers, studied every application. Each applicant's expectations and what the convenors thought were realistic were compared. If it seemed, in the staff's judgment, that a prospective participant could contribute to the group's objectives and could benefit from the experience, she was invited to participate in the workshop.

Doubtless, participants and convenors alike had multiple expectations. They came for personal growth, to alter their style of living, with intentions to benefit humanity, to become effective professionally, to feel good, to see what happens, to overcome the tedium of a dull relationship or unrewarding work, for attention, to have an adventure. Nevertheless, convenors (a more appropriate term for staff members because they are also facilitators and organizers) and participants agreed to work on a common goal: let's say, 'to examine through direct experience, in a large group, the approach that gave birth to client-centered therapy.' Probably this phrase would have meant something different for each participant, but each would have agreed to do *something*, and to do it *together*. 'We are all in this together; let's see what we can accomplish,' seems to be close to the attitude which reflected their common expectation. It may be that they learned what that 'something' was only after it had been accomplished. To begin, this shared expectation and the natural biological connection that unites all people may have been the participants' only tangible unifying thread.

Nevertheless, those who lacked even this thin tie, whose expectations were radically different from what convenors imagined could be reasonably expected from the workshop, were not invited to attend and were referred to alternate activities which might more closely match their goals. No one was refused on the basis of age, sex, race, religion, political opinions or an inability to pay tuition.

For these large group workshops, as for encounter groups, no claim was made that they were psychotherapy. The workshops frequently *were* therapeutic for some people, but they were not proposed, nor intended, as therapy. Indeed, the most common reason for not inviting a participant was that he *expected* therapy. If this was an explicit goal, the person was referred to psychotherapists in his region. The emphasis on expectation would seem justified based on the observations of Allport (1924). He suggests that in collective behavior, one of the prime mechanisms is the expression of people's similar predispositions that has been released by their co-presence.[3]

The possibility to explore expectations was always open. During the workshop, with the support of the convenors, participants continued to ask, 'Is this the right experience for me?' 'What am I getting from this?' 'What am I learning?' 'What will I take home with me?'

Staff members were attentive to small details in an effort to allow participants (with whom they counted themselves) as much freedom as possible in determining their own experience. Careful thought was given to the choice of accommodations and meeting rooms (for both privacy and accessibility), to food (with vegetarian options), to child care, transportation, and a network of communications to keep everyone informed.

Before deciding on behalf of the participants, staff members asked themselves, 'Does making this decision oppress or empower the person?' The convenors did not wish to make any decisions which might infringe on individual freedom, no matter how trivial the issue might seem (for example, assigning people to living quarters or allowing them to choose for themselves). Also, when necessary, the participants should be able to alter staff decisions to conform to the group's needs as they changed. This was only possible if the staff made only decisions that they could not refer to the whole group when it was united. Thus, convenors made as few decisions as possible but did not neglect simple decisions which, when submitted to it, would throw the large group into hopeless and chaotic immobility.

Although the organizers' desires determined the beginning, when participants arrived and were finally face-to-face in one room, a group-centered process guided the deliberations. The convenors ceased to function in a leadership role. Their influence (though doubtless colored by previous associations with power) was brought to bear as separate involved participants. It was not that there was *no* structure, as some imagine, it was that the staff and the participants together structured the greater part of the event.

The staff members did not hold themselves apart as directors, consultants, or encounter group facilitators, but joined enthusiastically as full-time participants. Their unwillingness to function as traditional leaders brought varied reactions. Some participants felt respected, liberated and motivated. Others sometimes felt abandoned, deceived, manipulated, and confused by this position. At other times, the staff's involvement as participants was mistakenly perceived as a 'modeling intervention': 'I do my thing, *you* should emulate me and do yours; that's the way to build community.' But rather than a planned intervention with an intended affect, it was usually merely the staff members being how they usually were. Doubtless they were a little more attentive than normally, in order to see the other's point of view and, were a little more enthusiastic to realize an efficient and wise group.[4]

The therapist's sensitive empathic listening in the therapeutic relationship may be expressed through an intimate dialogue with the client in which they follow the unifying thread of the client's inner experience. In the small group, the facilitators sensitive listening turns to include those who are not at the center of the group's attention; at times, to open the opportunity for their self-exploration; at times, to solicit their help in facilitating a constructive interaction. The facilitator's listening also turns toward these communications *between* small group members as well as within each one. In the large group, the convenor's attention may concentrate much more on the emerging pattern of the group. As an entity, what are we doing now? what is the meaning of this movement? what is being avoided? what is the consequence of this action? As well as, what am I myself feeling and doing?

The power of empathic understanding is striking—whether it comes from an individual or from a group. In a meeting of 250 persons (not one of the ones under consideration here), a man spoke of his loneliness brought on by emigration. His blood pressure, which was being monitored as part of a demonstration, immediately fell from a startling 205/115 and 130 heartbeats per minute, while talking of his loneliness, to 115/55 and 60 beats per minute as he listened to citizens of his adopted country express their understanding of how he must be feeling (Lynch, 1985: 178).

In client-centered therapy, the therapist does not pretend to know what she does not know. Her actions are not based on the authority of role or on a claim to expertness or on a theory, but on their relevance to the therapeutic process and the significance they have for the client. The therapist's outward behavior matches her inner experience. In the small group, the facilitator expresses himself honestly and openly, confronting and trying to resolve conflicts and facilitate open communications. The convenor's genuineness may be expressed in the large group by being responsible for her actions. She is willing to abandon 'what worked last time,' even the form and method of the latest version of 'person-centered approach' in order to do what is necessary to facilitate constructive learning. She is a *full* participant, willing to be involved, to influence, to be influenced, by what takes place.

Though this fact is difficult to grasp for people who have not experienced it (such as clinical psychologists who only work with individual patients), the convenor's (or therapist's or facilitator's) attitude and will to realize this attitude are not different in client-centered therapy, small group or large group. The form is different to accommodate different situations. The same approach is being applied. Rogers (circa 1983) answering a critic who had implied that his 'sensitive empathic listening,' so characteristic of client-centered therapy, had been abandoned in the large group workshop, replied, ' I believe I am the same person, guided by the same principles, in both situations. Whatever capacity I have for sensitive empathy and 'careful listening' was more fully called for in, for example, a group of forty than in the one-to-one relationship. How can anyone split the two experiences?'

Convenors shared with other participants the struggle to form an intelligent community in which each individual could be respected. Sometimes they were successful; sometimes, not. If any, the attribute which separated the convenors of these workshops from other group leaders—even those who report strikingly similar participant reactions, such as various 'Tavistock' approaches—was a willingness to enter into, as full-time participants, and *be changed* by, the experience they were living with other participants in the large group.

It was soon accepted, sometimes after bitter encounters, that the staff members were not abdicating responsibility but were simply admitting that, in spite of their experience, in most cases, they had no better answers than other participants to the knotty questions which arose concerning conflicting values, rights, interests, ethics, morals, and the complex crises that the community inevitably faced. The answers they thought would be of help, of course, they offered.

To convene people is not a light matter. Making careful choices on their behalf is an important duty. Eduardo Galeano (1985: 39) recounts the following story, 'Wiracocha, who had fled from the darkness, ordered the sun to send a daughter and a son to earth to light the way for the blind ... They carried a golden staff ... They tried everywhere to stick in the golden staff, but the earth bounced it back ... Finally, beside Mount Wanakauri, the sun's children stuck in the staff. When the earth swallowed it, a rainbow rose in the sky. Then the first of the Incas said to his sister and wife: *'Let us call the people together.'* [5]

A Large Group Meeting Begins [6]

'They're all from broken homes, you know, luv.'
'Yeah, the poor dears, some have adjusted better than others, too.'
     The cleaning women at a European workshop

Who knows how many voices these massive ceiling beams and mahogany-paneled walls have absorbed in their 75 years. Today nearly 150 persons fill the university's student lounge with conversations. Perhaps one-third of the group sits on the floor, surrounding a Mexican jar filled with flowers; the remaining persons sprawl on overstuffed sofas, shift restlessly on hard-backed chairs, and spill over into an uneven circumference of standing 'spectators.'

It is only their second day here, yet the experience is so compelling that many must strain to recover memories from beyond this room. The convenors are all present. The meeting has no leader to call it to order. Several conversations are being held in clusters of twos and threes as people chat and wait.

At last someone says, in a high-pitched breathless voice, 'I'd like to get started!'

An expectant hush falls quickly over the room.

The initial speaker (Mary is her name) shrugs her shoulders and adds, 'I have nothing specific to say, really. I just want to make *space* for anyone, who has a *need*, to speak to the whole group.'

Then Ralph, looking down at the floor, begins to speak. His slow words organize the group's nervousness into an attentive stillness. Ralph is 60, slight of body. Revealing only a hint of rehearsal he says, 'I have been a physician for more than 30 years. I thought I had stopped learning. But last night I discovered a new appreciation for *feeling*, for experiencing my own emotions. I only regret that I have been closed up for so many years of my life.'

Ralph looks back to the floor. Silence follows.

'It's wonderful; everyone is so *open* here. I can just be my real self,' someone finally says. In a tone of voice lacking conviction, she adds, 'Everyone outside should have this experience.'

A string of statements from different parts of the room unravels. The remarks are directed toward no one. Hardly a breath separates the commentaries.

'I want to continue what is happening now.'

'How am I going to apply what I learn here? I want to take something back to my work.'

'It is okay for us to love one another here, but what about the *real* world?'

'I can't speak in large groups like this and really feel oppressed here. I would like to form a small group where I could really be myself.'

To this seemingly unrelated lexicon of group members' thoughts is added the appeal for a schedule of activities to 'maximize the experience' for everyone. Another person quickly opposes any structuring, favoring 'letting it happen' as the best way to maximize the experience. Some wish the staff to make topical presentations.

Others feel they can learn more if the staff stays out of the way. Some want more people to speak. Others call for silence. Some wish to discuss Ideas and Theories. Others regard the discussions as already overly intellectual and wish that Feelings would be expressed more. Someone objects to creating a 'tyranny of emotions.' (Several people say later that they had felt a pressure to speak, to say anything, before this large group. It seemed that one had a place in the group if something could be said.)

Eventually statements begin to be related to one another and an argument arises over the value of the meeting. Marjory, a thirty-year-old secretary from Chicago, complains in her deep voice, 'I am not getting my money's worth. Nothing is happening or has happened so far that I can't duplicate with my buddies at Murphy's, the local beer joint.

'Any night of the week,' she continues over murmuring of objection, 'me and my friends can accomplish more than this group has so far. And we could have a few cold beers to boot, which is a helluva lot better than sitting cramped and thirsty, bullshitting in this hot room.' A young man from Seattle who had been trying to say why this experience was significant for him, folds his arms across his chest and frowns. He remains silent.

The group's brief honeymoon is over. People are speaking their piece. Their words mark a now familiar, at times unfathomable, stream of consciousness, which eventually reveals disappointing relations with loved ones, miserable childhood experiences, sadness, even despair, anger, rage, human suffering and eventually hope. These awkward communications characterize the beginning of the large group's stimulation which, once begun, is relentless, as if one of the laws of nature.

Anonymity

It is known that the more populous a group, the greater the proportion of its members will side with a speaker (Newton & Mann, 1980). Thus, with collaborators it may be easier for one to sway the sentiment of the group. For those who risk embarrassment, the large group may be friendly. But it is more often regarded as intimidating. It also seems to many as aggressive.

It is frequently explained that people behave aggressively in large groups because they are anonymous and therefore will not bear the consequences of their actions. Certainly this explanation can account for the acts of vandalism of marauding teenagers. When no one is looking or when one is hidden by a crowd, an individual may act destructively through what become anonymous acts. But does this view fit the large groups discussed here?

Not quite. In these groups, the aggressors are not anonymous. Everyone knows who they are. Each one may be held accountable by the group. Nevertheless, a surprising amount of verbal aggressivity is tolerated. Many statements which pass unchallenged in the group would doubtless lead to a fist fight, if delivered outside this context. Why is this?

A key to a plausible explanation may be the observation that the aggressivity is frequently directed toward no one. Even when one person is directly aggressive toward another, they are often launching an attack on one of their pet grievances and merely using the other person as a springboard. For example, 'I don't agree with what so and so said, I feel ...' What they feel and what so and so said may be difficult to connect. In this sense, there is anonymity, but it is the victim who is anonymous. That is, someone in particular is aggressive to no one in particular. The people who are used in this way do not always escape the disagreeable effect: thus, it is aggression. Also, there seems to be a special arrangement in large groups that allows people to speak with more immunity than in direct one-to-one confrontations and there is thus a higher level of aggressivity which group members tolerate. Perhaps this toleration even facilitates the resolution of difficult conflicts in the group by allowing people to express and understand all the varied feelings without prematurely reacting.

Speaking and Not Speaking

Besides aggressivity, many people fear large groups because they exert 'social pressure' on their members. This is always a possibility that must be present in the minds of participants in large group activities. These groups, especially those without designated leaders, which emphasize free expression, reduce this possibility somewhat. Unlike smaller groupings, in a large group there are almost always allies for a person whose opinions or feelings defy the direction in which the majority sentiment is moving. People can and do defend each other's rights to be different, to participate or not, in their own way, at their own pace, to remain silent, even to withdraw.[7]

Contrary to many social groups and even groups for personal development, silence was not unanimously regarded as a defect in these large group workshops. This could be one of the constructive aspects. Meerlo (1956) has lamented the inflated value speaking merely for the sake of speaking has. 'I am convinced,' he said, 'that there are many wise men among us whose voices and learning would help us to correct that part of our thinking which is delusional. But their wise words are shouted down by an excess of noise from elsewhere.'

The popular idea about the therapeutic value of self-expression doubtless encourages some people to review and reinterpret their lives in front of others. Unlike coercive use of this fact, in large group workshops there is no *requirement* to do so. Staff members and other participants may support a person who wishes to express his feelings while discouraging another who merely thinks he *should*. Participants are not only *not* required to speak in meetings, they are not even expected to *attend* meetings, if they do not wish to.

Speaking or remaining silent, thus, usually does not become one of the criteria for group acceptance. More likely, honesty with oneself, integrity toward the group, sincerity in one's expressions would be more highly valued—whether speaking or silent. The individual may not be unanimously liked, but she is usually accepted for who she is, not who she should be. Of course, to *influence* the group in the direction of a minority opinion may require not only courage but enormous energy.

Naturally, some people want their voice to be heard, to speak about themselves, for others to listen. They want their ideas accepted. As to this frequent battle for attention, perhaps Hegel's explanation suffices, 'They must engage in this struggle, for they must raise their certainty of being for themselves to truth' (Sennett, 1980).

The more verbally inclined persons, as in most informal social gatherings, will normally initiate the conversation. A few people, thus, establish the topics for discussion and the rhythm of conversing. Frequently the conversations become boring or pointless to others and they interrupt. Some who are not speaking would like others to be quiet and 'sense what is happening now.' Some quiet ones are doubtless uncomfortable speaking, but others merely find no opportunity. Many simply do not wish to add to the 'word pollution.'

Each statement made in the group elicits multiple interpretations. Some hear the emotional tone in the utterance. Others respond to some aspect of the content of the message. Most people respond to what they themselves are feeling or thinking at the time or to some belief they hold dearly—regardless of how the communication may or may not fit into the discussion. A humorous and common example is provided by a person who speaks little of the group's predominant language. He thus becomes frustrated in his attempt to express himself. After encouragement from some persons in the group, he unleashes his native tongue. Several interpreters arise to translate his words. Since each has caught a little different version of what he has said, they fall into a dispute over what he *really* meant by the statement. He looks on; more bewildered than ever. On the one hand, confusion is multiplied. On the other hand, these multiple interpretations serve to widen our awareness of ourselves: we can begin to accept that each one feels and perceives many things, frequently quite different from others.

Chaotic, confusing and rambling conversations are broken and the mood shifts dramatically when a participant says something from his or her real urgency, something intensely *private* and, at the same time, *universal*. When a person speaks from some internal motivation, not to please the others, not to say the 'correct' thing, not to merely fill the vacuum of silence, participants begin to concentrate their attention on the speaker. If the person is aggressive, what seems important is that her expression is vital to her. If she is sad, what seems important is that expressing this sadness is urgent. She may express curiosity, compassion, surprise, doubt, a passionate belief, a fiery opinion, devotion to a cause, a thoughtful question. It does not seem necessary to always capture the group's attention with something dramatic. Emotionless statements that clearly have importance to the speaker may also be accepted as interesting to the group. It seems to be a compatibility with what one is thinking or feeling and what she is saying that is more readily accepted.

Science vs. Freedom

A college professor rises and announces in a practiced voice that he has brought a tape recorder and would like the group's permission to record its proceedings. He says he would like to refer later to what takes place and perhaps to write an article for a scholarly journal. Those who think this a good idea, support his request. They would like to have a 'record for science.'

However, there are many others who distrust the professor's intentions. They say they do not wish to be 'guinea pigs in anyone's psychology experiment.'

The people who are backing science say the recordings could be used to study, not individuals but, the 'psychological processes of the group.' Therefore, no one would be a guinea pig.

Others say they resent the intrusion of someone who wants to observe (even for science) and not to be completely involved in the life of the group. They do not want their actions controlled by 'specialists' and do not want to think about what they are saying or doing in the group. Most of all, they do not want their privacy invaded by electronic instruments.

'But you will be free,' the professor pleads. 'If you request it, I will erase any part of the tape you do not like.'

'That puts too much burden on me,' someone replies. 'I don't want the extra work of making an analysis and deciding what I want to keep and what I want to erase. That is even a greater infringement on freedom. I want to say anything I like. And if I like, to contradict myself. I don't want my words to be made part of a permanent record.'

'But it is exactly this type of record,' an adversary replies, 'that would be valuable for learning.'

Soon the bystanders to this conflict, who doubtless feel some sympathy for both sides, grow restless with the discussion. They seem annoyed as much by the professor's bullying niceness as by the lack of generosity in the rights-to-privacy camp. More than anything else perhaps they resent being controlled by a dispute in which they have only a passing interest.

Although no decision is reached, tape recorders do not appear in subsequent meetings. This example is cited because it illustrates the weight that objection can carry and so as not to give the impression that every issue is resolved intelligently and to everyone's satisfaction, even though it may be resolved.

Aside from the topic of breaking into smaller groups, the debate over tape recording the large group meetings is perhaps the most popular subject of discussion in the early stages of the workshop. Though the debate may be predictable, there is no fixed pattern to the group's reaction. Sometimes the group has explicitly prohibited recording; sometimes it has been permitted with little discussion; at other times, recordings have been made even without requesting permission and this was allowed. On other occasions, participants who tried to record without asking the group's permission were humiliated in a long guilt-ridden harangue involving accusations of treachery, espionage or simply bad manners.

The values which help to shape such situations do not invade from the outside. People who attend these large group meetings already share many values in common. They place a high value on the individual, the right to be who one wants to be, the right to freely express one's opinions, beliefs, feelings, the right to better oneself—including developing one's potentialities, the right to equal opportunities and social equality. They value the confrontation of problems head-on and solving them quickly, active participation to achieve one's goals, fighting for one's rights, trusting the future. They believe that others should be helped to help themselves without encouraging dependence. They believe the individual must look after himself and is not obligated to serve society, to work for its objectives, nor to conform to its formalities.

This latter proposition, which most North Americans may find difficult to admit and more difficult to deny, presents many problems to the group. Participants want a cooperative group but do not want to be bound by its rules.

In the hurriedly constituted workshop culture, a strong value which emerges is 'to really be yourself,' to speak exactly what is on your mind. There is a tacit belief that 'we can relate different than the ordinary society.' Although they are largely associated with North American culture, these values were also common to workshops in Europe and South America.

Values and beliefs, of course, may conflict with each other—even within the same person. It is clear to some that one value outweighs another, but many remain undecided. They agree with both. Of course I want knowledge to expand, through science or otherwise. Of course I want to retain rights to privacy. Is this being wishy-washy? I don't think so. Why can't we have both? How to reformulate values and integrate those in conflict may be one of the group's major tasks. And quite often the conclusion is not spoken nor explicitly acknowledged. It is an aspect of non-verbal behavior and, as Hall (1959) has observed, it is 'in accordance with an elaborate and secret code that is written nowhere, known by no one, and understood by all.'

The Meeting Concludes

This morning's meeting has endured nearly three hours when Ralph again expresses his personal feelings about the experience he had the night before. He has learned, he reports again, but now with more intensity, how important it is for him to make real personal contact with other persons.

Ralph has come to the realization, he claims, that all theories of helping, of counseling, are incomplete. He will use any theory, even one which emphasizes expressing one's feelings, if necessary, to make *human contact*.

In the morning, participants sat expectantly and were interested that something (anything?) was being said for the first time in the group. Now, it seems that they are really interested in what *Ralph* is saying and many seem to understand and even feel an affinity for Ralph.

A few more or less political statements are made. They are passionate, but lack the dramatic resentment that accompanied earlier expressions. The speakers seem less rehearsed and their voices ring with originality. After Ralph, the others speak only briefly. Someone cracks a joke about what is happening and most people laugh heartily to put an end to the meeting.

The Crowd

It can be seen that the people gathered are not especially prepared for the enterprise they undertake. Despite their associations with the helping professions, they are surprisingly *inept* in communicating intelligently in the large group workshop setting.

On the deficiencies of specialists outside their area of specialty, but not aware of this fact, LeBon (1895), in his 19th century classic on crowd behavior, has spoken forcefully, 'The decisions affecting matters of general interest come to by an assembly of men of distinction, but specialists in different walks of life, are not sensibly superior to the decisions that would be adopted by a gathering of imbeciles.' On this score, groups have evidently not advanced much in the last 100 years.

During the early days of the workshop, meetings generate emotions, rather than integrate feelings. Moralizing, chaotic expressions of opinions, provocative ideas, the threat of violence, all make reasoning difficult and issues seem rationally unresolvable. The group, when emotionally aroused, can convincingly demonstrate not only its ability to act forcefully as one body, but also its destructive capabilities. This part of large group behavior has been described by William McDougall (1928) as,

> excessively emotional, impulsive, violent, fickle, inconsistent, irresolute and extreme in action, displaying only the coarser emotions and the less refined sentiments; extremely suggestible, careless in deliberation, hasty in judgment, ... devoid of self-respect and of a sense of responsibility ... its behavior is like that of an unruly child or an untutored passionate savage ... and in the worst case it is like that of a wild beast, rather than like that of human beings. (p. 64)

Even at its most creative, the process of the large group is rarely smooth and at its worst never reaches a high level of intelligent functioning. Misunderstandings widen the chasm between factions, and instead of clearing the air, personal expressions can end in unfair judgments and even insults. Out of frustration and exhaustion the group sometimes settles for hasty and arbitrary decisions. One would not suspect that sophisticated and well-intentioned people, with a childlike desire to express their beliefs in front of one another, could create such a graceless activity.

Frustration

Faculty meetings, committees, business conferences, formal social gatherings and many other occasions also provoke inefficiency, alienation, boredom, frustration, confusion and irritation in their members.

When the group is not enduring long flat discussions that run in circles, it seems to be completely intolerant of them. At times, the group has limitless patience; at other times, none at all. Individual's trying to exert their will to influence the group one way or the other are frequently frustrated. Participants in a research on personal experience as related to large group workshops did not even mention empathic understanding as significant to their experience (Stubbs, 1992). Indeed, the most common observation in large groups, up until the final hours, concerns the disappointing *lack* of empathy in the large group encounters.

Recalling constructive and joyous moments in group experiences, one may be hesitant to propose frustration as the *most* prominent feeling from group participation. Nonetheless, it may be.

Participants adopt many means for dealing with their relationship to the group. Many regain, according to Bion (1959),

> a sense of individual independence by total repudiation of the group and that part of the individual's mental life which is incessantly stimulated and activated by the group.' Others, acknowledging the benefits they derive from their participation, 'achieve a sense of vitality by total submergence in the group.

Simply repudiating the group does not change the fact that one is still physically and mentally part of the group. Similarly, one is already submerged in the group and this 'total submergence' frequently leads to the unrealistic expectation that everyone should feel good and cooperate joyfully. The actual fact that these self-deceptions are intended to hide seems closer to that proposed by McDougall (1928) in his classic book on group psychology:

> Individual minds which enter into the structure of the group mind at any moment of its life do not construct it; rather, as they come to self-reflective self-consciousness, they find themselves already members of the system, molded by it, sharing in its activities, influenced by it at every moment in every thought and feeling and action in ways which they can neither fully understand nor escape from—struggle as they may to free themselves from its infinitely subtle and multitudinous forces.

Perhaps it is in this endless play between a satisfying sense of personal potency and the surrender of that very individuality—its transcendence, that is—that leads to much frustration. If I cannot be completely myself, but must conform to the group's demands, I feel frustrated. On the other hand, if I am enjoying a sharp individuality but not integrated with the group or if the group is not harmonious, I am also frustrated. It takes time to find this harmony in the constellation of diversity which individuals bring to their meeting. Withdrawing from the meeting, insisting on obsolete principles which worked in some other group in the past, competing for power, are individual expressions that may slow or prevent the group's development. On the other hand, to ram through unjust, though quick decisions, to appease favored members, to ignore the ideas and feelings of the less powerful may destroy a healthy individuality.

By pooling their knowledge and skills, it has been observed, participants may solve problems none could solve alone. A group reporting an event (such as a jury report of an accident) is likely to be less complete but more accurate than its individual members' reports. Groups may produce ideas that occurred to none of their members previously in private. There is even some evidence of 'group learning': after people participated in various groups, the *group's* decisions were found to be greatly improved, even though the members' performances were not (Kelley & Thibaut, 1968). The superiority of judgment of a group may not be so much a reflection of the wisdom of the group's superior members as it may be a result of 'psychological factors inherent in discussion' (Barnlund, 1957).

On the other hand, everyone knows that at times, and depending on the heads, two heads are *not* better than one. An individual's production can also be better than his colleagues' and better than the group's. In tasks which require following a consistent, patient, strategy of solution, for example, the group falls short of the performance of its members acting independently. Centrally organized groups, with easily distinguishable leaders, may perform certain tasks more consistently than bodies not so organized. In some activities, group members get into each other's way, as when pursuing different lines of thought or 'contributing' to a discussion even when their comments are unhelpful or counterproductive. When a group tries to solve a problem better left to individuals, naturally there also may be frustration and discomfort (Kelley & Thibaut, 1968). A participatory approach to problem-solving or decision-making may also fail if participants cannot surmount the technical difficulties they encounter. For example, after 15 months, a group of educators had failed to develop an innovative product. In this same study, it was also found that the group preferred to satisfy social relationships, sidestep conflicts, avoid outside work and become more committed to the group as a group than to the group as a means to perform a task (Wood, 1989).

Thus, there are situations where group performance is superior; others, where individual performance is superior. For effectivity, the group uses both the advantages of cooperation and individuality. Participants in the group must measure their capabilities both as a *body* and as *individuals* in order to be sensitive to the most efficient course. This kind of learning is not smooth. It is awkward, though at times also elegant, unpredictable in its details. In its vagaries, it is not unlike nature. As Rene Dubos (1981) has observed, 'Nature is not efficient. It is redundant. It always does things in many different ways, a number of them awkward, rather than aiming first at perfect solutions.' The large group is similar.

Individual Frustration and Satisfaction

In a workshop I did not attend involving educators and helper-oriented people from both the black and white races in South Africa, Carl Rogers, one of the convenors, recounts an episode in which a black woman 'broke into a torrent of anger ... [and] said that she felt cheated in this meeting and disappointed in it and that she was never again going to open up to a white person. It was a real tirade of anger against the workshop ...' What followed appears to have been a deeply emotional period in the group. Reflecting on the situation, Rogers (1984) says, 'I felt that at last a very deep level of hostility had been brought to the surface.'

This kind of 'tirade of anger against the workshop,' is not uncommon in large group meetings. The source of a person's feelings varies. He or she could be having a bad day. There could be 'latent' personal feelings that suddenly surface. Or feelings may be provoked by a frustrating situation in the group itself. In the case mentioned above, Rogers seems to imply that the feelings are latent (perhaps with racist origins and present in more than just this woman): '*at last* a very deep level of hostility had been brought to the surface.' Perhaps this was the case. However, the participant said she 'felt cheated in this meeting,' suggesting that it was the activity of the group in that situation that provoked her outburst. Psychologists have had a tendency to over-emphasize the 'deep-seated personal feelings' and ignore structural factors, incompetencies of the staff and other sources of frustration that may be present in the *group*. The same amount of attention should be paid to each hypothesis. Participants can help a person express private anger and they can also accept responsibility for their part in provoking frustration in each other through the agency of the group. In a social provocation, such as this, helping a person deal with personal feelings (though it may) does not always help change the social situation.

Though frustrating and confusing and giving intelligent, sensitive persons reason to be wary, the large group can also be constructive. (Otherwise, why bother with it?) Either way, it always presents a compelling attraction. A participant put it this way: 'I go to these meetings where nothing happens, really. Mostly confusion, frustration. Nothing is decided. And still, today when I went downtown, planning to have dinner and watch a movie, I could not stay away. When the time for the meeting was near, I was *compelled* to return. I could do nothing about it; even from my years as a psychiatrist, I could not resist. When it seemed like the community was about to gather, I was pulled back like a reluctant magnet.'

Out of its characteristically awkward and graceless beginning, the large group can constructively confront many of civilization's perennial concerns: power and authority; scarcity, discovery and distribution of resources; violence and security; competition and fairness; sexual equality; competent health care; effective education;

relevant religion; freedom of expression and frequently—though not always—can develop elegant and equitable means of self-regulation and inventive resolution of crises. There is also delight in problem-solving, a taste for justice, for play, occasionally for beauty. Actions of the group can be humane, intelligent, entertaining and also transcend the proposals of any single participant. The workshop may be a puzzle, a spectacle, nurturance, learning, inspiration.

These large group workshops expose the futility of disputes over the superiority of either an individualistic or collectivistic viewpoint. The advantages to be gained from the perspective of the individual can be matched by the, often radically different, perspective of the group. And, a level of stupidity, impulsivity, and cruelty, equal to that found in a mob, may also be found in the lone individual. On the general superiority of the two viewpoints, judgment must be reserved.

Structure or Non-structure: Anticipating the future

You know, my friends, with what a brave carouse
I made a second marriage in my house
Divorced old barren Reason from my bed
And took the Daughter of the Vine to spouse
            Omar Khayyám

In the following morning's gathering the question of how to organize time for the large group meetings and other activities is once more raised. The suggestion to formulate a time schedule is met with various reactions. To pleas for a flexible organization of time, Terry replies, 'I think we need *more* structure than ordinary daily life. We want to have a definite plan whereby people can learn and solve problems arising in the course of our workshop. I envision breaking into small groups and reporting back to the large group according to a definite organizational pattern.' Many people nod in sympathy with this suggestion.

Linda agrees: 'This workshop must be organized, at least minimally. We have a limited amount of time. We can't take a chance that nothing would happen and this entire venture would be a waste of time and money.' The group appears convinced by this line of reasoning. Linda, Terry, and Paul volunteer to form a committee with others who work with organizational planning and business consulting. The committee promises to present a plan by 2 PM The meeting adjourns.

In the afternoon, a compelling presentation is made to the large group. Diagramming their plan on large pieces of chart paper, the committee reviews with the group the tedious democratic deliberations that preceded each point in the final proposal. Through scheduled blocks of time, it is proposed, workshop participants will be able to attend community meetings of the large group, small group encounters, special topic presentations, have time to eat, sleep and play. In short, everyone will be able to 'learn and meet personal needs in an orderly and efficient manner.' The proposal is applauded.

The planning committee, its pride swelling from victory, suggests a brainstorming session to list possible topics for the special interest groups—from which it is imagined most of the learning will take place. A sort of fair, where sample philosophies and remedies may be displayed, is envisioned. An eager response from participants generates a bulging 'shopping list.' Such subjects as education, healing, male and female relations, couples, men's liberation, women's rights, international issues, gay life styles, parapsychology, networking, open relationships, communal living, death and dying, children, movement, body therapies, co-counseling, person-centered gestalt therapy, psychotherapy, music, dance, art, nutrition, magic, Marxist politics, are some of those written down on newsprint with magic marker [felt-tipped pen] and taped to the wall.

At the peak of consumer excitement and as congratulations are being exchanged, a few timid voices begin to rise, challenging not the specific proposal, but the very *concept of planning*. Julie, a shy young woman who has not spoken before in the meeting, and a soft-mannered middle-aged man, Anthony, speak up. They express a vague uneasiness that something, perhaps an opportunity, is about to be lost. Was anything genuinely *new* being attempted in this workshop? Is this plan the most ingenious that the community is capable of envisioning?

Julie asks, 'What would it be like to live for awhile *with others in a community* in a truly new way, governed by our natural relationship, one to the other, and by our collective organic possibility—whatever that may turn out to be? What would it be like to be free to flow and connect with others with similar interests and perhaps discover our common purpose? Do we really need a schedule of activities to do this?'

Here and there, people nod in agreement.

'Adopting a schedule,' Anthony adds thoughtfully, 'would give us an "efficient" workshop. But those who did not fit into the scheme would have to go their own way. Sure, the proposed structure allows them this freedom. If you don't like the society, you can always drop out. But can we all go our *own* ways *together*, wandering, without a preconceived plan, but sensitive to the hidden purpose of this whole collection of persons?'

At first, peculiarly detached from active involvement in their own destiny, participants had contagiously accepted the committee's careful, though familiar, approach to self-governance. Early opposition was seen as a disruption of the group's progress. Yet, when people listened carefully to the dissenters, it was clear that innovation, not disruption, was their motive. Not fanatical anarchists, but thoughtful, quiet, explorers were advocating an albeit unreasonable, but somehow appealing, alternative. Could it really work? The meeting ended without setting an hour or place for the next gathering. Even the committee that had worked so conscientiously to produce an orderly program excitedly anticipated the outcome of this unexpected turn of events.

A participant's journal records the following: 'That evening, while reading in my room, a vague restlessness overcame me. It must be time for a meeting, I whispered to myself. Unconvinced of my real motives, I left my room and headed toward the meeting place where we had met in the afternoon. Joining me were a half dozen others who were also strolling down the hill. Entering the doorway, we were surprised to find over half of the entire group, assembled and buzzing with excitement. In a few minutes nearly the complete community was present and someone was speaking of his incredulity that this "crazy scheme" might actually be working.'

In the days that followed a general pattern was established out of initial wandering. The group was able to efficiently satisfy its members' social and productive needs. 'Knowing what's happening,' which would have been provided by the carefully conceived communication system of the planned program was now accomplished by participants sharing their immediate thoughts, opinions, feelings in the large group meetings.

A participant wrote later about her ambivalent feelings with this approach: Perhaps the group had 'gone off on a tangent' by not accepting the carefully planned schedule, she reflects. With amazement, she then continued, 'I noticed the schedule of each day was beginning to fall into place: small groups in the morning, special interest groups in the afternoon and community meetings in the evening. This was becoming the same schedule that had been thrown out earlier!'

This example illustrates what is possible with patience and the willingness to be changed—not by mere novelty but by a new reality. The members of this community did not just exchange philosophies, but allowed themselves to organize in a fundamentally different way. Participants became aware of not only their individual patterns of behavior but also the pattern of the whole. A seemingly private impulse, for example, to go to the meeting room, was shared by many. It was not only an isolated act but represented the group's volition.

Beyond Democracy: Participatory intuition

Democracy is a superstition of statistics.
    Jorge Luis Borges

Without permanent leaders and without previously organized plans, the group *can* learn to coordinate its activities and deal effectively with problems that may arise. Even very specific issues may be 'decided' in an innovative manner.

In the middle of a large group workshop, many are feeling the pressure of the busy self-imposed schedule of activities. They wish to take a day's rest. While some readily agree, many others also oppose the idea.

'I like the way things are going,' Francis replies. 'I would like to continue this schedule.'

'I am afraid,' Lillian says, nodding agreement. 'Back home, I live alone. Next year I will be seventy. All my best friends have passed on and I spend a good deal of time by myself. I am afraid. I don't know. If we take a holiday, my new friends here ... well, they might leave me. I couldn't bear to be dropped after feeling so much love.'

Some say that a free day is as much a part of the workshop as other days, just organized differently. No one has to be alone. A day off can provide learning opportunities also.

'We can take a day off anytime at home,' George objects. 'I came here to work, not to loaf around.'

'I don't want to legislate a day off,' Chip remarks. 'To legislate, to me, seems phony and structured. I want to just flow with it. When I feel like taking time off, I will do so.'

'But you're not so free,' observes Michael. 'We are presently *flowing*, as you call it, to a lock-step schedule. Yes, it is of our own making. Nevertheless, it holds us to its demands.'

It is also suggested, by some of the more psychologically minded present, that 'existential fear' may be behind the 'resistance' to doing nothing.

A proposal was made. Different implications of adapting it were heard. Positive and negative opinions and feelings were expressed. After everyone, who wished to be, was heard, the topic was abandoned. The meeting ends without an explicit decision.

Two days pass. Suddenly, one morning the routine is broken. Hardly anyone shows up for the morning small group meetings. No late morning general assembly forms. Today, there are no meetings at all. Instead, a group of music-makers surrounds Lillian at the pool; people are going to town for shopping; some go on a picnic; some sleep late. The accumulated result of these independent acts: a day off.

Holiday or not is of little consequence. However, that an informed intuition might bring about constructive coherent action, is noteworthy.

This collective action was *spontaneous, but not impulsive*. It was not the 'tyranny of spontaneity' which rules mobs. Nor was it people simply going their own way separately. This was a coordinated effort, but not driven by contagious emotion. Each knew the other's opinion from the previous exhaustive discussions. The final outcome was tempered by these earlier conversations. Thus, the group was cognitively prepared for an informed choice when the right time came.

Also, the final action could be considered *intelligent, but not strictly logical*. It did not follow from a linear sequence of logical steps. It included participants' 'illogical' sentiments. Feelings and emotions, as expressed in earlier deliberations, apparently influenced the outcome. Every need, desire, feeling, seems to have been considered in the eventual outcome. Lillian, for example, showed no signs of being left alone. George was doubtless 'flowing.'

Furthermore, the result was arrived at by a *democratic process, but was not legislated*. In this process, the power resided in and was executed by the people.

Those whose lives would be affected were involved in the steps leading to the final action. Unlike most processes called 'democratic,' no compromise had to be made. The communal reality was not defined by a statistical summing of individual positions, but by unified action which respected both the interdependent relationships of individuals and the individuals themselves. In this example and other examples given here, we see, as Becker (1968a) imagined for ideal government, 'an anchoring of power in as many subjectivities as there are those who fashion it.'

No plan was made, decision stated, or vote taken, prior to the eventual action. There was no agreement regarding time, place, or conditions for acting. In workshops such as this, it is common for meetings to end without a stated agreement, but with a consensus expressed through a collective action (everybody looks around at everyone else, slaps their thighs with their hands and stands up to leave). As a matter of fact, when a debate over an issue with diverse and strongly held sentiments and opinions has come to this point and someone says, 'I'd just like to see a show of hands to see if this really is a consensus,' the group will likely be thrown into renewed disagreement and factions. The unified act which expresses the group's sentiment becomes separated by words such as 'yes' or 'no.'

Koch (1970) has expressed concern that encounter groups shape the individual's self-definition through group responses and that behind this activity is a perversion of democracy, 'a sense of democratic process as an egalitarian merging of happy, well-met, mutually voyeuring people, rather than a system of agreements guaranteeing maximal dispersion of social control and minimum invasion upon both self-determination and privacy.' Though this shallow alternative is always possible, and should be guarded against, the foregoing example illustrates that in the large group workshop a person's self-definition is not only not always endangered, but may actually be enhanced and used in the dispersion of social control. It also illustrates that democracy may function in a manner that is neither a perversion, as Koch fears, nor a fixed system of rules which is the usual alternative.

In the foregoing example the process did not result in democratic policies but did result in wise action. The group did not adopt an 'organic model of consensus management.' Rather, each person expressed a unique individuality in an efficient collective effort which promoted the well-being of the whole and of the individual.

As one might suspect, when groups have *tried* to make decisions 'intuitively' or through an 'organic process,' no matter how well meaning they might be, they have rarely succeeded. Workshops in which the staff's primary purpose was to demonstrate 'an application of the person-centered approach' or 'to give participants an opportunity to experience a person-centered approach to group facilitation,' except for the personal victories of a few participants, could not be said to succeed in all the dimensions under consideration here. (See previous chapter.)

If individuality is focused upon, self-preoccupation and chaos are the predicted outcome; on the other hand, if individuals exhort each other to 'work as a team' or to 'build community,' oppression or immobility may as easily result. Again, two emphases at once are desirable: one on the individual; the other on the group-as-a-whole.

It must also be noted that the results of large group workshops were *not* always positive. Sometimes the large group did not become capable of governing itself. A group in Europe, for example, was immobilized by chaos and until the final moments never supported more than extravagant harangues and unresolvable conflicts. However, in general, Kirschenbaum's (1979) claim was realized, 'even with eight hundred people in a foreign culture [foreign to Rogers and most of his colleagues] and speaking in a language different from most of the staff's ... The groups *did* find a direction. The participants learned to listen to one another. The workshops allowed diversity, yet experienced a powerful sense of community. And the experience seemed to have important political consequences which were always close to the surface of the group's consciousness and were at times verbalized explicitly by community members.'

Big Group, Small Groups?

'I can't speak in this big group,' a large blond-haired man with a booming voice says firmly to the 150 or so persons assembled for the morning meeting. 'I would like to be in a small group of 10 or 12 persons.'

At this moment, of course, he *is* speaking in the large group. What, then, is he communicating? 'I can't do what I am doing?' 'I have feelings which are difficult to control; at the same time I cannot release them in this setting?' Or perhaps he just doesn't *like* to speak with so many people around.

'I don't feel anyone listens here.' 'I can't feel close in this large group.' These are other familiar statements which precede a discussion of dividing the group. To provoke this tendency, the size of the group does not seem to matter. Participants in T-Groups (T, for training) in the 1940s would meet in a group of 10 or 12 and someone would inevitably say, 'Let's break into smaller groups. I am freer to discuss and express myself with just two or three others' (Bradford, Gibb & Benne, 1964). At a workshop in Rio de Janeiro there were more than 800 persons present and many expressed the desire to break into small groups in order to speak together more intimately. I was quite surprised to find the mood in the 'small' groups (of 150 or so members) to have many of the characteristics of closeness and openness that can be found between participants in groups of 10 or 12 and that were doubtless procured earlier in groups of two or three, divided out of the *big* group of 10 or 12. As far as an ideal size for a group, Plato's advice could still be followed: 'I would allow the state to increase so far as is consistent with unity; that, I think, is the proper limit.'

Forming Small Groups

In the first workshop convened, 60 participants were invited, 12 per staff member. Before the participants arrived the staff divided the 60 participants into 5 small groups, trying to balance age and sex. A facilitator (staff member) was assigned to each group by a lottery drawing conducted by participants.

In the following programs participants became more involved in this decision. Finally, no prearrangements whatever were made. The staff did not even assume that small groups would be convened. As it was left to the large group, the process of dividing into small groups was very uneven. Some workshops managed an orderly division which included all participants. For others, the divisions were marked by controversy. Some never divided the large group into formal smaller numbers nor did the subject raise much interest among participants.[8]

Crises

Only when every means has collapsed does the meeting come about.
     Martin Buber

The workshop is approaching its midlife. Members of the group are asking, 'What will happen to these new feelings when I separate from all of you and leave this place?'

Galin, one of the participants, has not joined the community meeting today. He is said to have become very aggressive and is acting strange. Some people are concerned. Outside of the group meeting, community members either discuss the subject of Galin energetically or avoid it altogether. Two physicians compare tranquilizing medication that Galin could be given. Down the hall, two psychologists agree on the hazards of medications. They think there might be alternative interventions which could put Galin right. A registered nurse and a social worker put their heads together: might there not be a tougher screening test which would guarantee that 'weak' people would not be allowed to enter such a workshop?

Galin, small, quiet, arrives late for the meeting. He approaches the center of the assembly. He does not speak but stands when everyone else is seated. He enters near the edge of the circle, while there is a debate about Xeroxing address lists. He inches his way into the center, his eyes drink in the sky. Voices begin to hush as faces turn expectantly to Galin. He does not speak.

The group pulls in closely around the still figure. He forms the axle of a giant disc of silence. Though the center continues to remain sacredly still, the outer edge of the large circle buzzes with whispers.

'They know what to do.'
'What's the matter with him?'
'What should be done?'
'The doctors are taking care of him.'
'Poor thing.'
'Is he dangerous?'
'It's just a play for attention.'

Healing Capacity of the Group

Galin kicks the soft drink machine, sings in the middle of the night, runs screaming and half-naked through the hallways. He tells people he is on drugs, or off medication.

'Hold this book at a 45-degree angle,' Galin says. Then he feathers the pages and states, 'Now you have all the knowledge in this book.' He leafs through the pages repeating, 'See it? See it?' Arriving at the final page, he turns the book upside down and flips back through it once more: 'See it? See it?'

Galin makes sense, but it is an illogical sense. What's worse, he scares people, people who make their living as psychotherapists and social workers. 'Illogical' sense might be expressed like this:

> Sit down here my boy; relax.
> Okay, someone may please speak.
> Pain and Suffering are facts,
> Not companions we all seek.
> Joy and Happiness, they're weak.
>
> And where would this not be so:
> I want that! I don't want this!
> You are right—perhaps he—no,
> I am sorry, the mark you miss.
> Madness is our only bliss.
>
> Each thinks his Jackstraw true,
> A pulsing fount of knowledge.
> But why false this way of you?
> While mine ascends to truth's edge,
> Vainly gripping certainty's ledge.
>
> He who knows can claim this right.
> But you and I, we cannot fight
> The long day and empty night,
> Till surrender joinders sight
> And transforms that morning light.

'I am worried about Galin,' Francisco confesses to the community as it quiets for a meeting. 'He is not here and he was acting aggressive earlier.'

'Yes, he was very upset,' Sally adds. 'But now he is in his room resting. Lois is also suffering. Some people are staying with her.'

'You seem to be really concerned about Galin, Francisco,' Rosa observes.

'I'm very worried,' Francisco says. 'I am afraid he may need hospitalization for treatment. It is horrible to think of that happening to anyone. At the same time, I fear he may hurt himself or someone else. I want to treat him like a person. I don't know what is best to do.'

Is Galin sick or not? Some say he is. Among those who believe otherwise there are two different opinions. One is that Galin has 'chosen' to enter an altered state of consciousness for personal (and mysterious) reasons of growth. 'He should not be interfered with in order to learn whatever this experience may teach him.'

The other view (more in vogue during this workshop, though doubtless also held by Cicero) is that Galin, responsible for his mental state, is not motivated toward growth, but toward madness. This amounts to a self-defeating 'manipulation.' 'He should be confronted strongly and not permitted to take time and energy from the community with this behavior.'

A retired psychiatric nurse, a cardiologist, and the brother of a psychiatrist who had once spoken with C.G. Jung give their (contradicting) 'expert' opinions for how Galin should be treated.

Another participant suggests using the 'spiritual healing power' of the community. 'Let's all unify our hearts,' Betsy urges, 'visualizing Galin, and send him positive energy.' The group reacts as if no one had spoken. Betsy slides down in her chair.

'I am really angry at the facilitators,' Sally says, 'for not taking charge of this problem. They are supposed to know what to do.'

Before a facilitator (that is, a convenor) can respond, Barbara replies, 'This is a community problem. Francisco is a psychiatrist and he doesn't know what is right to do. We all have a responsibility here. Not just those who are *supposed* to know.'

'I would still like to see a facilitator handle the problem,' Robert replies. 'After all, he is trained.'

'The last person I would want to be helping me is someone who is *trained*,' Norma says. 'The best person to help me is *myself*. The strength inside of me is more than I could get from another person, no matter how well *qualified* he is. I am going to do what I can to help myself and to help others.'

'I don't know the *best* way to handle this situation,' a convenor replies. 'I am concerned about Galin and Lois *and* about the health of this whole community. I hope we don't panic. I hope we can find a wise course together. We need to know, I feel, each person's (including Galin's) perception of the 'problem' and really *understand* that point of view. If enough persons become 're-centered' in a new more complete perception, perhaps our best judgment will prevail and we can choose a course which treats Galin, not like a sickness, an enemy, nor a guru, but as he really is, in all his complexity and simplicity.'

The convenor is not in the role of leader, but he is leading at the moment. Just like anyone who advances his thought. He wants to do all he can, but not what he cannot. The convenor admits he does not know what to do. However, he is not giving up. He is not eager to make matters worse with misunderstanding. Perhaps he heeds the advice Freud gave Jung. He cautioned, 'Keep a cool head, for it is better not to understand something than to make such great sacrifices to understanding' (Lieberman, 1985). Can we all apply ourselves to find a decent solution to this crisis of our group?

From descriptions, convenors and facilitators always seem calm and efficient. Mostly in the interest of efficiency, authors report only the effective words. Thus, facilitators always appear to be under control whether they are or not at the moment. When the convenor says he doesn't know what to do, he is not just being clever or political or saying what he always says in such situations. He is saying he *doesn't know* (he *wants* to know; he won't give up *trying* to know; but just now he doesn't know). He feels awkward and uncomfortable not knowing. Remaining confident in situations which provoke speechlessness and trusting that someone in the group will have an intelligent suggestion can be extremely difficult. Rogers, speaking about his part in the decision to convene workshops where the staff must experience the same anxious moments as any other participant, said, 'Either I had helped launch an incredibly stupid experiment doomed to failure, or I had helped innovate a whole new way of permitting … people to sense their own potentialities and to participate in forming their own learning experience' (Kirschenbaum, 1979: 428).

Since the experience he writes about is over, we all know that it was successful, so his words sound a bit self-congratulatory. I am sure, however, that a profound doubt was part of his feeling *during* those moments of crises.

Let's return to the large group's deliberations: Frederick is speaking in a low, thoughtful voice. 'I could be helpful to Galin in this crisis. I left his room the other night and I'm sorry now I did that. I yielded to the 'experts' and the 'trained persons,' thinking they could help Galin more than I. Now, I am beginning to see that maybe at a time like this there aren't any experts; there are only people who can help and people who can't help, and he needs *my* support.'

The mood becomes quiet and pensive as others begin to speak of their willingness to accept their fear; they can live with it. Although, thank God, not everyone feels a genuine desire to help Galin, they can imagine ways to relate normally to Galin. A long silence concludes the meeting.

Surmounting Crises

The following day Galin disturbs sunbathers in the courtyard. He breaks a drinking glass in the kitchen where he walks barefooted. Later, a beer bottle, he sails across the patio, shatters on the bottom of the shallow wading pool. Reportedly, he tries to bite Enrique on the arm.

Most group participants are tolerant. They accept Galin and his antics. Others are annoyed and grow distant and fearful of him. Whether she likes it or not each person is living a relation with Galin.

The evening meeting begins with a long silence. A few persons finally speak. From subject to subject the conversation wanders with no real life in it.

After a clumsy silence, Frederick brings up the subject everyone else is avoiding: Galin. 'I had a very good experience with Galin today. I got into his trip. It was exquisite. At the university I teach philosophy, and being from a German family I've always used my head. Today I used my body without thinking. I am tired now and drained of energy but very enlightened by this day.' Fredrick and Galin had skipped, danced, growled, spit, and sat together in silence. He had entered Galin's world and feels he has learned a lot; perhaps, even helped some. 'Galin was my teacher today,' he concludes. Although he seems to have genuinely befriended Galin, is it also possible he is using Galin to satisfy his personal needs? to learn from Galin's crisis? or rescue him from it? or police him?

Several persons relate anecdotes of *encouraging* behavior they had glimpsed in Galin today. Positive remarks he made are recalled. Some relate touching moments of innocence. Others give accounts of how *wretchedly* Galin has behaved, the insulting comments he made, his obscene gestures.

'It sounds to me,' Louise says, 'like we are putting Galin on trial. He did many things right and many things wrong. I don't think it is necessary to judge him 'good' or 'bad.' What's important is to decide what to do about this problem in this community.'

Another one of the convenors speaks strongly, with conviction, 'This is hard to say, but I am really fed up with Galin around here. I've had it with that creep. He is manipulating the hell out of us and he's a damned nuisance. I want him to shape up or to ship the hell out.' Again, though with a different perspective, a convenor's expression matches his inner experience. He is participating as he is.

Michael says, 'I am just a lay person, not a psychologist. I am furious with the psychologists here. The entire group has been made into some kind of classroom type of diagnosis about community. Aren't you just trying to precipitate a crisis with this technique of non-directiveness? Why don't you give Galin some medicine and let's get on with what we are here for? I am exhausted with these endless discussions.'

Another convenor speaks, 'What are we here for, if not this? This problem is thousands of years old and yet to be mastered by civilized peoples. It would be very easy to cart Galin off to a mental hospital, to kiss him off and get rid of the problem. It's much more difficult to realize a collective wisdom which will regard him as a respectable person and also leave us all with a sense of dignity. How we accomplish the mobilization of a decision is crucial, I think, to humanity's future; how we treat ourselves, even in madness, is extremely important.'

'I agree,' Mario replies. 'The issues we are facing are some of the central aspects of living as humans with each other. Insanity, freedom, respect, responsibility—both with regard to individuals and to the collective—how to live wisely and cooperatively, what could be more urgent for our attention? Any road is not easy. We are trying to uncover our own best way together?'

'And any way we uncover,' adds a convenor, 'has to be right for Enrique, and Michael, Louise, Mario, Galin and all other participants. We are all part of this problem.'

Many add their advice in an explosion of statements:
'We should treat Galin like a *person*.
'I think he should be left to do as he pleases.'
'We should go to him, support him.'
'Take him away, get him out of here.'

It seems the earlier opinions are about to multiplied.

At this moment Galin himself arrives. He has decided to join the meeting. He moves slowly. Several persons go to welcome him. Many persons candidly express their anger, fear, and their caring. Francisco confesses that he thinks Galin is acting strangely, frightening a lot of people, and he is worried. He is also worried about the toll these behaviors are taking on Galin. Others who are worried about him say so.

Galin is visibly touched by the concern expressed for him. He says he thinks the best course might be for him to leave and return home. He will think it over. With nothing more to say the people rise from their seats, hug one another, and go off to dinner discussing a party that may be organized tomorrow.

At the following morning's meeting, Galin arrives clean shaven—for the first time in several days. His hair is shampooed and combed and he is wearing a clean suit. He speaks without any hint of peculiarity. He has spent several hours last night (as on previous nights) in a discussion with Frederick, Mario, and Sally with whom he has formed close friendships.

Galin speaks in a strong voice, 'I have learned a lot about myself here. I had to do it. I had to let loose. But I really need to go home *now*. I need to rest, to get away from this noise, from these people, from the 'energy' here. At home I can be quiet in my garden with my own music, my own personal things around me. Me and Saturna. Did you know I have a cat? In my own home I can reflect on what has happened to me here. I've asked Frederick and Mario to drive me home.'

The group accepts this decision. It is fitting for Galin and for members of the group. Most of an hour is spent in tear-filled farewells.

Arriving home safely Galin telephones Sally to tell the group he is with his family and friends. He is tired from the trip. He feels he has done the right thing. That same evening Lois, with color returning to her pale face, addresses the large group: 'I want to thank my small group. As I went through my 'dark night', they stayed with me, especially you Sally, I want to thank you. I think it saved my life. I entered the depths of my being and returned ... an incredible birth ... really. I can't thank you enough for letting me be *me* and sticking through it all.'

The large group had faced the disruption of its community in a courageous way, making (under the circumstances) what participants thought the best possible decisions. Each person was part of the deliberations. No one, least of all Galin, was kept apart from the discussions. Galin made his own decisions. No one decided for him. Yet, each person contributed to the eventual answer. Moment by moment the course was 'decided.' Many persons' values were reformulated. The meaning of mental illness, aggressivity, freedom of expression, security, human rights, social responsibility were among the concepts reformed. The culture could be said to have been transformed also and the eventual solution (which in itself was not extraordinary) was suited to this new culture. In *this* process, in healing itself, even transcending itself, the community was completely 'successful.' For a different time, location, and another group of individuals, no doubt the outcome could be different. But if the people spoke honestly, remaining together and open for surprise, this group concluded, the best decision could not be avoided.

In terms of curing someone with 'mental illness,' the group confessed its inadequacies. Though Lois 'came back,' Galin returned home. Even in confronting the limits of their abilities, group members behaved differently from the 'outside' society. They did not take an easy way out. They faced their limits and accepted responsibility for their actions.

Crises are well known for demanding the best of human compassion and ingenuity. The large group is capable of precipitating a crisis. At times it is also capable of resolving crises in a manner both intelligent and humane; respecting the security, well-being, and dignity of both the individual *and* the group.

A Real Problem

As long as the problems the group faces are real and not contrived, the possibility to resolve them creatively exists. Though simulations, demonstrations or situations where a number of persons are observers may provide ideas and diversion, they do not always contain the vitality needed to resolve very complex problems. It is not necessary to rigidly organize the group beforehand, to establish a theme, or to set an agenda. The group, as has been illustrated, can organize itself around its necessities. If participants have an urgency, such as the personal crisis of one among them or a regional conflict to resolve, they can organize themselves quickly and efficiently. If a crisis occurs in the group, participants mobilize their resources to deal with it. If nothing more urgent than the *question* of how to organize exists, the group will occupy itself with this.

Innovative Learning

One person alone is nothing.
When two are together, there is a unity.
      From a small Brazilian village

Learning in unknown situations might require accompanying change, exposing the whole as well as the parts, perceiving multiple causes and effects as well as inter-relationships between key elements. This learning has been called 'innovative learning' (Botkin, Elmandjra & Malitza, 1979). The inventiveness that occurs as a reaction to sudden shock, crisis, dangerous scarcity, adversity gives the most well-known examples of this learning. Is there a way to cultivate this type of learning before a serious crisis occurs?

One experience that could serve to illustrate a developing understanding of innovative learning is the following.

Carlos, a twelve year-old orphan from a poor family, was not enrolled on the workshop. He lived temporarily with his brother, a handyman employed by the institute which housed the workshop participants.

Some of the participants report that they have lost jewelry and some small sums of money; Carlos is suspected. Also, someone says they saw him trying to drown a stray dog in the wading pool. A woman complains that he was sexually aggressive toward her. 'Something has got to be done about this boy,' she demands.

A long and frequently heated discussion which involves the entire group ensues. On the one side, the list of suspicions of the boy grows. One person says that Carlos made an insulting face towards her. Another says he thinks the kid has a bad character. Someone else reminds the group that thousands of homeless marauders, just Carlos' age, are robbing and murdering citizens in the cities. This group of speakers concludes that the boy is a threat to the security of the community and should be immediately removed.

On the other side, some participants in the workshop say that they have not found him offensive. He has been courteous in encounters with them. He even helped one lady with her luggage when she arrived. She defends his offenses as childlike and innocent, as not meant to be aggressive, merely playful, and unjustly misinterpreted. Some suppose that the lad is clever, and judging from paintings he has made in the art room constructed by participants, he could even possess artistic talent. They argue that Carlos has no adequate supervision at home and if he remains with the workshop group, he has a chance at least for a positive experience with responsible people.

Though some see him as good, others as bad, the group reaches the conclusion that it does not have to judge between these extreme alternatives. It must, however, decide what to do about participants' strong sentiments surrounding the lad and what course of action to take regarding his presence: If he is sent away, the group can relax; but he faces poverty and frequent beatings at home. If he is allowed to stay, he may benefit; but there may be a danger to participants.

A few people insist that Carlos is, in fact, a member of the community and that the fair course of action would be to consult him in any decision that affects him. 'We are a family,' someone finally suggests. Around this metaphor participants can rally and integrate their values. It is agreed that those who feel more intensely (both for and against Carlos' presence in the workshop) will put the group's concerns before him. They will discuss with him how they feel, find out how he feels, and see if some solution can be worked out to everyone's satisfaction.[9]

In the meeting, Carlos says that he did not realize his behavior was frightening anyone. He was acting in his accustomed way. When he realizes others are threatened, he wants to change. Also, however, he wants to participate in the workshop. He wants to study dance with Grace; to learn massage with Laura; with Clare, to learn music and art; and with his brother, to learn to drive a car. They all agree. He agrees to behave according to the behavior which governed all participants.

Carlos stayed in the workshop. He not only abided by the consensual rules, but became an exemplary citizen. Those who previously feared him became his friends. Those who initially supported his point of view were not disappointed. In the end he made one of the more pointed observations of the group, 'This year there was lot of drama and not much adventure. I expect that next year there will be more adventure and less drama.'

Integrating Conflicting Values

We do naturally abhor not only endings but also never ending, that we not only fear change but the unchanging.
Jessie Taft

Anticipation—The early signs of a problem were detected: a minority of the group was suffering. This fact was not ignored. The group anticipated more serious problems. Also, participants in the group thought about (indeed, argued over) various alternative actions the group might take and what consequences those actions might bring. In the phrase of Botkin, Elmandjra, and Malitza (1979), these group members were 'seeing the present in terms of the future, instead of the future in terms of the present.'

Participation—Every person in the community was involved in the decision-making process, including Carlos. People showed an empathic understanding for each other's feelings. They were honest: their statements matched their thoughts and sentiments. They respected the dignity of each member of the community, even a 12-year-old who was not even officially registered in the workshop. And, this participation included a good will toward cooperating and using dialogue to reach an intelligent solution.

Values in Conflict— Maintenance learning is 'the acquisition of fixed outlooks, methods, and rules for dealing with known and recurring situations ... It is the type of learning designed to maintain an existing system or established way of life.' Maintenance learning is essential to the continuation of much of civilization's infrastructure (Botkin, Elmandjra & Malitza, 1979: 10).

What distinguishes maintenance learning from innovative learning is the role of values. Maintenance learning reinforces the values of the system it is designed to maintain and ignores others. When values are in conflict, learning opportunities are present. For this reason, values are called, 'the enzymes of any innovative learning process' (Botkin et al., 1979: 40).

In the example above, a dialogue of values brought conflicting sides into focus:

'A citizen has a right to live free from threat.'

'The community has a responsibility to protect its members and to govern the behavior of its members.'

'The individual should be free to act differently and still be accepted. We should not have to conform to someone else's opinions of proper behavior.'

'The community is responsible for looking after its children.'

'The group should be governed by humane feelings, not by cold rules.'

'Security is more important than anyone's feelings. If people are concerned about the boy's feelings, that's their problem, not mine.'

'If any member of the community has a problem, it is the whole community's problem.'

In many conflicts that arise within a group, such as this one, I can say, 'yes,' to each side of the conflict. When I heard the members of the community call for greater security, I said to myself, 'Yes, I want security.' When I heard their opponents call for greater respect for the individual, even if it is a 12-year-old, I said, 'Yes, let's respect the individual. Let's give him a chance.' I was thus required to find a position that could be backed by action and support these values. Could we have security and respect the individual? When the process was complete we did not have to settle for one against the other: for winning or for losing. With patience, the willingness to withstand frustration and confusion, and the ability to extract from complex human relations a fair solution was found. The group strived for the best and surrendered to the better.

Insisting on 'Yes' or 'No' positions in a conflict divides members of the community into two camps. On the other hand, a metaphor, that accommodates an elusive conjunction of diverse values, may be accepted by everyone. Within the metaphor of 'family,' for example, a range of values may be accepted together. 'Family,' for example, is more general because it can incorporate not only more values, but conflicting values as well; at the same time, more specific, since each person has a very specific notion of family. Group participants may agree on solutions consistent with the metaphor. A person's perception is radically changed by accepting the metaphor. For example, a person who was skeptical of the boy's trustworthiness after accepting him as part of the 'family,' saw him not as someone to fear but someone he should help to improve. It is also thought that using a metaphor to make an idea clearer tends to convince, not on the basis of the idea's merits but, due to the familiarity of the metaphor (Bowers & Osborn, 1966).

The reformulation of values, through metaphors, may account for one of the most powerful transformations the group can experience at a point of crisis. Each person's needs, each one's ideas, feelings, beliefs, each voice contributes to formulating principles which the group follows. Usually the complexity is not expressible in simple words. But it may be expressed by: The 'group is like an orchestra,' for example, with each one playing his own composition, but also listening to the others to blend in making music. The 'orchestra' gives both structure and freedom. Participants can agree to 'make music together' and see whether they like it or not.

To avoid premature conclusions, members of the group needed patience. They needed time to carefully formulate the problem, to let all the various perspectives come to light, to hear every voice. They needed strength to withstand the sheer weight of lengthy discussions, to avoid collapsing emotionally during their chaotic moments, to avoid the temptation to push forward hasty and radical solutions (such as ignoring the 'irrational' fears of some or sending the 'menace' away without further thought).

In the best moments of these workshops, participants were equally responsible for what took place. No leaders were appointed, but they did emerge. If organization was needed, someone helped it take shape. If technical knowledge was required, a person with expertise usually appeared. The one who could sharply express a certain emotion that others only vaguely sensed, the person who could compose a thought that captured what was eluding the group, the person who could provide a fact, a significant insight at the right moment became the group's leader.

Although its conditions for realization may be rare, this emergent leadership is not unknown. Xenophon described his comrades, ten thousand leaderless Greek soldiers, who returned safely on the perilous march from Persia to Greece, as drawing on individual intelligence and initiative, each one a leader, 'free individuals unified by a spontaneous service to the common life' (Hamilton, 1930). They survived by throwing off the rules and regulations which had been drilled into them. Whoever had a better plan spoke up. Their aim was the safety of all. In Edith Hamilton's words, 'The ten thousand leaders became ten thousand judges, ten thousand servants to suit the needs of the group.'

When Innovative Group Learning Fails

In most groups individual learning will take place, but group learning is a more delicate endeavor and can easily fail. In the United States, for example, a workshop was conducted in which a legal activist was present. In the midst of a conflict in the group he put forth (like other participants) his opinion. However, unlike others, he continued to insist on his point of view beyond all common sense. He pushed this same point of view (which by now had become a policy) into all future discussions, whether it was relevant or not. This crusade, he admitted, was a 'test' of the person-centered approach to see if it was 'tolerant of diversity.' From my experience, innovative learning *needs* diversity to find creative solutions. What it cannot tolerate, as this fellow proved, is bad will. It is a subtle cooperative venture. Naturally, without his constructive participation no integrated solution could be found. Diversity was plentiful. What was missing, and was impossible under the circumstances, was creative integration.

In another workshop, a participant, in an arrogant and self-centered tone, announced that he wished to tape record the meetings. Some participants accepted his proposal. Those who objected, he tried to bully into conformity with his desire. The objectors also held stubbornly to their feelings. A long discussion ensued. No decision was reached, but he withdrew his request to tape record. He sulked through the remainder of the workshop. Here, the situation was not settled to the satisfaction of one of the community members. He did not show the necessary humility to pursue a mutual solution. Other members of the group did not show the necessary autonomy to reopen the problem when they saw that he was alienated from the group.

There have also been cases, when the staff of the workshop was very diverse and the goals of the workshop were very unclear, where the group occupied itself with a unification such as one finds at football matches: strong emotions in a mindless conformity. In all these examples innovative learning could not take place.

Group Learning: The culture transformed

My desire to hear the truth was complicated with my fear of knowing it.
    Joaquim Maria Machado de Assis

Learning to function as a system that can face complexity and unpredictable changes and resolve its problems through intelligent reorganization may be one of the most important functions of these large groups. Though group members can be uninvolved in the group or merely indulge in self-serving activities, they can also be intensely involved in group decisions. They may even be able, unwittingly, to transform the group culture to one more fitting to a confrontation with uncertainty. The following example illustrates this.

A participant confronts the large group with a furious need to 'stage a happening.' Members of the group are eager at first to support what they imagine to be a psychodramatic emotional display—beating pillows, kicking, screaming—a norm of behavior that has been established in the small group meetings of this workshop. The man (let's call him Marvin) proposes a 'play.' He will take the part of his wife. Another person will play the husband. The group will look on.

Though they cannot explain it, several persons in the group express discomfort with the man's proposal. Others grow impatient to 'get on with it.' A sensitive and profound dialogue ensues between members of the group and the protagonist. The play that takes place is not what Marvin had in mind. No one moves from their chairs as the group draws out of him an agonizing story of how he sadly witnessed his wife sink into an emotional breakdown over the death of a friend, which led to her own eventual hospitalization.

'In doing this psychodrama, do you intend to live what your wife felt?' Marvin is asked.

'Yes, in order to better understand her experience and my love for her,' he answers.

'Do you intend to do something that could end in your hospitalization?'

'I don't know the outcome, but I am prepared.'

'Could anyone be hurt in this play?'

'It is not my intention to hurt anyone.'

To some, his answers seem reassuring. They believe he is 'taking responsibility' for his actions. To others, his replies are elusive and signal alarm. The tension builds up steadily. Some urge him to 'go ahead, dive in; the risks are worth it.' Others wish to support him, but do not 'feel comfortable' about their involvement.

Little by little, as Marvin pushes his project forward and the group sides with him or opposes him, he reorganizes his perceptions of what took place with his wife and what action he wishes to take at the moment. The play has progressed substantially.

'I am beginning to see something new,' he says.

'Did your wife break things?' a participant suddenly asks.

'Yes.'

A long still silence … dim incandescent lamps have rearranged the shadows in the room giving the people in the group a bolder outline. Minutes have turned to hours. As the group had awaited the principle actors, Lori and Marvin, to make their appearance, the play had already taken place. He and the group were the actors, struggling, step by step, in a drama of mutual invention, searching for an outcome fit for all. The drama which was enacted was less and, at the same time, more than Marvin had in mind.

Marvin interrupts the stillness. Thoughtfully, he says, 'I have realized something already. I am ready to give this up. It has been enough. It is complete. I have what I need. This is it. I am grateful.

'I don't need to act out my wife's trauma, as I thought. I *feel* what she felt, right now, and *you* feel it with me. I needed you to be accepting. I needed you to go with me. But I needed you to be strong, to push me, so I could be strong, so I could face myself. I needed you to care, in order to feel my caring. And I needed you to be *responsible*, as I was not. I've got what I needed, not what I thought I wanted. Suddenly I understand the love of two strong people.'

The path, not the destination, had changed. The group was transformed. In a search for truth, psychodramatic magic was replaced by the emergence of real human involvement. Marvin's shoulders drop as he lights a cigarette. He understands.

Marilyn breathes deeply. Virginia slumps in a chair. Steve stretches out on the floor, his hands behind his head.

No one had to go through with 'it.' Yet, everyone had gone through something together. The 'it' was faced. The group entered the chaos with Marvin and all came back.

'What exactly had Lori done?' someone asks as the group shuffles from the library where it has been meeting. Passing through the swinging glass doorway,

Marvin replies, casually: 'Exploding insanely, she threw loose objects at me and, tearing off her clothes, shattered a plate glass window with her naked body.'

Somehow the group sensed that Marvin's intentions might be dangerous. Even if he assumed responsibility for his actions, the group would not accept a harmful outcome. But perhaps Marvin, as he said, had no specific intentions. His drama depended on the group. A mutual creation. Everyone felt his way together; danger was part of the experience. Together they created a constructive alternative.

Conventional thinking might regard the change of direction as the 'group will' putting 'pressure' on the individual to conform his behavior to the group norm. But one must not forget that Marvin began with the intention of conforming to the cultural norm of explosive display of emotions and the group initially supported this approach, prepared to assist in the action.

However, another way to look at it is that in one coherent act, the established ideas of the group—that is, the culture—were transformed by coming into conflict with the group's new reality. The 'traditions,' the 'heritage,' the 'design for living,' in this group was changed. Members of the group had first established and then changed their social system. They did not merely participate in this system but, when needed, revised some of its underlying values.

Marvin followed his desire to understand himself and it took him in a surprising direction—not toward violence but away from it. Perhaps the community could have handled the crisis of an 'emotional breakdown,' if he became a 'problem.' This group, however, demanded more. Participants were sensitive to the pattern of the group and its consequences to the person. In a sense, they empathically 'lived' the experience with him. They changed together. He related afterwards that he understood more clearly the relationship with his wife, not only during the group but later when he had returned home.

We could not have survived as a species were we not able to be conditioned. Changing the culture, however, is perhaps as natural a function as adapting to it. Midgley (1978) has observed, 'When people resist and change the culture they were brought up with, they do so because their nature demands it. Conditioning fails here, because that which was conditioned is stronger than its conditioning.'

Earlier, an episode was related in which individuals, apparently moved by a private impulse, decided at the same time to go to the meeting room. The result was a spontaneous gathering of the community. That is, the pattern of many conscious private actions resulted in a coordinated action of the group. In the example just related, participants showed a sensitivity to the pattern of their actions. Although their individual thoughts and feelings and behaviors were not unusual (in fact, they were perfectly consistent with the existing culture), the pattern which was forming was not what they expected.

It is exactly this *perception* of the pattern that is unfolding, at the same time that each individual is expressing her individuality, that is important. It is important because it may lead to turning unwanted patterns into desirable ones without overt control over individual choice. The facility to perceive the group's patterns decreases the likelihood of group members ignoring their responsibility for the consequences of their collective action. A common pattern in large groups, for example, is the rejection of a member by the group, when individually everyone seems to accept the person. An awareness of the pattern of this rejection may make it more difficult for groups to commit injustice while their members shrug their shoulders and look at each other in amazement. Moreover, this awareness may also contribute to more intelligent collective actions.[10]

More Metaphors

Today there is silence in the group meeting. It is unlike the tense noiselessness of the early meetings. This quiet is peaceful. People seem to accept that they have nothing to say.

When we arrived at the workshop we all seemed to know what we wanted and how to go about getting it. If we were to have success, we had to work fast, to press hard, as there was not much time. Now it is not necessary to get anywhere. We can be where we are, even if where we are is nowhere.

To try to describe the good and the bad, the ups and downs, the various complexities of the experience, people again resort to metaphor. Ralph, for example, likens the workshop to a pearl, formed from a piece of dirt, an impurity. Out of our fears, our petty problems, our conflicts, our negative emotions, something pure and valuable has formed.

Sally says the workshop seems like an amoeba, a primitive form of life, sometimes round and integrated, sometimes elongated, irregular, yet always changing shape, flowing and organic, living.

Betty feels the workshop has been like a childbirth. It was conceived nine months ago by the convenors. The idea germinated in each participant's mind, out of sight, taking shape. Then with our congregating in this place it was given birth and it grew as a single being, struggling with its emotions, its selfishness, its adolescence, its place in the world as an adult with its midlife crisis, joys and disappointments and finally maturity.

Using metaphors to clarify understanding, not to lead to the resolution of conflict, is still an attempt to capture diverse characteristics in one comprehensive image. However, if carried too far, the result can be confounding. For example, the constructive workshop may be like a 'pearl' in the sense that it is rare and takes time to discover. But, in what sense, if any, is it like a 'pearl' that is clamped shut in a shell and buried in the sea? The continued use of a metaphor, after its initial integration of perceptions, may take away as much as it gives to understanding. Whereas, using metaphor as a device to integrate opposing, though necessary, values may be useful in dealing with crises the group confronts.

Opposites that Merge

Last day's gathering
Purple shadows trail their gaze
A golden exit.

It is the last time in this workshop the whole group will meet together. Sally is speaking and concludes, 'I don't know what this experience means to me yet, but I am excited. I haven't felt this way since I was a child.'

'I *disliked* every meeting intensely from beginning to end. All community gatherings seemed to bring out the worst in everyone, despite the clear, active presence of enormous trying and caring. And yet,' David concludes, 'I wouldn't be anywhere else. This is where I belong!'

From my journal notes:

The people who speak are familiar to me. Though I do not know them very well, I feel close to them. But also I feel close to the group, *to this community, to our collective presence. My attention returns to the conversation of the meeting. Some people speak of how much they like what is happening to them. Some still press to the end to have their questions answered. Others attempt to provide the missing answers. Others make suggestions for better organizing future workshops. Some express impatience with this line of talk. 'What are you really feeling?' they wish to know. Others are impatient with this fascination for feelings, 'What is wrong with thinking?' Some call for a union of the two. One woman says it is impossible. Another says, no it isn't, it is happening here. I agree with all of them.*

The complexity of the group's discussions, the mind-boggling problems and their multiple alternatives for solution are bewildering. Nevertheless, my mind is clear. I am very concentrated on the subject under discussion. My thoughts are intimately connected with the question being considered, with the problem to solve, with the search for understanding one another in conflict. My attention follows the faces of the speakers, their words, an abstract thought, a fleeting memory, my own inner feelings. Though my attention is focused, my thoughts are peculiarly diffused.

Every statement has a ring of truth to it. It is not completely satisfying to me, but close. When someone else speaks, offering the opposing view, I can also say, 'That's right, I agree.' But how can I agree to both? Paradoxically, at the same time I know I cannot, I do!

With each statement my sense of understanding grows and my sense of the truth becomes sharper, even as my ability to formulate them is escaping. I can feel the impending answer, yet even when I try to offer in words my enlarged understanding, it also comes up short of satisfying. It is with a sense of surprise and disappointment that I find my thoughts useful but inadequate to describe the complexity. Relief comes only when these same concepts are polished by the discussion into something that does serve.

So I sit alert, involved, concentrated, bewildered, straining for the formulation of words that will exactly fit this burgeoning 'it.' Though no words seem to describe completely 'it', increasingly the silence is capable of saying what we all wait to hear. Sometimes only the silence can express it and we settle for that.

But sometimes, as if the silence itself had spoken, we realize that the group has expressed a statement that fits. All the comments, the incomplete pictures, words, taken altogether, along with the silence, the squirming, movement in and out of the room, are a complete statement, an expression of who and what 'it' is.

I am whole and I am part of a whole. I begin to notice similarities between what is happening in the group and what is inside of me. I 'know' what will happen next in the meeting, what topic of discussion, what common feelings people will have, what concerns will be raised, what action is due. I can preview the next event. I can look to myself, not as an expert, not a teacher, but a simple source of insight. Yet, I am following, not guiding, the flow of events. I am following something that follows my own thoughts.

After experiencing the large group in its cumbersome way delicately formulating a just decision or taking efficient fair action, I began to respect the state of mind and the ability of a group of people to deal with complex problems. I could participate as any other member of the group knowing that in so doing, I was contributing to the group's ability. Did I trust *the group? I had more reasons to trust the group than not to. But I did not always see how the group could possibly deal with the* current *crisis. This time the group is surely doomed to failure. When the way was found out of the dilemma, I was once again impressed; enough so to organize other workshops. In this sense, I trusted the group. Perhaps, what I cultivated was a tolerance for discomfort and an openness for the possibility that the group could find a way.*

Satire

Tonight a group of persons gathers on the steps of the dormitory porch. No one has arranged the meeting. A few people begin to talk together, telling jokes. By and by they are joined by others. They make fun of the workshop. They laugh. Spontaneously they create a play. They imitate the convenors and the main characters of the workshop, and re-enact some of the more dramatic moments of the group. The most sacred acts are exposed to their bizarre side. The most sensitive moments are exaggerated and satirized. The timing of this activity is perfect. Had they performed yesterday it would have been inappropriate; tomorrow, too melodramatic. Tonight participants can laugh at themselves and really enjoy it.

Every workshop has had such an event. In some it is a skit, a talent show, all very organized. Enterprising participants in one workshop had tee-shirts printed with the group's slogans. They made costumes and wrote songs for a theatrical presentation before the community. Most of these expressions contained a refreshing iconoclastic humor. Whether these activities are planned or spontaneous, they are surely some of the group's most creative inventions.[11]

By concentrating so much on what happens within the group meetings may give the impression that this is the most important aspect of large group workshops. It is perhaps the most public, and therefore most easily described as the 'group.' The general assemblies are part of the, one could say, 'formal' ritual. However, some of the most significant events occur outside of this setting. The workshop is closer to daily life than many other applications of the person-centered approach: a conversation over a meal, a stroll along the beach, a small group dealing with an emergency, informal activities of the entire community may be extremely significant, not only for participants but for the community itself. Rogers (1986c), in describing a workshop, has suggested that perhaps the most significant unifying event was a night when the entire group participated in a wine drinking celebration at a local inn. In that workshop, the lack of an impressive unity in the meetings themselves was evident from a participant's report that there was 'rarely a consistent thread in the discussion.'

From the first letter the organizers send to prospective participants to the last encounter between participants is all part of the workshop.

Follow Up and Evaluation

Returning home, in addition to the many positive reports, participants in workshops sometimes report being at odds with their families, friends, and work. They may be like strangers to their loved ones and friends and find it difficult to return to routine life. The feelings they experience are not necessarily new, but the workshop may have strengthened certain of their narrower convictions.

In Chinese thought reform projects, in religious cults, in 'training seminars,' activities aimed at conditioning human behavior and attitudes, participants are not only obliged to confess in public and to undergo indoctrination, but the relief they feel (which may be taken as proof of, say, spirituality) is reinforced with follow-up meetings, 'advanced' seminars, or 'support' groups.[12]

In Wesley's religious movement, for example, 'Once conversion had been achieved in the large meetings, the converts were split up into groups of no more than twelve, who met once a week to talk over difficulties, deal in detail with their problems, and with a 'class leader' continued their indoctrination' (Sargant, 1957).

Clinical psychologists are often concerned with follow-up procedures to 'support changes' made during intensive psychotherapy treatment. The therapy is cast into a surgical metaphor: first, 'opening the person up,' second, implanting certain changes, and finally a closing or 'follow-up' to 'integrate the changes.' However, if the group is not intended as psychotherapy but is, for example, for educational purposes, follow-up activities should be evaluated differently.

Reinforcements that might be considered constructive when applied to *remedial behaviors* engendered by the group treatment, when applied to *new perceptions* gained in the group setting for education, could be destructive, if the group values are at odds with family values or career values or social values in the participant's life. To reinforce these perceptions and continue the compelling emotional states experienced in the group through regular 'support groups' could bind the person to a system of values which are not in his or her total interest. The person may need uncluttered time to integrate into the wider structure of his life important learnings from the group experience. Cults prevent this: they provoke an emotional experience, convert the participant to the cult's values, reinforce these values through regular interaction with other cult members and indoctrination. To prevent the person from integrating a powerful learning experience into his normal life, letting its meaning find its own place in this context, could be *unethical*. Robert Lifton (1961), commenting on brainwashing practices, observed that, 'What we see as a set of coercive maneuvers, the Chinese communists view as a morally uplifting, harmonizing, and scientifically therapeutic experience.'

A therapist reports on the damaging effect of conditioning activities that may be labeled 'psychological support.' A patient of his had joined a 'consciousness raising' group. Her initial gains—loss of feeling alienated and confirmation of identity— were reinforced through regular meetings. After a year, however, participants in this group were being chastised if they wanted to be attractive or if they liked to do things for a man. 'Purification,' writes Sabo (1975), 'of her feelings, loyalty to the group, in short, a rigid morality began to replace the original confirmation of her identity.'

Thus, the preoccupation with the means of producing change may eclipse the realization of a truly creative experience for participants. There is the danger (even within the life of a group) that the system or technique or the group itself will come to be regarded as 'the truth.' When passed on to the next 'generation,' instead of cultivating a more complete person, the group experience could simply result in another form of 'religious' conditioning. Coulson (1980) was asked by a participant in a group, 'Why do we have to be "person-centered," can't we do what we want to do?' Coulson's advice, in this regard, is, 'Perhaps we can aim for an uncluttered experience of life which for some will turn out to match the definition of effective therapy in vogue, while for others the experience will yield benefits we may never be aware of.'

Domination of participants can localize around an enemy, an ideal, belief, practically anything. In large group workshops it tends to centralize around the free expression of feelings. In follow-up groups it might focus around some set of qualities of a 'fully-functioning person.' Considering the ease with which people may deceive themselves, may be coerced, wittingly or unwittingly by groups and their organizers, I think that follow-up activities, especially support groups to reinforce changes produced by a large group workshop should be approached with care. Workshops should not aim at conditionings or reinforcement of conditionings, but in constructive change which is part of the person's ordinary life. A person truly self-directed does not need systematic 'social reinforcement' to change her real-life situation, if she desires to do so. A wedge of reinforcement should not be driven between the person and her family by psychological conditioning methods.[13]

In recent years, large groups in the person-centered approach have tended to lose their creative edge and to become stylized, focusing largely on therapeutic aspects in small groupings and a kind of public ranting in the general assemblies. There are many explanations for this, including the commercialization of such activities where participants are no longer invited to discover something together, but rather are invited to 'receive' an experience.

What is needed is much more understanding of large groups, their advantages and disadvantages, their effects, their relation to therapy and learning and a way to evaluate them. A large group workshop cannot fail, if the purpose is 'to give people an experience of the person-centered approach.' They had an experience didn't they? Then, it 'succeeded.' If the group is for, say, 'cross-cultural communications,' as long as people from different countries conversed, the group was 'successful.'

If the workshop 'aims to provide an environment which will enable people from many cultures to understand and build skills in using the PCA in cross-cultural communications,' as a brochure advertising a European workshop announced, it cannot go wrong. It aimed; even if it may have missed the mark. If the intention were taken seriously, however, the workshop could be evaluated. Was the environment provided? Did people from many cultures build skills in using the PCA in cross-cultural communications? How many did? What level of skill? What are they doing with these skills now? And so forth.

In the evaluation of these events another unfortunate trend has developed. It has become common practice to assume that some sort of 'facilitator attitudes' are causative and set about citing successful interventions. Such attitudes must be put into perspective with the total phenomenon. It is informative to know how an athlete, for example, approaches an important competitive event. However, this tells you little about the event itself, a phenomenon that consists of the athlete, other participants and spectators, a certain place at a certain time. The phenomenon does not depend *entirely* on the athlete's behaviors and certainly not on his attitudes alone. It can be noticed that beliefs and attitudes that are expressed by such acts as rubbing a little dust between the hands, making the sign of the cross with a bit of grass from the edge of the field, adjusting the uniform and wearing the same socks he wore in the last victory are *superstitions* whose principle effect is to contribute to a 'proper state of consciousness' in that individual, certainly a contributing factor, but hardly the principle cause of the outcome of a very complex activity.

It has also become common practice, if evaluated at all, to evaluate workshops only in personal terms. For example, in 1986 Carl Rogers (among others) convened large group workshops in Europe, South Africa and the Soviet Union. Although the principal goals of these events varied considerably, in evaluating success, Rogers relied heavily on the testimonies of a few participants who had very positive experiences (for example, Rogers, 1986c).

Is a positive experience unexpected? No. But neither is a negative one. The little research that has examined participant's reactions following a person-centered large group workshop suggests that, although most do not feel negatively, there will likely be a few participants who feel exceptionally good *and* a few who will feel very disappointed regarding their experience (Barrett-Lennard, 1977; Bozarth, 1982).

A large group experience which cannot benefit its members as *individuals* in tangible ways, definitely should not be considered a success. On the other hand, if *all* that can be shown to have been accomplished is that (predictably) a few people feel better and a few feel worse, is this to be considered success?

Clinical psychologists too often try to understand person-centered groups in a reductionistic manner: nothing but the sum of properties and behaviors of their members that result in 'treatment outcomes.' However, what medical treatment (such as large groups) would be approved that would be effective for only one or two percent of the population to which it was applied?

Because of its inefficiency as psychotherapy, it cannot be justified as a *method* for this purpose. However, this should not obscure the fact that for those individuals who *do* experience it as therapeutic, it may help more than a lengthy psychotherapy.

Although many large meetings may be no more than a rowdy public platform for spouting opinions and their full potentials may never by realized, the large group is capable of much more than watered-down psychotherapy or public ranting: it may provide a multi-dimensional learning-by-doing experience. None need be satisfied with mere novelty: it is long past the time to be amazing ourselves with the observation that citizens from such and such many nations, speaking so and so many languages, can survive a meeting together. How many times must it be discovered that, 'folks over there are just like folks over here?' It is more important to know *what* exactly was accomplished by such 'international meetings.'

These statements are not intended to dismiss large group workshops. On the contrary, as there are many things that large groups *can* accomplish (whether they are called 'workshops,' 'forums,' 'conferences,' 'congresses,' or whatever), I would like to see a broader evaluation and, thus, a broader and better understanding of these events.

People in large groups follow rituals, extend their ordinary abilities, perhaps restore mental health, promote personal development, improve social relations, stir transcendental longings, and may also succeed in self-governance, resolution of problems and adapting to uncertainty.

What dimensions might be evaluated?

Personal

I would begin, as Rogers, with the personal. How successfully were individual goals achieved? Organizer's goals? It would be wrong to say that therapy *always* occurs in large group workshops. Likewise, it would be wrong to say it *never* occurs. This dimension should be evaluated. How successfully (as in client-centered therapy) was the discrepancy between a participant's self-concept and her organismic experience reduced? What were other group members or members from the participant's family able to add to her evaluation of personal change? Did participants learn about their stubbornness, competitiveness, passivity, how easily they can be influenced, how they felt differently in the group than alone, their need for attention, or their flexibility, cooperativity, their honesty, respect for others, ability to help others, their creativity? Did they become aware of their fear and desire for contact with others? their ability to obstruct as well as facilitate the progress of the group? Did they find the group just? unjust? whimsical? that one individual can be both helpless and all-powerful in shaping the group's movements? Did participants feel autonomous and at one with the group? Perhaps Freud's criterion could be used: Do individuals enjoy work, love and play more? These could be some questions to consider.

Interpersonal

How successfully were interpersonal communications improved? How much 'greater understanding of self and others' was achieved? How did interpersonal relations—both within the group and beyond the group—change? How well were interpersonal conflicts resolved?

In these low-structured activities, the group is usually called on to govern itself. How successful was it at *self-government*? How effectively did the group *resolve problems* with which it was confronted? conflicts of values? Peacefully resolving a dispute over tape recording (or not resolving a dispute) in a manner which does not defeat diversity and does not permanently frustrate participants may be more significant than formulating resolutions.

How flexible was the *culture* of the group? How successful was the group in transforming the culture to a more appropriate form that would meet participant's changing needs?

How effectively could the group learn as a body or *adapt to uncertainty*? Did the group react with the primitive instincts of a herd? the logical precision of a jury? the self-assertiveness of a nation? Did it employ instincts, logic, assertiveness, intuition in wise and effective actions? Did it function to improve social organization and relations, as medicine (helping to improve the well-being of its members), as science (solving problems), as government (making decisions) and religion (helping its members understand their existence)? What was in fact accomplished by the group? If the group is for, let's say, 'cross-cultural communications,' how well did it accomplish its goals? If for 'conflict resolution,' how successful was it? Were the organizers' goals also realized?

Transpersonal

At what level was transpersonal awareness provoked in participants? Participants in large group workshops, in addition to extraordinary insights, often become aware of their relation to the group, the society, the species. They may become aware of not only the patterns of the group but the patterns of their life. An awareness of life and death, of 'oneness,' of a 'universal feeling' and other religious manifestations are frequently reported. What is the difference between genuine spirituality and artifacts of emotion provoked by the large group experience? Was there evidence of 'altered states of consciousness'? How were these experiences described? Could they be distinguished from 'spirit possessions' or psychosis?

What impressions did the physical setting make? What was the 'effect of group'? This may not be a one-time analysis, but on-going questions. If Sheldrake (1988) is correct, that, 'The invisible organizing principles of nature, rather than being eternally fixed, evolve along with the systems they organize,' we will be continually trying to understand new principles as well as new systems.[14]

Notes

1. The initiators of these large group workshops were Natalie Rogers, Carl Rogers, John K. Wood, Alan Nelson, and Betty Meador. After the first year's programs, Nelson and Meador undertook other pursuits and the staff was reconstituted. In the next six years the most consistent staff group consisted of Natalie Rogers, Carl Rogers, John K. Wood, Maria Bowen, Maureen Miller O'Hara, Jared Kass, and Joann Justyn. David Aspy participated on the staff of one workshop and Dick Vittitow and Marion Vittitow participated in that and one other.

2. Community, by definition, is a society of people having common rights and privileges or common interests. Thus, despite their temporary nature, we can call these large group workshops communities. They are especially, communities for learning.

3. In recent years it is more difficult to find examples of significant learning in some of the workshops called person-centered. Doubtless, two factors have contributed to a trivialization of these events. One is that staff members are not always chosen on the basis of competence. Political and commercial back-scratching, the weight of a local big shot's reputation, and a variety of other considerations have been involved in forming staffs. In more than one European 'cross-cultural' workshop, people were guaranteed a position on the staff if they could bring a certain number of participants from their province.

The second factor is the lack of screening practices for participants. Apparently anyone who can pay the enrollment costs may attend. Thus, workshops may be paralyzed by seriously disturbed persons, by fanatical groupies, by sensation-seekers, by merely misinformed persons, or by any number of other people (well-intentioned or not). Usually, both they and the group would have been better off had they not attended. One fellow told me that he attended one of these workshops thinking, on the basis of the name and the advertising promotion, that it was an innovative gathering for single people to meet while on holiday.

4. In relinquishing authority to the group, the convenors avoided the undesirable (as well as the desirable) effects of direct manipulation of participants. However, the possibility of indirect manipulation remained. Confusion, which may have been provoked in some participants by the convenor's refusal to lead or facilitate in conventional ways may have increased suggestibility in these group members. Jerome Frank (1961), referring to such as client-centered therapy, has noted that:

> The therapist's steadfast refusal to assume active leadership tends to create an ambiguous situation for the patient, who has only a vague idea of what he is supposed to do, how long he is to keep it up, and how he will know when he is finished ... The resulting unclarity may enhance [the therapist's] influencing power ... [as] a person in an ambiguous situation is impelled to try to clarify it ... To the extent that a person cannot unaided construct a clear set of expectations in a situation, he tends to look to others for direction. This may explain the finding that confusion increases suggestibility.

Convenors in the large group workshops described here did not *try* to provoke confusion. On the contrary, they tried to reduce unnecessary confusion by announcing to participants what they intended to do—at the outset and during the meetings. They admitted what they knew and what they did not know about the process they were all experiencing. They participated. If there was confusion, it is because the convenors were confused also.

Organizers also behaved differently from conventional non-directive group leaders. They accepted responsibility for preparations they had made for the workshop and what they did during the workshop. They were confrontable, not aloof. They even talked back; occasionally they disputed with one another, or with participants. They entered the dialogue, expressed their opinions, feelings, reacted spontaneously to new situations, and generally were not different from what they were in 'ordinary' life. They did not separate themselves from the experiences other participants were involved in. If the conditions provoked a change in consciousness, the organizers were exposed also.

This enthusiastic participation expels some doubts but may raise others. May this not actually encourage the acceptance of the organizer's goals—stated or not? Perhaps. However, a corrective may also have been functioning. An open and continual acceptance of criticism towards all aspects of the workshop, its organizers, its organization may have prevented an unwitting provocation of blind acceptance.

Many ambiguities may be noted. Leaders (convenors) do not lead. The group expects participants to speak (that is, symbolize their experience in linear patterns), but not to intellectualize (that is, form symbols in a logical manner). The group's problems provoke an intense need to understand, while at the same time asking participants to detach from thoughts, words, emotions. Be spontaneous! Such paradoxes effect the large group workshop.

However, instead of being an agent of manipulation, ambiguity could actually be a preventative for conditioning. There is evidence, for example, that ambiguity may *prevent* the hidden suggestion that participants should produce whatever is demanded by the organizers of the workshop (Orne, 1962).

5. Stable large groups have doubtless contributed to the evolution of the species. For example, since large groups possess definite advantages over smaller ones, evolution would seem to favor larger groups. Furthermore, Dunbar (1991) has proposed that human language evolved due to the necessity of maintaining large groups.

6. To illustrate some of the patterns, strengths and weaknesses of these large group events, this chapter will present one composite workshop. To insure participants' privacy, names and certain circumstances have been altered. The dialogues and general features are faithful to events I am personally familiar with from actual workshops. Episodes, which may have taken place in separate workshops, may at times be presented together to illustrate the general pattern of one such event: beginning, middle, and end.

In order to generalize some of the learnings, the majority of episodes have been drawn from a form of workshop which was developed in La Jolla, California (1974); Santa Cruz, California (1974); Oakland, California (1975); Ashland, Oregon (1976); Sagamore, New York (1977); Princeton University (1979) in the United States and Rio de Janeiro, Brasil (1977) and Nottingham, England (1978).

The form of workshop described here vanished around 1980. When their spirit of discovery, their adherence to careful screening processes, their avoidance of commercial influences, their careful preparation by confronting factions and problems between themselves began to falter, the convenors dismantled their institute devoted to convening large groups.

However, variations continue to be convened. For example, Rogers participated in large group events in Austria, South Africa, Hungary, as well as in the United States and the Soviet Union. These events did not have the group-centered character of the workshops from which I have drawn illustrations though they doubtless contained many similar qualities.

Presented here is an approach to group work with which I am familiar. This is not to suggest that this is the *only* way intelligent and creative groups come about. Nor that the groups described are necessarily superior to any other similar events. However, many of the observations presented here doubtless apply to other large group encounters.

7. In a series of experiments, Asch (1951, 1952) studied the effects of 'group pressure.' A group of 'confederates' were employed to make unanimously incorrect

judgments in simple perceptual tests. Their purpose was to influence the public statements of the experimental subject. About one-third of the participants in the experiment went along with the judgments of the majority in their group. However, if only one other person agreed with the subject, this 'yielding to the majority' was almost completely wiped out.

8. It was amusing to hear accounts of some similar workshops where the organizers wished to but could not relinquish control. In one program, for example, the staff members divided the participants into smaller groups before participants arrived, one group for each facilitator on the staff, and placed the lists of names on the floor in the center of the large group. As a staff member described it to me, 'The group sort of *intuitively* milled around and then participants passed by, picked up the assignments, and went to their meeting rooms.'

9. Although part of this final solution contained the well-established custom of a committee appointed by the larger body, this was not done, as is frequently the case, to relieve the larger group of cumbersome discussions. The group had already heard the various sides of the problem and had experienced the 'loss of time' and circular confusion of such deliberations. Rather, the committee was formulated so that the boy would not be paralyzed by a confrontation with a large and formidable group. At the same time the committee consisted of those who felt strongly for each side of the dispute. Thus, it was a true confrontation of the group, not merely investigative. As the large group had thoroughly participated, it did not (as often happens in parliamentary bodies) have to cross-examine the committee's findings or to reject its conclusions.

10. Many people become very nervous with talk of 'the group.' A psychologist friend of mine once said, 'What makes me uneasy about collectives is the realization that they don't make statements or interpret positions; only individuals do that. Individuals declare the collective higher than the individual and then speak for it. Collectives don't have a conscience (that I have noticed). Thus, God does not whisper in their ear, but only in the ear of individuals. One who is interested in the whole, would do good to defend the privileged position of the individual.'

I agree with him. *And* I think it should be remembered that although collectives do not interpret positions, they do *create* them, the same way they make statements, by their actions. The group may not be an 'organism' (at least not in the strict biological sense) but it is doubtless reality. For example, the United States Supreme Court has ruled, based on statistical analysis of racial distribution of employees in the organization, that a black former employee was discriminated against. Although no single individual was found to have been discriminatory, the *group* had discriminated against the individual. (*Time Magazine*, July 11, 1988: 13) I share my friend's uneasiness with individuals who declare the collective higher than the individual and pretend to speak for it. This, however, is a problem of individuals, not the collective.

Some cultures do not confirm the right of the individual to personal expression, to a body or mind of his own, to his own space. The concept of an autonomous individual in sociocentric cultures must seem a 'bizarre idea, cutting the self off from the interdependent whole, dooming it to a life of isolation and loneliness' (Kakar, 1978).

Except in specific cases where it is deserved, throwing the blame on either the individual or the collective does not seem productive. Kierkegaard is widely quoted as saying, 'The crowd is untruth.' (My friend quotes him also.) But, Buber (1957) replied, 'I do not know if Kiergegaard is right when he says that the crowd is untruth—I should rather describe it as non-truth since (in distinction from some of its masters) it is not in the least opposed to it.' Any warning against the group, Buber urged, can be only a preface to 'the true question to the single one.'

11. Here is an example of Client-Centered Workshop Blues, 1974:

>Oh the process is the thing that we must face
>Oh the process is the thing that we must face
>We must learn to make decision
>Without too much derision
>So shut-up and keep your ass in your own space !!!
>
>Oh you really should do this and this and that
>Oh you really should do this and this and that
>You have got to be so fluent
>Or else you're not congruent
>So how the hell will you know where you're at?!!!
>
>Oh that resonates a feeling deep inside
>Oh that resonates a feeling deep inside
>Now I know you share by bleeding
>And that is what I'm needing
>But I can't avoid the feeling that you lied !!!
>
>We have unconditional positive regard
>We have unconditional positive regard
>We have learned to be accepting
>EMPATHIC—not rejecting
>We're congruent when our feelings have been jarred.
>
>I respond to your resentment, yes I do
>I respond to your resentment, yes I do
>Although I really feel it
>I will not try to heal it
>But my gut response is still—Fuck You !!!!
>
>Oh I really do not want to lay a trip
>Oh I really do not want to lay a trip
>As a client-centered person
>I need some more rehearsin'
>So let's check it out before I flip !!!!

> I saw you in the bathroom last night
> I saw you in the bathroom last night
> Oh I almost took a peek
> But I felt like such a sneak
> And all I cared to do was take a leak.
> (I'm Pissed)
>
> I will never make a judgment or I'll quit
> I will never make a judgment or I'll quit
> You have shared your deepest feeling
> It's really got me reeling
> But my gut response is still—Bullshit!!!!

12. Frank (1961) presents a general review of systems of personality change and the aspect of control they may exert over group members: 'The means by which changes in the [trainee] are brought about include a particular type of relationship and some sort of systematic activity or ritual. The essence of the relationship is that the [trainer] invests great effort to bring about changes in the [trainee's] bodily state or attitudes that he regards as beneficial. The systematic activity characteristically involves means of emotional arousal, often to the point of exhaustion. This may be highly unpleasant, but it occurs in the context of hope and potential support from the [trainer] and the group ... The [trainee] may be required to review his past life in more or less detail, with emphasis on occasions when he may have fallen short of the behavior required by the world view, thus mobilizing guilt, which can only be expiated by confession and penance. This serves to detach him from his former patterns of behavior and social intercourse and facilitates his acceptance by the group representing the ideology to which he becomes converted.'

13. This argument is not meant to be against all follow-on meetings. Some may be useful by providing additional time between learning experiences. Nor is it meant to criticize follow-up for patients given psychotherapeutic treatment where the *intention* is to change and reinforce behaviors. What is criticized is the application of what may be useful psychotherapeutic practices to people who are not choosing to be in psychotherapy and may be adversely affected by such treatment. To integrate his learnings within the context of a person's social relations is not trivial. Indeed, Caplan (1981) defines *mental health* as just this: 'the potential of the person to solve his problem in a reality-based way within the framework of his tradition and culture.'

14. Rupert Sheldrake (1981), a plant physiologist and respected scientist, has proposed the hypothesis of *formative causation* to account for the observation that subsequent workshops (that is, separated by time and space) with different participants, seemed to know what the earlier groups had progressively learned. Sheldrake's hypothesis proposes that 'morphogenetic fields [analogous to other fields in physics] play a causal role in the development and maintenance of the forms of

systems at all levels of complexity.' This hypothesis would predict that learnings from a large group workshop separated in time and space from another large group workshop would be possessed by the second workshop.

The implications of this hypothesis are widespread. A society, for example, may be an abstraction that can be defended by individuals or groups. It may be an empirical fact by virtue of the consequences of individual acts when considered together. (For example, no individuals were singled out as guilty in causing the death of astronauts during a spacecraft launch. The entity NASA, the organization in charge of the United States space program, was to blame.) Though it may not be an organism, perhaps it can be said to have a 'consciousness.' Perhaps a collective consciousness?

The hypothesis of *formative causation*, although not energetic itself nor reducible to the causation of known physical fields, imposes a spatial order on changes brought about by physical causation. It is likened to a blueprint that, though not energetic, *causes* the specific form of the house. It is not the only cause and without materials, builders, and tools the house would not come into being.

In 1920, William McDougall, in the hope of testing the Lamarckian hypothesis that learning was inherited, began to experiment with the Wistar strain of white rats that had been carefully inbred under laboratory control for many generations.

The rats' experimental task was to learn to emerge from a tank of water through a darkened gangway. By attempting to leave through the alternate brightly lighted gangway, they received an electric shock. The two passageways were alternately illuminated, the bright one always giving the shock. Learning was determined by the number of errors made before the rat learned to exit through the non-illuminated passage. McDougall noted that as many as 330 immersions might be necessary before a rat learned to avoid the lighted pathway. Eventually, there came a point in the rat's training when he decisively chose the darkened route; afterwards, he rarely chose wrongly again.

Thirty-two generations of white rats participated in the experiment that lasted fifteen years. In accordance with Lamarckian theory, there *was* a tendency for successive generations to learn more quickly. The average number of errors for the first was 56; for the second, 41; the third, 29; the fourth, 20.

The experiment was repeated by W.E. Agar and colleagues in Melbourne. They tested 50 generations of rats over a twenty year period until 1954. McDougall's results were confirmed. The trained rats showed a marked tendency to learn more quickly in subsequent generations. However, the *untrained* rats *also* showed the exact same tendency.

Although the Lamarckian hypothesis had to be rejected, the findings support the hypothesis of formative causation that predicts that a form learned by one population of rats in one location would also appear in another population separated from the first in time and space.

An experiment was devised to test the hypothesis on people, using pictures containing 'hidden' images—the kind used in gestalt experiments: once you see the alternate image, it is very clearly distinguished. Two pictures were shown to people in different parts of the world under standard conditions. The number who spotted the hidden image within one minute in each picture was recorded. One of the pictures was then broadcast by television to two million viewers who were asked to look for the hidden image. After they had time to consider, the image was shown to them. According to the hypothesis, the change that took place in the minds of those who now knew how to perceive the hidden image, would affect all people.

After the TV broadcast, people in different parts of the world were tested with both pictures. Neither the ones viewing the pictures nor the ones showing them knew which had been seen on TV. There was no significant change in the percentage of those who could quickly see the hidden image in the picture that had *not* been shown on TV; but there *was* reported a statistically significant increase in the number who recognized the image in the picture that had previously been broadcast on TV.

CHAPTER SEVEN

A Rehearsal for Understanding the Phenomenon of Group

It is much better not to be pedantic, but to let the science be as vague as its subject, and include such phenomenon as these if by so doing we can throw any light on the main business in hand.
William James

Because the literature regarding non-European, international, trans-national, leaderless large group workshops from the person-centered approach is so sparse, the following report has been made. It is hoped that it may provide both valuable information on this phenomenon and encouragement for future studies.

In April 1988, I participated in the *IV Encuentro Latinoamericano de la Orientacion Centrada en la Persona* at the hotel La Pedrera in Uruguay. On the seaside, 210 kilometers from Montevideo, 62 psychologists and educators from Argentina, Brazil, Uruguay and Venezuela attended this meeting: 35 participants used Portuguese as their first language; 27, Spanish. It was a week-long event with the stated purpose, 'to meet and share experiences in order to reflect on distinct applications of the person-centered approach within the reality of Latin Americans.'[1]

We each paid our own travel and living expenses. None received a fee. Except for meal times (which were frequently changed), no other program of events was decided before the first plenary meeting of the group. There was no discernible leader—not appointed, elected, nor elevated by virtue of the strength of personality or reputation.

Since still little is known about this type of activity (see Rogers, 1977; Rogers & Rosenberg, 1977; Bowen, Miller, Rogers & Wood, 1979; Rogers, Wood, O'Hara & Fonseca, 1983; Wood, 1984, 1985, 1988 for reports on related events), after this workshop, I asked participants to write whatever they wished about their experience of the *Encuentro*.

Participants were requested to consider all significant aspects of their personal, interpersonal, transpersonal experience with regard to the *Encuentro*. For example, level of satisfaction with the workshop, significant changes in personal behavior and relationships, extraordinary experiences, perceptions of the group as a whole

---

This chapter was published previously in *The Person-Centered Review, 1* (3), 18–32, 1988.

and its behavior: in realizing objectives, problem-solving, governing, integration, etc. Participants were requested to relate whatever they wished but, if possible, to illustrate their comments with specific examples. The replies followed no common pattern. Most were written in a sort of stream-of-consciousness style, touching on subjects which interested the participant the most. Twenty-nine percent replied: twelve in Portuguese, six in Spanish. One Uruguayan replied partly in English.

Participant remarks deal with feelings (before, during and after the *Encuentro*—including disappointment and satisfaction, frustration and joy, 'good' and 'bad'), and with perceptions (of self, of individual behavior and collective behavior, of the structure of culture, of time and space, of life and of a timeless trans-individuality). Commentaries also discuss significant changes and learnings that participants experienced.

While contemplating each statement I received, I asked myself, 'What does this declaration communicate about the phenomenon of group?' In the spirit of *discovery-oriented research* which has been proposed by Mahrer (1988), I tried to be open to, 'what is new in the data, to what is out of the ordinary, different, unexpected, exceptional, surprising, challenging, disconcerting (...) to what does not seem to fit, to what is hard to grasp, organize, explain.' I attempted to be, 'sensitive to the discoverable.' I derived the meanings of 'out of the ordinary,' 'different,' 'unexpected' and so forth from comparisons with the way such events as the *Encuentro* are usually portrayed. It is from considerable first-hand experience with large groups from the person-centered approach that I felt qualified to categorize the 'exceptional,' 'the surprising,' 'challenging.' (Mahrer, by the way, presents convincing arguments that the approach he proposes is a viable alternative to more conventional research. He goes as far as to declare that, 'All in all, hypothesis-testing research does little more than confirm or fail to confirm the knowledge that we already firmly believe we have, as supported by powerful lobby groups.')

Although the categories into which the material seemed to organize itself are disputable (I would welcome other suggestions), it is clear from their responses that, from the point of view of participants, the phenomenon of group is rather complex and possesses dimensions that are rarely noted by group facilitators. Indeed, many group leaders assume that they themselves are the most significant factor in the group's success (but rarely in its failure). Out of participant commentaries regarding the *Encuentro* a sketch can be drawn of one perspective of the phenomenon of group which I hope will enlarge the field of investigation and help us gain a clearer understanding.

From the present data it can be seen that the phenomenon of group includes individuals with personal attitudes, intentions, feelings and perceptions who relate to one another in social activities. Their interactions, the moment, and the place have an effect on their consciousness. Their presence constitutes a culture (shared knowledge, values, customs and behavior) which favors certain collective actions (through separate, or so it is agreed, autonomous acts). Individual perceptions sometimes exceed what would be expected from the limitations of time and space. Participants' experiences may result in significant personal learning and changes of behavior.

What now follows are comments of participants which illustrate common perceptions and give body to this summary. Comments are unaltered except for what may have resulted from translation and from the inevitable distortion caused from taking them from their original contexts and placing them into categories.

Feelings and Perceptions

Before the *Encuentro*: Varied expectations

From the participant commentaries it is evident that personal objectives other than the official intention stated for the *Encuentro* also motivated participants to attend. As one person commented, 'I wanted to meet people who have the same vision of Man that I have and who are trying to develop their work from this vision.'[2]

Some had participated in previous 'Latin encounters' and wished to 'see old friends' among other things. But several readily admitted they merely wanted, as one person put it, 'to recuperate energy. I was wasted, not able to work or anything.' And another said, 'I simply wanted to let myself be and accumulate positive energies that I was desperately in need of.'[3]

During the meetings: Frustrated expectations

Naturally, the expectations of some would clash with those of others. One person illustrated this thus, 'Some people came to La Pedrera with the sole intention to relax on the beach, take it easy, get a tan and meet a soulmate with whom to share their cares and loneliness ... it made me feel uncomfortable because, ... when I returned I had to report to my university 'the results' of the *Encuentro* and the 'significance' for my area of work.'

Various persons expressed disappointment that they had not learned new theoretical formulations, as they would have liked to. In spite of this, the *Encuentro* did, for many of them, as one participant related, 'serve to solidify and enhance that which I had already learned.'

One participant announced at the first plenary session the desire, 'to win the group over to the idea of Latin American integration. Specifically, I would like to know if anyone was interested in transcending their private, local and national experience.'

This objective was frustrated, at least in the form that it had been pursued, since this person was interrupted by others who were irritated by these remarks. After the *Encuentro* the participant related a significant learning, 'never to develop such high expectations in this type of encounter.'

After some time and reflection had passed, this person added that, 'I eventually became more serene, less impulsive and having less need to incorporate other people into my projects.'

The large group encounter: Frustration and euphoria

From their commentaries one may note that the large group meetings provoked very intense emotional experiences in many participants. One participant, for example, expressed frustration because, as this person saw it, 'People seemed to fulfill very well their expected roles: the *Encuentro* includes large group meetings; in these meetings one shares feelings ... so, let's get on with it. But they were "speech feelings" and not "felt feelings".'

Another person expressed global disappointment because, 'I felt disappointed and without hope for psychology. We did not go beyond what is known, and not even that could we reach. I did not feel I could use everything I have.'

The first few days of the large group meetings were frequently described as aggressive and several persons reported disagreeable experiences. For example, 'Those who felt more emotionally charged and had the courage would express their feelings, risking that others would grant legitimacy to what was felt or thought. In this whole activity I felt badly because I always had the fantasy that they had rejected me on that first night when I expressed so openly my expectations of the *Encuentro*. I felt that the irritation I had engendered persisted during the whole time.'

Another person regretted that such a state of affairs could occur, 'I expected that people there would know how to "listen" better to what others had to say. I thought that ... people there would be more apt to respect the limits of each individual. Even when disagreeing with someone they could do so without invading the other's space or feeling threatened by everyone. I was very disappointed in the first three days. The large group meeting was very aggressive and it was impossible to "hear" what people were really saying. I saw a big fight over the power of knowledge, which made me fantasize those participants who were or wanted to be the most notable.'

Another, recognizing these aspects, also observed, 'I don't believe we had a great encounter. I did not experience the formation of a community [but] something Latin was lived. I believe that this was important: each could be who he or she wanted to be.'

However, another person seemed to regard as constructive an outcome that others felt was disagreeable: 'I don't know if the *Encuentro* was equally satisfactory for everyone. To tell the truth, I really hope that it hasn't been. I don't believe that a group must always be homogeneous; I believe that the group will be more beneficial, if it can promote sharing on its highest levels, where differences are not only accepted but effectively discovered and developed. After all, not being satisfied is as motivating as being satisfied.'

Near the end of the *Encuentro*, many noticed a change in mood having occurred. One participant remarked, 'It could be observed that many people showed an amazing amount of attention and solicitude toward others in the last few days. All this and more gave the group a distinctly different face from its initial one. On the last night, even I felt comforted and returned to expressing my feelings. I noticed that the group listened more sensitively and empathically.'

Participants' emotional experiences were varied, ranging from deep disappointment up to oceanic feelings. On the lighter side, one person related, 'The large group meeting began with a heaviness in the air, but after a little while a bird suddenly entered an open window. It flew around above our heads and tried to go back out, but banged up against a window pane. Everyone's attention was captured. Someone ran to the window and opened it and the bird flew to freedom. Coincidentally, after this event the group also liberated itself. Or, at least, I liberated myself, perhaps. The fact is it seemed the group had searched for a unity, that in my view can only be found when it transcends words. ... I noted that "language" was not very important when you really want to "listen" to someone. I felt that in the final days of the *Encuentro* this came to pass and people could converse and know each other better.'

And another reported what sounds like a profound experience, 'The silence that followed [an outburst of indignation] and the subsequent reflections by members of the group formed for me a genuine unity. I was touched emotionally and totally "plugged in," belonging to the group. It was as if all our consciousnesses were one thing only, alive and promising.'

Feelings, perceptions and significant changes after the *Encuentro*

Many people noted improvements in their ability to relate to others. One person said, 'The effect of the *Encuentro* on my relationships is basically to turn them each time more honest, more truthful.'

One person reported to have returned home with a, 'force and energy that had been awakened in me.' And, 'little by little I was discovering that what I felt was closely connected with the convivial experience of the *Encuentro*.'

Some of those whose relations improved also felt more efficient in their counseling practices. 'I see myself as more open to the communications of the other,' one participant remarked.

Also changes in perception of self were noted. For example, 'I discovered that I can be beautiful, even though for long periods of my life I believed that I would never again "be beautiful." And this new beauty is independent of how much one weighs, their age, curves or being fortyish or fiftyish.'

Significant Learning

Cognitive integration: A surprise from the spontaneous small groups

One participant, unsatisfied with some of the other aspects of the *Encuentro*, reported that: 'The small groups satisfied completely the intellectual aspect. There you could know what each person is living and what each one thinks, which were his or her problems and preoccupations in applying the person-centered approach. For me, it was very gratifying to participate in the small groups and share with those present.'

Another related that, after being unsuccessful in attempts to communicate effectively in the large assembly: 'I proposed [a small group] workshop which was really good for me for I got in contact with the participants and with myself. From that day on my energy cycle flew again, I could be on my own or with the rest of the group. So on the night ... when a lot of the group were feeling uneasy and began to explode I was very astonished for it was the first time I was feeling good in the silence of the great group, and I experienced what was going on as somebody who was in the group but [for] whom the cannon balls flew over her head.'

Another participant found the spontaneously organized small group meetings favorable to the integration that this person felt was missing in the first days of the *Encuentro* in other activities, 'The spontaneous philosophical discussions in small groups were the best. At the conclusion of each I had a feeling of integration and closeness.'

Psychotherapeutic learning: Cognitive–emotional

Participants also reported psychotherapeutic effects. For example, cognitive integration: 'I felt alone. And I discovered that solitude was a right that I possessed, just like the right to have all the other feelings that I might want ... anger, fear, jealousy, envy, love, friendliness, tenderness, respect, shame, timidness, anything that would come to my heart. Solitude is the recognition of my absolute life, and the recognition of my relative limits.'

And behavioral changes of an emotional nature, as reflected in this comment: 'I am more open to meet and converse with whatever person, even strangers on the street. I have the sensation of being an old friend of the whole world.'

One can also find indications of a mixture and perhaps integration of emotional and cognitive learning. This same person expressed: 'I could live and integrate completely my personal experience with my theoretical perspective. To live out the question of transference in the group and [at the same time] to discuss how to deal with transference in the counseling practice was very important for me.'

Learning in interpersonal relations

One person commented, honestly, 'My preoccupation in getting ahold of my personal experience did not permit me to get a good sense of the group.'

Nevertheless, one can also find indications of interpersonal learnings in the *Encuentro*. For example, one participant observed, 'I can understand others better and mainly I can also accept when I don't understand. Not always I am able to understand, but certainly I am better able to respect the other in each group that I live.'

Another related that, 'I perceived the possibility of utilizing aggressivity constructively through confrontations and the free expression of feelings.'

Another shared that, 'The more significant learning was to relearn to trust. I find that I am always relearning this.'

One of those who came to the Encuentro to recuperate energy, related that, 'I think that I had an important learning in this moment, between others: to be open to the perspective of the other. Perhaps to be really empathic. And to live the encounter really taking into account the other. The other isn't better but he is equally important. ... I am enjoying the discovery of the process of giving, simply giving, without eminent expectation of return.'

Others concluded that interpersonalness was not merely an attribute of humanity but is humanity. For example, 'To be in contact with our own experiences is the same as to be in contact with the other or with the group, since they are part of us.' And another put it, '[The experience of the *Encuentro*] left me more sensitive to my and to the other's humanity; I feel I belong more to the human species ... I returned with more availability to be transparent in various relationships and to begin to take better care of my significant ones. In brief, I perceive myself more available for others, for me, and more ready to receive.'

And another, 'I listened and reflected more on myself and I felt very good *alone*, in the company of me. I tried to accept the different positions and manners of *being* and *to be* in the world and was able to understand without judging and each day this makes me feel better.'

Some people reported that they felt closer through understanding others. A participant expressed it this way, 'I was surprised to see people discussing things that hitherto I thought were only mine, so personal. And I was touched by this. I think that there was a communion (unity) between us, which did not exist in the other group settings. I went for a walk on the beach to reflect. I wept without knowing exactly why.'

Not only emotional closeness, but through differentiation, an enhancement of personal values was also reported, 'I was able to feel closer to certain persons ... and more distant to others.'

Sexual relations

The subject of sexual relations, usually controversial and rarely mentioned, was touched on by several participants. For example, one participant said, 'References that came to me concerning the intense hidden sexual activity between different members caught my interest. Perhaps this should be a subject to reflect on.'

Another stated, 'More people who were involved in intimate relationships in the end were more able to share this with others, although not in the large group meetings. In the beginning they either were not involved intimately or they were trying to hide their love relations, including me.'

And another observed, 'The group was continually more eroticized, each time occurring more erotic situations of all types: triangles, incest, seduction, platonic, etc.'

Perceptions of Time and Space, Shared Values, Collective Behavior

Space: The environment

Also, there are indications of a sensitivity to the influence of the environment on participants' experiences. Many people mentioned the sea, the beach, the starry nights. Some examples:

'Of the first two days the image that remains with me is of the beach ...'

'The sea was a dimension of energy, beauty and melody.'

'I treated myself with care by abundant swimming in the sea and the swimming pool.'

And, another person mentioned the effect of activities which are infrequently considered part of events such as the *Encuentro* (but of course are): 'Some of the behind-the-scenes activities (such as occurred around the birthday of Carmen) helped demonstrate to me that there will always exist mini-groups and that one can belong or not depending on how secure the group is.'

Culture: Shared values

With this last observation, we enter also the area of culture. In the many 'international conferences in the person-centered approach' that I have attended, the cultural differences were much fewer than admitted. Differences provoked by language were largely circumstantial and quickly dispensed with after paying the customary obeisance to the inevitable nationalist who felt obligated to defend a dying empire's mother tongue and to the translators' self-serving needs to be featured in the limelight. The culture that prevails is the group culture.

It can be noted that participants became sensitive to this, 'The group consisted of persons of three different nationalities (Argentines, Uruguayans and Brazilians, on the whole very young) who possibly had participated in previous encounters together and had consolidated friendships. I had little possibility to share socially.' [Actually there were seven nationalities represented in the *Encuentro*.]

One person felt he found evidence of cross-cultural understanding, 'I believe that the people from the northeast of Brazil giving in to the Argentines to hold the next *Encuentro* in Argentina is a good example of cross-cultural understanding. Personally, I was very comfortable with the Brazilians. The predominance of Portuguese language in the meetings required an effort from the Uruguayans and Argentines but was lived with acceptance and sympathy.'

But one of his compatriots did not agree, commenting that, 'We did not arrive at a primary unity beyond nationalities and regionalisms.'

One person felt a distinct lack of intercultural understanding. 'In my case, my main interest was to understand the other participants from their point of views. Nevertheless, I did not feel understood myself, interculturally. When I shared my expectations and my desire that the objectives of the group would transcend our present limits, some people showed they felt irritated, molested and uncomfortable. It did not occur to them to ask what was happening in my country and why I would like them to do so. My preoccupation continues. Perhaps I am overestimating the importance that Latin American helping professionals feel towards contributing to the mutual understanding and growth of people and to strengthen the humanistic movement in our countries where so much is done to degrade the human being. ... For how can you talk about person-centered approach when the relation between the individuals at all levels is centered on authority? ... This was what I wanted to discuss. Perhaps for us it is better to be directed, perhaps the best political scheme that fits us is the dictatorship and the humanistic perspective is only rhetorical.'

Nevertheless, others perceived a significant transformation of the culture of the *Encuentro*. One person described, ' A new culture whose language was "portunhol" and that communicated as well as possible thoughts and feelings [was formed]. ... This is how I see it, with the group process being a process connected to the external reality, in this case the Latin American reality.'[4]

This perspective was challenged by another, 'I still don't know if I understand this thing about 'Latin American-ness'. A Latin American conference must deal with Latin American subjects? Or is this only a geographic criterion, of proximity? What do we Latin Americans have in common? The things we are lacking? Lack of democracy, lack of respect for human dignity, lack of attention to education, to health, lack of food? Are we united through these deficiencies? Thus, if a group of persons without mother or father meet together, they formulate and institutionalize an 'orphanage.' We are together because we have the same deprivation? Or because we have the same needs for democracy, dignity, education, health, food? These needs are typically Latin American or are they human necessities of every person? ... Uniting ourselves through what we lack seems to me decreeing our own failure; as if we would not have united through our potency, but through our impotency. We are such poor little things. Whereas, if we unite through our potent characteristics (that are characteristics of all people and not only Latin Americans), finally we are able to create.'

Another commented on the experience of meeting a few persons who had previously attended other Latin American encounters in which this participant was also present: 'It is interesting and delightful to get together with people that are also part of this process. In most cases, I don't know anything about their personal daily life outside of these meetings. But I know a lot about the person, the person that he or she is in that space ... They are persons that I meet each year, every two years and they have such big importance in my life and I in theirs. And when a new *Encuentro* begins it is as if the previous one had only ended yesterday.'

Trans-individuality

Also a perception of the group as a system that behaves cohesively can be found in the commentaries. One example: 'I had the impression that the group as a whole was present in every moment. I felt that the group was with me in every instant, not only when the large group met, but also when I was alone, with only one other person or with a small group. This group of which I speak was not formed by these or those persons. It was as if it were something beyond those individuals that together formed the group, as if it were an organism that had its own identity independent of the particularities of those who formed it. And for that reason, I don't think it was very important, if some persons felt more integrated in the group than others. Even those more quiet, more isolated, more alienated with respect to the group, were a part of it with their silence, their isolation, their alienation. I believe that it doesn't work to believe oneself to be outside the group when one is in it. To be alienated, isolated, silent already are ways to be in the group. I think that I am speaking of the unity that I felt in the group even when someone said that it still wasn't a group. Already we were a group when we actually met together in La Pedrera, and none of us was immune to its effects, neither from leaving nor staying to the end. I see the group as a sharing. We can share at many different levels. From the beginning at La Pedrera we were sharing the same space, the same food, the same beach, we already were a group.'

And, how this system made decisions and regulated itself or did not regulate itself was frequently commented on. For example, one person thought that the problem of cigarette smoking was resolved creatively: people smoking would stand by the window and afterwards would return to the circle of participants in the center of the room. Others, however, thought that the matter was not really dealt with effectively. One participant observed, 'Both the smokers and the non-smokers seemed to consider the problem as an aesthetic one (smoking is ugly or dirty) or as a moral question (smoking is bad) instead of discussing how to deal with a practical problem: how to provide the quality of air that each participant desired. Very little discussion took place and after an initial conformance with the requests of the non-smokers (to smoke by a window), the smokers seemed to feel they had earned the right to return to smoking in the group by having submitted to the morality of the non-smokers. The non-smokers at this point felt insulted that smokers were not following the established rule. The question did in fact become a moral one. This rendered the problem more difficult to resolve than had no solution been proposed. Anyone who would want to reopen the discussion would have to exert a superhuman effort to get the two sides to search out an intelligent solution. Likewise, the decision for the choice of location for the next *Encuentro* suffered a similar failure by not discussing all the points of view. Before either group—the Argentine or the northeastern Brazilians—or anyone else could sufficiently present their feelings and thoughts, disinterested persons rallied the group to take a vote.'

Another thought that the group was, 'a little disorganized and impatient and inconsistent in its decisions (as to presenting or not presenting written work at the next *Encuentro*, as to the location of the next *Encuentro*, as to each participant providing copies of their papers, as to policy about videotaping the meetings). It seems there was a greediness for emotional harmony, for affective cohesion, that drove the group not to invest too much "intellectual energy" in decision-making, perhaps in order not to dismantle the emotional atmosphere, constructed through painful effort ... As if there were a preconception against "thinking decisions," as if there were a certain dread of divergencies, and it were necessary to pass over them rapidly in order to return to "goodness" ... If there isn't trust, the tendency is to make decisions by "majority rule," that doesn't seem to be the best criteria. Majority of persons present, or majority of 'pressures' exerted by the favored group members.'

Thus, there were comments which touched on 'the individual in the group,' of the 'group in the individual' and of an isomorphism—group and individual as one, 'We see ourselves reflected in the group that is a part of us, at the same time that we are a part of it. To be in contact with our own experiences is the same as to be in contact with the other or with the group since they make part of us.'

Perceptions Beyond Time and Space

Transpersonal reality

One may note perceptions of a transpersonal reality in the commentaries. One person observed, 'I confirmed that these encounters really make me feel in contact with the 'Other.' I am each time more 'religious.' For me, these encounters repeat the beginning and the end of the world.'

At times this illumination came out of a negative experience. One person related, 'I did not know exactly what it would be to encounter, but it suddenly appeared to me with the people discussing the silence the first time the group met. I felt as if that were a grand illusion, that the people did not have the capacity to see something larger that involved them and they would limit themselves to foolish discussions.'

One person realized, it seems, the effect of a transpersonal experience, 'We were talking on the beach ... we sat down and I heard myself saying things that I did not know that I knew, with a startling tranquillity.'

And, another expressed, 'In this *Encuentro* everything was very clear to me. It is as if I had succeeded in closing an important cycle. ... The sensation of almost total identity is startling, it is like a wave that in order to be fulfilled throws itself into its own tidal ebb. What I feel like doing is to weep, but it is neither from sadness nor joy. Perhaps the joy would be in those moments when this could be shared. They are rare moments which I still do not know how to find. Far from here, right here, the craziness of the traveler is full of wisdom. It surprises me to feel so different and at the same time it gives me an immense tranquillity, it is as if I were succeeding in being in touch with my center. I have the sensation of magnetism, I am able to feel what attracts and what repels. I don't have to think from here the thought that restrains me, that criticizes me. At the same time, I ask myself from where does this certainty come, this perception of time without limits?'

Trans or trance? A less 'real' reality?

Other indications of altered states of consciousness may also be found in the commentaries. One person noted an alteration of the perception of time, 'I have the sensation that this is like an island in time, a sort of dream. A week or a century, I could not measure.'

Others also shared similar experiences, 'I had the impression of a lot of time passing, not merely a week. It was a sensation of having lived outside of reality, suspended in time and space.'

Another recounted a perception involving physical sensation, 'I perceived in me ... something related to energy, as if it had been used up (or sucked out) by the participants, and I needed to recuperate it since I felt extremely tired.'

One person expressed concerns about this aspect of the phenomenon of group, 'I feel certain reservations about encounters such as this. Such sensations, although confusing intellectually, seem to me to be "situational reactions" ... that are not congruent with the person's perceptions, conduct and reflections outside of the group setting. Surely this does not apply to everyone, but particularly it applies to some of the excessive affection and acceptance.'

Another participant also perceived alterations of consciousness; however, this person believes this did not effect the ability to function logically, 'In this [intense group interaction] I surrendered considerably, I was very conscious of how I let myself go with the process. In this way I could experience in myself very strong feelings in the group. Like the chaos, at 2 AM, the group still meeting. The perception of my own power in proposing a group meeting during the daytime. The sensation of experiencing feelings that I don't know at what point they are mine or another's. The certainty of living things, that at the same time they are mine, are of the group also. The practice of being aware of this process in groups is what I believe makes me, when I return to my private practice, an excellent psychotherapist. I return more in contact with myself. ... Although I had let the process of the group carry me in the *Encuentro*, when I returned it still seemed real and genuine. It did not make me lose the notion of reality. The decisions I took during the *Encuentro* make sense back home—with different perspective, of course.'

A reality more 'real'?

A participant related the following, 'I saw some courageous, some wounded, some rejuvenated and living crazy fantasies and some other ones risking. This makes me admire them more, but not on a mystical level (as I had seen them before), but much more human. ... The relations are lived (as I see it) within a greater reality. The key word for this *Encuentro* was (for me) "demystification": mine, me in relation to myself, me in relation to others, others towards me. This demystification is related to freedom: of being and doing, searching creatively through meeting when the traditional approaches do not function.'

Another commented, 'It was not an island inserted in a different reality. It was a hard life process that took place in La Pedrera, more for some than for others, depending on the degree [to which] they took care of themselves.'

Another agreed, 'I discovered that what happened to us was also life, with difficult moments, with cowardliness, with aggression. It is worth saying that we had agreeable moments and others which were not, and that we allowed ourselves the freedom to experience and express almost all the feelings, emotions and passions that lead our lives.'

Creativity

Also indications of creativity could be found. During the workshop, a small group had written the words and music for a performance which they presented at the birthday celebration of one of the participants. Their song expressed humor and insight regarding the major events of the *Encuentro* up to that moment.

One of the members of this group described a personal experience of participating in this creative production, 'It was the only moment in which I felt myself completed, totally immersed in the experience, liberating my artistic creativity and playfulness, as if I and the group were one thing only.'

In terms of the lack of creativity in the large group meetings, one participant related, 'I was disappointed and shocked. It did not seem that they wanted to innovate—only to repeat what they already knew: sit together, smoke and express opinions. They were comfortable with the certainty of uncertainty, with what they are accustomed to: none knows what will happen, but whatever it will be, it will happen within this known structure.'

Another apparently agreed and offered this comment, 'I intuit that something is happening in professional groups and it has to do with the role of professional. I intuit that it has to do with roles that stick to us and that we fall into and it has to do with power, in the sense of political manipulation, with the power of control and has to do with the sense of *déja vu* that we have through the years. Thus, we cannot escape the role of facilitator that sticks to our skin. The old dilemma. To have to facilitate or not. Role or authenticity, etc. I think that all this has to do with losing freshness. There are always things to learn and above all they don't come through our old clichés: lectures to the group, endless haggling, long-winded speeches.'

Another added, 'It seems that many people can only conceptualize the *Encuentro* as group therapy. Perhaps this preconceived stance of making facilitative interventions and sharing polished personal anecdotes in order to animate the group, more than anything else, has prevented the group from becoming anything more than bad psychotherapy.'

Another person, however, observed various creative acts occurring in the *Encuentro*, but not necessarily within the large group meetings, 'I think that the group resolved its conflicts on various occasions in a way that was not explicit or verbalized. For example, there was the change of quarters, the rearrangement of tables in the dining room, the flexible hours of the large group meetings, all this during the whole time of the *Encuentro*.'

And another remembered an event in the large group meeting that this person considered to be creative, 'I think the work of art [installation] presented to the organizing committee at the end was extremely creative and integrative. In the beginning someone put a mattress from the couch covered with strange and unrelated objects on the floor. It looked more like a *macumba* offering, with cooking pots, bones, leaves, etc. After that I designed that "Alondra" of peace (did you know Alondra is the name of a bird?), I think that there erupted an opportunity to integrate all expressions and all or many people got up and added to and modified the design such that something highly creative and integrative resulted.'

Reflections on the meaning of life

Some participants also reflected on the meaning of their lives. For example, one recalled, 'In these days I thought a lot about all of life: relationships, profession and day-to-day.'

And another commented, 'It gave me serious motives for continuing to work as I work, to live as I live, believing in what I believe in.' And this reaction was shared by people who had negative experiences as well as those who had positive ones.

Another expressed that, 'I feel stronger to live … to "taste" internally that it is worthwhile to live.'

Summary and Conclusion

Participants' perceptions of the *Encuentro* reveal much about the phenomenon of group. For example, their motives were varied: to socialize, rest, learn. The large group encounters were emotional: a source of both frustration and euphoria. The meetings were often chaotic and although creative moments were realized, much talent was wasted. Nevertheless, participants realized new perceptions of wholeness, interconnectedness and insights into life and its meaning.

Many reported psychotherapeutic effects such as improved understanding and appreciation of self and others. Relationships were improved. The ambiance was a strong factor in the experience. People were aware of the distinctions between cultures as they began and the culture that eventually developed in their gathering.

A perception of the group as a whole was apparent in the commentaries. Many felt a confluence between the 'group consciousness' and their individual consciousness. How the group governed itself and the quality of its decisions were observed. Transpersonal experiences that involve unusual perceptions (sometimes in altered states of consciousness) were noted.

These subjective views must provoke many thoughts in those unfamiliar with such events. One thought that may be worth pursuing is that activities such as the

Encuentro have substantial tribal qualities. With the customary rituals, in Uruguay, the meetings of the general assembly frequently began with a prolonged almost sacred silence. The traditional large group meetings, in spite of the apparent disorganization, the chaotic discussions and epidemic emotionality were regarded as the only formality of the *Encuentro*.

The hyperaesthesia common to tribal celebration and ritual may also be observed in such activities as the *Encuentro*. Some participants, often initiates, from lack of sleep, eating irregularly, prolonged dancing and other consequences of the heightened emotional atmosphere entered into altered states of consciousness which resulted in unusual behavior. Just as in traditional tribes this may harm the individual or others or it may serve to help him or her explore a level of consciousness more elevated and become more closely identified with the group and the cultural values. In the rites of passage, one can find veterans advising the initiate on how to go about properly expressing personal feelings (always say 'I,' don't intellectualize, and so forth). Exactly what is and what is not the attitude of this tribe (that is, what is and what is not person-centered) is continually debated by the elders.

The tribe uses art also to preserve its story: the song to commemorate the birthday of Carmen told the story of the group, and the art installation presented to the organizing committee also recounted the group's history and some of its values.

Recognizing this tribal aspect in behavior enables one to notice that many group activities take advantage of 'gaps' in our education (such as the fact that emotional excitement, fatigue and other factors render one receptive to new perceptions but also to indoctrination and foolishness). We can notice how much we have and have not changed, how much we are and are not different from other groups. I feel that learning more about the phenomenon of group—both from the internal point of view and from the external point of view—can make the experience of group more meaningful and more useful to members of the group. Not only this, the group itself may become more useful to humanity.

It is evident from this *Encuentro* that it is becoming more and more difficult to fit explanations for positive outcomes into the popular idea that only the behavior of the facilitator creates a climate for constructive personality change. The fact that there were no designated facilitators in the *Encuentro* and that the results were indistinguishable from those of other person-centered workshops practically finishes off this notion. Even if one attributes 'facilitative attitudes' to some participants (which undoubtedly was the case), still the phenomenon does not accord with the theory of client-centered therapy as applied to individual patients. The heaviness or lightness of existence, the influence of groupness, of the sea, the results of frustration, expectation, the peculiarities of the culture, which these people constituted by their presence together are all influential in the phenomenon. Since we are always part of groups (and sometimes ones that might be useful), there exists the possibility that knowledge of this phenomenon may benefit humanity itself.

Notes

1. Participants that were part of the Uruguayan organizing commission which arranged hotel lodgings, local transportation and all the many details that permitted the event to take place were: Abidel May, Alondra Mendizábel, Graciela Eichin, Magdelena Bravo, Maria Luisa Blanco and Richard Griesser.

2. I am responsible for the translations of participants' comments into English from the Portuguese or the Spanish. In this endeavor I received the invaluable assistance of the Brazilian artist Lucila Machado Assumpção.

3. Even in the great religious revivals, there was evidently a variety of motives for attending. Cleveland (1916) quotes a witness, '[These camp-meetings] were doubtless attended for improper purposes by a few licentious persons and by others with a view of obtaining a handle to ridicule religion. ... The free intercourse of all ages and sexes under cover of the night and the woods was not without its temptations. It is also to be feared that they gave rise to false notions of religion by laying too much stress on bodily exercises, and substituting them in place of moral virtues and inward piety. These were often considered as evidence of a change of heart and affections, though they neither proved or disproved anything of the kind.'

4. Portunhol: a contraction of Portuguese-Espanhol. There were no translations. Each participant spoke the language most comfortable to him or her. Listeners made an effort to understand the other's language and communication.

CHAPTER EIGHT

Learning about Learning
The person-centered approach applied to education

There is impressive research evidence in the United States (Aspy & Roebuck, 1983) and West Germany (Tausch, 1983) that suggests that students who have teachers who are empathic, congruent, and warmly accepting are likely to improve on most of the indicies that interest the school systems.

For example, these students:

- miss fewer days of school.
- have increased scores on self-concept measures.
- make greater gains on academic achievement measures, including both math and reading scores.
- present fewer disciplinary problems.
- commit fewer acts of vandelism to school property.
- increase their scores on IQ tests (K-5).
- make gains on creativity scores.
- are more spontaneous and use higher levels of thinking.
  (Aspy & Roebuck, 1983)

Carl Rogers (1983), in the revised edition of his celebrated book, *Freedom to Learn*, divides learning into two categories: rote-memory of material which is meaningless to the student (which Rogers detests) and experiential learning (for which he is passionate).

For Rogers, experiential learning involves the 'insatiable curiosity that drives an adolescent boy' to discover, for example, all he can about engines to improve his motorcycle's performance. It includes making what the student is discovering 'a real part of *me*.' Furthermore, the student's personal feelings guide this pattern of discovery: 'No, no that's not what I want! ... Ah! here it is! Now I am grasping and comprehending what I *need* and what I want to know!' (1983: 19).

In this notion of experiential learning, the student, for purely personal reasons, chooses the subjects she wishes to learn, becomes emotionally involved with them, and evaluates her own learning progress. This type of learning, Rogers justifiably points out, has deep significance for the learner and may even change her personality.

The goal of learning, Rogers says, is to become the 'fully functioning person.' This is an idealized person of the future who would cultivate the capacity to relay every stimulus through the nervous system without distorting it through a defense mechanism. This person is, thus, said to be 'open to experience.' Furthermore, his personality and self 'would be continually in flux,' living in the moment, in an 'existential fashion.' Finally, he would do what feels right in the moment, 'trusting his organism to find the most satisfying behavior' in each existential situation (Rogers, 1983).

These views of significant learning emphasize *some* important aspects of learning, but not all. The ideal person which is said to result from this learning would be amply suited for a particular time and situation, but probably not for every future time and place. Rogers' views of learning emerged from a society whose predominant values had suppressed or undervalued the perspective of experiential learning he emphasizes.

What were those societal values? A list would include the following:

- *stable interpersonal relations*: marriage was not to be broken; the individual was to remain closely involved with the family; homes, jobs, and friends were not to be changed frequently.
- *external orientation*: individuals were to think of others before themselves; young people were to prepare for roles in society.
- *superiority of thinking*: emotionality was a weakness; feelings were to be controlled by logic.
- *delayed gratification*: work now, play later.

Today, however, we have societies quite different. Values have changed somewhat and are continuing to change. Marriage and families may not be so stable. Interpersonal relationships may be more casual. Individuals may think of themselves first and may be much more mobile. Feelings, not logic, may be used to guide decisions. Young persons may shun societal roles for a 'free' life. Even when they assume traditional careers, they may want to play now, pay later.

In a society with relatively stable personal, social, and political structures, Rogers aimed his educational approach at the development of a person who appeared to have more flexible dimensions. He followed the direction in which his psychotherapy clients, confronted with fixed opportunities and changing necessities, were changing. However, for societies with more flexible structures, do we not need, in addition to an approach for facilitating this person's development and helping him learn, also an approach for those who are facing a new reality and a new future? I don't suggest dismissing Rogers' concepts—they are still needed. I do suggest their amplification, to suit the pluralistic demands of peoples and societies which now have greater diversity.

Rote Memory: The advantages

Gazzaniga (1985) reports about an unfortunate man who had the hippocampus structure of his brain removed in a surgery intended to control epilepsy. As a result, the patient lost all ability to remember beyond a few minutes. This created a pitiful existance for this poor man. For example, if he could not remember that his mother had died, whenever he would learn of her death, it was as if for the first time and he would undergo a painful grieving. The next time he inquired of his mother, he would receive a new shock, another agony.

What makes this person's suffering noteworthy in the context of learning is that although he could not remember tasks which he had to be taught again and again, he *was* able to learn them. He learned to solve, for example, a complex parlor game requiring the manipulation of concentric rings in a sequence of thirty-one precise moves. Each time he worked through this problem, he denied any previous knowledge of it. Nevertheless, each time he improved his ability. Learning was taking place in spite of no conscious mental retention.

This example is meant to illustrate what we all know about normal people as well: they learn, especially physical skills, by doing, sometimes over and over and that teacher attitudes may have very little effect on this process.

Puluwat navigators in the South Seas are said to be able to guide their native canoes among the many islands through the use of an impressively developed intuition. Familiarity with the sensation of moving over the waves, knowledgeable perceptions of wind and weather, the appearance of the waves, the color of the water, the location of the sun and stars help these master navigators in their art. Although their intelligence must integrate many categories of information, initially, the knowledge of the positions where certain stars rise and set on the horizon, one of the key factors, had to be committed to memory by rote (Gardner, 1985). Thus, in order to benefit from the experiential learning, first the rote-memory of very likely uninteresting material was necessary.

Rote-memory or repetitive exercises or otherwise unglamorous methods should not be ignored. All methods should be evaluated in terms of their value to learning.

Personal Choice: Its limitations

The student's curiosity and personal whims in choosing what to study should not be exaggerated. It is necessary to learn some facts and information before the time when one may have an interest in the subject. This point was painfully demonstrated following a disaster at a Soviet nuclear power station. A person, apparently uninformed of the dangers, received very serious injuries from radiation while bicycling in a contaminated area. Particularly in matters of survival one cannot wait until her interest is aroused to learn the threats that surround her. One must understand (without indulging in groundless sensational rumors, nor in unnecessary fear) the dangerous effects of radioactivity or the breeding habits of disease-carrying mosquitos or the risks certain behaviors may have in the transmission of AIDS *before* a problem has manifested—otherwise, when a symptom appears, it may already be too late to prevent tragedy.

Society has the responsibility for establishing educational processes which prepare its citizens for known eventualities and, now even more so, unknown eventualities. The educational system has a responsibility to know what it wants its students to learn, beyond merely the skill of going to school. Those applying the person-centered approach would do well to accommodate learning for eventualites known and unknown, and learning which is *less* personalized as well as more personalized.

Principles of Psychotherapy Are Not Enough

Ironically, Rogers' interest in teaching (as it is in psychotherapy and facilitating groups) is in what the teacher (psychotherapist or group facilitator) *does* to improve learning. This is ironical because this approach is called *student*-centered (client-centered, person-centered). Yet, it is most often the qualities of the teacher (psychotherapist, group facilitator), not the student, that are considered. Should not more also be known about the complexities of the learner and the conditions that surround learning?

Yet, even in terms of the teacher, Rogers' concepts do not seem to me to reach far enough. When I was a graduate student in mathematics, some teachers, with whom I learned the most, had serious emotional problems. One of them could not look students in the eye, he was so shy. Another grew so furious, if anyone interrupted with a question, he would abandon his lecture and storm out of the room. One admirable quality these both had was an *intense* involvement, not with the student's emotions, but with the subject. Where should this quality be put in the person-centered approach to learning?

In fairness, it should be noted that my math professors, though they possessed limited ability to show it in conventional terms, also *were* empathic. They understood my confusion and frequent frustration, my occasional victory, not because they were sensitively attending to my experience, but because they had faced and overcome the same obstacles I was then encountering. In their exaggerated emotional reactions they were congruent to a fault. Though they were unmovable in their mathematical perfectionism, they were totally accepting of my personal weaknesses, as well as my intelligent thought.

Nevertheless, they had neither a therapeutic attitude nor behavior, as Rogers would understand these qualities. If one listened to electronically recorded intervals of their classes, I doubt that it would be concluded (using psychotherapeutic criteria) that they had any 'facilitative attitude' whatever. (Once I mentioned to a professor, from whom I learned enormously, of my anxiety in facing his difficult examinations.

He said, 'You just have to relax. Take a drink or something.') Should not the complexities of these different attitudes and behaviors be better understood?

Any application of the person-centered approach to learning, if it is to be other than mere personal conviction, must include more than interpersonal aspects and at the same time avoid becoming too abstract. Thousands of years of religious and political movements have amply demonstrated that when people aspire to a moral code without a context in which to make it a reality, hypocrisy is more likely achieved than a true way of being. Any effective way of being may be the *end product*, not starting point, of (in the case of teaching) devotion to learning and the acquisition of the skill of teaching as well as, in some cases, the emotional sensitivity to students.

Locus of Control: For those who have it

The learning process described by Rogers is a good fit for a very special kind of student: one who is guided by an internal locus of control or evaluation. But what about persons who may be different? Should this approach be applied to everyone? Even in psychotherapy, where the person-centered approach enjoyed so much success, the response may not be so simple. Studies of group therapy suggest that persons with higher levels of *external* locus of control respond less favorably to non-directive or less-structured group experiences (Abromowitz et al., 1974). Research also suggests that an inner-directed learning experience may be difficult for people with higher levels of external locus of control (Kilmann, Albert & Sotile, 1975). If we insist on a one-sided approach to learning that favors inner-directiveness aren't we abandoning those who may learn differently?

Even what is here called experiential learning is approached differently by different people. Some are able to experience a process such as, for example, psychotherapy, and afterwards theorize about its various interrelations and similarities to other conceptualizations and to generalize the experience to other aspects of life. While other persons may have difficulty generalizing and making connections from an experience unless they have received a preliminary understanding of the framework being used.

Although learning may involve a biochemical process in which brain neurons sprout new synapses and dendritic spines in response to outside stimulation, everyone knows that not every person learns in the same way. For persons with a strong auditory preference, for example, it may be sufficient to merely hear a language to learn it. On the other hand, visually orientated persons may have to *see* the words written before they are fixed in memory.

To prescribe the same approach for every student by insisting that he have a 'significant experience,' that he be 'self-directed,' or that he avoid certain methods of approaching learning would be as insensitive as the North American public schools seem to have been toward the inner-directed student. Is not a larger perspective needed in this approach to remain person-centered and not philosophy-centered? A *more* personalized approach, in this case, could include those who learn in different ways.

The Fully Functioning Person

The description of the 'fully functioning person,' bouncing about in the swirl of sensory stimulation, following her feelings from one satisfying situation to another, living an existential philosophy surely would be ideal for living in the urban centers of the United States in the 1960s. She could deal efficiently, therefore, with (what is now) the past; but, could she deal with the imponderable future?

Even by proposing an 'ideal person' Rogers treads on thin ice. This approach backfired for the Chinese communists with their 'new man' and the Soviets who used to speak of the 'new civilization.' Of course, when some formulation of human functioning becomes an ideal, it is bound to be less than the real possibilities. Sensations from sensory stimuli are not always more important than other aspects of consciousness. One self is not more valuable intrinsically than another, nor are the whims of an unstable and shifting self necessarily a reliable judge for a positive contribution to civilization. There are more meritable causes than mere momentary satisfaction that seemed to be the principle guide for the 'fully functioning person.'

Karl Kraus, the Viennese satirist, once quipped, 'Life is an effort that deserves a better cause.' With so much effort involved in becoming an 'ideal person,' couldn't she have a better cause than mere momentary self-satisfaction? For what purpose is this ideal person living? Would a purely *process*-centered person, for instance, really be able to act in concert with others in completely unforeseen situations offered by the future?

It is precisely in the area of values that any 'person of the future' may have to have great sensitivity and perhaps some kind of ability to perceive the essentially equal qualities of seemingly opposing values. There are some four of five billion people in the world, more than 150 nation states, in which many more cultures are entertwined. Cultural values are in conflict all over the planet. To settle many disputes, common values—which outweigh the values in conflict—might be found. If your neighbor has built a system on a value for 'development' and you have built yours on a value for 'ecology,' his 'destruction of nature' (as you see it), will eventually conflict with your 'obstruction of progress' (as he sees it). A more complex value might be found on which the two could unite (shared prosperity and planetary salvation?). Does an 'ideal person' with a mere 'existential perspective' have the necessary breadth of vision, the flexibility, the diversity of interests and abilities to be a competent participant in the resolution of such problems?

Innovative Learning*

How are we to deal with these problems of conflicting values? Furthermore, how are we to deal with problems such as air pollution and decadent institutions; problems in which the individual has a hand in creating, but once created, is powerless (alone) to resolve?

Learning in unknown situations might require accompanying change, exposing the whole as well as the parts, perceiving multiple causes and effects as well as interrelationships between key elements. This learning has been called 'innovative learning' (Botkin, Elmandjra & Malitza, 1979). The inventiveness that occurs as a reaction to sudden shock, crisis, dangerous scarcity, adversity, gives the most well known examples of this learning. Is there a way to cultivate this type of learning before a serious crisis occurs?

This question is one that has been addressed in a series of large group learning programs from the person-centered approach. Let me sketch, briefly, one experience that could serve to illustrate a developing understanding of innovative learning.

A few years ago such a workshop was convened in Brazil. Carlos, a twelve-year-old orphan from a poor family in São Paulo, was not enrolled on the workshop. He lived temporarily with his brother, a handyman employed by the institute which housed the workshop participants.[1]

During the early days of the workshop, some of the participants report that they have lost jewelry and some small sums of money; Carlos is suspected. Also, someone says they saw him trying to drown a stray dog in the wading pool. A woman complains that he was sexually aggessive toward her. 'Something has got to be done about this boy,' she demands. 'The child must be sent home,' someone else concludes.

As there are no official leaders and no agreed upon procedures to follow in this case, a long and frequently heated discussion which involves the entire group ensues. On the one side, the list of suspicions of the boy grows. One person says that Carlos made an insulting face towards her. Another says he thinks the kid has a bad character. Someone else reminds the group that thousands of homeless marauders, just Carlos' age, are robbing and murdering citizens in the cities. This group of speakers concludes that the boy is a threat to the security of the community and should be immediately removed.

On the other side, some participants in the workshop say that they have not found him offensive. He has been courteous in encounters with them. He even helped one lady with her luggage when she arrived. She defends his offenses as childlike and innocent, as not meant to be aggressive, merely playful, and unjustly misinterpreted. Some suppose that the lad is clever, and judging from paintings he

---

* The text from here until the Conclusion is repeated in Chapter 6, between pages 117 and 122. This is due to the fact that some of the chapters in this book have been previously published elsewhere as separate works. This text differs slightly from that included earlier and we have reprinted it here in its entirety.

has made in the art room constructed by participants, he could even possess artistic talent. They argue that Carlos has no adequate supervision at home and if he remains with the workshop group, he has a chance at least for a positive experience with responsible people.

Though some see him as good, others as bad, the group reaches the conclusion that it does not have to judge between these extreme alternatives. It must, however, decide what to do about participants' strong sentiments surrounding the lad and what course of action to take regarding his presence: If he is sent away, the group can relax; but he faces poverty and frequent beatings at home. If he is allowed to stay, he may benefit; but there may be a danger to participants.

A few people insist that Carlos is, in fact, a member of the community and that the fair course of action would be to consult him in any decision that affects him. 'We are a family,' someone finally suggests. Around this metaphor participants can rally and integrate their values. It is agreed that those who feel more intensely (both for and against Carlos' presence in the workshop) will put the group's concerns before him. They will discuss with him how they feel, find out how he feels, and see if some solution can be worked out to everyone's satisfaction.[2]

In the meeting, Carlos says that he did not realize his behavior was frightening anyone. He was acting in his accustomed way. When he realizes others are threatened, he wants to change. Also, however, he wants to participate in the workshop. He wants to study dance with Grace; to learn massage with Laura; with Clare, to learn music and art; and with his brother, to learn to drive a car. They all agree. He agrees to behave according to the behavior which governed all participants.

Carlos stayed in the workshop. He not only abided by the consensual rules, but became an exemplary citizen. Those who previously feared him became his friends. Those who initially supported his point of view were not disappointed. In the end he made one of the more pointed observations of the group, 'This year there was lot of drama and not much adventure. I expect that next year there will be more adventure and less drama.'

Individuals, as usual, learned many things during this workshop. Furthermore, the *group* could be said to have learned also. Participants applied their customary solutions to no avail. What was successful in the last workshop, failed this time. Many believed it was impossible to resolve this conflict without alienating someone. Yet, together they did what they did not, at first, believe they could do.

Some Aspects of this Innovative Learning Experience

Anticipation—The early signs of a problem were detected: a minority of the group was suffering. This fact was not ignored. The group anticipated more serious problems. Also, participants in the group thought about (indeed, argued over) various alternative actions the group might take and what consequences those actions might bring. In the phrase of Botkin, Elmandjra, and Malitza (1979), these group members were 'seeing the present in terms of the future, instead of the future in terms of the present,' which is what 'person of the future' idealizations tend to do.

Participation—Every person in the community was involved in the decision-making process, including Carlos. People showed an empathic understanding for each other's feelings. They were honest: their statements matched their thoughts and sentiments. They respected the dignity of each member of the community, even a 12-year-old who was not even officially registered in the workshop. And, this participation included a goodwill toward cooperating and using dialogue to reach an intelligent solution.

This participation involved an aspect of human consciousness that, at the moment, I am only able to characterize with two seemingly contradictory, but actually complementary, concepts. One is *autonomy*; the other, *humility*. Each person experienced herself fully, as she actually was and gave freely of her opinions, sentiments, and her information. She expressed her feelings and reactions to others directly and forcefully, in an effort to bring forth the best she could in terms of a solution. Also she refused to contribute to injustice and to accept a solution that jeapordized her freedom or security or personal satisfaction. Her faculties of critical judgement were applied to every phase of the process. In other words, she acted as an *autonomous* person.

At the same time, whenever her critical judgement discerned a superior suggestion to her own, she surrendered her own opinion or idea for the superior one. She could be sensitive to the emergence of interrelationships of concepts as well as sentiments and the formulation of a more complete picture, without insisting on her personal view. She was willing to change her beliefs and values. She could put aside personal glory for the satisfaction of an intelligent outcome for all involved. This state of *humility* is not at all easily explained. To scramble an old saw, it may be easier *done* than *said*.

Perceptions, it should be noted, were not only shared through words in the formal meetings. Music, art, and other media to express images probably contributed insight to bear on the solution as well.

Values in Conflict—Maintenance learning is 'the acquisition of fixed outlooks, methods, and rules for dealing with known and recuring situations ... It is the type of learning designed to maintain an existing system or established way of life.' Maintenance learning is essential to the continuation of much of civilization's infrastructure (Botkin, Elmandjra & Malitza, 1979: 10).

What distinguishes maintenance learning from innovative learning is the role of values. Maintenance learning reinforces the values of the system it is designed to maintain and ignores others. When values are in conflict, learning opportunities are present. For this reason, values are called, 'the enzymes of any innovative learning process' (Botkin et al., 1979: 40).

In the example above, a dialogue of values brought conflicting sides into focus:

'A citizen has a right to live free from threat. The community has a responsibility to protect its members and to govern the behavior of its members.'

'The individual should be free to act differently and still be accepted. We should not have to conform to someone else's opinions of proper behavior.'

'The community is responsible for looking after its children. The group should be governed by human feelings, not by cold rules.'

'Security is more important than anyone's feelings. If people are concerned about the boy's feelings, that's their problem, not mine.'

'If any member of the community has a problem, it is the whole community's problem.'

In many conflicts that arise within a group, such as this one, I can say, 'yes,' to each side of the conflict. When I heard the members of the community call for greater security, I said to myself, 'Yes, I want security.' When I heard their opponents call for greater respect for the individual, even if it is a 12-year-old, I said, 'Yes, let's respect the individual. Let's give him a chance.' I was thus required to find a position that could be backed by action and support these values. Could we have security and respect the individual? When the process was complete we did not have to settle for one against the other: for winning or for losing. With patience, the willingness to withstand frustration and confusion, and the ability to extract from complex human relations a fair solution was found. The group strived for the best and surrendered to the better.

Courage and Patience

The members of the group needed patience in order to carefully formulate the problem, to let all the various sides of the problem surface, to hear every voice, to withstand the sheer weight of lengthy discussions, to avoid falling into despair during chaotic moments. Although they were often tempted by hasty and radical solutions, such as ignoring the 'irrational' fears of some or sending the 'menace' away without further thought, participants could allow an understanding of the whole problem to find its own dimensions. To Carlos and to those threatened, the dimensions were personal and direct. To others, inasmuch as the outcome of this problem would define the kind of community in which they lived and the kind of community which eventually might judge them also, the dimensions were personal and ideological. They were creating *their* society, for better or worse.

When Innovative Group Learning Fails

In most groups individual learning will take place, but group learning is a more delicate endeavor and can easily fail. In the United States, for example, a workshop was conducted in which a legal activist was present. In the midst of a conflict in the group he put forth (like other participants) his opinion. However, unlike others, he continued to insist on his point of view beyond all common sense. He pushed this same point of view (which by now had become a policy) into all future discussions, whether it was relevant or not. This crusade, he admitted, was a 'test' of the person-centered approach to see if it was 'tolerant of diversity.' From my experience, innovative learning *needs* diversity to find creative solutions. What it cannot tolerate, as this fellow proved, is bad will. It is a subtle cooperative venture. Naturally, without his constructive participation no integrated solution could be found. Diversity was plentiful. What was missing, and was impossible under the circumstances, was creative integration.

In another workshop, a university professor, in an arrogant and self-centered tone, announced that he wished to tape record the meetings. Some participants accepted his proposal. Those who objected, he tried to bully into conformity with his desire. The objectors also held stubbornly to their feelings. A long discussion ensued. No decision was reached, but he withdrew his request to tape record. He sulked through the remainder of the workshop. Here, the situation was not settled to the satisfaction of one of the community members. He did not show the necessary humility to pursue a mutual solution. Other members of the group did not show the necessary autonomy to reopen the problem when they saw that he was alienated from the group.

There have also been cases, when the staff of the workshop was very diverse and the goals of the workshop were very unclear, where the group occupied itself with a unification such as one finds at football matches: strong emotions in a mindless conformity. In all these examples innovative learning could not take place.

Conclusion

People applying the person-centered approach to learning may amplify their vision. Different people learn in different ways. They should not be forced to choose the subjects they wish to study, have a passionate experience, or evaluate their own experience. We *must* learn many things whose significance we may not be aware of and consequently we do not *want* to learn. It is probably not sufficient to facilitate the learning of all students that the teacher show empathy, congruence, and acceptance in the narrow context of psychotherapy research. Learning also occurs from doing. Rote exercises should not be shunned merely because they are disagreeable or unfashionable. They should be evaluated on the basis of their value for learning.

Although there probably always will be, in the struggle over competing ideas, those who may use these comments to discredit or dismiss the person-centered approach to learning. My intention is not to provide fuel in these disputes. I think a broader outlook can be taken toward learning, one that incorporates what Rogers has proposed and more. Devotion to the subject, to learning, to truth may also be factors in successful teaching. Whatever these factors are, the teacher's responsibility is not to be merely a pleasant person, but to do what is necessary for the student to learn. Teachers must learn how to teach; students, how to learn.

Caution should be exercised in trying to cultivate 'a way of being,' in the field of learning and also in the wider field of life. The goal of learning perhaps *should* be a 'fully functioning person' but this person would need to be capable of meeting the requirements of the time and place in which he must function. His values must support this task.

Thought should be given to the relation of individual learning to group learning. In the case of pollution, for example, individuals are not learning how to protect their health as fast as the group is learning, through its members' collective actions, to produce dangerous air pollutants. Individuals must learn *as a body* how to resolve problems as well as irresponsibly and thoughtlessly creating them.

Rogers' ideas of personal development came about within a relatively stable society. The person's subjective world had little space in that society. Today, respect for the person's subjective world and the stability of societies has changed. A personal attitude that is aware of the context in which it is formed is also needed. Anticipation, participation, empathy, congruence, acceptance, good will, how to deal with conflicting values and work cooperatively without sacrificing autonomy and critical judgment might be desirable as part of individual learning experience; not as another formal course or classroom simulation game, but as a background that is continually kept in the individual consciousness.

Notes

1. This low-structured workshop convened 80 persons, mostly from the helping professions. It was an experience of self-governance, learning how to learn as a group, and learning how to resolve collective problems which arise during the workshop, as well as for personal and interpersonal development.

2. Although part of this final solution contained the well-established custom of a committee appointed by the larger body, this was not done, as is frequently the case, to relieve the larger group of cumbersome discussions. The group had already heard the various sides of the problem and had experienced the 'loss of time' and circular confusion of such deliberations. Rather, the committee was formulated so that the boy would not be paralyzed by a confrontation with a large and formidable group. At the same time the committee consisted of those who felt strongly for each side of the dispute. Thus, it was a true confrontation of the group, not merely investigative. As the large group had thoroughly participated, it did not (as often happens in parliamentary bodies) have to cross-examine the committee's findings or to reject its conclusions.

CHAPTER NINE

Effect of Group

Sobriety doth rob me of delight,
And drunkenness doth drown my sense outright;
There is a middle state, it is my life,
Not altogether drunk, nor sober quite.
            Omar Khayyám

That many of the benefits of client-centered therapy and of small encounter groups were also realized in large group workshops was not surprising. However, these large group workshops did present two related surprises. The first was that a group of educated, good-natured people, largely from the helping professions, could behave, at times, no better than an unruly mob and that members of the group, though stable in other situations, could suddenly become deranged in the group setting.

The second surprise was that, given this and the sometimes hopelessly chaotic nature of the group meetings, quite delicate, intelligent and participatory actions could also be carried out by the group with a sensitive respect for each of its individual members. A large group, with participants in a creative state, could resolve crises, find solutions to complex problems, intelligently coordinate its activities without plans, legislation, or parliamentary procedures, and even transform its culture in a compassionate and efficient process that involved, respected and benefited its members and itself.

Expectations

A large part of my surprise at the chaotic behavior of large groups stemmed from my own expectations. Having lived in a relatively ordered and individual-oriented society, I had little experience with large groups of this type. I had, of course, been part of crowds and had felt the strong contagious emotions of religious services, political rallies, music concerts and championship athletic contests. Yet, I grew to expect that the bizarre and destructive acts of mobs were the result of hoodlums who, carried by the wave of contagion and hidden in the crowd's anonymity, unleashed their aggressivity. Good citizens, educated people, on the other hand, when they gathered together, so I imagined, would continue to act in a civilized manner.

When I discovered that frequently they did not, I accounted for their strange behavior and the tangled logic of their deliberations as a function of one or two bad characters who took advantage of the group's good nature to cause trouble. In cases where this explanation did not fit, I suspected, as many participants do, that the chaos of group activities was due to the organizers and their methods who, directly or indirectly, frustrated the group, thereby provoking aggressive actions.

Although all these explanations are plausible, there were still many cases for which none would fit. Little by little, I began to suspect that the behavior of participants and of the group as a whole in these large group workshops, though unfamiliar, may not be extraordinary—in fact, it was an ordinary aspect of human nature. Ordinary people with the intention to do good, not seeing the complete picture nor realizing the full consequences of their actions, or with misguided motives, can even do harm (Milgram, 1974).

Effect of Group

Gathering together apparently has an *effect* on persons, an effect that can translate into collective behavior which may be destructive (or may also be constructive). Or it may be merely troubling, as in the following common occurrence.

The large group has completed deliberations on a knotty issue. The pros and cons have been passionately aired; the problem attacked from various angles. The exhausted assembly grudgingly accepts a compromise proposal.

Leaving the meeting room a participant's glance meets that of a friend: 'I feel awful,' he says, surprising his companion.

'So do I,' the other readily admits, a puzzled look on his face.

'I went along with things in there, but now I don't feel good about it.'

'Why didn't you object or speak out more forcefully? Why didn't I, for that matter?'

'I don't know. I didn't feel so strongly about it till just now. In there it seemed okay; I had nothing to say.'

They are perplexed by their own actions. They were free to speak up in the group. They felt no pressure to remain silent. They did not feel afraid. Still, for some reason, they did not feel the conviction to speak. Once outside the meeting room, however, they became immediately aware of a strong sentiment running counter to the group decision. In spite of doing everything they felt necessary at the time, they are nevertheless feeling regret. It is as if each was two different persons; one, the group person, with his values; the other, the solitary individual, with his frequently different values.

A report on a workshop, which I did not attend but which was similar to person-centered large group workshops in many respects, also illustrates this effect on participants who have a group personality and an individual personality and how they effect one another. In this group, some participants turned against one of their more active colleagues and he was 'unquestionably wounded and angered' by this action. Other participants were later ashamed that, through their failure to act, they indirectly contributed to this man's humiliation. 'I just cannot forgive myself that I let this happen to him,' one person apologized over and over (Doob & Foltz, 1973).

Heinz Kohut (1985), in an analysis of groups, has observed that a portion of the membership of any large group is allowed, by the group as a whole, to heckle, ridicule, suppress, or even insult a member—acts which the ethics of the whole group would not permit. Group members who do not like the victim, but whose sense of fairness would not permit silencing him, do nothing to prevent others from doing so. Thus, at times, a person or a small group may assume leadership to accomplish an unpleasant goal which the group as a whole wants but also wishes to disown. When the act is completed, a sense of guilt would naturally occur to those whose desires conflicted with their ethics, even though they did not participate directly in any crime.

This ambivalence may be studied more or less directly. For example, Asch (1955) found that people profess opinions according to their perceptions (even incorrectly), if among others who profess the same opinions. Verplanck's (1955) research suggests that a person's tendency to offer an opinion may be strengthened or weakened, depending on the rate at which the listener agreed. And the research of Zimmerman and Bauer (1956) suggests that what one remembers or believes depends on the audience he or she is addressing. Juries and other authoritative bodies often reach decisions which each member supports by vote but were he to have acted, not as a 'representative of the people' but as a private individual, he may have decided oppositely.

In another workshop, a similar divergence between public opinions and private opinions was noted. 'Again and again,' the workshop organizers write, 'we witnessed instances of the same person's inconsistently expressing, for example, conciliatory views in his T-group and then being silent or defending a more rigid position in the General Assembly' (Doob, Foltz & Stevens, 1970).

Individuals in the group may also feel *no* remorse for their aggressivity. John Allaway (1971), speaking of similar large groups, from his work with the Tavistock Clinic, observes, 'In the large group hurtful things are done by individuals and the group to other individuals without arousing any compassion for the victims. And, quite commonly, those who do these things blandly deny any responsibility for them' (p. 5).

It is not uncommon for participants to like other members of the group individually and even have very good relations outside of the group meetings and, at the same time, to hate the *group*. As one participant expressed his surprise and disappointment with the phenomenon, 'I enjoyed good relationships with many people as individuals but in the group we flopped around like fish trying to learn to walk.'

Even what is spoken in these large group meetings apparently is not always entirely the choice of the speaker. I have observed several times the following event: Without invitation, a person speaks; seemingly voluntarily. He expresses some opinions, personal feelings, private thoughts he says he wants to share with others. Group members react normally. Some look at the fellow and nod their heads, some show no interest. The group, in general, treats the speaker as it has previous speakers in the meetings. Although one or two persons may ask for clarification on some point or other, the person is not apparently coerced into continuing to speak.

At the end of the episode, he appears satisfied. He says many things that were on his mind, some details of his life, he has revealed for the first time. This pleases him.

At the following meeting of the group, however, he announces that he feels 'betrayed by the group.' He felt good last night, but today he feels that the 'group took advantage of me' and 'pressured me into going too far.' He feels 'exposed' and ashamed and wishes he could take back some things he said. Group members are astonished. They deny they had any special interest in his affairs. No one persuaded him, they say. They thought he was saying what he wanted to say.

This phenomenon has been made more clear through the vivid description of a university graduate student who had a similar experience upon being interviewed by Rogers in front of a large group workshop. The day after the 'demonstration therapy interview' that Rogers conducted with her as the 'client,' she began, 'to feel slightly uncomfortable.' 'I felt extremely shy,' she related, and spent the day avoiding Rogers and her friends. 'It seemed like people were watching me,' she added.

Doubts about having 'hogged the show', troubled her. Then, she 'remembered the silences during the interview and how each time they occurred, I rushed in and "spilled the beans" about myself. I began to feel vulnerable and sensitive about my experience ... It still seemed impossible that I had participated willingly. The whole experience seemed out of character to me' (Slack, 1985).

Her statement not only clearly illustrates that her state of consciousness was different during the therapy interview than the day afterwards, but also the effect of group. A large part of her worries dealt with what others in the group were thinking about her. When she was pressed to participate in a second interview with Rogers she was reluctant. She said she felt, 'like a rock star must feel when his or her career suddenly rises to fame.' It is obvious that both in and outside the large group setting she felt both allured and coerced by this experience. See also (Rogers, 1986b) for another example.

In these examples, group participants are aware of their actions. They do not feel anything is wrong at the time, but later, under different circumstances, they regret their behavior. However, it can happen also that the group participant will have no awareness of his actions. For example, this statement from a meeting between members of conflicting factions illustrates a dissociated state of consciousness also found in intensive group meetings: 'One man stood up in amazement at a large group session and recounted that he had just walked out of a campus shop in a daze and then discovered he had taken a ballpoint pen without paying for it. Another found himself "walking around outside just talking to myself—I've never done that before"' (Doob et al., 1973).

Though at times participants may act with little individual awareness, at other times they may launch into conscious acts which disrupt the possibility of group solutions. Although highly satisfying for the individuals, the result is often disastrous for group effectivity.

For example, in the summer of 1981 hundreds of persons gathered in the Great Hall of City University, London. They came from some 30 nations to attend the First Assembly of the Fourth World—a conference of 'small nations, groups working for their autonomy and independence at all levels from the neighborhood to the nation ... which are struggling against the giantism of the institutions of today's mass societies for a human-scale and non-centralized, multi-cellular, power-dispersed world order' (O'Conner, 1982). Perhaps a sensible motive.

Papers were received from 255 participants. The assembly divided into special interest groups such as 'Arab/Israel,' 'Decolonizing the Great Empires,' 'Women and the Fourth World,' and so forth. From descriptions, the participants' behavior was probably not unlike what could occur at a large group workshop of the person-centered approach. Certainly the interaction was intensive and many participants were serious-minded and with ambitious goals.

When the Fourth World conferees brought back their small-group findings to the large group, they fell prey to the same infection of giantism they protested. Under the weight of their ignorance of the group's invisible institutional forces, a dispute broke out over whether to vote or insist on consensual agreement on key issues (as discussed earlier, a common, frustrating, but nevertheless manageable, occurrence in large group workshops). After an hour of haggling someone asked for a 'show of hands' (but not a *vote*, the suggested was quick to add) of those who thought voting for the proposal was in order. Some of the members favoring consensus withdrew from the proceedings at this point by joining hands and forming a circle in the center of the assembly hall and chanting 'Om.'

'In short order,' writes a reporter at the conference,

> comic-opera warfare erupted on the floor of the assembly. The Celts were angrier than ever, the Om was louder than ever, and tempers continued to rise ... As the minutes passed, more and more people began filtering out of the hall. The worst moment came when the Latvian representative ... tried to intervene on the part of the Celts, and was repeatedly interrupted by an Englishman who proposed that everyone stop talking and simply hug one another ... Thus, the First Assembly of the Fourth World ended. Nothing was decided, nothing was declared, and nothing, in fact, was done. (O'Conner, 1982)

This scenario is not uncommon. It may be inevitable unless participants have won the necessary hard-fought experience from large groups in which more intelligent outcomes have occurred.

Contagious or even euphoric feelings, resulting from such experiences, are also common. A sense of 'oneness' may even be so great that a person crosses the boundary into states of consciousness quite different from the ordinary. In so doing, he may frighten himself and others. It is not uncommon for several companions to nurse him for a few days until he returns to a stronger sense of self.

Nevertheless, some of the same factors that lead to destructive, or at least negative, outcomes for the group may also contribute to constructiveness at times. For example, though it can be disruptive, the flight of awareness from the present moment may also result in unusual insights and integrative emotion. During a large group workshop meeting, for example, a woman shared a 'vision': a sharply outlined mental picture of a 'forest scene.' At that moment another group member was silently weeping. Through the suddenly flooding tears, this person told of the startling effect of having her 'mind read.' She had, at that very same moment, been grieving for her 'beloved wooded land' that had recently been taken from her in a legal action.

Participants in large group workshops may think and act differently (even at times to the contrary) from the way they think and act alone. In the group they may behave in ways that make them feel proud or that they may come to regret. Though they may behave in ways that surprise, perplex, disappoint, and even embarrass themselves and others, they are normal people, often from the helping professions in Europe, North and South America, who merely sit in a circle and talk. It appears that with no prearranged system of conversing, no special effort, when people speak of personal concerns, politics, inflation, virtually any subject (but especially when they simply express honestly what they are feeling at the moment), they can begin to behave as if they are not 'themselves.'

The Ritual

As the Pilgrim passes while the Country remains.
So Men pass on; but the States remain permanent forever.
    William Blake

In these person-centered large group workshops, the system of personality change and learning is more apparent than in either client-centered therapy or the small group meetings. The convenors of the workshop are less active and, therefore, more apt to be symbolic in the perceptions of others. The ritual is much more extravagant and inventive in its circumstances. The setting is likely to be much more influential since it is usually both more elaborate than and more remote from the setting of the participant's daily life.

Workshops were most frequently convened in beautiful surroundings: the gardens of a university campus, in the mountains, by the sea. The middle of summer guaranteed abundant sunshine. The consciousness of participants in these large groups was doubtless effected by this congenial ambiance. The effect of the people themselves, the effect of group, also exerted a strong influence on the consciousness of participants. Duerr (1985) has observed,

> To say that the ritual has its own life and expresses itself in each succeeding generation, may be too strong. But is it no stronger than to say that an individual came to some conclusion or system of thought free from those around him and free from the thousands of years of tradition that preceded them?

In the large group workshop it is difficult to ignore that group members are experiencing exceptional states of consciousness that may result in either destructive and constructive consequences.

The names applied to the effects of altered states of consciousness in large group members have not been complimentary: 'contagious behavior' or 'mass hysteria,' a wild, uncontrolled excitement which spreads through a group of people; on the less dramatic side, 'social conformity,' the convergence of initially divergent responses of individuals in a group setting. Though these terms do not explain the why or how of such phenomena, they do suggest ways in which we think *we* would never behave.

However, there is a good chance that we *would* behave similarly under the same conditions. Most of us behave much less logically and much less consistently than we imagine. An abundance of fascinating observations have been recorded on this subject. For example, people are much more likely to be influenced to do something they do not wish to do, when the persuasive request merely includes the word 'because,' than when the exact same request is made without this word (Langer, Blank & Chanowitz, 1978).

A small concession or the appearance of concession tends to provoke reciprocity, even when it is illogical. For example, in a large group workshop, a participant asked the group for permission to film the meetings. There were several strong objections and therefore the man said he would wait until the group could reach a consensus before filming. (Permission to film was eventually granted after a week of, at times intensive, discussions.) In the meantime, could he tape record the group's discussions? Although the objections to sound recording were identical to those of filming, the man's request was immediately granted by the group. He had first made a concession to the group by delaying his filming; the group reciprocated by allowing sound recording. (For similar examples and analyses, see Cialdini, 1985).

The group's apparent lack of concern, at times, for a member's suffering has been explained as 'pluralistic ignorance': each person looks at the others and thinks, 'Since no one else is concerned, I guess there is nothing wrong here' (Latané & Darley, 1968).

As noted in Chapter 4, promising development in psychology is the trend to relate to evolutionary biology. Findings in brain researches, cognitive psychology, neurology and such areas suggest 'modules' of mind rather than a single mind. Our subjective experience gives us the illusion of consistency, as if we have one integrated mind. Instead, proposes Ornstein (1986), for example, we possess a 'multimind,' several 'small minds' being 'wheeled in and out' to deal with different situations and necessities of the organism. Thus, a person, under the influence of one of these minds that has been invoked to deal with a special situation, may behave in ways which are inconsistent with the image of the 'governing mind.' When this occurs, there is 'cognitive dissonance' and the person reinterprets the behavior in a way that causes it to be consistent with this image (Festinger, 1957).

Thus, the young man who tells the group more about himself than he later wishes he had done, may have been under the influence of a mind invoked by social conditions. Operating under its rules, the individual spilled out information that the governing mind later found dissonant. Thus, the man blames the group for drawing out of him an incorrect image. And, in a way, one of him is right.

The perspective that unusual behavior of individuals in groups can be explained as people behaving in a 'trance' or an 'altered state of consciousness'—when the person's thoughts, feelings or behavior deviate significantly from a general norm of subjective functioning (Ludwig, 1967)—may have accumulated the largest literature, to date, on the subject.

According to Shor (1959), a researcher of hypnosis, the usual state of consciousness—what is termed the ordinary waking state—is characterized by a certain frame of reference called the 'generalized reality orientation,' which, in the background of attention, 'supports, interprets, and gives meaning to all experiences' of the person. In special states of mind, this orientation can temporarily fade or disintegrate and become non-functional. Following Shor's definition, a trance is, 'any state in which the generalized reality-orientation has faded to relatively nonfunctional unawareness.' Sleep and daydreaming are everyday examples.

An altered state of consciousness may be produced in various ways. Some states are so common they are rarely considered exceptional mental states. As William James (1896) observed, even 'sleep would be a dreadful disease but for its familiarity.' Thus, merely lying down, relaxing, falling asleep induces a trance. Dreaming is the vivid experience of this state. Daydreaming is another example. In daydreams, consciousness of the external world is diminished and, in a more receptive state, thoughts become more fluid, sometimes offering new ideas and insights (Singer, 1976). Going *without* sleep may also induce this state. Prolonged sleep deprivation may even provoke psychotic-like reactions. After only 40 hours without sleep, 70% of the participants in a research project had already experienced illusions, delusions, and hallucinations. Even after only the second night without sleeping, sporadic disturbances in thinking were common to all subjects. Participants were often embarrassed afterwards when informed of their behavior during the experiment (Tyler, 1955).

In large group workshops that last more than a couple of days, it is common for people, caught in the flurry of activity and emotional stimulation, to go without regular sleep. Participants also may experience euphoria, various shifting moods, including depressions. Lack of sleep, of course, is not the only variable. Participants may be using alcohol and drugs as well as abundant quantities of stimulants such as coffee.

The ingestion of alcohol and drugs is a common means of inducing different states of consciousness. It is thought that mind-altering chemicals may have been used in religious rituals and prophesying since the seventh century BC. Supplicants would ask the priestess at the temple of Apollo at Delphi for predictions of the future after which, according to Arnold Ludwig (1964), 'Pythia would mutter some magical words while inhaling fumes emanating from poppy leaves or hempen ingredients. She then would fall into a 'hypnotic' trance during which Apollo wrestled with her, but she finally succumbed to his power. Awakening from trance, she would utter the famous oracles, known for their ambiguity and *double entendres.*'

Field (1960) has suggested that the Hebrew prophets may have also entered trance states through breathing mind altering fumes. Moses, for example, in the Old Testament record, '... brought their cause before the Lord; always enveloping himself in fumes before giving utterance ... And the Lord spake unto Moses face to face as a man speaketh unto his friend' (Numbers, 11: 25).

The notion that the oracles were produced by the use of hallucinogenic chemicals is disputed by Jaynes (1976) who explains their effectiveness by virtue of a 'collective cognitive imperative,' a belief system of 'culturally agreed-on expectancy or prescription, which defines the particular form of a phenomenon and the roles to be acted out within that form.'

The elaborate induction to enter trance, the loss of consciousness, the proclamations in the name of Apollo were also carried out in the context of accepted belief and ritual. As many as 35,000 people a day are said to have journeyed to Delphi, purifying themselves in readiness to meet the oracle. For over a thousand years, it was, according to Plato, the 'interpreter of religion to mankind.' Jaynes believes, 'It was something before which skepticism would be impossible as for us to doubt that the speech of a radio originates in a studio that we cannot see.'

Our beliefs and fears may certainly influence our state of consciousness. People in groups seem to be particularly vulnerable to the effect of these states. Virtual epidemics have been initiated by provoking fear reactions. In 1787 in Lancashire a woman put a mouse down the neck of a female co-worker in a cotton factory. The victim who was terrified of mice, entered a fit of violent convulsions lasting 24 hours. The next day the contagion affected three more women who entered a similar state. By the fourth day 24 persons, including a man who exhausted himself restraining the others was similarly effected. Even two children were among the victims. Accompanied by a rumor that 'cotton poisoning' was the cause, the malady spread to nearby factories. The cotton workers, as is still practiced today with persons similarly affected, were electrically shocked out of their fits.

From his investigations in treating soldiers in World War II who had 'broken down' following a traumatic battle experience, Sargant (1957) concluded that, 'in states of human fear and excitement the most improbable suggestions can be accepted by apparently sensible people.' By imposing stress, 'one set of behavior patterns in man can be temporarily replaced by another that altogether contradicts it.' Normally aggressive people may feel cowardice; timid people may display impressive courage. Stressful and confusing events, as well as strong emotional experiences, may also be present in large group workshops and may instigate a change in state of consciousness.[1]

Even without extreme circumstances, many individuals conform to the opinions and behavior of other group members, in spite of violating reason by doing so. When questioned about this behavior, following psychological researches, some participants said they lacked confidence in their own judgments and decided to trust the group's; others simply did not want to appear different from the majority; and some convincingly denied that their perception was erroneous (Asch, 1951, 1952, 1956).

Sherif and Sherif (1969) have reported that from their researches:

> If a person is placed alone in a dark room, he will report movement (of a stationary light). If a number of trials are conducted, in which he is asked to tell how far the light 'moves,' he will tend to establish his own range of movement, on each trial seeing movement that deviates from a certain typical amount.

If several people participate together, hearing each other's reports, their reports of movement will merge into a 'group perception,' even if they had each already established independently his or her own judgment.

The authors conclude:

> New qualities arise in social interaction which are not identical with the properties of behavior of the individual prior to their interaction. Once the group 'anchorage' has been established, it will tend to persist in group members. Even if tested alone, they will tend to see movement in terms of the group norm. (ibid.)

Participants easily adopt respective roles and behaviors within the group. Even when group roles are arbitrarily assigned and represent extreme deviations from one's ordinary life, participants seem to be exceptionally agile at adapting to the requirements of role. (See, for example, the prisoners and guards experiment at Stanford: Haney, Banks & Zimbardo, 1973) Thus, group members may also be influenced without their conscious knowledge to behave in ways in which the group approves.

The reactions to this assertion are noteworthy. Some group participants say, 'This is nonsense. I am not so easily influenced. I am free to choose how I shall behave.' However, what people think of as uniquely held opinions, feelings and beliefs, when investigated, may be found to be shared by others. For example, college men and women in the United States were found to believe that their personal values and beliefs are what made them unique. However, the surprising result of a research of 200 male and female university students investigating this hypothesis showed that the belief that an individual thought set him or her apart from others was, in fact, what that person most had in common with the others. The men thought their unreligious views distinguished them from one another and the women thought what marked them as different was their liberal sexual attitudes (Brandt & Fromkin, 1974).

Furthermore, the importance of maintaining an illusion of uniqueness was illustrated by researches that showed that individuals will begin to change what they believe is a private view when told that their (previously imagined unique) attitude, in fact, is held by their colleagues (Snyder & Fromkin, 1980).

In groups, some people who have acted in a manner they later consider to have been unusual, will invent elaborate ritual or magical explanations to account for their behavior. On the other hand, some participants, in fact, do not come under the group's influence. They may be so busy trying to surrender to the contagious emotions that they are unable to do so. All of these reactions have also been observed in laboratory studies (Hefferline, Keenan & Harford, 1959).

As stable as ordinary consciousness appears to be, it is remarkably easy to enter other states of consciousness such that one's behavior and thought patterns are significantly different. Relevant to the induction of such states of consciousness among members of large group workshops are: fatigue (Tyler, 1955), emotional tension (Sargant, 1957), anger and frustration (Goodman et al., 1974), relaxing of critical faculties (Ludwig, 1966), fasting (Field, 1960), ambiguity and confusion (Frank, 1961), boredom (Heron, 1957), concentration on a dynamic or charismatic speaker (Ludwig, 1967), listening to music, singing, and dancing (Deren, 1970), public confessions of feelings (Lifton, 1961), as well as being isolated from routine daily life, being intensely engaged in artistic creation, problem-solving, meditation, fervent prayer, long vigils with a troubled friend or enduring intensive group meetings, and the ingestion of alcohol, caffeine, and other mind-altering chemicals. Even eating a meal together may alter significantly the perceptions of participants (Razran, 1938). Thus, there are physiological factors, psychological factors and sociological factors which affect consciousness and behavior, all of which may be present in large groups, as well as in the course of psychotherapy. Considering the possibilities, it would be surprising, if people in large group workshops did not experience an altered state of consciousness.

Many other factors influence consciousness. Space may provoke significant changes in mood and behavior (Mintz, 1956; Barker, 1968). In spite of praising the qualities of the location (breathtaking sea, romantic Greek island, alpine freshness, old-world charm) in their accounts of person-centered workshop experiences, it is *very* rare that participants credit the *space* itself as influential in their experience. The place is thought of as merely 'icing on the cake': What a great group. And weren't we lucky to be in such beautiful surroundings at the same time.

Except for accounts of religious retreats to a remote area for self-reflection, little is heard of the effect of place. It always surprises me to hear (as I did recently at an international conference) a psychologist, while promoting his technique, relate that the most astonishing results were being obtained in *workshops* which had begun to be held in resort settings. Lavishing praise on his own invention, he showed no apparent awareness that merely gathering a group of purposeful people in a stimulating ambiance could account for the major part of his amazement.

If the effects of trance are considered more closely, one finds that in such states of consciousness people have reported experiencing changes in perception, a sense of unreality, a melting into their surroundings, blank-mindedness, a loss of control, disconnection from parts of their bodies and other strange sensations. Also, feeling happy, powerful, feeling like a different person, being fascinated with certain thoughts, and feeling under the control of others have been reported (Ludwig & Levine, 1965). Supposing that through participation in a large group workshop, one's ordinary state of consciousness is altered and he may engage in behaviors that are disruptive to others, perhaps even destructive and that he may later regret, how can this be worthwhile? When one considers the nuisance and dangers of drunkenness, of spontaneous possession, of homicidal binges by those in psychotic states, the tragedy of Charcot's hysterics, as well as the frenzies of mobs and their impulsive crimes (LeBon, 1895; McDougall, 1928), it may be difficult to imagine what value varied states of consciousness may have in human adaptation. On the other hand, it is difficult to accept, as Ludwig (1966) quipped, that it is merely to provide subjects for nightclub hypnotists that humans have developed the capacity to enter trance.[2]

In such states, habitual patterns of thinking are not in force and the person may be highly suggestible and may experience 'reality' in completely different ways. What he once regarded as 'impossible' becomes possible: superhuman feats are even possible. Ludwig (1967), a researcher of special states of consciousness, says of such experiences:

> The person no longer seems bound to the necessity for syllogistic reasonings ... the distinctions between cause and effect may vanish, the notion of time may become more relative, opposites can coexist and not seem contradictory ... A type of 'perceptual cognitive restructuring' tends to occur in which the individual has available new avenues of experience and expression.

Thus, what is also possible in such states is the experience of extraordinary abilities and creativity, not only destructiveness. Indeed, creative activity involved in plastic art, literature, music, science often results from perceptions that exceed 'the generalized reality orientation.' The effect of group, then, can result in other unexpected benefits: new perceptions, even special insight, resolution of difficult problems, and delicate and intelligent decisions. It is within the nature of humans in collectives to act mild or violent, purposeful or senseless, constructive or destructive, wise or foolish. In order to consider the potential value of the effect of group, it is perhaps worthwhile to review briefly groups that have cultivated trance states and the positive uses to which they have been put.

Traditional Groups

In the context of an organized system of personality change or religion in which they are usually found, trance states are not necessarily regarded as manifestations of pathology. Ribeiro (1956), analyzing the Rorshach tests of *Xangô* mediums in Brazil, concluded that they were in the normal range and were fairly well adjusted. Stainbrook (1952) concluded that, though hysterical characters could be found among the Brazilian *candomblé* mediums, a schizophrenic could not function in the controlled and complex structure of the *candomblé* rituals.

In addition to Afro-Brazilian systems such as *macumba* (Bramly, 1977) and *umbanda* (Camargo, 1961), several other traditional systems of personality change have been amply described: such as that practiced in Bali (Belo, 1960), the French colonial versions of Voudoun (Ravencroft, 1965; Deren, 1970), fundamental Christianity (Cleveland, 1916) and Pentacostalism (Goodman et al., 1974).

The practices of traditional systems in facilitating personality change vary from solitary quiet meditations to such as the Salish Indian tribe of North America where, in a specially designed place, troubled members are blindfolded, restrained, beaten, lifted, lowered and whirled about as part of a violent and noisy ritual in which they undergo 'death and rebirth' (Jilek, 1974). Expressing one's feelings to a kind listener in a private room would fall somewhere between these extremes.

The ritual, in addition to preserving the knowledge of the system, provokes an altered state of consciousness in participants that probably renders them more receptive to the commanding principles of the system. The ritual also projects these principles by virtue of a specifically selected place, decorative symbols, music, and behaviors of participants and representatives. Ravencroft (1965), from studying Voudoun, observes that, 'Social structure, ritual activity, singing, dancing, drumming, and ceremonial focus on specific gods combine to create a dramatic social atmosphere and mentality which redefines reality. Individual thought and feeling are transcended by collective action and sentiment.' With appropriate changes in the ritual's description, perhaps this could serve to describe a large group workshop as well.

Although in trance states the 'generalized reality orientation' may have little influence, it apparently is maintained by the organism. In sleep, for example, in the midst of a vivid dream one may suddenly have the realization that one is dreaming, without interrupting the dream. In hypnosis studies a 'hidden observer'—some part of the person's mind that can communicate with the hypnotist—has also been discovered to be aware of 'unconscious' activities performed while under hypnosis (Hilgard, 1977; James, 1890).

William James (1890), describes the 'lower phases' of the phenomenon which is perhaps most relevant in considering large group workshop experiences.

> Mediumistic possession in all its grades seems to form a perfectly natural special type of alternate personality, and the susceptibility to it in some form is by no means an uncommon gift, in persons who have no other obvious nervous anomaly ... Inspirational speaking, playing on musical instruments, etc., also belong to the relatively lower phases of possession, in which the normal self is not excluded from conscious participation in the performance, though their initiative seems to come from elsewhere.

Traditional groups have discovered various ways to discipline this state and to use it constructively. For example, in the Nubian Zar ceremonies of Ethiopia, the Nile Valley, and Southern Iran, through singing and dancing the group leader and participants enter trance states in which symptoms of mental illness are said to be alleviated and cured (Favazza & Faheem, 1983).

Fasting, in addition to singing and dancing, has also been used in a group setting to induce trance states in Ghana; not for curing the individual patient, but in developing the healers themselves. Healers and 'spiritual guides' are also trained through the use of trance states in Afro-Brazilian cults such as *candomblé* and *umbanda*.[3]

'Primitive' does not necessarily mean wise. Without the guidance of a tradition and disciplined learning, these same trance states manifest in bizarre ways. For example, Sargant (1957) describes how in West Africa the Soughay migrants, returning to the Ivory Coast from a visit to the Gold Coast where ritual possession is practiced, when aroused to suggestibility by drumming were possessed, not by the spirits of the ancient tradition, but by the governor general of the Gold Coast, or senior officers in the West African Rifles, or even by the impressive railway engine which transported them to and fro. The fledgling mediums, in the possessed state, mimed the gestures realistically of whatever 'spirit' possessed them. The lack of consistent wisdom among 'spirits' may have prompted Maria José a *macumba* cult leader in Brazil, to say, 'No one is going to make me think that all you have to do is to die to attain knowledge' (Bramly, 1977).

For the specialists of the tradition, the constructive trance is easily distinguishable from other manifestations. Maria José, a *mãe do Santo*, takes action to quiet mediums who enter a destructive trance.

> Whatever the motive of the trance may be, the personality of the medium has nothing to do with it. One minute the medium is herself and the next minute, she no longer exists: the god has entered her body. But these moments are easy to tell apart. (Bramly, 1977: 45–6)

Thus, a great deal of training and discipline goes into making the trance a productive experience both for the medium and the community.

Although workshop participants may enter into a profound trance or even exhibit psychotic-like symptoms, it is probably the 'relatively lower phases of possession' that are likely to be of constructive value and should be studied. The more extreme versions of trance are presented here not to *describe* large group workshops but to suggest the range of possibility of such events and the need to understand further these phenomena.

The large group also exposes many of its tribal characteristics—both positive and negative. Perhaps it could be called an 'acephalous tribe,' inasmuch as there is no single leader and the members participate in decision-making and are supposedly equal in status. Although many participants are atheists, an exact belief is unwittingly practiced. For the sacred autonomy of the individual, for example, the tribe will fight fiercely—both within and without its own ranks. Part of the ritual that produces hyperaesthesia consists of breaking with ordinary life, confessing feelings in public, confronting diverse values in tedious sessions that are frequently indecisive, experiencing confusion, ambiguity, strong emotions, prolonged silences in the general assemblies, going with little sleep, irregular meals, celebrating and other means of emotional arousal. Having been rendered suggestible, the individual is assisted by the group to explore 'elevated consciousness', a closer identity with the group, just as in the more readily recognizable tribes. The person-centered tribe does not lack legends, myths, tradition, initiation rites, councils of elders debating the finer points of law ('therapist conditions') and so forth.

Value of Trance States in Human Functioning

In traditional systems, the trance state occurs in an accepting cultural framework. A ritual both helps to induce these states and to provide the critical faculty for understanding and channeling the medium's behavior into useful acts. As Maya Deren (1970) states:

> The individual participates in the accumulated genius of the collective, and by such participation becomes himself a part of that genius—something more than himself. *His exaltation results from his participation*, it does not precede and compel it. (p. 229)

Thus, individuals under the 'effect of group' participate in a collective activity which changes both the individuals and the society in which they live. Large groups from the person-centered approach also deal with stress, promote individual awareness, and advance the social order of the community and, as in traditional systems, the person may emerge more complete, with 'a strengthened and refreshed sense of his relationship to cosmic, social, and personal elements' of life (Deren, 1970).

Healing

One of the functions of traditional groups seems to be the promotion of healing. Medical practices, in traditional systems (and perhaps in modern systems as well), have realized their effectiveness when patients (and sometimes the healers and sometimes both) are in trance states. Tart (1969) adds that such practices are also the society's way of creating 'modes of reducing frustration, stress, and loneliness through group action.'

The Zar healing ritual is said to alleviate and cure symptoms of mild depression, anxiety, somatoform disorders, and chronic schizophrenia in (usually) female patients as a 'last resort' form of treatment. Favazza and Faheem (1983) state, 'The Zar ceremony results in neither insight nor verbalization of social-psychological problems nor working through conflicts. Rather, emotions are aroused and intensified through the dramatization of a dangerous confrontation with evil spirits. The special ceremonial atmosphere, the rituals, and the wearing of new clothes heighten the drama.'

Personal development

In Haiti, participants in the Voudoun ceremonies, 'learn love and beauty in the presence and person of *Erzulie*, experience the ways of power in the diverse aspects of *Ogoun*, become familiar with the implications of death in the attitudes of *Ghede*. A participant sings in the chorus, and feels in his own person that surge of security which is harmonious collective action. He witnesses the wisdom of ancestral and divine counsel, with its history and experience, for his own guidance in action. In effect, he understands the principles because he sees them function.' 'The ritual,' further observes Deren (1970), 'reaffirms first principles—destiny, strength, love, life, death; it recapitulates a man's relationship to his ancestors, his history, as well as his relationship to the contemporary community; it exercises and formalizes his own integrity and personality, tightens his disciplines, confirms his morale. In sum, he emerges with a strengthened and refreshed sense of his relationship to cosmic, social and personal elements … *The miracle is, in a sense, interior. It is the doer who is changed by the ritual, and for him, therefore, the world changes accordingly.*'

Though the 'miracle' of change may be interior, the system and its organization appears to be important. An overly organized or unintegrated system can be quite banal. It has been reported, for example, that the Cree Indians use TV soap operas, such as the *Edge of Night*, to make predictions and future decisions (Gransberg, Steinbring & Hamer, 1977).

It is not to be 'high'—in an altered state of consciousness—nor only to heal, that the ritual finds value. 'For in the final analysis, what is important, is not only what the servitor does (which might conceivably be the right thing for the wrong reasons) nor what he consciously understands (which would vary according to his intellectual capacity) but *what he has become* as a result of his participation in those ceremonials' (Deren, 1970).

To organize the community's values, direction, decisions

In Haiti, in the Voudoun cult, *Legba*, the principle of Life; *Carrefour*, the young man at the crossroads; *Ghede*, life which is eternally present; *Damballah wedo*, the ancient venerable father; *Simbi*, the patron of magic; *Agwe*, ruler of the sea; *Ogoun*, the warrior hero; *Erzulie*, goddess of love, are archetypes which on occasion are expressed through mediums and imparted to the community.

Deren (1970) observes, this

> system of mental and emotional convictions upon which the very survival of the community is dependent, does not, and *could* not require of them that they perceive and understand its principles on an abstract, metaphysical level in order that they be inspired to participate in it. On the contrary, every possible physical technique—particularly drumming and dancing—is used to involve the individuals in activities in which those metaphysical and moral principles are structurally implicit, so that these are, in a sense, unconsciously absorbed by the participant. This is no more, but certainly no less, than a highly developed form of 'learning by doing' educational method ... Indeed, it is precisely because these concepts have been unconsciously absorbed and have become the very premises of their subsequent thought-patterns, that the individuals are least aware of them as explicit concepts.

The Afro-Brazilian cults, such as *macumba*, also constitute a system which preserves the community's accumulated knowledge in ritual. 'My son,' says Maria José, 'our gods and spirits are all we have. We have nothing else, no sacred texts, no monuments, no enduring references. That is both our weakness and our strength.' How the medium feels, personally, is not significant to Maria José. The trance benefits the community. The medium volunteers her body and self to the spirit (Bramly, 1977).

In Ghana, when a spirit 'takes' a person and drives him furiously into the forest, this is thought to be a sign of a strong calling to the priesthood. The one who survives the ordeal is apprenticed to an experienced priest. Under the elder's guidance using the discipline of traditional rituals and values, the initiate learns to speak coherently in the trance state, becoming the oracle of some *obusum* and thereby bringing messages to the community. The priest's utterances develop through what Field (1960) calls, a 'curious blend of gainfully directed hysteria and patient self-discipline.' They have the authority to speak for public opinion and the society's moral code with personal immunity. A productive trance seems to be shaped by a mature or stable personality in the medium and by self-discipline under the tutelage of the commanding principles of the tradition.

Discipline and knowledge are essential. Maria José herself no longer enters trance. Her role now is to facilitate the ceremonies. 'I am there to make sure the gods help everyone. I do whatever I can to control the trances so that they are neither dangerous nor ineffective.' Though she controls, she does not pacify the spirits or the mediums. 'The trance should be harmonious. And that does not necessarily exclude violence. It's in the nature of the possession of certain gods to be brutal' (Bramly, 1977).

The personalities of the archetypes are necessary for the community's needs, but just like community values, they are not necessarily harmonious. *Exu*, in *umbanda,* a foreigner who had led a wicked life, in *macumba* is a sort of lovable scoundrel. He plays tricks on people and makes fun of some. Maria José defends him:

> But he isn't necessarily wrong, is he? People are often ridiculous. *Exu* tries to exalt the parts of us that are most alive. He is very close to us. I would even go so far as to call him the most human of the gods ... People weren't made to be machines. Part of us is madness, a necessary madness *Exu* is master of—this is the most creative part of us. It is the source of our evolution. Without *Exu* what would our lives be? Nothing but a monotonous repetition of passionless acts. (Bramly, 1977)

Exu specializes in the 'art of letting one situation spill over into another, and so giving things a new dimension. This also gives him his reputation of mischieviousness' (ibid.).

Adapting to uncertainty

The mass religious movements of Europe, particularly those surrounding John Wesley's preaching, have also been viewed as functioning to serve to advance social and political forms. Political scientist Frederick Davenport (1968) claims that the 'very gathering of such masses of men with a common purpose was in unconscious sympathy with the drift of the age. It's like had never been known before in England. The fundamental democratic right of assembly was not yet evolved.' Thus, people falling in trance states in mass meetings did not serve the church so much as it served democracy. 'The mass meeting, the platform speech, the political pamphlet freely and widely distributed—these were the very organs of public opinion in the democratic movement, and they were in large measure the outgrowth of the revival.'

Groups functioned in ways that were not for merely social or religious purposes. Those revival groups, in 'unconscious sympathy with the drift of the age,' may have allowed people to pick up information and ideas out of the air, so to speak, allowing for the social and political development of the community.

Transpersonal awareness

'The Ntwumuru and Krachi peoples,' writes Williams (1971), who studied the Sokodal West African dance, 'like the people of most post-industrialized societies, are not expressing *themselves* in their dances so much as they are *expressing a set of values.*' The ritual thus serves purposes which transcend individuality. 'To worship the Loa,' writes Deren (1970), 'is to celebrate the principle, not the matter in which it may be momentarily or permanently manifest ... The function of and purpose of such divine manifestation is the reassurance and the instruction of the community.'

The ritual contains not only the means for inducing trance states but also a framework—a different reality orientation—within which the consciousness of the participant may function constructively. Through apprenticeship there is always a living representation of the ritual, who, unlike elected figureheads, has experienced the effects of the ritual and learned their significance and perhaps how to teach mediums to discipline their trance state in order to inform the current collection of individuals. Thus, through the community, the ritual framework, with its grand archetypes, finds a voice in an individual who can express its wisdom in terms of that particular community at that time. In turn, the individual instructs the community. The individual creates the group that creates him.

A harmonious group may be a starting point, not end-point, of transpersonal awareness. The special state of consciousness is a capacity for greater purposes:

> in all this cosmic variety, the constant is the mind of man ... It is as if the mind, by-passing the particularities of circumstance, the limitations and imprecisions of the senses, arrived, by paths of metaphysical reason, at some common principled truth of the matter. (Deren, 1970)

Under the influence of the large group workshop, the ordinary reality orientation is relaxed and participants' perception, concentration, mental powers may also be extended. What once was regarded as 'impossible' becomes possible; 'opposites can coexist and not seem contradictory'; the person has 'new avenues of experience and expression.' The boundary between self and others may relax and a feeling of 'oneness' might even be experienced. Thus, although wild or uncontrolled crowd behavior is always possible, the group's traditions and a few people who have experienced a successful workshop are helping to facilitate a context for constructive actions. Participants, through their *participation*, may become part of the accumulated knowledge of the collective, be healed, resolve personal problems, 'confirm their morale,' and gain an increased sense of their relationship to each other and even perhaps to cosmic elements. The experience participants live together also provides guidance to the group through a 'learning by doing' education and helps them adapt to uncertainty. The form adopted by these workshops is determined by the people who participate and their customs. Thus, democratic principles are served in the group's innovations of self-government and problem-solving. Each individual is respected as the group strives for efficiency and wisdom.

Thus, healing, personal growth, resolution of personal problems, increased self-confidence, improved relationships, adapting to uncertainty, guidance for the community, transpersonal awareness, are some of the dimensions along which the large group workshop might progress. The first few, which concern the individual and relationships between individuals in the group are the same outcomes as in the therapeutic relationship and the small group.

The large group, though frustrating, confusing, even exasperating at times, may be a teacher for the seeker, a therapist for the client, provider of alternatives to the problem-solver, inspiration for the artist. The essence of its creative state may come not from one person, with the answers, but out of a group of persons with inquisitiveness, good will, shared expectancy, not fully realizing that a wisdom may be hidden in their searching.

Participant's Creative State

> [F]or true community presupposes freedom in action and freedom to renounce one's right as an individual for the sake of one's fellow men. Masses are made up of passive beings, driven together by equal needs and equal anxiety ...
>   Kurt Goldstein

On the level of the group, Ruth Benedict defined 'synergy' as a group which fused selfishness and unselfishness 'by transcending their oppositeness and polarity so that the dichotomy between selfishness and altruism is resolved and transcended and formed into a new and higher unity' (Maslow, 1965). Though rare, some groups seem to have had, and continue to have, this ability to develop the consciousness necessary to reduce stress, facilitate self-realization, make intelligent decisions, serve religious and social functions, facilitate perceptual and social changes, and to guide and instruct the community from sources of knowledge which transcend the private person.

In the resolution of crises, problems, in intelligently coordinating its activities without plans, legislating or parliamentary procedures, and in group learning, the person-centered large group workshops allowed each person (including a protagonist, if there was one) his own say; each person influenced the outcome. Conflicting values were reformulated and frequently the culture was transformed. Eventual solutions being found within the new cultural matrix. In such cases, the group functioned coherently, effectively, with wisdom and efficiency and what resulted were just actions. The successful group is not bound by its own previous organization. Originality, not mere novelty, is a mark of its actions. The right to be out of step is also respected. The group allows each person to add his own contribution—no matter how incomprehensible it seems at the moment, no matter how timid, forceful, sensible, delinquent, or even contradictory it may seem. Each autonomous utterance, though it adds to the complexity, has significance. Without compromising, the group settles for only intelligent actions which are just, growth-promoting or healing for the individual and the community. The group, at these times, consists of the spontaneous cooperation of diverse individuals applying initiative. The individual's awareness of the group's patterns—the coherent thoughts and actions of the group brought about by all the individual thoughts and actions—gives the group a self-consciousness. The thoughts, sentiments, possibilities of the community and the isolated human consciousness may not be the same; they may not be *one*, but they are not *two*.

Neither a collective point of view, nor an individualistic point of view need be favored. The advantages to be gained from the perspective of the individual can be matched by the often radically different perspective of the group. Likewise, since a level of stupidity, impulsivity, and cruelty, equal to that found in a collective, may also be found in the lone individual, no judgment may be made on the superiority of one of the two viewpoints. Both are necessary at the same time for an effective group. If one insists on only the collective point of view, people may be bullied into conformity by the majority, while the group flounders in ineffectivity. Robots, not persons, may be produced. Group wisdom falls to the lowest common denominator and individual initiative and talent are often wasted. On the other hand, to insist only on the individualistic viewpoint is equally perilous. The 'deeply personal' perspective often ignores the fact that we are inextricably intertwined with others. By ignoring this fact, a unity is less likely. Greed, corruption, injustice, ineffectivity are the well-known side effects of this extreme.

What is the attitude of participants which allows one group not only to surpass the accomplishments of individual members, while others end without ever reaching the level of capability of one of their individual members? Speculations would include that participants seem to be intensely involved, both autonomously *and* cooperatively. Their expectations, attitudes, values, beliefs, capacity for empathic understanding doubtless affect the outcome. They are sensitive to one another's feelings and thoughts as they follow together a thread of consciousness *and* sensitive to the overall patterns created by the group.

Good Will

A lack of good will, such as in the organizers rigidly imposing psychological techniques and not re-adapting to the needs of the group or the participants, or adhering to a predetermined position with no intention of changing, may prevent the group from functioning constructively. This point is illustrated in the Fermeda Workshop which brought together members of three African states involved in a border dispute. A participant made this observation, 'there is no direct relationship between the development of empathy and the extent to which the delegates were able to free themselves from commitments to the policies already held by their respective governments on the issue' (Okumu, 1970).

He goes on to say:

As long as participants from the Republic of Somalia adhered to their government's policy that the Ogaden (in Ethiopia) and the North Eastern Province (in Kenya) should become integral parts of Somalia, the Fermeda experiment did not convince them to the contrary ... In other words, the opening up of the self during the training phase and the free and open discussions relative to the problem, its magnitude, and its costliness, together with the effort expended in the T-groups to suggest possible ways and means to achieving lasting peace came to naught. (ibid.)

Compared to the atmosphere of mutual trust and confidence in the small groups, the general assembly or large group

> became an anti-climax: many individuals spoke up mostly for purposes of exhibition, a characteristic of public negotiations and parliamentary procedures. Perhaps for this and other covert reasons the consensual basis of group action exhibited in the small T-groups was totally lacking. The General Assembly thus fell short of the expectation that it would be an integral part of the process of generating better communication and understanding of vital questions. (Doob, 1970)

One of the T-groups made 'notably greater progress than the other: brainstorming sessions were more serious and productive, the disputes were examined more carefully and with less avoidance behavior; the solutions proposed were more specific; and the group stood more solidly behind its own recommendations.' In the 'laggard group' there was an individual whose

> aggressive, uncontrolled behavior, often exacerbated by drink, seemed most probably to be idiosyncratically, not culturally determined. This group never developed a means of reducing or neutralizing his erratic and sometimes calculatedly disruptive behavior, which seemed to manifest itself most when some progress or agreement was close at hand. (Doob, 1970)

It is not a matter of disagreement or being out of step with the majority or contributing differently than the others that is disruptive. Silence is not necessarily disruptive and may even contribute to the group's functioning. For example, the report continues, 'Although at times distressing to the organizers and some of the Africans, the silent deviants in that T-group proved non-disruptive, and the group learned to function effectively without their (verbal) contributions.' The unity of consciousness is quite fragile. It is so subtle and vulnerable that anyone with the intention to do so, can sabotage it. One need not be talkative, nice, agreeable, congenial or cordial to preserve unity, only good-willed.

Personal Voice

Though the usefulness of the metaphors of 'organism' or 'group mind' as applied to large groups can be controversial, the large group nevertheless can be seen to *act* coherently. Though the members of the group may bring this about through the sum of their individual actions, this does not necessarily come about through the *coordinated* effort of common thoughts or common feelings or in accordance with personal motives. Participants may have different values and feel quite differently about what they are doing. The sum of their actions, however, brings about a group action.

In fact, the large group restores some of the process of 'individual self-definition' that may be diminished by the small group.[4] In the large group a person may formulate his own thoughts and responses, not a group response. Though his autonomy is apparent, the large group does not allow the illusion that one is not *socius* (a member).

Autonomy/Humility

The description attempted here does not represent how people *should* be, but how they appear *to be* during constructive periods in the meetings. The intense involvement of participants in creative crisis resolution, problem-solving, self-government, seems to be accompanied by what are usually regarded as contradictory (but really complementary) aspects of consciousness occurring together in the individual. One aspect will be called *autonomy*. The person is capable of self-governance, independent thought and action, and expression of her unique thoughts, opinions, beliefs and perceptions in reacting to the group. The person can maintain a separate identity, experiencing personal values and feelings and thoughts in a larger context than merely the present moment. Thus, in the example related in Chapter Six, Julie and Anthony illustrate autonomy by confronting a movement toward unanimity with, 'Wait a minute. This does not feel right to me as an individual.' If the group enthusiasm is moving toward injustice, an expression of autonomy would be, 'I will not take part in this activity and I urge the group to find an alternative.'

What may seem paradoxical, the person is at the same time able to live fully in the moment, abandoning pride, a sense of personal significance, to surrender to something of greater value, something that transcends himself. This aspect will be called *humility*.

One who vigorously puts forward his best idea for a solution to a serious problem the group faces and then, in the next moment, relinquishes his idea, belief, doctrine, perception for one superior in moving toward a solution, would illustrate the convergence of autonomy and humility. One offers her best, then surrenders it for what's better.[5]

Humility

In its ordinary meaning, and one that is intended here, 'humility' signifies an unpretentious absence of pride or self-assertion. It is derived from the word 'humus,' earth. 'Human' came from the word for earth by way of 'humility' and the quality of humility remains deeply human.

As has been mentioned, in intense encounters in the large group, with a narrowing of attention to one speaker, to one vital question, to a compelling dilemma often under soft lighting, participants are doubtless exposed to conditions which provoke a relaxation of the 'generalized reality orientation.' To allow oneself to enter a state of consciousness with broader horizons, would represent an aspect of humility.

The positive outcome of this 'lower level trance' state is the ability to extend powers of physical agility and strength, and, in the case of crises in the large group, to extend concentration, perception, insight, and creativity—to assist the collective. What is called humility allows the person to yield to the creative prospects of different states of consciousness (or different minds), to relax the critical faculties, to surrender opinions, convictions, perceptions, to those superior in inching the group toward just and intelligent outcomes for both individuals and the collective. It allows the mind to bypass 'the particularities of circumstances, the limitations and imprecisions of the senses,' to arrive at 'some principled truth of the matter' (Deren, 1970). This humility allows a voluntary submission of the person's individuality to the group's necessities. The individual is willing to change. She is able to surrender impatience and easy answers for an attentive waiting—alert to follow *or* to lead *or* to remain still.[6]

In this state, the person is able to live unattached to a particular form: at one time, favoring no structured activities; at another time, a highly organized structure. Since solutions which worked before or were successful in other groups are not necessarily effective in a different situation, the person may surrender even the understanding gained from past experience, to live with doubts, with fears, but without being governed by them.

The meaningful meeting of one person with another is part of this humility. Erich Fromm (1956) has called interpersonal fusion

> the most powerful striving in man. It is the most fundamental passion, it is the force which keeps the human race together, the clan, the family, the society. The failure to achieve it means insanity or destruction—self-destruction or destruction of the other.

While not every person in the group may be attracted to each other, may not be admired, or even liked, humility allows each person's existence to be *accepted*, as one accepts the world, without trying to decide if it is to be believed or not. People are able to put themselves in the other's shoes, to sense the meaning of the person's expressions, both for the individual and for the group. Negative feelings are accepted as a reality and not *always* a prelude to destructive action. Different interpretations of the same phenomena are used, not to fuel disputes, but as a basis for inventions. A way is found to blend contradictory facts.

Autonomy

It does not hurt to repeat that groups are capable of destructive as well as constructive acts. Reason is vulnerable. A group of people is always capable of thoughtless behavior.

> Reason and arguments, are incapable of combating certain words and formulas. They are uttered with solemnity in the presence of crowds, and as soon as they have been pronounced an expression of respect is visible on every countenance, and all heads are bowed. (LeBon, 1895)

The same conditions which result in the relaxation of the generalized reality orientation of participants, opening the possibility of creativity, can also, through weakening of critical judgment of group members, open the way for foolish conformity or even mob behavior. This humility can be manipulated if the person gives up a 'dynamic, changing, viable and useful kind of cognitive response' for 'certain kinds of routine and stock thoughts which he is unwilling to examine critically' (Schein et al., 1961: 262). Doubtless, each of us is vulnerable to this tendency. Simone Weil (1951), an ardent anti-Nazi recognizing her need to be wary of her own weaknesses, states, 'I am aware of very strong gregarious tendencies in myself. My natural disposition is to be very easily influenced, and above all by anything collective. I know that if at this moment I had before me a group of twenty young Germans singing Nazi songs in chorus, a part of my soul would instantly become Nazi ... It is wrong to be an "I,", but worse to be a "we."' Without humility to transcend differences, the group lacks the fact of creativity. Without autonomy to express conflicting feelings, the group lacks the tension of creativity.

People who are not susceptible to hypnosis complain that they are unable to forget the situation *as a whole*. They cannot help but think of the absurdity of the suggestions and what friends will think of them afterwards (White, 1941). Sometimes in large group workshops a participant will complain that he cannot 'get into the experience' or that 'people seem to be faking their emotions'; he cannot become cohesive with the group. This is autonomy: too much prevents one from entering the experience and learning from participation; too little, leaves one in the hands of emotional contagion.

Both autonomy and humility are always present. As Meerlo (1956) has observed, 'every individual has two opposing needs which operate simultaneously: the need to be independent, to be oneself; and the need *not* to be oneself, *not* to be anybody at all, *not* to resist mental pressure. The need to be inconspicuous, to disappear, and to be swallowed up by society.'

Autonomy, with its isolated, personal view point, protects against the development of 'true believers.' The private perspective which can take a longer range view, beyond the immediate moment and its attractions, challenges the objectives and fundamental values and processes which guide the group.

The group, to function justly and effectively, needs this attitude even though members expressing it can appear to be at odds with the collective will. With autonomy, the person looks 'at the world from his own independent viewpoint, to tell the truth as he sees it, and so to keep watch and ward in the interest of society as a whole' (Milosz, 1985).

With this critical perspective the person is also less likely to be 'swallowed by efficiency' or 'sacrificed to the higher good' or pressured into becoming 'the correct member of society.' To keep watch over and respect the interest of the group, both as critic and enthusiastic participant, is not a simple matter. One never knows if he is doing the right thing. Nevertheless, he must apply his strength to what he thinks is right (autonomy) and at the same time reserve a corner of doubt; ready, if evidence appears to support it, to counteract his own ideas and even their guiding principles (humility). Inevitably, he will, at times, be at odds with his friends and other group members and will stand alone.

Being able to experience one's own feelings of the present drama of the group *and* have an awareness of a larger context, a sense of life outside the meeting, one is able to express his indignation against violence suffered by a group member, but also make sure that the true criminal is apprehended and not an innocent bystander.

Humility may involve a diminished I–You distinction, timelessness, obliviousness to personal desire; autonomy implies courage, responsibility and intelligence to prevent mindless resignation. It is in the balance of autonomy and humility that dividuals become individuals, in which one may, as Dubos (1981) suggests: 'Live individually, act locally, but take a global perspective.'

Humility and autonomy are two sides of the same coin: the person is vigorously expressive, lucid, delineated *and* functions in a spontaneous congruence, diffused with an intelligent, effective collective of persons. The participant, as Konner (1985) has described behavior in a Kalahari tribe ritual, 'is at once exotically self-involved and heroically selfless.' The conjunction is more than either face. It does not obey the private or the universal. This conjunction faces life with the energy of expectancy but with few expectations. It is interested in *being* community, not 'forming community,' striving for 'unity' or trying to 'create community,' which will likely end in the opposite. Contrary to conventional expectation, its autonomy functions for unity of the whole; its humility functions for individual expressions and growth.[7]

Notes

1. It was even discovered that results could be obtained by provoking emotions of fear and anger, not from the actual, but, from imaginary events. For example, a patient who had collapsed in a tank battle was given the suggestion that he had to fight his way out of a burning tank. Outbursts of fear and rage led to emotional collapse, followed by dramatic relief of nervous symptoms. (It is worth noting that little was reportedly gained by inducing a melancholic patient to weep.)

2. Recalling that the word 'mob' comes from *mobilus vulgus*, negative aspects of this phenomenon have been amply supplied by Trotter (1915). What is sought here is an explanation that includes the positive aspects as well.

3. In Brazil, mediums frequently enter trance (even on the first occasion) merely by spinning themselves around a few times. (Goodman, Henney & Pressel, 1974). As I witnessed in the Philippine Islands, practiced mediums can enter trance with only a moment's concentration and a flick of the head (see also Belo, 1960).

4. This is a major criticism of encounter groups. (Koch, 1970).

5. Koestler (1978) has proposed a polarity of 'tendencies' in human beings: the 'self-assertive tendency' and the 'integrative tendency.' In this view, each of us is a 'holon,' asserting our individualities as a whole in our own right and also as a part integrated into a larger whole.

More recently, Diekman (1990), writing about modern North American cults, uses 'compliance' and 'dissent' to describe the two modes of consciousness that, when used in contradiction result in less effectiveness than when used complementarily. He gives a very convincing example of a group of American government officials which, acting in a compliant way, made a decision that resulted in a diplomatic disaster. This same group, reconvened to decide on another similarly urgent and complex problem, changed its manner of deliberations to respect defiant opinions. Compliance based on this respect for defiance resulted in a decision which, this time, produced a successful action.

Here I have preferred to approach these relations from the subjective viewpoint because that is how most group participants understand their experience. The important aspect of any consideration of these relations is their intelligent expression—appropriate for the individual and for the larger whole. The creative state does not seem to be so much one tendency winning out over the other, as both tendencies expressed fully together (perhaps this constitutes a *third*). It may be possible to cultivate such a division of consciousness into one comprehensive act. Hirst, Neisser and Spelke (1978) found that, with training, two persons volunteering for the experiment could be taught to read with normal speed and comprehension on one subject while *simultaneously* writing on *another* subject.

6. LeBon (1895) says that the crowd is not dependent on numbers but on the 'disappearance of conscious personality.' Doubtless there is a diminishment of 'conscious personality' in the group, just as there may be a diminishment of 'conscious sociability' when a person is isolated. A creative state may exist when participants in the group are conscious, at the same time, of both their individual and social selves and have summoned the best qualities of both.

7. In the paradigm of multiminds (Ornstein, 1986), one might say that the governing portion of the mind, which has yielded to other portions more suitable for cooperative tasks such as problem-solving, continues to function at the same time: the person is using more than one mind at once!

One may also recognize in autonomy, the 'congruence' of the client-centered therapist; in humility, the 'empathic understanding' and 'unconditional acceptance.' Learnings about their conjunction in the large group setting might also improve the function of psychotherapy.

CHAPTER TEN

On Becoming a Culture

[A] mode of truth; not of truth central and coherent, but of truth angular and splintered
De Quincey

Rogers reorganized the way he had been taught to practice psychotherapy (Freudian orientation, taking case histories, etc.) and built up an understanding of the success of his new system of personality change in terms acceptable to the North American culture. Reorganizations of knowledge and the consequent improvement of technologies are continually taking place. The pattern is all too familiar, but nevertheless worth studying. Although indisputable at the time, when viewed in retrospect many treatments appear ridiculous.

Systems of Personality Change and Success

In the history of 'successful' medical practice, for example, one finds reputable and honored doctors confidently prescribing, among other things, crocodile dung, frog sperm, eunuch fat, fly specks, dried viper lozenges, furs, feathers, hair, human perspiration, oil from ants, human and animal blood and excretions, and moss scraped from the skull of a victim of violent death (Shapiro, 1971). In not too distant times, cold water immersion, flogging, disorienting patients by swinging them in all directions, electric shocks, and puncturing the frontal lobes of the brain with an icepick have been popular and 'effective' treatments for psychological disorders.

Although many of these treatments were doubtless harmful to the patient, some probably facilitated the cure of some people (the placebo effect would predict a certain number). The developers and representatives of such systems should not always be considered charlatans (although doubtless a certain number are, as in any profession). They may be sold on their own approach, may be reluctant to accept new information, may refuse to revise their concepts, may defend and promote their techniques even after they are shown to be wanting and may tend to regard the worth of their own shaky theories as superior to others'. This could be due to sordid commerciality, to fiery ambition, to simple self-deception or merely to *unexpected success*. As the system develops more complexity and convincingness and as the techniques become more reliable, even the founder may become astonished by the effectiveness of his or her system of personality change or healing. The following account is an example of such startling success and how it can produce a confident advocate.

In 1930, Franz Boas published the biography of Quesalid, a Kwakiutl Indian from the region of Vancouver in Canada. Quesalid, a skeptic who was curious to learn the tricks of shamanism in order to expose them, allowed himself to be tutored by a shaman and initiated into his system. Quesalid learned the sacred songs, methods of inducing vomiting, the deployment of spies to pick up bits of information about the illnesses of various people. Most of all, he mastered the technique: the shaman concealed a tuft of down in the corner of his mouth and, after biting his tongue to make it bleed, he sucked at the body of the patient, finally spitting out the 'bloody worm' as evidence that the infection had been removed.

Even before Quesalid had completed his studies, he was summoned to treat a sick person who had dreamed of him. No one was more shocked than Quesalid himself to find the method he employed successful. Still, he interpreted the miraculous cure as due to the patient believing 'strongly in his dream about me.'

Quesalid was astonished even more when he witnessed the methods of shamans in the neighboring Koskimo region who, instead of producing the bloody down as evidence of exorcized illness, merely spat a little saliva into their palms. Anticipating the current disputes over differences between rival schools of psychotherapy, he wondered, 'What is the value of such a method? This cannot be a real treatment. What is the theory behind it?' Afterwards, Quesalid treated a woman for whom the Koskimo treatment had failed. Through *his* method, he gave the patient something. His rivals only *claimed* to have captured the illness. Not only that, his approach *worked*. His faith in his own approach having been bolstered, he set about exposing all imposters and their 'false methods,' earned pride in his achievements and staunchly defended his practice against all competitive approaches (Levi-Strauss, 1967).

Originally, Rogers had applied his *approach* to the treatment of problem children. The principle of his psychotherapy, that there is a self-sufficient 'drive toward mental health' within each person, was derived from a basic belief of the approach. It was used to mount forceful and persuasive arguments *against* psychotherapy. He argued that viewing the use of foster homes, for example, as inferior to psychotherapy in the treatment of problem children was 'both unrealistic and unfortunate.' He declared:

> We shall not be inclined to look down upon treatment involving manipulation of the environment, if we recall the fundamental axiom upon which it is based, namely, that most children, if given a reasonably normal environment which meets their own emotional, intellectual, and social needs, have within themselves sufficient drive toward mental health to respond and make a comfortable adjustment to life. (Kirschenbaum, 1979: 75)

As Quesalid, Rogers rejected the accepted forms of treatment of the day. In Rogers' case this was psychoanalysis. Likewise, when he had achieved successes and his system of psychotherapy had become evolved, Rogers defended it against competing schools—including the behaviorists who favored 'manipulation of the environment'—and even competing currents of thought. For example, a student, Fred Fiedler, proposed a research that might show that expert therapists from *different* schools were more alike in their practice of psychotherapy than they were to those less expert from their *own* schools. Rogers, according to Fiedler, said that, 'he wouldn't believe this study even if it came out the way I said it might' (Kirschenbaum, 1979: 204).

Fiedler's (1950) research *did* show that the therapeutic practice of nationally known expert therapists from psychoanalytic, client-centered, and Adlerian therapy lines were more like each other than like those of non-experts within their own line. The therapist's intervention or non-intervention, activity or passivity, did not prevent a good therapeutic relationship from forming in which, among other things, the more practiced therapist remained sensitive to the feelings of the client, while the less experienced one was more likely to wander to his own concerns. The accomplished therapists (experts) could better understand what the client was trying to communicate and what meaning this had for him. The Fiedler study, though not confirming his beliefs, still could support Rogers' theory and perhaps helped to awaken more interest in the therapeutic relationship. It is likely that Rogers' protectionism was based on a belief that developed from success he had witnessed with his own eyes. He was not so sure of the others, but his approach really worked. William James (1948), commenting on the advantages of the self-centered perspective, observed, 'Science would be far less advanced then she is, if the passionate desires of individuals to get their own faiths confirmed had been kept out of the game' (p. 102).

Doing Nothing

Although effective in his own time, one of the reasons Quesalid's methods (and perhaps this may be becoming true of Rogers as well) would be unpopular today is that the healer would be seen as not *doing* anything—according to the perspective determined by present cultural values. On close examination, however, it may be noticed that 'not doing anything' also may work pretty well for modern North Americans when the ritual happens to conform to their current beliefs and expectations.

Consider the following research conducted in the United States: All patients were prepared exactly alike for surgery to relieve *anginas pectoris*. At the moment the operation was to begin, the surgeon was given instructions to perform either a real or simulated operation. In the simulation, the chest was opened and without doing anything else was closed again; in the real operation, the procedure then thought to be curative was followed: the chest was opened, an artery tied off, the chest closed again. It was found that the simulated surgery was equal to the standard (or 'real') operation in reducing symptoms (Beecher, 1961; Cobb et al., 1959; Dimond et al., 1958, 1960).

In common with the healers of other epochs and cultures was a complex trusted procedure involving not only charismatic personalities but also places of high reputation—if not of cathedral proportions, a location maintained in meditative silence—instruments carefully crafted from rare and expensive materials, analyses decipherable only by masters, elaborate cleansing practices, precisely trained apprentices who must prove their devotion to the sacred doctrine, which, if not secret, is largely inaccessible to the laity. A powerful ritual is conducted within the cultural possibilities—a ritual that both doctor and patient believe they must perform for healing to take place.[1]

Cultural Setting

What is called culture is an agreed-upon pattern of thinking, feeling and behaving that each individual learns and shares with others in a particular group. As Kluckhohn (1949) has observed, 'It is one of the important factors which permits us to live together in an organized society, giving us ready-made solutions to our problems, helping us predict the behaviors of others, and permitting them to know what to expect from us' (p. 27). When a person revises her values and behaviors, she is revising the culture.

Client-centered therapy was developed largely in response to a specific culture and responded to the particular necessities of its individuals. The focus on individualism was empowered by a value enunciated by Ralph Waldo Emerson (1929) and also became a principle of client-centered therapy's system:

> To believe your own thought, to believe that what is true for you in your private heart is true for all men—that is genius. A man should learn to detect and watch that gleam of light which flashes across his mind from within, more than the lustre of the firmament of bards and sages.

Van Belle (1980) has suggested that Rogers began to practice psychotherapy when a prominent cultural value might be expressed as, 'the individual should free society.' Client-centered therapy responded to 'an idea whose time had come,' or rather to the need for a corrective, promoting the value that instead the 'society should free the individual.' This was a shift in morality: instead of helping each other, it was now emphasized that each should be himself. But was this new? No. The culture already contained provisions for justifying this emphasis in values. In around 1859, John Stuart Mill had proposed that the person who is more valuable to himself is also more valuable to others.

Opposing values may coexist or come into conflict. For example, in the late 1980s, the insistence on an exclusive 'right to life' divided one segment of the population of the United States from another segment whose members insisted on 'freedom of choice.' Upon each value was mounted a radical movement bent on destroying the competing value. Though they had been brought into confrontation by two warring factions, according to opinion polls at a significant point in the struggle, the average citizen was more likely to continue to favor *both* values, not one over the other. Thus, two values the culture had accommodated were put into conflict by two opposing groups of true-believers.[2]

A system of personality change may also incorporate both accepted beliefs and marginal beliefs that may also be contradictory in certain contexts. Contrary to the norms of society, systems of personality change are much more accepting of a person's actual behavior, although much more exigent of his ideal state of being. Thus, a social deviant may be accepted by the system as a person who is capable of being reformed internally to adopt and conform to the system's principles.

By 'placing greater stress' on the 'feeling aspects,' client-centered therapy was engaged in an activity that was yet to become part of polite company. In this sense, it varied from the main stream of social behavior. At the same time, the intimacy between therapist and client expressed a special aspect of culture that may have already been changing. Client-centered therapy, in a certain sense, was also an agent of this change. In client-centered therapy, 'the selection, emphasis, and positive valuation of certain aspects of human reality,' Barton (1971) recognized, 'come to have primary weight and reality for others.' Thus, client-centered therapy became a 'special form of general cultural process.'[3]

Client-centered therapy, in its formation and transformation have not differed significantly from the general patterns of cultural evolution. The culture, in a strict sense, may not have *caused* client-centered therapy, but neither did client-centered therapy *revolutionize* the culture. They evolved together. Moreover, the principles of client-centered therapy evolved along with the system of personality change they were organizing. The practice of therapy was improved in accordance with new learnings as they were perceived through experience with that very practice. The problems client-centered therapy confronted, the methods used to try to resolve them, and the patterns of thought and language used to formulate theoretical constructs and test them were all of their time and place and of the person-centered approach.

Some of the values shared by client-centered therapists in North America today, for better or worse, include a respect for the uniqueness and worth of the individual, the right to be who one wants to be and to develop one's potentialities, the right to equal treatment by authorities and the same opportunities for wealth as others. Also valued are: active participation in working to achieve one's goals and standing up for one's rights, a trust in the future and a better life and the belief that problems can be solved through effort, concentration and introspection. Though according to these values, others should be helped to help themselves, (paradoxically) one is not obliged to help the society, work for its objectives, nor conform to its formalities. (This latter value may be changing as the person-centered approach is applied in a wider context.)[4]

The client-centered therapist also represents honesty, integrity, peacefulness, strength, and the value expressed by the question, 'Am I living in a way which is deeply satisfying to me, and which truly expresses me?' (Rogers, 1961a).

Most of what we know about client-centered therapy has come from clinical observations and research studies of interviews between a clinical psychologist with attitudes of genuineness and non-judgmental acceptance and certain intentions to help through understanding and support and a client who is anxious due to an incongruence between her self-concept and her actual organismic experience.[5] The ritual called 'psychotherapy' took place in a university counseling room and was determined by the shared beliefs, habits of thought and social conventions of the mid-western United States in the 1950s. The ability of participants to enter a special state of consciousness called 'empathic understanding' figured in success. The purpose was to improve the client's self-concept.[6]

Morality

The cosmology of client-centered therapy includes the belief in a

> formative directional tendency in the universe, which can be traced and observed in stellar space, in crystals, in micro-organisms, in more complex organic life, and in human beings. This is an evolutionary tendency toward greater order, greater complexity, greater interrelatedness. In humankind, this tendency exhibits itself as the individual moves from a single-cell origin to complex organic functioning, to knowing and sensing below the level of consciousness, to a conscious awareness of the organism and the external world, to a transcendent awareness of the harmony and unity of the cosmic system, including humankind. (Rogers, 1980)

It is thought that this tendency will 'actualize' a person's potentialities, if it is not thwarted in some way. It is only necessary to simply 'be.' One need only ask oneself, 'Am I living in a way that is deeply satisfying to me, and which truly expresses me?' (Rogers, 1961a). A social value that may be derived from this might be, 'One has a right to develop his or her potentialities.' And then, 'One has a right to be who he or she pleases.'

It is easy to slip from here into the reasoning: 'If you are not living in a way that is deeply satisfying, you *should* be. Be yourself!' Thus, a morality—what accords and does not accord with the standards of right and wrong—has been formed.

One may find the enforcement of this morality in many activities dealing with the person-centered approach. It is not uncommon, for example, to witness someone say in a group, 'I feel that the group is experiencing a difficult time just now.' Another person will surely add a corrective, 'Wait a minute. You cannot speak for *me*. Don't include me in your *we*. Don't you want to say, "*I* am experiencing a difficult time."?' Such a challenge may have been useful in the days when participants were not in touch with their own feelings and 'projected' them onto others or onto 'the group.' Perhaps the first speaker did intend to say that he was having a difficult time. And perhaps he really wanted to say the *group* was. To automatically challenge the words, without understanding their meaning, is part of enforcing a morality.

It may be acknowledged that this therapy morality has doubtless contributed to advancements in according more respect and dignity to ethnicity, women, to personal sexual preferences, and so forth. Also, atheism or 'new age' religions are now more or less accepted in Rogerian groups.

Nevertheless, such a morality may still obstruct the progress of some participants. As Bergin (1991) has observed, 'many clinicians do not understand or sympathise with the cultural context of their client's [usually more traditional] religious world view, but instead deny their importance and coerce clients into alien values and conceptual frameworks.'

This not only applies to the acceptance of, say, traditional Christianity, but also broad religious questions. For example, a person in a discussion group on the person-centered approach said, 'This approach does not say enough about death.' A therapist in the group immediately replied, 'Well of course we do. If the client brings the subject up.' But what the group participant meant was that for most of what psychotherapy (and science) considers reality, one is 'dead.' According to present scientific doctrine it was not for fifteen billion years after the universe began that life appeared on earth. An individual who was apparently nonexistant during this time, lives some few decades and then dies. This infinitely small slice of time is the only part called, 'reality.' Is there any other reality? Surely this reflection deserves the same consideration as others.

The kind of individual more likely to be accepted within the range of applications of the person-centered approach would be the 'fully functioning person,' a person 'open to experience.' A person not open to experience might easily be considered immoral.

For example, I once witnessed a dispute between two people who were conducting 'person-centered training courses' for health-care workers. After a lengthy, and sometimes heated, discussion, involving charges and countercharges over infringements of territory and other commercial considerations, one of the disputants said he did not wish to discuss the matter further. The other became furious and said, 'You are *unethical*.'

He was not unethical because of the way he conducted business, but because he refused to continue to 'share his feelings.'

A principle derived from client-centered therapy is that the therapist does not take responsibility for the client's feelings, decisions, behavior, and so forth. It is the client who decides what is right for him or her. It is easy to see how, 'The client decides for himself,' may be turned into, 'The client *should* decide for himself.' That is, take responsibility for yourself. Indeed, one could notice Rogers gently nudging his clients toward accepting themselves as worthy of respect. (See his interview with Gloria, for example.)

In a group not long ago, a young woman was trying to convey a complex experience to the others. She said that 'the group' had helped her and she wanted to thank the participants. She said she was aware that she had her part in what had happened, but she was trying to express something *more*. The group had helped her to change the image she had of herself. She felt this would not likely have occured without the others. She did not know how it happened. By bringing it up in the group at this time, she was trying to understand the experience.

A therapist sitting at her side insisted that she rephrase her statement to give herself credit for the change. He was nudging her toward acknowledging the belief that, 'each one has within herself the wisdom and power for self-directed change.' However, she had already made it clear that she acknowledged this and was now trying to explore beyond this point.

His intervention, far from facilitative, was actually impeding this exploration.

Many of the therapeutic attitudes thought to facilitate personality change in psychotherapy have become skewed into rules of behavior. For example, genuineness also becomes, 'Be yourself,' and non-judgmental acceptance becomes the mind-bender, 'It is wrong to make judgments.'

It is ironic that an approach that helped therapy clients move away from 'oughts' and 'shoulds' of the morality of their day to live more their organismic experiencing, would manifest in its applications a morality that could be every bit as enslaving. To be concerned with this aspect of the person-centered approach is not of mere theoretical interest. As Mary Midgley (1991) observes:

> Judging is not in general simply accepting one of two ready-made alternatives as the right one. It cannot be done by tossing up. It is seeing reason to think and act in a particular way. It is a comprehensive function, involving our whole nature, by which we direct ourselves and find our way through a whole forest of possibilities. No science rules here; there is no given system of facts which will map our whole route for us. We are always moving into new territory.

This 'comprehensive function' should be found in all aspects of human nature, even those which are disagreeable. Rogers did not seem to be able to accept that human beings, even when they set out to be helpful, could be harmful. For example, he admitted to being dumbfounded by Milgram's (1974) experiment in which ordinary people applied what they thought were extremely harmful electric shocks in order to jolt a person into learning for his own good. It is not surprising that Rogers was startled. Thirty-nine psychiatrists who were consulted prior to the research said that not one in a thousand subjects would react as Milgram's did. What occured was almost the exact opposite. Not one participant in the experiment refused to execute the procedure and merely walked out of the lab. On the other hand, Greene (1969) in a study with white rats who had within their means (though against their best interests) the power to prevent other rats from being shocked, eight out of ten did so. Is there not something missing in a cosmology or even a system of personality change that does not understand such basic behaviors as these? A human being should have as much altruistic tendencies as a white rat. Shouldn't it? And if it doesn't, how come?

When the person-centered approach was being applied to psychotherapy and to small groups, therapists and facilitators seemed to be conscious of its 'comprehensive function.' Coulson (1972) describes an ethic of group facilitation: 'The group is in a better position for multi-directional, life-implicated learning, if the facilitator is in it with them than if he is exempted, standing back, arranging for them to go into areas that he hasn't charted ... or will not bear the consequence of exploring' (p. 78). Thus, since this has not continued to be the case in all applications of the person-centered approach, it has not been immune to the same cultural process that has occured with many other noble innovations (religion being the most ready example): a simple morality replaces the comprehensive function of judging and signals the end of innovation.

The Creation of a 'Person-Centered Approach' Culture

The Center for Cross-Cultural Communication (based in Europe, but apparently with no headquarters) has recently boasted that it has taken up the American psychologist Carl Rogers'

> search and work from where he left off. [And,] in this regard, the cross-cultural workshops [this Center conducts in Europe] have been a flagship of discovery and creativity in the constructive possibilities and opportunities which they can provide for staff members and participants alike. (McIlduff & Coghlan, 1993: 23)

Is there any evidence for these claims? In the cross-cultural communication workshops to which I have been invited and from all reports I have seen regarding others, I have not detected Carl Rogers' mantle having been passed, nor any extraordinary amount of 'discovery or creativity' having taken place.

Even if the Center's assertion were not pure hyperbole, it nevertheless raises a crucial question. Have cross-cultural communication workshops improved communications between cultures any more than say, tourism, university exchange programs, trans-national business negotiations or military occupations? If the workshops have improved communications at all, that would be commendable. However, should not a project that suggests that it consciously aims at improving communications between cultures do it better than activities for which this is a mere byproduct? Furthermore, the central theme—cross-cultural communication—does not appear to be of great interest in most of these workshops. According to various staff members it has rarely, if at all, been discussed or commented upon during the various workshops. In more than 20 years of promoting the subject, the Center has produced little, if any, literature on the specific subject of cross-cultural communication (although the subject of the 'facilitation' of groups has been touched on several times: this will be discussed later).

Were they not to have had much to say about cross-cultural communication, what these workshops seem to have done splendidly is to create their own culture. One may attend a workshop in Bristol, Brussels or Barcelona and be assured that the same jargon will be spoken, regardless of the languages used (one of which will always be English), the same traditions will be respected, the same rituals enacted, the same social conventions and even the same habits of thought will be followed. It is also likely that familiar people will recount familiar stories, a predictable haggling over points of order will take place and the group will endure the expected 'process' as it 'unfolds.' In other words, a portable culture is ready and waiting. Like your credit card, you needn't leave home without it.

Intracultural more than Intercultural Communications?

Aside from language differences, what, if any, are the significant barriers to communications between the various European cultures today? Even though two groups may speak different languages, they may share substantial cultural similarities: consider the United States and Brazil. Whereas, speaking the same language does not guarantee identical cultures. For example, the culture of Portugal (who colonized Brazil) is European. Thus, it may be more similar to Spain than to Brazil, where the same language is spoken, but where the culture has been influenced by the Americas.

One wonders if cultural differences between European nations are not fewer than between what constitutes a European culture and non-European cultures. Certainly Germany has historical and perhaps diplomatic or philosophical differences with France. However, it would appear that the cross-cultural communication problems Germany is currently suffering are more due to differences between 'guest workers' from Turkey and other non-European cultures, than between neighboring countries.

Surely to a non-European, it is as much the *sameness* of European countries as their *differences* that is striking. Besides a preference for thick granite and its dark shadows (which perhaps is really a desire for stability), a taste for formal clothing, and a suspicion of novel ideas, European communities share many things in common that they do not share with, say, Japan, Zimbabwe or Bolivia. The noted French historian Fernand Braudel (1994) suggests a fundamental difference between Europe and other groups is that, 'European civilization is based on wheat and bread—and largely white bread—with all the constraints that this implies.' The organization around the neighborhood bakery, the corner bar, the use of the knife and fork, do not differ significantly from Amsterdam to Budapest.

In many ways Europe is becoming more and more a single culture by the day. Certainly the conventions that workshop participants are likely to encounter—that is, those surrounding the use of taxis, buses, trains, hotels, restaurants and so forth—differ little from one place to another. Non-European travellers quickly catch on how to make their way between European countries. It is not so easy in Asia, Africa or South America.

Of course, individual differences between nations are extremely important. Not only to the inhabitants of local regions, but to anyone who would try to understand intercultural exchanges. Underlining this point, the eighteenth-century German prince Hermann Puckler-Muskau has given this advice to travellers: 'In Naples, treat the people brutally; in Rome, be natural; in Austria, don't talk about politics; in France, give yourself no airs; in Germany, a great many; and in England, don't spit' (Newby, 1986: 16).

Traveling aside, there are issues that frequently arise in cross-cultural communication workshops that Europeans regard as obvious evidence of cultural *differences*. For example, organizers of cross-cultural communication workshops have reported that

> over the years [participants' statements in the workshops] display great thematic consistency. [These recuring themes include] collective guilt arising from the Second World War, suffering and the Holocaust, power issues at home, at work or in relationships, power and the position of women, social discriminaton and stereotyping, ethnic conflicts within and between nations, the aftermath of the overthrow of totalitarian governments, and the organizational and financial considerations of the workshop staff. (McIlduff & Coghlan, 1993: 25)

These are subjects of indisputably vital importance to participants in these workshops. Also, they touch on deeply universal human concerns. They are therefore *general* issues, and logically should be noted as such by everyone else. Nevertheless, to non-Europeans, especially those not from the United States, with their own local emergencies, these may understandably appear as provincial European preoccupations and, in this regard suggest the *particularity* of European culture.

Not only what is meant by 'cultural' but also the term 'international' may need substantial clarification. A meeting in Bern, involving participants from Austria, Switzerland and Germany, is technically an 'international conference.' However, on any continuum of internationalness, it would be closer to the 'provincial,' than to the 'worldwide' end.

Reports on cross-cultural communication workshops make a good deal out of the number of different nationalities represented in their gatherings. However, what does the mere summing of the different countries of origin of participants really imply? In terms of significant differences, it means less and less these days. And, it could even be insignificant. For example, if one did a headcount at the latest Florida tennis club that specializes in training future champions, who would be surprised to find a dozen or so nationalities among the young aspirants, each one more American than the next?

These days, almost any workshop could be said to be 'international.' In a workshop held in Warm Springs, Georgia (in the United States) where I have been recently, there were participants from Brazil, Egypt, France, Great Britain, Greece, China, Israel, Japan and Slovakia. There was even someone from Cleveland. Who could deny that it was an 'international' workshop, featuring people from ten countries, speaking eight or nine languages? Nevertheless, to claim anything special about 'cross-cultural communication' would doubtless be misleading. The majority of participants (there were no facilitators) were from within a radius of a few hundred kilometers of the workshop site, in the southeastern part of the country. The topics were intensely personal; the opposite of what might be thought of as 'international.' Is it often otherwise? Whatever the location, the majority of participants come from nearby and internationalness plays a relatively minor role.

A Cross-Cultural Communication Workshop Culture?

Although evidence of significant accomplishments in cross-cultural communication may not have come to light and the distinctions between whatever cultures are being 'crossed' has not yet become clear, there are considerable indications of a *cross-cultural communication workshop culture*.

A people with a history

There are apparently no restrictions on participation in these workshops and a great many people make a habit of attending year after year. This familial population both creates and preserves the culture's oral history. 'Typically, at the beginning of a large group workshop,' former organizers and facilitators of cross-cultural communication workshops write, 'some participants speak of their experience of others who are already familiar with the "group culture," who know "the rules," the correct way to speak in order to be given attention' (MacMillan & Lago, 1993: 26). A facilitator for more than a half-dozen workshops reported that he could 'predict with great accuracy,' when a certain regular participant would rise to recite a poem, when another would complain that he did not understand what was happening at the moment, and another would begin to accuse the organizers of incompetence.

Though not explicit, this workshop culture is also well-known to the organizers, who are understandably concerned with its implications. For example, they try to imagine 'the impact that the regular, familiar attendees tend to have on those persons who are newcomers to the process' (McIlduff & Coghlan, 1993: 26). Organizers have further noted that, 'The workshops are novel and sometimes strange experiences for new participants who understandably arrive with a mixture of uncertainty, keen expectations and perhaps a little fear'(p. 21). This is similar to the experience of army recruits arriving at boot camp, children who have been sent away to boarding school, and any number of other 'immigrant' experiences.

Language

The cross-cultural communication workshops, as a subculture, let's say, have their own distinct and effective language. 'English' is used between staff members. No, not standard English. Since the majority of the staff members speak English only with difficulty—as a second language—their version (with its guttural accents and latinized syntax) has become specific to this culture. Whatever the exact convention might be, it is clear that a technical language, inaccessible to the masses is used. Anthropologists might call this a language of the tribal council or priests.

In the 'community,' that is, the plenary sessions, another convention is followed. English is spoken and then translated by specialists into the language of the host country and also into French and perhaps German, and vice-versa. Minorities who do not understand these tongues must cluster in the corners and whisper Polish or Portuguese or whatever. Clearly, communication within the workshop promotes Anglo-European cultural values. For example, translation itself encourages the convention of one person talking and others listening in silence. This is not a habit of many other cultures. Not even all Europeans adopt this manner. Italians, for instance, often prefer to talk and listen at the same time.

Translators are sometimes facilitative and sometimes not. The Italian expression *traduttore traditore,* though well-worn, is nevertheless appropriate for what often takes place. In addition to outright, though more likely unwitting, betrayal, translators slow down communication in general, introduce significant changes of rhythm and inject their own individual personalities. Frequently, the speaker's ideas and feelings are *interpreted*, instead of translated.

There is inevitably a point in the deliberations when the translator feels moved to speak as a 'person.' Everyone applauds this assertiveness and break with authority. After all, he or she is not a mere instrument, but a person. (This is one of the culture's most prized values.) Now the translator has become a personality in the group. To return to being faithful to translation is not easy. Naturally, some love the spotlight more than others. They may mimic the speaker or emphasize suggestive words, if the talk is light. If it is serious or tedious, they may make editorial comments or nit-pick fine points of grammar with other participants who know the languages. And should they tire, they may suddenly 'forget' what language they should be using and repeat what has just been said in the same tongue. A rest interval is surely indicated. In the worst case they upstage the person trying to communicate something to the group and dilute his or her words.

It should be noted (as those who have attempted this task know only too well) that translating is a demanding, tiresome and for the most part thankless job. Though there are many heroes in this field, it should not be assumed that translators, even excellent ones, are always devoted to the facilitation of communication. Not only personal, but national influences may intervene. For example, once a likeable Frenchman, who made his way around workshops with his elegant style and unmatched translation, sat silent through a good portion of a large group meeting in which there happened to be no other French participants. Suddenly, he rose and announced to the assembly that he had a desire to hear his native tongue spoken at the meeting. Thusly, he launched a tedious discourse in French. The group listened respectfully. Then, as there was no one as qualified as he to translate, he interpreted himself.

For better or worse, these language difficulties are this culture's reality. Nevertheless, should they not be further explored? For example, what are the implications for a program of facilitating cross-cultural communication in the choice of English as the insider's language? What are the political implicatons? What are the implications of promoting a system (the person-centered approach) which is built on principles of honesty, openness, transparency in interpersonal communications using a code that is frequently inaccessible to the majority of participants? In 22 years of the cross-cultural communication workshop 'tradition,' could not a genuine multilingual staff have been developed? But let's move on to perhaps one of the more distinct marks of a subculture: its jargon.

Jargon

Articles on cross-cultural communication workshops reveal an abundant jargon. To start with, the phrase 'cross-cultural communication' itself, surely qualifies as 'confused, unintelligible talk' or 'a specialized notion of those in the same way of life,' that is, *jargon*. The literature on cross-cultural communication workshops (as on many activities of the person-centered approach) is replete with words such as 'process,' 'climate,' 'experiencing,' 'personal power,' 'experiencing personal agendas,' 'deeply personal,' 'checking understanding,' as well as such metaphors as 'flowing,' 'unfolding,' 'growing,' 'emerging.'

In Europe, additional jargon has been generated, such as refering to the person-centered approach as a 'philosophy of being,' or mentioning 'the philosophy, theory and practice of the person-centered way of being.' The workshop staffs have been said to be 'attitudinally and behaviourally committed to the person-centred approach' (McIlduff & Coghlan, 1993: 27). The expressions, 'the person-centred worker' and 'the person-centred way' have been used. And for the more gullible there is even said to be a 'person-centered arena.'[7]

Beliefs

Many of the beliefs that seem part of cross-cultural communication workshop culture have been inherited from client-centered therapy: 'Society causes the individual's problems.' 'Through *personal power*, the individual can be free to *stand up for his or her rights.*' Other principles participants encourage each other to, 'Trust in the future and there will be a better life.' 'Problems can be solved through effort and introspection.' 'Others should be helped to help themselves. However, (paradoxically) the individual is not obliged to help the society, work for its objectives, or respect its formalities.'

Traditions

Officials of the Center for Cross-Cultural Communication are proud of their tradition. They state, 'For over twenty years cross-cultural communication workshops have been held in various European countries,' and, without foundation, add that the workshops, 'have, over time, become a familiar annual event to the vast majority of [European] persons interested in the person-centred approach'(McIlduff & Coghlan, 1993: 21).

The aspect of tradition most discussed by the organizers of cross-cultural communication workshops is the activity they call 'fragmenting into small groups.' The consistency of this phenomenon and the establishment of tradition is suggested in this statement. 'Despite an overall attendance of more than 3000 participants [over 22 years], the workshops have developed a fairly predictable pattern ...'

1. The 'community' spends considerable time discussing the merits of moving into smaller groups, facilitated by the (at times, rather intimidatingly large) staff that has been assembled for this purpose.

    Some participants are in favor; others, opposed. The discussion which can become rather intense really decides only *when* and *how,* and never what it purports to decide: *whether or not.* This will be discussed later.

2. 'Optional topic-based workshops and interest groups are organized.'

3. Social activities, such as, eating a meal together, 'provides the occasion for much useful interaction and meeting new people' (p. 24). One may think, 'Did we really need cross-cultural communication workshops to discover this?' However, this may be one of the most facilitative event the workshop provides.

    That a frustrating experience is inevitable, due to the structure of the workshop, is illustrated by this comment: 'The staff from previous experience, also suspected strongly that the process of fragmentation would be arduous and painful as the community decided *how* and *when* to fragment' (McIlduff & Coghlan, 1993: 85).

The 'process of fragmentation' frustrates participants and facilitators alike. Probably because it is deeply contradictory. On the one hand, people are trying to decide in a democratic manner (an important cultural value, though perhaps understood differently between 'east' and 'west' Europe), whether to break into small groups or not. On the other hand, reports of 22 years of cross-cultural communication workshops suggest that the 'community' has never *not* 'fragmented' into small groups (fairly well eliminating the hypothesis of chance). This suggests that the exercise, if not futile, is merely one of deciding, not *whether* but, *how* and *when*. In a free society, this would suggest that 'fragmenting into small groups' might be a cultural value that outweighed the process of choosing. However, these workshops are not free societies. They are structured traditions that, through their very structure, may oppose a democratic process.

Leaving aside the obvious barriers to democracy, such as centralized power and so forth, the workshops' foundational concepts have within them a requirement for small groups. This constitutes the basic contradiction. There is really no need for discussion. Small groups are inevitable. To see this, it is helpful to understand the history of development of these activities. The cross-cultural communication workshops were inspired by and patterned after the La Jolla Program of the Center for Studies of the Person in California. Even jargon has been imported. The authors of a recent article on cross-cultural communication workshops conclude that for facilitators of such events, 'There is the need to be empathically in touch with the overall situation in the community … There is the crucial need to stay grounded, centred, and in touch with the self, with emerging feelings and thoughts' (McIlduff & Coghlan, 1993: 30). The new-age adept at the latest California growth center could not have put it better.

Once introduced into the European culture, the workshops, of course, took up their own concerns and adopted their own political agendas. Outside of psychotherapy these were considerably different from the Americans' (recall the Holocaust, ethnic conflicts and other recurring European themes mentioned earlier), while in the context of psychotherapy, much has been the same. For example, at the time of writing this chapter, the two cultures share concerns about child abuse, the homeless, AIDS, women's issues, and politically correct speech.

When cross-cultural workshops were getting underway, Carl Rogers, with his own hands, was himself applying the person-centered approach to large group workshops. In this endeavor he was fully involved, not merely in an honorary role as 'consultant' or 'co-founder.' He conceived of, planned, wrote brochures announcing the workshops and participated completely as any participant. In fact, it was the heavy schedule of North American workshops that contributed to his cancelling a European trip in 1974.

Unlike the La Jolla Program's emphasis on small encounter groups, the focal point of Rogers' workshops became the large group itself: that is, the total community. The change in philosophy required to make this step separated Rogers' approach from the La Jolla Program. It was participants, not the program directors, who planned, as much as possible, the structure and activities of the workshop. The La Jolla Program did not adopt this innovation since it was not consistent with its philosophy and goals. The heart of the La Jolla Program was the small encounter groups and that continued to be the case.

On the other hand, the cross-cultural communication workshops did adopt the innovation, but without changing their philosophy or goals. Thus, like the La

Jolla Program they featured small groups with facilitators and some plenary meetings where people could say pretty much what they please, but the meeting was not expected to 'go anywhere.' It is just a *big* group encounter as opposed to a *small* group encounter. In Rogers' own programs, the large group could and did *decide* every possible aspect of its life. And herein lies the roots of the cross-cultural communication workshop contradiction and the source, both for participants and group facilitators, of substantial frustration. Participants are under tremendous structural pressure to form small groups since they are a built-in requirement of the structure of the program. Participants are free to discuss *when* they will do what the authorities have planned. But this freedom appears to be only in how long the inevitable can be held off.

Another aspect of structure that discourages democracy is due to the practical realization of the foundational principles. That is, the small groups need facilitators to lead them. And when you have small group facilitators, the old addage applies: If the only tool you have is a facilitator, you can bet someone will be facilitated.

All these facilitators (18 in at least one of the recent cross-cultural communication workshops) waiting around for hours or sometimes days for the group to decide if they will use them or not are bound to experience frustration, especially when they are not so sure what they are doing anyway. (We return to this subject in the final section on philosophy and goals of the workshops.)

One would expect that the facilitators would directly or indirectly push for the formation of small groups. And there is evidence to support this hypothesis. For example, in one workshop there was the expected lengthy and at times irritating discussion of when and how to fragment into small groups. Just before the issue had been settled to everyone's satisfaction, a staff member stepped in and urged participants to go into small groups. Many were disappointed. As this participant expresses it, 'I'm feeling quite lost. Adding so much structure to no structure is a little weird. Somehow something is not quite right in what happened. The struggle was so hard and then suddenly 'The Staff' emerges. I don't understand' (McIlduff & Coghlan, 1989: 86–7).

Another participant related, 'I went to the large group really anticipating strongly the last bit of the process of getting into small groups and felt let down when I heard that the staff had decided to solve the problem for us by telling us to go into small groups' (p. 87).

Even when facilitators were not trying to rush into small groups, they may still have tended to manipulate the 'process.' Indeed, a staff member reported that in one workshop a group of participants, having decided to form a small group, arrived at the designated room to find it locked. An afternoon was lost trying to find out how to enter the room only to discover in the end that a staff member had the keys in his pocket the whole time. He had refused to reveal this fact as he was waiting for a 'group consensus to emerge.'

The British counselling psychologist Colin Lago (1990), who has substantial experience in both facilitating and organizing cross-cultural communication workshops, also suggests that the staff group may unwittingly influence the group process solely through its constitution. Lago states:

> It could be argued that the culture of the staff team, already dominated by English and staffed by sophisticated travellers, joined together in their person-centered philosophies and working practices, successfully overrode concerns about cultural identity, cultural understanding and patterns of culturally determined behaviour.

Another person who has participated in several of these workshops goes further than questioning the influence of systemic values and expresses a global lack of confidence in their morality:

> I think I have a mistrust of the genuineness of cross-culturals ... I have a mistrust of what the practice is and what the theory is ... I really go for it, I really want it, and it does work for some people, but I always don't get in love with it because someone could come and practice in a way and call it person-centered and manipulate me. And I find it more with the men in the approach ... They use the approach for power. (Stubbs, 1992)

One can understand the facilitators' dilemma. Afterall, they have been called on to facilitate a small group and doubtless want to do so to the best of their ability. Nevertheless, it is difficult at times to be sympathetic with their self-centeredness, and at times, arrogance. For example, in one group, facilitators decided not to introduce themselves. The workshop participants spent many frustrating hours with the banal question: 'Who are the facilitators?' This had occured in the 1960s in the La Jolla Program when its proposal was, in part, to test the limits of facilitation and its definition. It is difficult to believe it was necessary to repeat this exercise some 30 years later. Especially when it seems to have served no constructive purpose whatever. To the contrary. How was a workshop helped by *blocking* essential communications?

Of course, the question, 'What is a facilitator?' is legitimate. And each person who intends to confront this challenge must take it seriously and answer it. But not at the expense of participants. To set up such a crazy situation, why wouldn't it provoke frustrating feelings? It would be a miracle if it did not.

One more note on facilitation. In this era of eclecticism, it is not always easy to detect the person-centered approach in the behavior of facilitators. McIlduff and Coghlan (1989: 80) assert that, 'One well-established dynamic of all person-centered groups is the function of the staff as a model of facilitative behavior.' A long list of references, all but two or three from organizational psychologists (only one from the person-centered approach), backs this up. This notion has been mentioned by Rogers, perhaps to suggest that being a good example is better than being a bad one. Nevertheless, it has never figured in his serious thought. 'Modeling' is in fact a tenet of behavioral psychology. It runs counter to the person-centered approach which prefers to encourage the 'actualizing tendency' inherent in the person and not his or her human tendency to mimic someone in authority. It is certainly not 'a well-established dynamic in *all* person-centered groups.'

Ritual/stylized behavior

Perhaps the rituals that are most important in preserving the culture are those that appear as personal, but also speak for the culture. For example, one 'first-time participant' observed, 'Some experienced large group talkers were doing their thing or performing their ballet dance. It did not encourage me to trust them. Rather, I thought I witnessed people's needs becoming at times so overwhelming that they burst forth irrespective of the level of comfort or ease or trust that they felt towards the group.' The 'experienced ones' were, by trying to establish how one carries on social conversation in this culture, perhaps ritualistically establishing the insiders and outsiders of that society.

The formal rituals are easy to note: a bouquet of flowers placed conspicuously in the center of chairs arranged in a circle. Perhaps more characteristic, a sacred silence, eyes directed to the floor or roaming the other faces, that begins each meeting after someone has brought to a sudden halt the whispering chit-chat.

A woman in one workshop confronted an important aspect of ritualized behavior and, since what she is making is not an uncommon observation, perhaps even a significant characteristic of the workshop culture. She had related that she had joined the workshop to discuss certain issues. She was disappointed that her ideas, opinions and views were not given the same weight as others' feelings. 'Why do feelings come before these things?' she wanted to know. 'It seems that there is a tyranny of feelings here' (McIlduff & Coghlan, 1989: 81).

Rolling hand movements that simulate a waterwheel, while the eyes are cast to the heavens, as if searching desperately for the right word, characterize the ritual for introspective 'genuineness.'

In the small group meetings, the healing ritual of psychotherapy most often prevails. The practitioners may espouse gestalt therapy or whatever, but the ritual is the same.

Morality

In addition to the morality developed through client-centered therapy, pointed out earlier in this chapter, it seems the cross-cultural communication culture emphasizes what may be an even more severe self-centered ethic of individuality. This has even alarmed the organizers themselves who state, 'It seems to us that the person-centered approach does have a moral and ethical duty to promote a communal attitude toward personal freedom' (McIlduff & Coghlan, 1993: 95).

Other values have also been confounded. Confidentiality was an old encounter group value. For those rebelling against a rigid and hostile society, it was essential that their secrets not be revealed. In cross-cultural communication workshops, this value has both been ignored and elevated to a morality.

For example, in Hungary in 1984, the organizers bulldozed the community into allowing a television station to film the proceedings. The TV crew stationed itself at the entrance to the meeting room while the organizers applied the pressure to workshop participants. 'Let them televise.' Slogans flowed freely: 'Very important to democracy in this country.' 'A merging of East and West.' 'Symbol of an end to the Cold War.' 'Ground-breaking historical event.' Finally, 'You have five minutes to decide, because as you know television has a tight schedule.' The group's weak opposition caved in. Filming was allowed.

No sooner had the TV cameras departed, an over-zealous facilitator who was trying to uphold a personal version of confidentiality, stood up in the plenary meeting and denounced a young Italian student who was innocently tape recording the proceedings. The student had thought (logically enough), 'If a television crew can burst into the meeting and film what they please and present images, interpreted in a manner that only God knows how, to the population of Szeged, why could I not tape record?'

And why not? Because she had violated the 'group process.' The requirement established by several years of workshops that fed into its morality, was to say, 'please,' to ask for permission, to let a debate take place, even if it were to be a rubber-stamp of the political decision of the organizers (as it was, in the case of local TV coverage). The earlier decision was not universal. It applied to Hungarian television, not to students. The youngster was thoroughly tongue-lashed by the self-righteous facilitator.

Summary

The nations of Europe, whose members participate in these cross-cultural communication workshops, doubtless have many cultural differences, including language differences in some cases. The question is: how significant are these differences in the workshop?

On the other hand, the similarities, not only in customs and daily life, but also biologically are numerous. As Desmond Morris (1994) has put it:

> We may wear different hats but we all show the same smile; we may speak different languages but they are all rooted in the same basic grammar; we may have different marriage customs but we all fall in love. Despite our different skin colours, religious beliefs and social rituals, we are biologically astonishingly close to one another. (p. 6)[8]

Furthermore, whatever cultural differences that may exist between participants, they are effectively neutralized by the influence of the workshop culture itself. In considering a list of activities and conventions, suggested by the American anthropologist Edward T. Hall (1959, 1966), that differ between cultures, virtually every one is determined by the *cross-cultural communication workshop culture* and not by the native cultures of participants. For example, verbal behavior is unified by translation and non-verbal behavior—the grunts and gestures expressed while groping for words—quickly becomes a familiar pattern. Furthermore, the comfort level due to metric distance between people (each may choose where he or she sits), to odors (no smoking convention), to the arrangement of the space (a large circle), to appointment times (a half-hour after the stated hour), to the timing for establishing acquaintances (instantaneous, we are all 'persons'), to discussions (reveal your true feelings, or at least opinions), to time schedules (flexible), to touching (encouraged), to contextual meaning (a place to be yourself) are all determined by the workshop culture and take precedence over the participant's native cultural conventions.

So what is so surprising, if a cross-cultural workshop demonstrates that 'folks over there are just like folks over here'? They are anyway. And even if one wished to accentuate the national differences effectively eliminated by the group culture, how many times must it be proved that so-and-so-many nationalities, representing such-and-such-many different languages survived a few days together in a resort hotel?

Philosophy and Goals of the Workshops

The cross-cultural communication workshops have claimed to have provided opportunites 'for persons from many diverse cultures to meet together with the goal of improving personal communication and understanding' (McIlduff & Coghlan, 1993: 21). The two published journal articles that begin with this phrase contain a total of 36 pages. In those 36 pages there is not *one word* about results. Do these workshops improve communication between cultures? Do they even improve 'personal communication and understanding'?

The articles move quickly to professional matters. The authors assert that

> the lifeblood of research topics in the person-centred world [are the] vital issues concerning the nature of group facilitation and co-facilitation, group process, learning, adapting, communication, language differences, intercultural complexities and confusions, staff support and harmony, the nature of power— both organizational and personal. (ibid.: 22)

Again setting aside the hyperbole, this list, already top-heavy with a 'how-to' emphasis, anticipates articles on facilitation of groups and group process which occupy some *two-thirds* of the content of the combined articles.

A major part of the discussion on facilitation concerns the facilitators. From 'feedback received over the years,' the organizers offer facilitator questions they regard as, 'of huge significance in understanding the facilitators' perceptions of their function.' Furthermore, the facilitators' comments reproduced are unashamedly self-centered. There is not one word of concern for participants—how they might get on, what the experience might mean for them, not even whether or not the experience might be constructive or not. Not one word about the outcome they would hope for participants, not even in global terms. It is all *me, me, me*.

For example:

'Am *I* really hearing each individual that speaks in a way which enables *me* to grasp their personal meaning, feelings and thoughts.'

'What about *my* needs and personal power?'

'Am *I* being influential without controlling or directing these persons?'

'What factors, circumstances, behaviours or situations will prompt *me* to respond to a given individual or remain silent?'

How much does it seem appropriate for *me* to speak in the community of 200, given that *I* have twelve or more co-facilitator colleagues?'

'What shall *I* do if *I* get caught up in the ongoing process and *I* am very much put in touch with *my* own vulnerabilities? '

'Can *I* be truly *myself* in this group?'

'Will *I* be judged if *I* make a mess of things out in the community room?'

'When *I* intervene will *my* colleagues, especially the experienced ones, evaluate and be making judgements about *my* competence or will they accept *me* and *my* way in the moment?'

'If one of *my* colleagues wants to give *me* feedback, particularly negative feedback, will he/she actually do it, if so, in what way?'

'If necessary can *I* find the appropriate support, acceptance, help and understanding in the staff group?' (ibid.: 29–30).

If the staff are not truly first concerned with themselves and only secondly concerned with the participants and the goals of the workshop, then the reporters have not felt it important to record staff members' comments to the contrary. Either way it suggests a *staff*-centered and not *person*-centered perspective.

The second hypothesis may very well be valid, since one of the most explicit value statements that emerges from these articles is that 'The presence of a group of facilitators demands a committment to the well-being of colleagues' (ibid.: 31).[9]

Conclusion

The Center for Cross-Cultural Communication has been promoting the 22-year tradition of cross-cultural communication workshops. Articles have been published demonstrating no more than that these workshops accord with what has been previously known about large group workshops from the person-centered approach. Virtually nothing has been reported on the main subject in hand: improving cross-cultural communication. In fact, since these workshops are concentrated in Europe, the question has been raised as to what significant cultural differences really exist in this rather provincial workshop population?

Although not much light has been shed on their effectiveness, the workshops seem to have effortlessly created their own culture. This is perhaps inevitable when there is virtually no effort at self-reflection and criticism. Distinct traditions, including an oral history, specific language and social conventions, a particular belief system or world view, values, morality are all noticeable in the constitution of this culture.

A good deal of what has been written on the subject of the workshops has dealt with professional concerns, mainly the 'facilitation' of the 'process.' These questions seem premature. First, the essential question must be answered: 'In terms of improving cross-cultural communication, what have been the significant specific accomplishments of cross-cultural communication workshops?' The proposal to improve communication between diverse cultural groups certainly seems to be worthwhile. And it is to further this reality that the subject has been taken up here.

Notes

1. The comparison of 'modern' behaviors with primitive 'rituals' is not as fanciful as it may seem at first. For profound and convincing images and comparisons, see Morris and Marsh (1988), Shah (1987, 1988). Deren (1970) also draws the following similarity of the modern magician and his formulae (immediately familiar to those who live in large cities):

> He conceives his plans in almost solitary secrecy, or with a few cohorts; he is feverishly protective of the exclusive right to exploit the power of his discovery or invention; he is frequently concerned with an almost occult effort to divine that special twist of public taste which makes for a hit or a best-seller; he is devoted to the idea of magic combinations of words in a certain just-so order, which is a catchy slogan; he labors to create a skillfully obsessive image of material or sexual seduction and involves himself in a complex and formal series of cabbala-like manipulations involving 'contacts,' publicity incantations, and even what might be accurately termed the cocktail libation.

2. The culture may be an abstraction which can be defended by individuals or groups. It may be an empirical fact by virtue of the consequences of individual acts when considered together. Though, strictly speaking, it may not be an organism, it may 'learn.' Perhaps it could even be said to represent consciousness, a collective consciousness? See Sheldrake (1981, 1988).

3. One indication that the culture sanctioned client-centered therapy and other systems of psychotherapy is that a few years ago there already existed more than 160,000 professional therapists in the United States alone. It has been estimated that 30% of the population of that country has sought some kind of psychological counseling in their lifetime.

4. In the case of the person-centered approach to individual therapy (that is, client-centered therapy), much of the ritual of American medicine has been incorporated: electronic telephone messages, computer billing and appointments made by a professional secretary. A waiting period in a special chamber that (through the use of music and reading materials) prepares the client's mind for the subsequent session in a quiet and dimly lit consulting room that is usually decorated with books, diplomas, aphorisms, oriental carpets, potted plants and amply projects the principles of the system.

Successful therapy doubtless satisfies the expectations raised by the client's previous adaptation to the culture and prepares him for modifying that culture. Outside of client-centered therapy one may be expected to conceal true feelings; inside a session, to express them honestly and completely. Outside, chit-chat may be socially desirable and even define a person's value; inside, it may impede progress. Thus, the process is similar to what happens in society in general: our individual consciousness derives from the culture; our collective behavior in turn modifies the culture. The psychotherapy ritual produces a relaxed state of 'empathic understanding' in which the client's experience may be reorganized. We apparently follow and are influenced by a culture that we are creating.

5. In the theory described by Rogers (1959), 'experiencing' did not yet play a part. The theory postulated a mechanism of change revolving around 'the communicated unconditional positive regard of an empathically understanding significant other' (Barrett-Lennard, 1979).

'Experiencing' is a later concept that draws attention to the inner process of the client (or the therapist). This is a process through which a person becomes aware of the incongruence between the self and the organismic experience and also the means through which the discrepancy may be reduced (Gendlin, 1961, 1978; Gendlin et al., 1968).

It is a bodily felt process of concrete ongoing events to which the person may always refer directly. For example, if one wishes to restate, for a puzzled listener, what has just been related, but in different words, she must inwardly attend to the 'felt meaning' of the communication. By 'focusing' on this 'direct referent', one may arrive at different words that associate with it and a new statement may be formulated (Gendlin, 1978).

Although the concept is a brilliant clarification of an interaction between the self and the organism and even for reformulating the self-concept, this 'focusing on the bodily felt direct reference' is probably not an adequate foundation for relating to others or for becoming a complete human being (not that any psychothereutic process is). Yet, as with many promising innovations, including applications of the person-centered approach, it is becoming suggested as a panacea. A recent advertisement claims that focusing, 'offers: A way of listening to oneself and others, a means to personal insights, a resource for spiritual growth, a path to healing and reconciliation, a catalyst for healthier relationships, a method for reducing stress and preventing burn-out, a means of getting in touch with one's creativity, a tool for phenomenological research.'

There are other similar important bodily processes, such as 'remembering,' that doubtless do the same. Although there are courses offered on improving one's memory, there is no movement to promote remembering as there seems to be for 'focusing.' Also, there is an excellent antidote for remembering: forgetting. For too much focusing, I don't know what the remedy might be, although it surely must be needed for people who cannot have an ordinary conversation without pausing 'to go inward.'

Of course, the philosophical insight of 'experiencing,' the therapeutic innovation of 'focusing,' and the good-willed efforts of people trying to help others better themselves should not be blamed for these excesses. They are part of the apparently unavoidable tendency toward vulgarization that seems to follow every worthwhile enterprise.

6. Doubtless the times influenced greatly. Many have pointed to his North American Protestant upbringing as having influenced Rogers' thinking. Notably, the concept of unconditional positive regard is popular with certain kinds of critics. But one may also note cultural influences all the way through the development of client-centered therapy. In the widespread social applications of client-centered therapy in the 1960s and 1970s, one may see the influence of that period. Early in the development of his system, one may note the influence of World War II on the construction of concepts. Rogers usually worked with a *staff* ('a group of officers serving a military commander'). In an *encounter* ('sudden face-to-face meeting between combatants'), group participants and facilitators would *confront* ('face boldly, meet in hostility') each other and their own behavior. Therapists had a regard for the client that was *unconditional* ('surrender without conditions, absolute'). And the goal of therapeutic activities was that the client would become *aware* ('from *waer*, cautious, as the general was aware of the enemy's designs'). Therapists would *free* people by emphasizing (as in wartime) the *immediate situation* (since past and future had little meaning for those facing battle, particularly after the invention of the nuclear bomb).

Too much should not be made of such observations. They merely verify the obvious: everyone uses the patterns of thought, science and technology that are available for his or her time and place. After some 25,000 years, the paintings on the walls of ice-age caves such as Lascaux, continue to be a source of beauty and inspiration, in spite of the crude perspective and materials used to conceive the work. An effort should be made to understand the essence of a person's work without regard to local color.

7. When a friend of mine from the interior of Brazil read a phrase containing, 'the person-centered world,' she said, 'Oh my God, are the Europeans planning a Rogerian theme park? I can see it all now: The *Empathy* House of Mirrors, where you can find your true self reflected. The *Genuineness* Roller Coaster, where you can experience the real ups and downs of life. No horror house is needed. It will all be a nightmare.'

8. An immense class of human regularities (including their social lives)—both statistical and structural—has been catalogued. For example, 'Adults have children; humans have a species-typical body form; humans have characteristic emotions; humans move through a life history cued by observable body changes; humans come in two sexes; they eat food and are motivated to seek it when they lack it; humans are born and eventually die; they are related through sexual reproduction and through chains of descent; they turn their eyes toward objects and events that tend to be informative and adaptively consequential issues; they often compete, contend or fight over limited social or subsistence resources; they express fear and avoidance of dangers; they preferentially associate with mates, children, and other kin; they create and maintain enduring, mutually beneficial individuated relationships with nonrelatives; they speak; they create and participate in coalitions; they desire, plan, deceive, love, gaze, envy, get ill, have sex, play, can be injured, are satiated; and on and on' (Brown, 1991). Even language may be classed as a universal. The renowned North American linguist Noam Chomsky has proposed that in spite of observing the 4,000 to 6,000 languages being spoken on the planet, a visiting Martian scientist would conclude that Earthlings speak a single language (Pinker, 1994).

9. Even if the 22-year tradition of 'cross-cultural communication workshops' were to have yielded little tangible evidence of success in improving communication between cultures, this does not mean that the person-centered approach has no potential for improving trans-national understanding, facilitating conflict resolution, or for learning the nature of culture and its process of formation. In fact, in 1981 an extremely innovative workshop was organized in the shadow of the Swiss alps. In many ways this workshop represented the culmination of Rogers' own innovation, the series of carefully organized workshops that ended in 1980 or so. That is, it carried the learnings that Rogers had accumulated further.

This workshop was held in Zinal. Some 100 participants attended. It was organized by an extremely conscientious staff, coordinated in large part by the American art-therapist and Swiss citizen Elizabeth Dominice-Johnson. There were several other members of the organizing team, but I do not remember their names. This is significant, because, unlike most of such events, they did not wish their names to be remembered. They worked long hard hours to bring about a workshop that would not depend on personalities.

There was an organizing team, but there were no facilitators. In spite of the fact that people from at least nine different countries attended, there were no translators. Each person spoke the language he or she cared to speak and when someone did not understand, another would help that person out. This was doubtless facilitated by the fact that no participant did not understand at least English or French or German. Still: no official facilitators; no official translators. From observation and participant reports, the workshop process was indistinguishable from the constructive large group workshops I am familiar with.

In addition to this, the workshop featured many other innovations. First of all, every step of the way in planning the event was shared with participants. The organizers developed a kind of newsletter through which it could inform participants of what they were thinking and planning, but also that served as a network of communication that in effect allowed the encounter to begin before everyone was face to face. Participants wrote brief descriptions of themselves in their native languages, of what they wanted from the workshop, of what they wanted from life, of whatever. They included a photograph. It was a genuine encounter.

Another innovation was that several children participated in the workshop. Not merely attended, but participated. They formed a 'small group' and they took part in the plenary sessions just like anyone else. I think this is significant. Although there are many existential aspects of the person-centered approach, the presence of children in an Alpine village enlarged the scope of the workshop by avoiding the condition that the British philosopher Mary Midgley (1978) attributes to existentialists. She has criticized them for 'proceeding as if the world contained only dead matter (things) on the one hand and fully rational, educated adult human beings on the other—as if there were no other life-forms. The impression of *desertion* or *abandonment* which existentialists have is due, I am sure, not to the removal of God, but to this contemptuous dismissal of almost the whole biosphere—plants, animals and children. Life shrinks to a few urban rooms, no wonder it becomes absurd.'

10. Although it should not be assumed that he either endorses, or does not endorse, the ideas I am presenting here, I would like to thank Colin Lago, a counsellor at the University of Sheffield in Great Britain, for valuable comments on an early draft of this manuscript.

CHAPTER ELEVEN

What's Wrong With the Psychology of Client-Centered Therapy

We should make things as simple as possible, but not simpler.
    Albert Einstein[1]

Rogers' 'wrong ideas' such as 'permissiveness' and 'non-directivity' have been relatively easy to lay aside. However, (continuing to paraphrase Ernest Becker's (1973) observation about Freud's thought), the problem has been with those 'brilliantly true insights, which were stated in such a way that they fell just to one side of reality.' What does the psychology of client-centered therapy lack?

A Wider View of Human Nature

As the person-centered approach began to be further enunciated and applied to various endeavors besides client-centered therapy, the debate over the basic assumptions and their consequences widened. Rogers and B.F. Skinner, for example, argued over the question of free will; while Rogers and Rollo May squared off over essential human nature—good or evil. Rogers' discussions with real theologians, such as Paul Tillich, stirred little interest.

The Rogers/Skinner squabbles over determination finally ended in a stalemate. In 1962, Rogers concluded:

> I feel in thorough agreement with Dr. Skinner—that, viewed from the external scientific, objective perspective, man is determined by his genetic and cultural influences. I've also said that, in an entirely different dimension, such things as freedom and choice are extremely real ... And so for me, this is an entirely different dimension which is not easily reconcilable to the deterministic point of view. I look at it as being similar to the situation in physics, where you can prove that the wave theory of light is supported by evidence; so is the corpuscular theory. The two of them are contradictory. They're not at the present state of knowledge reconcilable; but I think one would only be narrowing his perception of physics to deny one of these and accept only the other. And it is in this same sense ... that I regard these two dimensions as

both real, although they exist in a paradoxical relationship.' (Kirschenbaum, 1979: 268–9)

Thus, it is not so simple, but still easily understood: we are determined by culture *and* free to choose; thus, determining culture in return.

If this understanding had been embedded in Rogers' system of personality change, who could fault the psychology of client-centered therapy? A mature person would assume responsibility for her contribution to the existance of inept institutions, restricting customs, incompetent leadership, workmanship, teaching, and other aspects of the society that damage individuals. She would also be expected to help to improve them. But participants in client-centered therapy did not always (nor were they encouraged to) assume responsibility for their actions.

The sociologist Ernest Becker (1969) describes the consequences of not assuming this individual responsibility:

> When men fail to act *individually* and *willfully*, on the basis of their *personal, responsible* power,' he states, evil 'comes into being on the basis of a real evolutionary development: man is the animal in nature who, par excellence, can create vast structures of power by means of his symbolic manipulation of the world of energy ... here is an animal whose means of creating power are such that they check his own free development ... The way out of this paradox is that man is [also] the one animal created by evolution who can use his power for further liberation of *individuals* from the continuing constraint of groups.' (pp. 110–12)

Thus, the personal, responsible power of individuals may support either the accommodation or reduction of evil in the culture—depending partly on the individual's awareness of the collective consequences of individual acts. Although client-centered therapy has been silent on this aspect, other applications of the person-centered approach have aroused an interest (Rogers & Ryback, 1984).

May (1982) took Rogers to task for asserting the sovereign freedom of the individual and then blaming society for the individual's woes. Rogers had declared, 'it is cultural influences which are the major factor in evil behaviors ... So I see members of the human species ... as *essentially* constructive in their fundamental nature, but damaged by their experience' (Rogers, 1981).[2]

'But,' May replies, 'who makes up this culture except these very persons like you and me? ... There is no self except in interaction with a culture, and no culture which is not made up of selves,' leading him to conclude, 'I propose that the evil in our culture is also the reflection of evil in ourselves and vice versa.'

May has apparently assumed a global perspective such as that of civilization. A person's views of time and space, right and wrong, of the purpose of life, of authority, freedom, hope, his source of pride and concern, his fears, relation to others, ways to deal with uncertainty, values, beliefs that are compatible with other members of society are learned from a culture that was formed not necessarily by his self, but by other selves before. The wider perspective of groups has also made it possible to recognize that one is determined by both genetical and cultural influences and also, through his own will, he may choose his destiny, to be himself. His life influences the world his grandchildren will inhabit. The technical description of the process is offered by Levins and Lewontin (1985): 'as the parts acquire properties of being together, they impart to the whole new properties, which are reflected in changes in the parts ... Parts and wholes evolve in consequence of their relationship, and the relationship itself evolves.' Or simply speaking: We are following something that we are creating.

In asserting his opinion about society, Rogers expresses the individual's perspective. He was doubtless extrapolating from what he had learned practicing psychotherapy where he sided with the client's perspective. Clients frequently felt that society was to blame for their problems. And to discover who one really wanted to be and what one wanted to do in life, they might have had to reject temporarily the authority and values of parents and society. Fed up with others controlling them, they did not want to hear about 'responsibility.' They wanted 'freedom.'

Thus, Rogers' assertion that cultural influences have damaged clients may not only represent the client's initial reality, it may even be a perfectly suitable hypothesis for the practice of client-centered therapy in the beginning stages. Nevertheless, as a member of this potentially destructive culture, where does the client's own responsibility for not damaging others come in? Furthermore, such an emphasis on the personal self as the *exclusive* reality does not provide a sufficiently broad perspective with which to understand groups of individuals and other phenomena that by their nature involve other realities.

Of course, debates such as the one that took place between Rogers and May might also have served to satisfy motives other than mere clarification. May's notion of the 'daimonic' illustrated his position on human nature: 'The daimonic is the urge in every being to affirm itself, assert itself, perpetuate and increase itself.' This did not differ substantially from Rogers' concept of the 'actualizing tendency.' Thus, it would appear that natural principles were not being disputed. Even idealism, how the person *should* be, did not seem to be at issue, since they both advocated a humanistic psychology. The crux of their disagreement appears to have been concerned with how human behavior was interpreted, or perhaps more precisely, how it was to be visualized. Perhaps they had taken up the preoccupation of Helvétius who believed that human qualities such as goodness or badness when encouraged in a person would come about. A sort of power of positive thinking debate. The *right* stress on the *right* viewpoint might influence the development of more perfect human beings and a more perfect culture. The problem was they disagreed on this 'correct' viewpoint.

A Realistic View of Individualism

Client-centered therapy has emphasized the *individual*, his subjective world, the enhancement and maintenance of *his* organism. Buber (1960) was critical of client-centered therapy because of the possibility of producing individuals instead of persons. He stated, 'I have a lot of examples of man having become very very individual, very distinct of others, very developed in their such-and-suchness without being at all what I would like to call a man.'

The myth of uniqueness

Barton (1971), in his phenomenological analysis of client-centered therapy partially confirms Buber's fear:

> Both therapist and client fall prey to a false individualism and a false individuality, since they do not recognize the cultural constitution of self. Imagining it to be an in-itself, independent of others, a force of self-actualization outside of culture, they can only negatively evaluate culture as an interference with self. The therapist therefore, blind to his own history as a rather democratic, usually American individualist fosters an individualism in the other, an idea of the non-dependence of the self, which is deeply false, even to the way in which the organismic self has actually developed in the theory.

Thus, client-centered therapy has helped people become aware of themselves as unique individuals. However, it has not noticeably helped them to realize that they are *also* not unique, as the novelist Joseph Conrad contributes, 'not the product of the exceptional but of the general—of the normality of their place, and time, and race.'

Effectively functioning groups from the person-centered approach reveal the necessity for not merely enhancing one person at the expense of others, but enhancing many persons and also enhancing their ability to produce something together, perhaps even enhancing their survival. Where would actions that do *not* 'enhance' or 'maintain' the organism, but nevertheless enhance and maintain the *group*, figure in theories which may grow out of the person-centered approach?

Not too long ago a jet aircraft, trying to take off with iced wings in a snowstorm, crashed into a bridge on the Potomac River. As the broken airliner slowly sunk into the icy waters, several people were rescued by a passenger who was sacrificing his own life.

Where would this act of altruism—sacrificing oneself for others—fit in the hypothesis of the self-actualizing tendency? This question presents difficulties not only to client-centered therapy's theory but to the theory of evolution as well, according to which the present species evolved through a process of natural selection of individuals best suited for existing conditions. If the most altruistic members of the species are willing to sacrifice themselves for others, then their genes would be lost and selfishness would be the trait selected. Yet, altruism hangs on. How can this paradox be explained?

Some refuse to believe that individuals would put the group before themselves. The biologist Paul Ehrlich (1986), for example, argues that, 'Favorable as certain behaviors are for the group, they will be selected against at the individual level if those that perform them are more likely to perish than those that do not' (p. 95). This view seems to have many counterexamples. Soldiers and many others, whether altruistic or not, select behavior that makes them more likely to perish than those who do not select this behavior. The philosopher Mary Midgley (1978) observes that the invention of ways in which altruistic behavior, 'can seem to benefit the agent himself arises only for Egoists, because only they have ruled that it has to do this to make him act' (p. 129).

Ronald Cohen (1972), an anthropologist, studying the Kanuri in Africa, found that in that culture, an individual is not valued if he is 'only a person, with no connections, no group to be responsible for him if he did something wrong' (p. 54). Cohen concludes that, 'Altruism is therefore not organismic, but originates instead as a learning response to sociocultural norms in a person's environment.'

Many others, including psychologists (Campbell, 1965, 1972), have had their say on this subject. None has improved on Charles Darwin's own suggestion that selecting altruistic individuals provides for the survival of the *group*. Groups with persons willing to die (or to put their personal advancement aside) for them will themselves survive; groups without such individuals will not.

What has frequently been forgotten in client-centered therapy's fascination with the individual is that Emerson in his (1929) advice (doubtless forming part of the person-centered approach) urged not only to, 'Trust thyself: every heart vibrates to that iron string,' but *also* counseled, 'accept the place the divine providence has found for you, the society of your contemporaries, the connection of events.'

The victim-of-society myth

The psychology of client-centered therapy revolves around the consciousness of self. In brief, society is seen to be the cause of the individual's problems. It distorts his or her personality. The natural tendency toward self-actualization is then released in a relationship with a client-centered therapist. Through this interaction, the individual may formulate a new self-concept that is more congruent with his or her organismic experience.

Nevertheless, for group applications there are serious problems with this hypothesis. First, in the group the society is no longer an abstraction. In a manner of speaking, it is the group itself, being created moment by moment by participants. Sure, people may be damaged by the group-society, but there are only the participants themselves to blame. Each participant cannot be only a victim. Some must also be victimizers.

The psychology of client-centered therapy proposes that, in a relationship with a therapist, the client may revise his or her concept of self in accord with organismic experience. This revision is based in part on a reflection such as, 'Am I living in a way that is deeply satisfying to me, and which truly expresses me?' (Rogers, 1961a). There is nothing wrong with this. *Carpe Diem.*

There is no problem, that is, unless *your* 'deep satisfaction' prevents any of your colleagues from living in this way also. Indeed, remember that although they may have become more confident individuals, people having completed client-centered therapy could not be shown to have gained more respect and acceptance for others. (Gordon & Cartwright, 1954). While participants in encounter groups from the person-centered approach apparently could be (Tausch, 1983).

The task in the group is not merely to reject the rules of 'society' and live as one pleases. It is to create a society in which every member may live as much as possible in harmony with his or her organismic experience.

The myth that the individual controls his or her own destiny

Client-centered therapy's psychology includes the belief that people may be counted on to do the right thing and that people are always in charge of their own actions. It is clear that this is not entirely the case. In large group workshops, for example, it is common for participants to behave one way in the group meetings and later, when alone, to regret their actions. Juries and other social bodies sometimes reach decisions that each member voted for but were the individual to have acted, not as a 'representative of the people' but as a private person, he or she may have decided to the contrary.

This phenomenon also occurs slightly differently, but even more regretfully, on a global scale. Urgent ecological problems have been created by many individuals unwittingly acting in concert. A major difficulty to resolving the problem is that nobody seems to want to give up their inexpensive food (which, in order to produce on a vast scale, wastes substantial soil, a principle patrimony of the planet), their automobile (whose exhaust pollutes the air they must breathe), their refrigerators or bug sprays (whose pressurized gases destroy the ozone, the planet's radiation protection layer), their personal computers (whose fabrication byproducts are among the most toxic). Some are ready to give up these things when everyone else does. The overall effect of this phenomenon is a marvel of cooperation, a well-organized and disciplined endeavor. The problem is that no central control exists. Millions of people conspire to create situations that no single individual admits that he or she wishes and whose solitary withdrawal from adding to the problems, accounts for practically nothing in changing the system.

The myth that individuals are rational and well-intentioned

Individuals may be rational, but they also continue to act nonrationally. They are still tribal. We form into tribes of motorcyclists, football fans, rock music fanatics, professors in academic departments, religious congregations. Each has its own uniform, myths, rites of passage, jargon and so forth (Morris & Marsh, 1988). Much of the behavior in large group workshops can be seen to be tribal.

And as far as good intentions goes, history is full of examples of well-intentioned people who are quite capable of damaging others (Milgram, 1974).

An Adequate Respect for the Client

A serious obstacle to using the psychology of client-centered therapy for applications of the person-centered approach is its therapist-centered perspective. The *practice* of therapy focuses on the client. Rogers also helped to bring respect for the client within the psychology profession. Nevertheless, in expositions of theory, research and practice, the emphasis has been distinctly on the *therapist* or the therapist's point of view.

The requirement in the theory of client-centered therapy that the client *perceives* the therapist's unconditional positive regard and perceives empathic understanding has not suggested so much an interest in the client's participation as it has been taken as a signal that the therapy is 'working.'

In discourses on researches, for example, one cannot help but notice the distinctly therapist-centered bias in the conceptualization of effective therapy. For example, 'We discovered that we could pinpoint,' Rogers (1980) proudly states, 'which response of the therapist caused a fruitful flow of significant expression to become superficial and unprofitable' (p. 138). The perspective of this research was the following: 'The therapist *causes* a flow of profitable or unprofitable expression on the part of the client; now, let's find out how.' Exposing the bias in this perspective, Quinn (1953) also reveals the startling fact that, from client-centered researches, the degree of empathy in a client-centered therapeutic relationship can be reliably estimated by judging *the therapist's statements only*, without any knowledge of the client's statements.

How is it that one can judge that the therapist has 'entered the private perceptual world' of the client, 'temporarily living in the other's life, moving about in it delicately,' as a 'confident companion to the person in his or her inner world,' as Rogers (1980: 147) has described empathic understanding, without even considering what the *client* is saying or feeling? Surprisingly, Quinn's disturbing revelation did not throw the research methodology into question nor did it provoke indignation concerning exaggerations of the therapist's role. Instead, Rogers (unconvincingly, yet effectively) interpreted this finding as support for the view that empathy is *offered* by the therapist and she is responsible for empathy in the relation (Rogers, 1980: 147).

Comments from Rogers and his associates regarding the client-centered 'relationship' were more likely to mean the *therapist's* relation to the client, rather than a relationship as such. The client's perception was of little concern. This view is not better expressed than in Rogers' own words: 'In client-centered therapy we are deeply engaged in the prediction and influencing of behavior. As therapists we institute certain attitudinal conditions and the client has relatively little voice in the establishment of these conditions' (Rogers, 1961b: 449).

Nevertheless, the client's personal experience does not always conform to the therapist's perceptions nor to his or her conceptualizations. Rennie (1988) found from extensive interviews of clients immediately following therapy sessions that personal relevance is not the sole motivation for a client to chose a certain topic to discuss.

For example, one person spoke on the subject of immaturity, not because of wanting to but, because she had 'built herself up to it.' Clients may speak about subjects with no particular urgency because they are involved in a private internal dialogue that they do not wish to reveal at that moment. Another client related a dream in order to 'convey that she was basically a normal, lighthearted, creative individual and not the kind of person the therapist seemed to think she was.' Clients may like the therapist to talk about herself to get to know her better and compare behaviors. On the other hand, the therapist sharing his feelings or observations when the client is worried about a personal problem is less likely to be tolerated. In general, clients tend to forgive the therapist's mistakes and maintain good manners, leaving time for the therapist to also talk (Rennie, 1988).

Furthermore, their own contributions do not go unnoticed by psychotherapy clients, even in behavior therapy. Ryan and Gizynski (1971) reported that patients felt, 'that most universally helpful elements of their experience were the therapist's calm, sympathetic listening, support and approval, advice, and "faith"'. However, from her side of the relationship, one client felt satisfied that her therapy was completed, but was 'willing to stay because I felt that [the therapist] was involved with me and that I would hurt her if I quit.' Transference? Empathic understanding on the client's part? A sense of a relationship that required reciprocal caring? A sensitivity to the complexity that is involved in every human interaction?

Confidence in the Therapeutic Human Relationship

The effect we have on each other goes considerably beyond transference and certainly beyond ordinary social interaction. By our presence, the other's perceptions, emotions, muscle tension, respiration, heartbeat and blood pressure are altered. We are so intimately connected to one another that one physiology researcher has been prompted to say, 'The autonomic nervous system is as much a social structure as a vegetative one' (Kamiya, 1981).

Lynch (1985) concludes, from research relating speech with the cardiovascular system, that, 'To be human means to live through a body that is both biologically incomplete without other human beings and utterly dependent on others for its emotional—that is, human—development and meaning' (p. 276). Using psychogalvanic reflex to measure anxious, threatened, or alerted reactions in the client, it has been found that whenever the therapist's attitude became even slightly less accepting, the number of abrupt galvanic skin responses significantly increased (Dittes, 1957).

'Rogers' greatest contribution,' declared Richard Farson (1974), 'has not been in giving us a technique to fix people, but in creating a new form, a new definition of relationship in which people can function more fully and be more self-determining.'

On this subject, Rogers was also ambivalent. He regarded the 'relationship' as both an *element* in psychotherapy and the therapy itself. At times he mentioned 'the character of the relationship between therapist and client.' By this, he suggested that he was using the analytical mode of consciousness. In these instances, 'relationship' is an abstraction, a convenience of the intellect. From this perspective, the relationship is not tangible. There is a client, a therapist. They do something together. Everything that might be attributed to relationship can be reduced to what two individuals do and the relationship disappears. They get along pretty well. They are said to have a good 'relationship.'

However, at other times Rogers has also refered to 'a relationship permeated by warmth, understanding, safety from any kind of attack ...' Or, he spoke of the 'present emotional relationship which exists between the two.' In these phrases he suggests that 'relationship' is now viewed from an holistic mode of consciousness. That is, relationship is now a phenomenon that relates client and therapist, instead of an abstraction that is formed by considering separate individuals together.

By claiming not to interfere in this 'emerging self' of the client, the therapist underestimated her legitimate value in the phenomenon of the effective therapeutic relationship. On the other hand, by claiming to 'create an environment' through mere 'attitudes' alone, the therapist grossly overestimated this part of her role. It is not *she* who creates an environment; it is constituted by she *and* the client *and* the situation. She does not create a relationship; she and the client and the environment *are* the relationship.

At times, Rogers was very much aware of the significant effect of the therapeutic relationship. He wrote:

> The process of therapy is seen as being synonymous with the experiential relationship between client and therapist. Therapy consists in experiencing the self in a wide range of ways in an emotionally meaningful relationship with the therapist. The words—of either client or counselor—are seen as having minimal importance compared with the present emotional relationship which exists between the two. (Rogers, 1951: 172)

After the humbling experience of trying to treat hospitalized chronic schizophrenic patients, he acknowledged the importance of clients in any effective therapy. Reviewing the research on psychotherapy with hospitalized patients, he noted that:

The characteristics of the client or patient influenced the quality of the relationship which formed between himself and his therapist. High levels of empathic understanding, genuineness, and warm acceptance in the therapist's behavior are more likely to be evident when he is dealing with a reasonably expressive individual with a socio-economical level closer to his own. The therapist's attitudes are clearly important, but the patient's characteristics appear to play a definite part in eliciting these qualities. High therapeutic conditions seem to be a product of interaction between the person of the therapist and the person of his client. (Rogers et al., 1967)

Nevertheless, client-centered therapy's theory and practice continued to have contradictory perspectives. Rogers promoted and, in practice, as much as the client cooperated and participated, *did* take part in a warm and significant human relationship that centered on the client and relied heavily on the holistic mode of consciousness. In this mode the phenomenon of the effective therapeutic relationship is not an element of anything, it *is* therapy. On the other hand, he came to regard almost exclusively the professional activity he was involved in as *essentially* centered on the therapist. How the client regarded this relationship, how the client contributed to it (beyond the material he presented), the client's subjective world (aside from what he told the therapist), was not of much interest. Did the client also adopt an attitude of 'trying to understand'? Did he experience empathy, congruence, positive regard? These questions did not interest client-centered therapists very much. However, they may be of considerable interest in applications of the person-centered approach.

A Full Appreciation of the Complexity of the Person

It is clear that the client's initial motivation is important to the success of therapy, as it would be to the outcome of most endeavors. 'Patient involvement, exclusive of the influence of both exploratory processes and therapist-offered relationship,' summarizes Gomes-Schwartz (1978) from her psychotherapy research, 'showed a consistant relationship with outcome.' Persons who begin client-centered therapy with an ability and disposition to seek inwardly for the cause and resolution of their discomfort and who have a strong need to relate to people are most likely to improve. Those who are 'overcontrolled' and look outward for the cause and resolution to their personal problems are unlikely to benefit from this type of therapy. (Kirtner & Cartwright, 1958) Clients who are more successful in psychotherapy are likely to begin therapy at a higher stage of psychologic functioning than the less successful ones (Walker, Rablen & Rogers, 1960; Tomlinson & Hart 1962).

But client-centered therapy is just this: helping people help themselves through seeking inwardly for the solution to their problems in relation with a psychotherapist. This may be true for all therapies with roots in Freud's innovation that combined the notions of Charcot (that life events affected the personality and psychological problems of the patient) and those of William James (that the subjective, personal, world of the patient is central to psychological health) into a practice which included a profound and loyal relation with the patient (Drinka, 1984).

Clinical experiences challenge the assertion that the client has little to do with establishing the conditions for effective therapy. For example, 'The client is not a blank tablet,' Barton (1971) observes,

> on which the therapist writes, but is moved by the therapist differentially and thereby elicits the therapist differentially. Thus a specific client may elicit from a therapist a much greater than average (even for him) degree of sympathy, tenderness, soft warm attentiveness; another client with the same therapist may bring out much more of the therapist's cool, objective, factual mode of responding ... The variability that was seen to belong quite properly to the therapist's side of therapy equally belongs quite properly to the client's side.

Research also supports this view, challenging the therapist-centered perspective. Moos & MacIntosh (1970), for example, in studying several therapists working with the same clients, have found that empathy is influenced to a greater extent by the *client and the situation* than by the therapist. Not only empathy, but the therapist's evaluation of prognosis, capacity for insight, liking, have all been shown to vary with how the therapist perceived the patient's motivation for therapy (Wallach & Strupp, 1960). A statement that may apply to both the client's influence and the influence of the therapist's belief and good will.

Mitchell, Bozarth and Krauft (1977) have concluded from their review of research on psychotherapy that empathy, positive regard, and genuineness are associated with therapeutic outcome in a much more complex way than mere cause and effect based on what the therapist does.

Moreover, summarizing their ambitious review of research studies, Smith, Glass & Miller (1980) go even further, urging

> [t]he possibility ought to be considered more seriously that the locus of these forces that restore and ameliorate the client of psychotherapy resides more within the client himself and less within the therapist and his actions. What the client brings to psychotherapy—the will to solve a problem or be rid of it, the intelligence to apprehend contingencies and relationships, the strength to face weakness, the confidence to trust another person—may contribute more to the success of the therapy than whether it lasts twenty hours or ten, whether or not there are other clients in the room, or whether the therapist pays obeisance to Fritz Perls or Joseph Wolpe. (p. 188)

This suggestion combines perfectly with the person-centered approach, even though it conflicts somewhat with explanations of the practice of client-centered therapy.

Also, a positive attitude toward the therapist and a committment to working at changing oneself *has* been associated with success in psychotherapy (Gomes-Schwartz, 1978).

A Clear Understanding of Method

Although every method has militant adherents, no one approach has been proved to be superior to the others. Indeed, all psychotherapies have severe limitations. As Strupp (1983) reminds, 'A number of psychopathological conditions are not helped significantly by available forms of psychotherapy (or any other known treatment modality). The extent to which intensive or prolonged psychotherapy produces radical reorganization of the patient's personality and therefore lasting change is questionable.'

Nevertheless, psychotherapy does appear to be more effective than doing nothing—for most people. In a study comparing psychoanalytic psychotherapy to behavior therapy, for example, Sloane and colleagues (1975) found that three groups of patients, one receiving psychoanalytic psychotherapy, one receiving behavior therapy and the third consisting of patients merely assigned to a waiting list, all 'improved significantly on the severity of their target symptoms.' There was no significant difference in the amount of improvement between the psychotherapy and the behavior therapy groups. Both treated groups, however, improved significantly more than the waiting list group. Further, Smith, Glass and Miller (1980) conclude their complex review of 475 psychotherapy outcome studies with the confidence that, 'Psychotherapy is beneficial, consistantly so and in many different ways. Its benefits are on a par with other expensive and ambitious interventions, such as schooling and medicine. The benefits of psychotherapy are not permanent, but little is.'

It is not known how much similar the so-called different therapies really are. Their differences may be largely due to what they choose to emphasize. For example, it is conceivable that 'cognitive therapy' may consist of revising faulty thought patterns in the context of a 'therapeutic relationship.' While, on the other hand, 'relationship therapy' may amount to providing a warm, reassuring relationship in which 'faulty thought patterns are revised.'

A study by Gomes-Schwartz (1978) supports the hypothesis that the therapist's technique is not the essential factor in therapy outcome. Thirty-five young men, mildly to moderately disturbed, were assigned on a rotational basis to three groups of therapists. Ten patients saw psychiatrists with an average of more than 23 years of experience in analytic therapy; ten more saw psychologists with an average of 15 years experience in experiential (Rogerian influenced) psychotherapy; and fifteen saw university professors (average of 17 years since the PhD) who had reputations of being good persons to talk with concerning problems but had no training in psychotherapy. The professors were from Mathematics, English, History, and Philosophy departments of the university.

The process of therapy differed considerably. The professionals spent more time than the university professors exploring the psychodynamic roots of patients' problems. The professors and the experiential therapists were warmer and more personal in their relationships with patients than the analytic therapists but the results were the same for each group. The conclusion was, 'Untrained professor/ therapists generally effected as much improvement as experienced psychologists and psychiatrists. Further, the variables that best predicted change were not related to therapeutic techniques but to the positiveness of the patient's attitude toward his therapist and his commitment to work at changing.'

However, even with such dramatic evidence, method cannot be discounted. Without a method or theory for what they were doing, the college professors in this research, had difficulty sustaining a therapeutic process *over the long run* (Strupp, 1986). That the effect of the therapist is probably stronger than her method obscures the importance of method. After all, strategy and interventions also 'importantly shape and define relationships' (Jones et al., 1988).

Furthermore, the successful therapist's beliefs and attitudes are likely to be integrated with his approach. The therapist's interest in the *treatment* has even been shown to be more important than his interest in the patient, in terms of involving patients in the therapy process. (McNair et al., 1963). It is difficult to understand the phenomenon of effective therapy by separating the therapist, client and the system they practice.

A Wider Concept of Self

The reinforcement of custom and the maintenance of the society's status quo is doubtless aided by a preoccupation with one's own self, to the exclusion of others. No sooner has one generation freed itself from the narrow-mindedness, prejudice and mass foolishness of the previous generation, then it begins to oppress the next generation with its own 'uniqueness.' As Bertrand Russell (1917) observed, 'Each generation believes that this difficulty is a thing of the past, but each generation is tolerant only of *past* innovations. Those of its own day are met with the same persecution as if the principle of toleration had never been heard of.'

The self which is made up of this sense of uniqueness and other features is not a very reliable entity. One may be autonomous one moment, and in the next, the self may be completely transcended through an intense involvement with others. Our thoughts and feelings are intimately connected to those about us. Everyone knows that one speaks differently, expresses another angle, other emotions—still the 'truth,' but a different facet—with different people. One may express strong feelings or opinions but they are selected, may even be constituted differently when with work colleagues, the boss, the spouse, or the lover, the parents, the children, the neighbors, strangers. Some other aspect of the story comes out, or is colored differently, appropriate to one's perception of the relation, the other's receptivity, the hour, one's own and the other's interest, the listener's ability to understand. The network of thoughts, feelings, opinions, concepts, values, the biological connection between persons influences what one feels and perceives and *how* one expresses himself. Indeed, this is so common an observation that William James (1890) declared, 'Properly speaking, a man has as many social selves as there are individuals who recognize him and carry an image of him in their mind.'

Not only is the 'social self' not consistent, neither is the 'personal self.' The literary artist Logan Pearsall Smith (1934) has described succinctly this observation, 'I look at my overcoat and my hat hanging in the hall with reassurance; for although I go out of doors with one individuality today, when yesterday I had quite another, yet my clothes keep my various selves buttoned up together, and enable all these otherwise irreconcilable aggregates of psychological phenomena to pass themselves off as one person.'

Other selves

Often we may not even be in control of ourselves. Consider the following experiment. Eight men and four women, ages 18 to 50 years, were divided into four groups of three persons each. The psychologist Ralph Hefferline and research colleagues (1959) at Columbia University attached sets of recording electrodes to members of the first group who were told they were participating in a study of the effects on body tension of noise superimposed on music. They were instructed to listen to the music through earphones and to do nothing.

The second group, with electrodes attached, were told that an invisible muscular movement would control the noise. They were to listen to the music and try to discover and make use of the muscular response. The third group, with electrodes in place, were told the effective response for controlling the noise was a tiny twitch of the left thumb (which it was). The fourth group was the same as the third except that its members also had a meter by which they could see the results of their responses.

Music was played and a disagreeable 60-cycle hum was superimposed upon it. Whenever the experimenter detected through the electronic instrumentation a thumb twitch, he turned off the noise for 15 seconds. If the noise was already off when the thumb twitched, it was surpressed for an additional 15 seconds.

Except for two people in the third group, all the subjects were trained to twitch their left thumb. These two were so busy twitching their thumbs, *trying* to make something happen, that nothing did.

Members of the first group believed that they had been passively exposed to music and were astonished that they had in fact controlled the frequency of the noise.

Two members of the second group gave up looking for a response, became passive, and allowed the conditioning to take place. The other member professed to have discovered a complex ritualistic movement for controlling the noise. The procedure consisted of rowing motions with both hands, infinitesimal wriggling of both ankles, slightly shifting the jaw to the left, exhaling, and then waiting. Probably in the interval the thumb twitched. Whatever else, he demonstrated the persistance of ritual in human activities. We know that trying to do good sometimes results in harm. But this example also shows that right actions may also come from mistaken intentions. Both of these observations are relevant to the practice of psychotherapy.

The lone member of the third group who was conditioned had not understood the instructions and spent his time gradually increasing pressure with the thumb on an imaginary switch.

A hidden observer

Ernest Hilgard (1977) at Stanford University has discovered a way to communicate directly with the 'self' who may control some of these hidden functions. He has called this entity the 'hidden observer.'

In a demonstration of hypnotic deafness, Hilgard hypnotized a blind student who was given the suggestion that he would be completely deaf to all sounds. Wooden blocks were clapped together next to the man's ears. There was no reaction. Blanks from a starter's pistol had also been fired in a previous demonstration. The man showed absolutely no sign of flinching.

Since the man's ears functioned perfectly well, another student asked if there was not some 'part' of the person that was 'conscious' of what was happening. To test this hypothesis, Hilgard spoke to the subject in a quiet voice,

> As you know, there are parts of our nervous system that carry on activities that occur out of awareness, of which control and circulation of the blood or the digestive processes are the most familiar ... Although you are hypnotically deaf, perhaps there is some part of you that is hearing my voice and processing the information. If there is, I should like the index finger of your right hand to rise as a sign that this is the case. (ibid.)

To everyone's surprise the finger rose.

The subject then further astonished those present by saying, 'Please restore my hearing so you can tell me what you did. I felt my finger rise in a way that was not a spontaneous twitch, so you must have done something to make it rise. I want to know what you did.'

Nearly 100 years ago, after careful consideration of dreams, hypnosis and other, what he called, 'exceptional mental states,' William James (1896) concluded that, 'the mind seems to embrace a confederation of psychic entities.' This fits well with modern thinking. As Robert Ornstein (1986) has observed:

> The idea that we have one rational mind seriously undersells our diverse abilities. It oversells our consistency, and it emphasizes the very small rational islands in the mind at the expense of the vast archipelagos of talents, opportunities, and abilities surrounding them.

A unification of all these selves or minds may be much more complicated than Rogers suggested; if, in fact, psychotherapy, with its limited perspective, is capable of such a project. Nevertheless, Rogers' intent was not bad: realization of human potentiality.

Although which self is apparent depends on moods, on the environment and may be subject to control which is outside of personal awareness, there may also be an 'observing self,' a basis for integrated and wise action. Though not suspecting its existence, did client-centered therapy appeal to its wisdom in the reorganization of the client's experience?

A Recognition of an Everyday Reality that Doubtless Affects Psychotherapy

As can be seen from studies of the placebo effect, a client's expectations and values play a major part in successful therapy.[3] For example, those from a culture which values superlatives in speech, individual effort and novelty in general, experienced more drug-associated changes from *two* placebo capsules than from one (Blackwell, Bloomfield & Buncher, 1972). Those who received *different* placebos in three consecutive two-week periods improved more on this concentrated and varied treatment than those on a longer, six-week, regime which featured less novelty and the same placebo (Shapiro, 1971).

A placebo (from the Latin, 'I shall please') in medical parlence is a substance inert in relation to the pharmacology of the disorder. Thus, what is considered placebo effect in medicine is the relief of symptoms or cure of disease that comes about from causes inexplicable through the biological theories which apply to treatment. Factors surrounding patient improvement through the use of placebos, such as the doctor and his relation with the patient, considered inert in medicine, may be considered *cause* in psychotherapy. Placebo effect in the medical treatment of some physical as well as psychological disorders, thus, becomes a validation of psychotherapy as treatment in those cases (Frank, 1973).

Surprisingly, even such subtleties as color may influence a client's experience, perhaps according to some finely tuned common expectation or conditioning. For example, in a medical school demonstration, a class of 56 students were given envelopes containing either pink or blue capsules, which contained no pharmacologically active ingredients, and told the capsules would cause sedative or stimulant effects. Drug-associated changes subsequently affected the expected 30% of the participants; pink capsules were more often associated with stimulant actions and blue with sedative actions (Blackwell, Bloomfield & Buncher, 1972).

In a study that used placebos to induce sleep, blue tablets were more effective for women, while orange ones were more effective for men. Testing the tranquilizer Oxaepam, anxiety was reduced more effectively by a green tablet than by a red or yellow one; depression, by a yellow tablet (Shapiro, 1971).

The client's expectation—or perhaps one might even say, his self-healing capacity—can exert a very powerful effect on experience, even overturning the effect of strong drugs. A patient suffering from nausea and vomiting, for example, was assured by physicians that the drug treatment they were administering would be successful. Symptoms (both clinical and subjective) immediately disappeared. This happened in spite of the fact that what the patient was given was actually a powerful drug that *induces* vomiting! (Wolf, 1950).

During the process of psychotherapy it is common to observe a client's incongruence: his bodily expression and his stated assumptions in conflict. This is also evident in placebo studies. In a research by Park and Covi (1965), fifteen newly admitted clients, diagnosed as 'neurotic,' were *told* that they were to be given a placebo for one week, after which further treatment would be offered. 'These pills,' they were instructed, 'with no medicine, only sugar, have helped others and we believe they will help you.' Patients were prescribed a dosage of one capsule three times per day at mealtime. On the basis of both doctor and client ratings of four different measures, all fourteen participants who finished the treatment were considered improved.

The way clients conceptualized their experience is illuminating. One client, after a dramatic improvement, replied, 'It wasn't sugar. It was medicine!' Another declared, 'They're not sugar pills, because they worked!' The evidence of their body is indisputable. The authority of the doctor, since they improved, is not shaken; and since they are not prepared to imagine they could improve *without* taking medicine, the clients cling to their assumptions and conclude there must have been a mixup in the prescription. Experience is not enough to overcome their beliefs and expectations. Thus, beliefs and basic assumptions may not always change, even as a result of successful psychotherapy.

Unexamined assumptions, that may pass for beliefs, may survive despite repeated confrontations with reality. Frederic W.H. Meyers published this observation: A religious woman, when questioned about what she thought had become of the soul of her recently departed daughter, replied, 'Oh well, I suppose she is enjoying eternal bliss, but I wish you wouldn't talk about such unpleasant subjects' (Russell, 1950: 108).

In the placebo study, convinced that the pills contained no medicine, a client ignored the complexities of medical theory and turned to expected results. She assumed without question, from the beginning, that the pills would help to 'ease my mind.' which indeed they did. Other patients may integrate the complexities of experience by shifting to a symbolic perception or ritual observance. Success may depend on how closely the treatment matches the ritual that doctor and client feel they must fulfill in order for healing to occur. When given the pills, one client remarked, 'Why would they help, because for people, each time they take a pill, it's a symbol or something of someone caring about you, thinking about you three or four times a day?'

A client, who considered the doctor reassuring, also decided that taking a pill in 'the right frame of mind' gives a 'moral support.' She also believed that the organism possesses a self-healing ability: 'I think I had a lot to do with it myself, to be honest. By knowing myself. By knowing that I had to control myself to keep myself in the right frame of mind.'

Another said, 'Every time I took a pill I thought of my doctor and how I'm doing. It just reminds you that you are trying to change yourself.' These examples reveal a great deal about not only how clients experience treatment but also, the influence of the culture on their expectations and the role of the system's commanding principles in the treatment.

The one participant who did not improve, dropped out because her husband had ridiculed her for spending money to take 'sugar pills.' Her symptoms worsened.

Attempts to define the kind of person who is likely to respond to placebo effect have only added to the mystery. Researches have been unable to correlate, for example, suggestibility, personality, age, or sex of patients with successful treatment with placebo. To further complicate matters, some patients do not respond to the first trial, but respond to the next. Some show more receptivity in a group than individually (Knowles & Lucas, 1960).

If you imagine that placebo effect is frivolous, you should read the report of a patient who became *addicted* to placebo tablets (Mintz, 1977). Placebos may even be dangerous, reportedly having caused a wide variety of *toxic side-effects* (Beecher, 1955).

The only clear signs for possible placebo effect in the patient are anxiety, agitation, and pain: the same indicators found for success in psychotherapy. Indeed, Gallagher (1953) found that clients with low anxiety tend not to become involved in the client-centered therapy process and drop out. Hence, the hypothesis of anxiety as a requirement in the client may be a sound one for client-centered therapy as well as for placebo effect in medicine.[4]

Thus, the client cannot be separated from the phenomenon. His anxious incongruence, desire to change, and his ability to enter into an immediate, personal relationship might even be prerequisites to success. His values and beliefs, motivations and intentions, his expectations, his contribution to sensitive empathic understanding and acceptance of the therapist or therapeutic relation doubtless also figure in effective therapy. A client may be healed by ingesting a chemical that has been scientifically established as curative. On the other hand, he may even cure himself by ingesting chemicals known to *cause* his symptoms. He may cure himself by ingesting completely innocuous chemicals or by using no chemicals whatever, merely conversing with a psychotherapist. In successful cases, evidence of the system's principles may be found in the ritual. For example, in the placebo treatments the following may be noted: 'When someone cares about you, you improve.' 'To improve, you must exert effort.' 'You have within you the power to improve.' 'Treatment is a reminder that you are trying to change yourself.'

In the case of the person-centered approach to psychotherapy, while the client may have intentions at odds with the therapist's, may keep many thoughts and feelings hidden, may carry on an inner dialogue while conversing on a completely different subject with the therapist, her belief in the treatment and the approach to therapy has been recognized as a factor in success (Kirtner, 1955). Respecting the therapist's equal 'air time,' forgiving her foibles, and realizing that 'they and the therapist are dealing with a highly ambiguous and complicated subject,' demonstrate both the client's involvement in and fairness in assessing the relation (Rennie, 1988).

Although James' (1896) observation that 'the mind seems to embrace a confederation of psychic entities' was passed over for almost a century, today there is much talk of interactive 'mental organs' or 'modules' of mind. Quite a list of supposed modules has already accummulated. It includes one for face recognition, for spatial relations, for tool-use, for fear, for social exchange, for emotion perception, as well as a 'theory of mind' module (Barkow, Cosmides & Tooby, 1992).

The enormous variety of patterns of thought, varied emotional reactions to the same social situation in large group workshops also suggests a complexity that exceeds the limits of the concept of self proposed by the psychology of client-centered therapy.

Research of thinking patterns confirms that we may indeed use 'modules of mind' to confront certain kinds of experience. However, these studies also suggest that the wrong module may be selected to deal with a problem better suited to another. Furthermore, modules may be 'triggered' by certain behaviors of others, even by the phrases they use, and even by certain words.[5] This view also explains why a person may act and feel completely to the contrary when within a group meeting and when solitary; all the time feeling that he or she is a single entity.

In a small volume of lectures, James (1896) has described various 'exceptional mental states.' Among the subjects he has discussed are dreams, hypnotism, automatism, multiple personality, demonical possession, witchcraft, insanity and genius. James (1890) also admitted that a person 'has as many social selves as there are individuals who recognize him and carry an image of him in their minds.'

Similar phenomena are readily verified in large group workshops and are not easily accounted for in the theory of client-centered therapy.

An Appreciation of the Effect of Environment

Rather than the human being affecting the climate, what has been more frequently noted is the climate affecting the human being. When Rogers was responsible for placing children in foster homes, he seemed to have grasped the notion of 'climate' or 'environment' as an agent in personality change. More recently, the concept of 'climate' became even more important in the scheme of Rogers' thinking. At the same time that this notion moved closer to a centralizing concept for his system, it became more vague. In the end, it appeared as nothing more than meager 'attitudes' held by the therapist as he enters into a therapeutic process with his client. Nevertheless, there are real and substantial aspects of the environment that influence our feelings, perceptions, thoughts, our consciousness, essentially, 'who we are.'

William James (1929) has noted, 'Our normal waking consciousness ... is but one special type of consciousness, whilst all about it, parted from it by the flimsiest screens, there lie potential forms of consciousness entirely different ... apply the requisite stimulus, and at a touch they are all there in all their completeness' (pp. 378–9). The environment can provide several such stimuli.

The most straightforward aspect of 'environment' is place. And place doubtless influences consciousness. Note, for example, Thoreau's (1929) description about Walden:

> One inconvenience I sometimes experienced in so small a house, was the difficulty of getting to a sufficient distance from my guest when we began to utter the big thoughts in big words. You want room for your thoughts to get into sailing trim and run a course or two before they make their port. In my house we were so near that we could not begin to hear ... If we are merely loquacious and loud talkers, then we can afford to stand very near together, cheek by jowl, and feel each other's breath; but if we speak reservedly and thoughtfully we want to be further apart.

Who hasn't noticed the effect of place? In a grand cathedral, and in spite of the distraction of clammering tourists, one's shoulders relax and consciousness, not bounded by the dark moldy corners of the dense building, soars to timeless reflections on life's meaning, one's purpose in a mysterious and inexplicable universe, humility, nobility. On the other hand, even though one may not perceive the cause (or even refuse to believe it when demonstrated), an ugly, crowded space, can provoke 'monotony, fatigue, headache, sleep, discontent, irritability, hostility and avoidance' (Mintz, 1956).

If, as Barker (1968) found, a drugstore or basketball game affects consciousness and human behavior in accordance with the *requirements* of their structure, how much more so does a workshop's beautiful resort setting or a psychotherapist's delicately arranged consulting room? (One may recall that Freud treated his clients in his home, not a sterile office. They were surrounded by ancient artifacts and symbols that by their very presence may have invited the deep and noble human desire for self-discovery.)

An extension of the setting might also include people close to the therapist or client who influence the therapy process. Therapy supervisors, for example, may influence directly the process of therapy (Steinhelber, Patterson, Cliffe & LeGoullon, 1984). Also influential may be family members, nursing or other support staff, and those involved in supplemental treatments the client may be receiving concurrently. Even in client-centered therapy interviews conducted before a group, the group may have as much or more influence as the therapist (see Slack, 1985; Rogers, 1986b).

The mere reduction of sunshine, as occurs from seasonal shifting of the sun in lattitudes closer to the poles, can cause significant mood changes. On the other hand, simple exposure to bright full-spectrum light reduces the depression that many people experience during winter months (Rosenthal et al., 1984). Color also appears to effect mood: pink-colored walls of a detention room, for example, have been claimed to calm a person in an aggressive state. Everyone would agree that sounds, especially music, affect our moods. But, scents also affect consciousness and bodily functions. The smell of spiced apple, for example, has been reported to reduce blood pressure on the order of that caused by meditation.

Gregory Razran (1938) demonstrated that a person's perceptions are significantly altered by merely eating a meal. He asked people (not all college students) to rate and characterize musical selections and paintings both while eating lunch and afterwards. In spite of realizing that their perceptions had changed, Razran could not convince participants in the experiment of any influence. 'All they could believe,' he disappointedly concluded, 'was that "the mind may work differently during a meal" or that it may "change after you've heard (or seen) something before," but not that it can change "because I heard or saw it during a meal." "Not me. What will professors think of next?"'

Though few clients will be eating a meal during traditional present-day therapy (though they will, during residential programs), all of them will be breathing. And the air they will breathe may have an affect on their state of consciousness and their emotional reactions. This has been noticed, for example, in certain weather fronts such as followed by the dry hot winds of the *sharav* in the Near East, the *foehn* in Central Europe, *zonda* in Argentina and *santa ana* in Southern California. These 'winds of ill-repute' have been associated not only with irritability, but migraine headaches, nausea and respiratory congestion in a substantial number of persons exposed. This type of wind pushes air with high concentrations of positive ions. The inhalation of air containing large numbers of small *negative* ions, on the other hand, relieves these symptoms and induces relaxed moods. Large amounts of negative ions are found naturally in the clean air surrounding beaches, waterfalls and glacial peaks. Perhaps it is no coincidence that these places often figure in inspirational experiences. Polluted industrial air contains the least amount of negative ions (Kreuger & Reed, 1976). Thus, the air in the therapy setting could profoundly affect a patient's mood: from irritable avoidance to relaxed introspection.[6]

Certain natural formations such as majestic mountains, expansive plains, the sea, lakes, apart from the effect of small negative ions, may also influence mood through some sort of structural effect on consciousness. Strolling through a well-designed park, even in a polluted city, may help a person to relax and experience peacefulness, harmony, beauty and perhaps reflective thoughts. There is even evidence that a view of nature through a hospital room window may facilitate a person's recovery from surgery (Ulrich, 1984). Furthermore, the presence of flowers in his or her room may also contribute to the improvement of the mental state and the rate of recovery of the patient (Watson & Burlingame, 1960).

Evidence suggests that even exposure to invisible low frequency magnetic fields, such as those that surround powerline transformers and computer stations, may (in addition to being dangerous to health) affect a person's memory and sense of time (Brodeur, 1989).

The therapy setting organizes the participant's space. It contains the presence of another, emotional and physical stimulation, images, sounds, smells, colors, changes in light, and the air itself that affect the participant's state of consciousness.

Thus, it might facilitate a person in perceiving beyond herself, reflecting on her life, realizing her true desires, gaining insight into personal problems, or arriving at new perceptions of her relationship to society—just as what might be hoped from good psychotherapy.

An Understanding of the Professional Role

Julius Seeman (1954), another of the founders of client-centered therapy, discovered that success in psychotherapy associates closely with a strong and growing mutual liking between therapist and client. Being liked, in psychotherapy as in most endeavors, is conducive to success (Stoler, 1963; Lipkin, 1954). In a study of psychoanalytic therapy, clients who improved more were more liked by their therapists, resembled their therapist's usual clients, and were considered 'suitable' for treatment. In a study of behavior therapy, clients who improved more had therapists who 'felt comfortable with them and found them interesting.' Though the style of the therapists in both psychoanalytic and behavior approaches were quite different (behavior therapists, for example, were more directive and talked more), 'successful clients in both therapies,' researchers conclude, 'rated the personal interaction with the therapist as the single most important part of their treatment' (Sloane et al., 1975).

The therapist proposes, explicit at times but also implicit, to share with the client a process of mutual discovery, to understand the meanings of the client's experience and for each to express honestly his feelings and values. Just as in any endeavor, how well the therapist does what she knows how to do affects the outcome. Thus, the *purity* with which the therapist executes his approach may affect the success of the therapy (Luborsky et al., 1986).

There also may be an association between the consistency of the therapist's belief system and effective therapy (Combs, 1986). For example, there is astonishing evidence of the physician's belief being related to success in medical treatment. In a double-blind research on placebo effect, the physician's intuition (guessing correctly when medicine or placebo was being administered) was associated with higher improvement rate among the more than 300 chronic schizophrenic patients being treated (Engelhardt & Margolis, 1967). One of the most striking anecdotes reported on the relation of a physician's belief and a patient's improvement is the following: after noting the positive effects of a new experimental drug on relieving a patient's symptoms of asthma, a physician substituted a placebo in the hope of establishing the new drug's validity. When the patient complained of renewed symptoms, the physician was satisfied there was no placebo effect and ordered more of the drug. However, the pharmaceutical manufacturer replied that the drug originally supplied was in fact a *placebo* (Ornstein & Sobel, 1987). The patient had been receiving a non-active substance all along. When the physician believed an active drug was being prescribed, the patient progressed; when the physician believed otherwise, the patient's symptoms worsened.

An Adequate Concept of Empathic Understanding

Empathic understanding, what the average person associates with a concerned involvement of therapist with patient, has been given various professional meanings. The anthropologist Clifford Geertz (1983) says that, 'understanding the form and pressure of [a person's inner life] is more like grasping a proverb, catching an allusion, seeing a joke, than it is like achieving communion.' Corcoran (1983), a researcher of this subject, suggests that empathy involves experiencing a feeling that corresponds with the feelings of another. Social psychologists have divided empathy into two types: 'affective' (I feel what you feel) and 'cognitive' (I comprehend what you feel) (Gladstein, 1983). Psychoanalyst Heinz Kohut (1978) calls the process of understanding another, 'vicarious introspection.' Empathy, he depicts as, 'the human echo to human experience.' Webster's English Dictionary says, since the word derives from *en* and *pathos*, empathy literally means 'in-feelings.'

Rogers initially defined empathy as a specific *state* of consciousness: 'The state of empathy, or being empathic,' he declared,

> is to perceive the internal frame of reference of another with accuracy and with the emotional components and meanings which pertain thereto as if one were the person ... Thus, it means to sense the hurt or the pleasure of the other as he senses it and to perceive the causes thereof as he perceives them, but without ever losing the recognition that it is *as if* I were hurt or pleased and so forth. (1959: 210–11)

The essential aspect of the phenomenon of the effective therapeutic relationship involves a creative interplay between the analytic mode of consciousness and the holistic mode of consciousness. Rogers (1955) seems to have perceived this when he confessed that he felt, 'an increasing discomfort at the distance between the rigorous objectivity of myself as scientist and the almost mystical subjectivity of myself as therapist.'

One is the linear, moment-by-moment fluctuating awareness of thoughts and feelings of the analytical mode of consciousness (to sense the hurt or pleasure of the client). The other is a timeless perception (to generalize the meaning, *as if* I had this hurt or pleasure) of the holistic mode of consciousness. Besides providing a context for meaning, the all-at-once awareness also diminishes narrowmindedness. Empathic understanding, in other words, is a state of consciousness in which one experiences and participates in a flow of thoughts and feelings and their meanings with another while *also* being aware of the larger context in which the two exist. In this state, opposites may co-exist without causing concern about contradictions. The therapist's awareness is active, not a passive acceptance. He is aware of both the moment-by-moment activity and the patterns that make up life. The falsification of this activity can be disastrous. For example, the therapist's passive acceptance of resistance, evasiveness, negativism, and not facing problems in the therapist–client relationship have been found to be predictors of failure in both client-centered therapy and analytic psychotherapy (Sachs, 1983).

In psychotherapy, it is not enough to merely attempt to understand the other's world, not even to feel something the client is feeling (and certainly not sufficient to dampen tears with 'support'). The client must also experience being understood. In participating in a state of empathic understanding, the therapist may even feel and say things that might appear strange (or at least unexpected) in other traditional therapeutic contexts. See examples of 'idiosyncratic empathy' cited by Bozarth (1984) where, for instance, to the doubtless initial horror of his supervisor, a therapist related to his client a long drawn-out story about repairing his Volkswagen engine. Although this violates the principles of client-centered therapy and conventional wisdom about empathy, in that moment, this was in fact an important experience of empathic understanding as confirmed by the client afterwards.

Rogers' empathic state of consciousness

Rogers describes an episode of empathic understanding that illustrates this integration of analytic and holistic modes of consciousness:

> [I]t starts with, and is preceded by, settling into this attitude of 'I want to understand every single thing that [the client is] saying; I want to really sense what it means to [him or her].' I feel [in moments of empathic understanding] all in one piece, as though I am all focused. Yet, in ordinary life, I think, 'God, how am I going to get everything done before I leave for Europe.' You know, pretty well fragmented. It is a very existential moment because, when I finish a really good interview, my memory for that interview is often very bad. Later, when I think about it, some parts of it will come back; but the intellectual side of me is not very much present. Well, the intellectual side is there too, but it is all focused in this moment with no intent of thinking about it, with no intent to remember it. So, all my abilities are there, I think. The best periods in therapy are timeless moments. I am not aware of time. Except for the fact that if I have another appointment at such and such a time, there is some background awareness of that. In an interview in front of a group, pretty soon the group disappears completely. They are not there. It is just the two of us. (Monteiro dos Santos, 1985)

The therapist and client participate in an integrative experience that transcends time, that transcends the boundaries of the presumed identity of both client and therapist. Through a single-pointed attention to 'every single thing' the client is saying, the therapist's everyday frame of reference becomes more flexible. In this state, he feels all in one piece as he 'settles into' the holistic mode of consciousness. He may lose awareness of his surroundings and even the sense of time. When returning to his everyday state, he may experience a partial amnesia. In other words, in these intense and vital moments he is, by definition, in an altered state of consciousness (Shor, 1959; Ludwig, 1967). This could also be what William James (1890) called one of the 'lower phases of mediumistic possession.' It is not a deep trance that possesses the person, capturing his will and incapacitating his thinking ability. Rogers' critical faculties are operating. It is a disciplined state in which the complementary modes of consciousness are both functioning optimally. It is a state that Field (1960) describes as 'a curious blend of gainfully directed hysteria and patient self-discipline.' In fact, in this state the therapist is apparently *more,* not less, aware than at other times. Rogers (1957a) verifies this when he indicates that he never felt 'as whole, or as much a person' as he did in his therapeutic interviews.

It is worth repeating that none has described the *complementary* functioning of the analytic and holistic modes of consciousness better than Rogers himself when he noted that, 'Beyond the immediate message of the person, no matter what that might be, there is the universal ... So there is both the satisfaction of hearing *this* person and also the satisfaction of hearing one's self in touch with what is universally true' (1980: 8).

Furthermore, this experience was apparently a quite normal, or unremarkable, part of client-centered therapy's practice early on. 'When there is this complete unity, singleness, fullness of experiencing in the relationship,' Rogers (1961a) describes, 'then it acquires the 'out-of-this-world' quality which therapists have remarked upon, a sort of trance-like feeling in the relationship from which both the client and I emerge at the end of the hour, as if from a deep well or tunnel ... a timeless living in the experience which is *between* the client and me' (p. 202). One of the most innocent and at the same time most striking verifications of this phenomenon, from the client's side of the therapeutic relationship, is 'We were mostly me working together on my situation as I found it' (Rogers, 1949).

Recently, Rogers put this experience into the current language:

When I am at my best, as a group facilitator or a therapist, I discover another characteristic. I find that when I am closest to my inner, intuitive self, when I am somehow in touch with the unknown in me, when perhaps I am in a slightly altered state of consciousness in the relationship, then whatever I do seems to be full of healing. Then simply my *presence* is releasing and helpful. There is nothing I can do to force this experience, but when I can relax and be close to the transcendental core of me, then I may behave in strange and impulsive ways in the relationship, ways which I cannot justify rationally, which have nothing to do with my thought processes. But these strange behaviors turn out to be *right*, in some odd way. At those moments it seems that my inner spirit has reached out and touched the inner spirit of the other. Our relationship transcends itself, and has become a part of something larger. Profound growth and healing and energy are present' (Rogers, 1985).[7]

Some time after his initial definition, Rogers (1980) redefined empathic understanding to be, instead of a 'state,' a 'process.' In fact, over the years Rogers has refered to empathy, not only as a 'state' and a 'process,' but also as a 'condition,' 'attitude,' 'quality,' 'ability,' 'aptitude,' and 'source of knowledge' (Quadros, 1979). The literal-minded have taken this as an indication of an ambiguous, poorly formed, concept. However, it is understandable, if one realizes that empathic understanding is a *condition*, in the sense that it may be necessary for the success of therapy. Trying to understand the expressions of the client and what meanings her thoughts and feelings have for her, the therapist adopts a particularly attentive *attitude* (and perhaps clients do this as well). Empathic understanding seems to be a *quality* of the effective therapeutic relationship. It is an aspect of the *state* of consciousness of the therapist and client who share a vivid perception of the world of the client. It is a *process* in the sense that this state of consciousness is not fixed, but exists in flux, just as the relationship itself. It becomes an *ability* or *aptitude* when one learns how to sense the deep personal meanings of another person and communicate this to him or her. It is a *source of knowledge* in the sense that this 'out of the ordinary' state of consciousness permits intuitively 'knowing what one does not know' and unexpected insights or discoveries.

More recently, Rogers conceded the obvious, that the client also participates in this empathic state of consciousness with him, relating, 'I feel that in the best moments of therapy there is a mutual altered state of consciousness. That we really, both of us, somehow transcend a little bit what we are ordinarily, and there's communication going on that neither of us understands that is very reflective' (Heppner, Rogers & Lee, 1984). Replying to Bergin (1991), Rogers, in a further attempt to understand this subject better, said:

> I believe there is some kind of a transcendent organizing influence in the universe which operates in man as well ... My present very tentative view [of humans] is that perhaps there is an essential person which persists through time, or even through eternity.

Other factors

The experience of empathic understanding is also related to culture, an observation missing from most explanations. For example, for a citizen born in the United States, ignoring his concerns for ideology and concentrating on how he *feels* (central to the method of client-centered therapy) may indeed lead to empathic understanding. For an African, on the other hand, such an emphasis could very well result in exactly the opposite: an experience of complete *lack* of understanding, respect and sensitivity for the client's reality—as North Americans trying to facilitate an encounter group of Africans found out (Doob, 1970; Doob, Foltz & Stevens, 1970).

The effect of empathic understanding is active at the biological levels of existence. As Lynch (1985) found, when one truly attends to the external environment in a relaxed manner or listens to others speaking, blood pressure usually falls and heart rate slows. Through dialogue, participant's heartbeats become interrelated and the cardiovascular measure of their relation depends, at least, on the expectations of each, the presence of support from the other, and actively attending to oneself or to the other.

The neglect in seriously considering the client's participation in empathic understanding or other aspects of the process of client-centered therapy is the major reason that after some 50 years of research the theory has yet to be validated (Watson, 1984). It is no longer sufficient to conceptualize empathic understanding, congruence and non-judgmental acceptance as merely therapist attitudes, if one wishes to understand their relation to all the effective applications of the person-centered approach.[8]

Diminishing the 'I–Thou' distinction, together they apply a highly refined attention on the client's feelings (and ocasionally on the therapist's). The organization of the client's experience is the goal. The centrality of the client's feelings is not merely unfolding, 'it is constituted in the lively attunement and emphasis of the therapist-together-with-his-client' (Barton, 1971). In this attunement the therapist as well as the client is changed. By denying her profound and vital effect, by claiming to be 'careful not to interfere' in the 'emerging self,' the client-centered therapist underestimates her legitimate value in the therapeutic endeavor. On the other hand, by claiming to 'provide an atmosphere' or 'create an environment' through her attitude alone, the therapist grossly overestimates her role. The therapist's values, indeed the values of psychotherapy itself, are part of the phenomenon of the effective therapeutic relationship. The experience of empathic understanding, congruence, even non-judgmental acceptance may be seen to be as much the *result* of the relationship, as the *cause* of it.[9]

Empatia interuptus: another view

The hills near Rome are veiled by blue haze that has drifted up the soft valley of the Sabines. Across the plaza the sagging terrracota façade of the village storehouse blushes in the late afternoon sunlight. On the cafe's terrace sweet drinks are being sipped reflectively. Cigarette smoke curls silently. The normally impatient weeping willows on the avenue are motionless. The land is still, expectant, as if on the verge to speak. Nevertheless, it merely listens.

Sabini? It is mountainous country east of the Tiber and north of the districts of the Latins, in the heart of the central Apennines. Tradition allies the people of this region with the beginning of Rome. The Sabines gave Rome the *populus Romanus quirites*, the individual citizen as contrasted to the community; in return, the Romans stole the Sabine women.

Quirinus, the Sabine deity, never attained the first rank, but did get chummy with Jupiter who guarded the path of duty and right doing. Jupiter's wife Juno stood for the female principle of life. Every man had his 'Genius,' every woman, her 'Juno,' divine double.

The broken silence, wrongdoing, and the divine double are elements in this story.

At a retreat center, in a lounge off of the dining room, an internationally known expert in 'cross-cultural communications' is holding forth in an encounter group. Although he does not become personally involved with his female students, his grey-templed charm and the promise of earning psychotherapeutic skills have attracted a large group of Italian women. They are mostly psychologists and have enrolled in a course of training in sensitive and accurate empathic listening. In this group they will learn from practice. The famous North American psychologist listens intently to each participant as she reveals some previously guarded fact about her life. Other members of the group make comments that are tolerated patiently. Then the psychologist contributes his observations, at times impressively capturing the exact sentiment the speaker intends to convey. Often the American offers home-grown wisdom or relates anecdotes from his university days which are received appreciatively.

The moment has arrived for a woman, who has served before as the great facilitator's translator, to tell of a long kept secret. Irani says she wishes to reveal 'something that she has held within her and is bursting to come out.' She says it 'frightens and excites her at the same time.' There is another woman present, Juliana, who has also translated the American. He knows them both well. Both are middle-aged, not unattractive. They live in industrious northern Italy; that is, they tend to be less talkative and more practical than their restless younger colleagues from the south.

It is decided that Irani, who has been translating, will speak directly to the American in English. Juliana will take over the task of translating Irani's words into Italian for the others. The psychologist lights a cigarette and examines his fingernails while this detail of procedure is settled. He doesn't understand one word of Italian but prides himself on his sensitive listening and his ability to reflect deep feelings, even through a translator. When the professional moment arrives, he will be ready.

Irani begins her confession. Squeezing her hands together, as if praying for the right words (or perhaps hoping that awkwardly chosen or even wrong words will be accepted), she begins to tell the psychologist how she feels about him. Over these years, as he worked, she translated. Through devotion to the message, she had become more and more close to the messenger. She does not hide her present disappointments with life. She admits that she may be feeling a bit more vulnerable than usual. In any case, she respects the way the facilitator conducts psychology. She has even applied his techniques effectively in her own modest practice.

Irani speaks in English. Juliana repeats in Italian. English to Italian. English to Italian.

She fights against the final wave of surrender: 'Is this real?' she wonders. 'I don't know what to say.' Finally, she gives in, 'Not only do I feel close to your work, I feel close to you! As a *woman*.'

English to Italian, English to Italian to English to Italian to English. The faces of group members veer from Irani to Juliana to Irani to Juliana.

With guilt and passion, Irani declares, 'After 20 years of marriage, I have these feelings for a man who is not my husband. What is to become of me?' With tears running down her cheeks, she leans toward the American, her arms open wide, her voice broken by sobs, and says, 'I love you.'

Irani's intimate feelings are nakedly exposed, her final words hang in a sacred silence. Juliana, choked with emotion, is not able to translate. Then the master of understanding rises, holds his arms out wide and, as if greeting his favorite aunt on her birthday, announces, 'Of course, I understand; and I love you too.' He then flings himself into the arms of *Juliana* who, terrified and speechless, is incapable of explaining this incredible act to the astonished group.

Irani's words were understood, they were accepted, yet an unthinkable tragedy has occured. The psychologist listened as he was accustomed to: English words which *followed*, not preceded, the incomprehensible Italian. He attributed the words of one admirer to the feelings of another. Irani, realizing what has happened, begins repeating, as if to validate the evasive reality, 'It's okay. Yes, it's okay. It could be her, yes.'

The dumbstruck Juliana, in the arms of the American, her dream come true, filled with both indescribable pleasure and immeasurable embarassment, screams, 'Oh, my God! It's all wrong. It's all wrong.' Members of the group stare, horrified; incapable of assimilating her words in light of what is taking place.

The master of understanding is reassuring, 'There, there, of course it's wrong. But that's okay too.' After the appropriate interval for such embraces, he glances at his wristwatch and says, 'Well, it's time to end this session. I'll be seeing you all in two months when I return.'

Irani and Juliana stare at each other as their colleagues file numbly from the room. Irani rises slowly and tenderly embraces the shivering Juliana. The bewildered psychologist shrugs his shoulders. 'What's the big deal? All I did was hug somebody.'

A summer shower begins falling. Hail stones splatter on the red tiles of the balconies. Rainwater refreshes the air. Splashing along the gutters of the tile roof and cascading onto the veranda it applauds the greater event: the effect of a warm and supportive empathy.

Two conclusions, from many, are apparent: One, even when one tries to do good, he or she may do harm. Second, even if one's actions are not the best, a good outcome might still result by virtue of the decent and pure intentions of others involved.

Notes

1. Cited by Crick (1994).

2. I don't know about Rollo May, but Rogers scarcely would have any direct experience of 'cultural damage.' He was the child of stable, intelligent and well-meaning parents. He attended upper-class primary school with the likes of Ernest Hemingway and Frank Lloyd Wright's children. He spent his youth in a spacious 8-room, 5-bath 'farmhouse' with a clay tennis court. At the university he studied with Goodwin Watson who introduced him to counseling. At the University of Chicago he worked during an enlightened era. He became wealthy from royalties on his best-selling books. On the other hand, from knowing him personally and from studying his writings—from diaries of a trip to China as a youth until his last essay on peace—it is clear that he had a deep compassion for the suffering of others.

3. Although one would imagine that psychotherapists would be delighted by information, such as learning more about placebo effect and human nature, many I know say they feel very uncomfortable with this knowledge. It seems in part that they cannot digest facts that fall outside their frames of reference or factors which they feel they have no control over. The psychotherapist's response, too often, is no better than the self-deceiving client who buries his or her head in the sand when confronted with uncomfortable facts.

4. The client's lack of urgency to resolve a real problem is what makes demonstration interviews so bland. Although the results are often disappointing, they may serve to illustrate the therapist's method and her steadfastness.

5. Cialdini (1985) relates many fascinating examples. For example, Langer, Blank & Chanowitz (1978) conducted a research in which a person 'cut' the line waiting to make copies at a library copier. When she asked the person using the machine, 'Excuse me, I have five pages. May I use the Xerox machine?' only 60% complied. However, when she asked, 'Excuse me, I have five pages. May I use the Xerox machine because I'm in a rush?' 94% let her skip ahead. It seems that 'because I'm in a rush' made the difference. But not so. When she asked, 'Excuse me, I have five pages. May I use the xerox machine because I have to make some copies?' 93% complied, even though no real reason was given. Merely the word 'because' is sufficient to 'trigger' action almost automatically.

6. One may note that the various activities (one-to-one psychotherapy, small groups, large groups) may appear different by virtue of the characteristics that become foreground and background in each. Thus, in one-to-one psychotherapy in the foreground is the therapist and client, their professional relationship, their attitudes, beliefs, confidence in the procedure. Empathic understanding is most often expressed through conversation. The effect of setting, certain social effects, the consequences of culture, for example, remain in the background for the most part. In small groups, the interpersonal relationship between participants comes forward. Cultural-related

factors also appear more prominent. The professional conversation recedes. Other group members may be more important in this setting than the facilitator. The environment becomes more important. In the large group, the therapeutic factors become less obvious. Interpersonal relations are important. The environment, the effect of group, cultural factors play a major role. In each, of course, Rogers is trying to facilitate the establishment of a 'climate' for a constructive outcome, both for individuals and for the group.

7. It is well to accumulate data and keep an open mind in regards to such phenomenon. William James (1896) has duly warned the investigator of exceptional mental states of the reactions that various phenomena may illicit. 'Some minds,' he observed, 'would see a marvel in the simplest hypnosis—others would refuse to admit there was anything new even if one rose from the dead ... of these minds, one pursues the idols of the tribe, another of the cave.'

8. Frequently people ask which is more important: congruence, unconditional positive regard or empathy? What is the *primary* condition? From the different perspectives: client, therapist and relationship, one might say that unconditional positive regard is most important to the client (to receive); that congruent is most important to the therapist (to be); and that empathic understanding is most important to the relationship (to be effective). However, the fact that there are three concepts does not mean that they necessarily *must* be ordered.

Behind this question is often a therapist's dilemma: If one does not like a person, what should one do? To be truly genuine, the therapist would react as he or she normally does in life. That is, he or she would not show acceptance toward the client. To pretend to accept the person would be incongruent. To try to resolve this problem logically, outside of the consulting room, is fruitless. The attempt ignores the fact that when the therapist is practicing therapy he or she is experiencing a special state of consciousness that may permit such contradictions to co-exist without provoking excessive worry. Empathic understanding, congruence and non-judgmental acceptance on the part of the therapist are functioning when the 'ordinary reality orientation' that raises such questions is relaxed.

9. There is a perplexing trend in North and South America to try to show that Rogers' psychotherapy is not 'phenomenological.' The reality may or may not be so. However, the disturbing assumption in such projects is that phenomenology is 'good' and that which is not is 'bad.' A graduate student at a South American university, for example, has concluded a thesis by saying that Rogers, by not having a 'phenomenological attitude,' compromised his practice of psychotherapy. This is a very strange accusation. To me, it is equivalent to an engineer building up an argument based on a certain airtight logic that leads to the conclusion that a hummingbird due to its unorthodoxy is aerodynamically unsound and therefore unable to fly. It is possible that Rogers' posture may not have been 'phenomenological,' that his theory may be mechanistic positivism, that it may be incomplete or even wrong, that his philosophy may be vague. Nevertheless, the

attitude with which he approached the study of the phenomenon of effective psychotherapy certainly was congenial to Heidegger's (1962) *phainomenon*—that which shows itself in itself. And most important of all, he was an *effective* therapist. His therapy was hardly compromised by whatever phenomenologicness he may have lacked.

As a matter of fact, I am attracted to phenomenology. I feel that, for example, the phenomenological science of Goethe is more elegant than Newton's science in describing the phenomenon of light. However, aesthetical preference is one thing and effectiveness in practice of psychotherapy is another. For critics who, as far as I can see, have yet to demonstrate an *effective* 'phenomenological psychotherapy,' to criticize Rogers' unarguably effective and successful practice is deplorable.

CHAPTER TWELVE

Toward a Psychology for Applications of the Person-Centered Approach

We must recollect that all our provisional ideas in psychology will someday be based on an organic structure.
     Sigmund Freud

The person-centered approach does not need anything, except to be applied effectively. It should no longer be confused with the principles of client-centered therapy. With more knowledge of human groupings, it no longer need be ineffective in applications involving groups. If it is *applied*, and not used to *give an experience,* it will take care of itself.

Nevertheless, the psychology of client-centered therapy is not adequate to account for most applications of the person-centered approach. Thus, there is a need for a comprehensive psychology. Rogers (1959) anticipated this need. While publishing the theory of client-centered therapy, he recognized his statement as inevitably flawed, inexact in the manner of most theories, and vulnerable to the effects of time. He asked for a revision of his explanation within a decade. It's already twenty years late.

The subject is complicated. Any theory must now include the complexities of large group workshops to improve transcultural understanding and transnational communications, large groups which meet to resolve conflicts, large groups that form communities for learning, encounter groups, classroom learning, group therapy *and* client-centered therapy. It must explain the various phenomena encountered in these activities.

William James (1890) considered psychology as, 'the science of mental life, both of its phenomena and their conditions.' In his classic text, he addressed among other things the subjects of stream of thoughts, consciousness of self, attention, concepts, discrimination and comparison, association, perception of time, space and of things, memory, sensation, imagination, perception of reality, reasoning, instinct, emotions, will, and exceptional mental states. Any psychology should include these subjects as well.

In light of the broad range of questions raised by applications of the person-centered approach, it would be both appropriate to current realities and consistent with the historical trend of Rogers' thinking regarding 'organismic experience' to base a psychology for these applications on evolutionary biology.

Perhaps something along the lines of 'evolutionary psychology' (Cosmides, Tooby & Barkow, 1992) might be a promising starting point for developing this psychology. Thus, it would assume there is a universal human nature, not as expressed through various cultures but, at the level of evolved psychological mechanisms which are adaptations brought about by hundreds of millions of years of natural selection. Also, it would assume that our present human body and brain—and therefore, mind—adapted to the way of life of Pleistocene hunter-gatherers over some two million years.

The social adaptations also evolved over millions of years of nomadic life but may no longer be suited for the social conditions that began only a few thousand years ago and are now changing at a mind-boggling pace. There has not been enough time for evolution to work its wonders on our minds in this short time. The few thousand years since the outset of agriculture and the beginning of 'modern' culture is less than 1% of evolutionary time.

Although our explanations to the contrary may be inventive, we may continue to be governed by certain, perhaps harmless (though at times destructive), adaptations from this substantial history. To enter in trance in order to learn from spirits of the dead, to envision directions for a desperate people, or go to war, may be a mere step away from painting the face and throwing oneself into a frenzy for a football match. Firelight dances in the middle of the forest and sideline theater at the Silverdome may both be the result of the same adaptation. Motorcycle gangs and high society, in choosing their uniforms, may both be motivated by the same impulse. 'Movements,' religious, popular, or whatever may be seen as attempts to incentivize the group to 'centralize,' 'intensify the will,' in order to 'move on.'

A psychology based on evolutionary biology would provide understanding for such phenomena. Also, it may integrate the mysterious placebo effect. Considering the millions of years of biological evolution within the atmosphere, its air, electromagnetic and gravitational forces, it would probably have explanations for these effects on human consciousness. Likewise, place may be influential by virtue of built-in preferences adapted over evolutionary time. Other exceptional states of consciousness may also be seen as evolutionary adaptations, perhaps to sense what was beyond the senses. Modules of mind were apparently developed to deal with special situations. Understanding them might help us to use our minds more effectively in our present realities.[1] Effect of group might be the result of evolutionary adaptations that provide the group with what it needs. Thus, individuals are 'moved' by the group to provide leadership, humor, sober reflection, daring, whatever is indicated for the group's effectivity at the moment. Contagion also might have served to mobilize the group for facing severe crises such as famine or war.

Finally, individual 'psychological mechanisms' also fit conveniently into this orientation. 'Material denied to awareness,' 'defenses,' and so forth (Rogers, 1959), may be seen to have developed to deal with the necessities of survival in the hunter-gatherer existence. For example, 'denial' may have been very useful for a people who had to cooperate for survival, had to move on quickly and had little opportunity to deal with personal differences or with living in a way that was 'truly satisfying.' (See Nesse & Lloyd, 1992, for discussion of this aspect.)

These speculations suggest powerful explanations for why, at the same time we are convincing ourselves to the contrary, there are forces over which we seem to have no control; for why tribal adaptations appropriate for thousands of years ago persist in marginal ways; for why we may be different people, while believing we are but one.

Nevertheless, we should not be overly impressed with these speculations. We should take time to test these perspectives, to investigate, to reflect, to learn. A point of view such as this may offer powerful explanations for large blocks of phenomena. However, history suggests that the more powerful a theory is, the more care that must be taken in its use. Remember the epidemics, not only in psychology, sociology and anthropology, but also in art and literature that followed Freud's powerful psychological explanations. Mercifully, most of the more ridiculous have now been retired. Nevertheless, the tendency doubtless still exists.[2]

Yes-Sense

Client-centered therapy was founded on Kurt Goldstein's (1939) hypothesis of 'the drive of self-actualization.' Rogers (1951) stated it this way: 'The organism has one basic tendency and striving—to actualize, maintain, and enhance the experiencing organism.' Client-centered therapy selected the person's subjective world as most fruitful for exploration, recognizing that 'human beings, by changing the inner attitudes of their minds, can change the outer aspects of their lives.' Although William James had long since contributed this impulse, it may be as valid today as then. Client-centered therapy learned to trust this inner world, to listen to oneself and believe in one's own thoughts and feelings, watching 'that gleam of light which flashes across his mind from within, more than the lustre of the firmament of bards and sages.' Ralph Waldo Emerson had previously uttered these words, but they are still worthy of noting. The person-centered approach contributed to a practice of psychotherapy whereby theory was left at the entrance to the consulting room, where only sincerity, a spirit of discovery and creativity were invited to enter; only constructive change was expected to exit. Although Otto Rank had established this practice earlier, it is no less timely now. Fredrick Allen and others had also opened the consulting room to the public by publishing transcripts of their therapy sessions. However, such openness in search of learning was embraced and promoted by Rogers. Client-centered therapy also promoted forthrightness, transparency, equality between people; it promoted self-sufficiency, tolerance of differences, that people should be helped to help themselves and a belief in a better future. Such values were part of North American culture, but so was client-centered therapy.

Although its innovations may not have always been totally original and some have not stood the test of time, client-centered therapy has been effective. Although many of its intentions may not be attainable through psychotherapy alone,[3] they may continue to be applied through the person-centered approach: helping people to know themselves, to become more of what they are capable of becoming, to participate in the perfection of humanity.

His perhaps overly materialistic perspective led Rogers to overlook hidden dimensions, dreams, subtle effects of environment, in brief, a large and important part of human existence. On the other hand, he did not become a victim of speculation or of false mysticism. Although he seemed oblivious to subtle and important details of the environment, he promoted a recognition of its theoretical importance. Although he did not know how to articulate the philosophy of phenomenology, to capture the beauty that Merleau-Ponty and others could effortlessly describe, what he offered people was more valuable than what he was, contrary to what many think.

To express the phenomenon in which Rogers participated as a therapist, he was fond of quoting an observation of Lao Tse. The Chinese sage wrote, 'It is as though he listened and such listening as this enfolds us in a silence in which at last we begin to hear what we are meant to do' (Buber, 1957).

'The more deeply I hear the meanings of this person,' Rogers (1980) said about clients in his therapy practice:

> the more there is that happens. Almost always, when a person realizes he has been deeply heard, his eyes moisten. I think in some real sense he is weeping for joy. It is as though he were saying, 'Thank God, somebody heard me. Someone knows what it is like to be me.' In such moments I have had the fantasy of a prisoner in a dungeon, tapping out day after day a Morse code message, 'Does anybody hear me? Is anybody there?' And finally one day he hears some faint tappings which spell out, 'Yes.' (p. 10)

Rogers was successful in developing a practice of effective psychotherapy. He was able to achieve such results in his personal efforts. He was, 'capable of being in uncertainties, mysteries, doubts, without any irritable reaching after fact and reason.' He was sincere. He believed that he could help and that to do so was the most important thing in the world at the moment. He even shut out the rest of the world to concentrate fully in the task.[4]

Rogers had a genuine respect for the best in persons and turned the purest in himself toward that part of the other, to accomplish something of lasting value that neither could do alone. He based his approach on appealing to the side of the person which he says he found, 'positive, forward moving, constructive, realistic, trustworthy' (Rogers, 1957c).

In his best work, he put aside dogma, self-interest, unsubstantiated beliefs, prejudices, to let reality 'show itself in itself,' to help people with the preliminaries to becoming human—that is, to be free from greed, anger, selfishness, to have a sense of humor, curiosity and openness to discovery. He asked what each of us should ask, 'Who am I?' 'Where did I come from?' 'Where am I going?' 'What am I doing here?' He allowed the minds of participants to contribute their unique brilliance. Like every artist, he unwittingly grasped the moment and the linear piece-by-piece construction of personal reality, while, at the same time, appreciating the all-at-once, 'what is universally true.' Thus, he bypassed 'the particularities of consciousness, the limitations and imprecisions of the senses,' to arrive at 'some principled truth of the matter.'

In his book, *On Becoming a Person* (1961a) he used the word 'isness' for what he was procuring in his work. 'Is' comes from the Indo-European root *es* (meaning, it is, it is true). From this, came *es-mi* in Germanic and *eam* in Old English, am. Old English also produced *sil*, meaning it is so, *sim* in Portugues, *yes* in English (Thomas, 1992). Thus, the simple, 'yes,' affirms also both truth and being. Ultimately, perhaps the most significant expression of his approach and the most important thing Rogers had to say was simply, 'yes,' to personal improvement, to real learning, to constructive behavior, to nourishing relationships, to honest thinking, to life.

Notes

1. The cognitive psychologist Merlin Donald (1991) has observed that, 'very recent changes in the organization of the human mind are just as fundamental as those that took place in earlier evolutionary transitions. Yet they are mediated by a new memory technology, rather than by genetically encoded changes in the brain. The effects of such technological changes are similar in kind to earlier biological changes, inasmuch as they can produce alterations in the architecture of human memory.'

Since only an evolution of consciousness appears to be a path through which we may possibly deal with our current realities as a species, this news seems encouraging.

2. The complete understanding of consciousness may never yield to 'biological' explanation. Although reductionistic efforts have been made to provide strictly biological explanation, they have yet to be convincing. (See Crick, 1994, for the latest and most uncompromising.) Whatever, we should keep an open mind.

3. There are some who, because of this, advocate its abolishment. For example, Masson (1990) declares, 'I believe that therapy is never honest … Most [therapists] want to be helpful; but what they actually can offer, under the best circumstances, falls far short of what they would like to offer. It cannot be otherwise. Because therapy depends for its existence on the postulate that the truth of a person's life can be uncovered in therapy, the therapist is rarely willing or able to acknowledge that the profession itself is fraudulent.' However, if the therapist admits that one may not become complete nor may the 'truth of one's life be uncovered' (how could it be in such a narrow enterprise?), psychotherapy may be useful for less ambitious

pursuits, including, perhaps in best cases, preparation for uncovering the truth of one's life.

4. Perhaps he had an inate ability. Jerome Frank (1978), himself a great figure in bringing sense to the field of psychotherapy, thinks there may be born healers. 'People like Milton Erickson,' he suggests, 'who had an uncanny ability to see what people need and give it to them. Maybe it's healing energy. Carl Rogers is another one.'

References

Abramowitz, SI & Abramowitz, CV (1974) Psychological mindedness and benefit from insight oriented group therapy. *Archives of General Psychiatry, 30,* 610–15.

Abramowitz, CV, Abramowitz, SI, Roback, HB & Jackson, C (1974) Differential effectiveness of directive and non-directive group therapies as a function of client internal-external control. *Journal of Consulting and Clinical Psychology, 42,* 849–53.

Allaway, J (1971) Explaining Human Behavior in Groups. Institute for Cultural Research monograph. Kent, England.

Allport, FH (1924) *Social Psychology.* Boston: Houghton Mifflin.

Asch, SE (1951) Effects of group pressure upon the modification and distortion of judgements. In H Guetzkon (Ed) *Groups, Leadership and Men.* Pittsburgh, PA: Carnegie Press.

Asch, SE (1952) *Social Psychology.* New York: Prentice Hall.

Asch, SE (1955) Opinions and social pressure. *Scientific American.* November.

Asch, SE (1956) Studies of independence and conformity: A minority of one against a unanimous majority. *Psychological Monographs, 70* (9), 416.

Aspy, D & Roebuck, F (1983) Researching person-centered issues in education. In CR Rogers *Freedom to Learn for the 80s.* Columbus, OH: Charles Merrill.

Barker, RG (1968) *Ecological Psychology.* Palo Alto, CA: Stanford University Press.

Barkow JH, Cosmides, L & Tooby, J (1992) *The Adapted Mind.* New York: Oxford University Press.

Barnlund, DC (1957) A comparative study of individual, majority, and group judgement. Northwestern University.

Barrett-Lennard, GT (1977) Toward a person-centered theory of community. Unpublished manuscript. West Perth, Australia: Centre for Studies in Human Relations.

Barrett-Lennard, GT (1979) The client-centered system unfolding. In FJ Turner (Ed) *Social Work Treatment: Interlocking theoretical approaches* (2nd edn). New York: Free Press.

Barton, A (1971) The client-centered transformation: A phenomenological approach. In A Giorgi, WF Fischer & RV Eckartsberg (Eds) *Duquesne Studies in Phenomenological Psychology, 1.* Pittsburgh, PA: Duquesne University Press.

Bateson, N (1966) Familiarization, group discussion and risk taking. *Journal of Experimental Social Psychology, 2,* 119–29.

Bebout, J (1976) Basic encounter groups: Their nature, method and brief history. In H Mullen & M Rosenbaum (Eds) *Group Psychotherapy: Theory and practice.* New York: Macmillan.

Bebout, J & Gordon, B (1972) The value of encounter. In LN Solomon & B Berzon (Eds) *New Perspectives on Encounter Groups.* San Francisco, CA: Jossey-Bass.

Becker, E (1969) *Angel in Armour.* New York: George Brasiller.

Becker, E (1973) *The Denial of Death.* New York: Free Press.

Bednar, RL & Kaul, TJ (1978) Experiential group research: Current perspectives. In SL Garfield & AE Bergin (Eds) *Handbook of Psychotherapy and Behavior Change: An empirical analysis.* (2nd edn). New York: Wiley.

Beecher, HK (1955) The powerful placebo. *Journal of the Amercian Medical Associaton, 159* (17), 1602–6.

Beecher, HK (1961) Surgery as placebo. *Journal of the American Medical Association, 176* (13) 1102–7.

Belo, J (1960) *The Trance in Bali.* New York: Columbia University Press.

Benson, HK (1996) *Timeless Healing.* New York: Scribner.

Bergin. AE (1971) The evaluation of therapeutic outcomes. In AE Bergin & SL Garfield (Eds) *Handbook of Psychotherapy and Behavior Change.* New York: Wiley.

Bergin, AE (1991) Values and religious issues in psychotherapy and mental health. *American Psychologist, 46* (4), 394–403.

Bettleheim, B (1989) *Freud's Vienna & Other Essays.* New York: Alfred Knopf.

Bion, WR (1959) *Experiences in Groups.* New York: Basic Books.

Bixenstine, VE & Abascal, J (1985) Another test of the effect of group composition on member behavior change. *Journal of Clinical Psychology, 41* (5), 620–8.

Blackwell, B, Bloomfield, SS, & Buncher, CR (1972) Demonstration to medical students of placebo responses and non-drug factors. *The Lancet* (June 10), 1279–82.

Borges, JL (1932) *Discusión.* Buenos Aires: M. Gleizer.

Bortoft, H (1986) Goethe's scientific consciousness. *Institute for Cultural Research Monographs Series 22.* Tunbridge Wells: ICR.

Botkin, JW, Elmandjra, M & Malitza, M (1979) *No Limits to Learning: Bridging the human gap.* Oxford: Pergamon Press.

Bowen, M, Miller, M, Rogers, CR & Wood, JK (1979) Learnings in large groups: Their implications for the future. *Education, 100* (2), 108–16.

Bowers, JW & Osborn, MM (1966) Attitudinal effects of selected types of concluding metaphors in persuasive speech. *Speech Monographs, 33,* 147–55.

Bozarth, JD (1982) The person-centered approach in the large community group. In G Gazda (Ed) *Innovations in Group Psychotherapy* (2nd edn). Springfield, IL: Charles Thomas.

Bozarth, JD (1984) Beyond reflection: Emergent modes of empathy. In RF Levant & JM Shlien (Eds) *Client-Centered Therapy and the Person-Centered Approach: New directions in theory, research and practice.* New York: Praeger.

Bozarth, JD & Temaner, B (1984) Client-centered/person-centered psychology: A statement of understanding. Paper presented at the Second International Forum on the Person-Centered Approach.

Bradford, CP, Gibb, JR & Benne, KD (1964) *T-Group Theory and Laboratory Method.* New York: Wiley.

Bramly, S (1977) *Macumba.* New York: Avon Books.

Brandt, JM & Fromkin, HL (1974) A survey of unique attitudes among college students: A state of pluralistic ignorance. Unpublished manuscript. Purdue University. Cited in

CR Snyder & HL Fromkin (1980) *Uniqueness: The human pursuit of difference.* New York: Plenum Press.
Braudel, F (1994) *A History of Civilization.* New York: Viking Penguin.
Brodeur, P (1989) The hazards of electro-magnetic fields. *The New Yorker,* June 12–26 (3 parts).
Brodley, BT (1994) Some observations of Carl Rogers' behavior in therapy interviews. *The Person-Centered Journal, 1* (2), 37–47.
Brown, DE (1991) *Human Universals.* New York: McGraw-Hill.
Buber, M (1957) *Pointing the Way.* New York: Harper & Row.
Buber, M (1958) *I and Thou.* New York: Scribner & Sons.
Buber, M (1960) Dialogue between Martin Buber and Carl Rogers. *Psychologia, 3,* 208–21.
Buber, M (1966) *The Knowledge of Man: A philosophy of the interhuman.* (MS Friedman Ed). New York: Harper & Row.
Buber, M (1979) *Das dialogische prinzip.* Heidelberg: Verlog Lombert Schneider.
Burton, A (1974) *Operational Theories of Personality.* New York: Brunner/Mazel.
Caine, TM, Wijesinghe, B & Wood, RR (1973) Personality and psychiatric treatment expectancies. *British Journal of Psychiatry, 122,* 87–8.
Camargo, C (1961) *Kardecismo e Umbanda: Uma interpretação sociológica.* São Paulo: Livraria Pioneira Editóra.
Campbell, DT (1965) Ethnocentric and other altruistic motives. In D Levine (Ed) *Nebraska Symposium on Motivation, 13.* Lincoln, NE: University of Nebraska Press.
Campbell, DT (1972) On the genetics of altruism and the counter-hedonic components in human nature. *Journal of Social Issues, 28,* 21–37.
Caplan, G (1981) *An Approach to Community Mental Health.* New York: Gruner Stratton.
Chodorkhoff, B (1954) Self-perception, perceptual defense and adjustment. *Journal of Abnormal Social Psychology, 49* (4), 508–12.
Cialdini, RB (1985) *Influence.* Glenview, IL: Scott Foresman.
Cleveland, CC (1916) *The Great Revival in the West.* Chicago: University of Chicago Press.
Cobb, LA, Thomas, GI & Dillard, OH et al. (1959) Evolution of internal mammary artery ligation by double-blind technique. *New England Journal of Medicine, 260,* 1115–8.
Cohen, R (1972) Altruism: Human, cultural, or what? *Journal of Social Sciences, 28* (3), 39–57.
Colson, DB & Horwitz, L (1983) Research in group psychotherapy. In HI Kaplan & BJ Sadock (Eds) *Comprehensive Group Psychotherapy.* London: Williams & Wilkins. (The authors cite a study by D Malan at the Tavistock Clinic.)
Combs, A (1986) Person-centered assumptions for counselor education. *Person-Centered Review,* l 72–82.
Corcoran, K (1983) Emotional separation and empathy. *Journal of Clinical Psychology, 39* (5), 667–71.
Corey, G (1985) *Theory and Practice of Group Counseling.* Monterey, CA: Brooks/Cole.
Cosmides, L, Tooby, J & Barkow, JH (1992) Evolutionary psychology and conceptual integration. In JH Barkow, L Cosmides & J Tooby (Eds) *The Adapted Mind.* New York: Oxford University Press.
Coulson, W (1970) Major contribution: Inside a basic encounter group. *The Counseling Psychologist, 2* (2), 1–34.
Coulson, WR (1972) *Groups, Gimmicks and Instant Gurus.* New York: Harper & Row.

Coulson, WR (1980) Personal communication. 29 June.

Coulson, WR (1989) Founder of 'value free' education says he owes parents an apology. *AFA Journal.* (April 20–1).

Crews, C & Melnick, J (1976) The use of initial and delayed structure in facilitating group development. *Journal of Counseling Psychotherapy, 23,* 92–8.

Crick, F (1994) *The Astonishing Hypothesis: The scientific search for the soul.* New York: Charles Scribner's Sons.

Davenport, FM (1968) *Primitive Traits in Religious Revivals.* New York: Negro Universities Press.

De Quincey, T (1890) *The Collected Writings.* D Mason (Ed) *Vol. xi.* Edinburgh: Adam & Charles Black.

Deren, M (1970) *The Divine Horsemen.* New York: Chelsea House.

Diekman, AJ (1990) *The Wrong Way Home.* Boston, MA: Beacon Press.

Dies, RR (1973) Group therapist self-disclosure: An evaluation by clients. *Journal of Counseling Psychology, 20* (4), 344–8.

Dimond, EG, Kittle, CF & Crockett, JE (1958) Evaluation of internal mammary artery ligation and sham procedure in angina pectoris. *Circulation, 18,* 712–3.

Dimond, EG et al. (1960) Comparison of internal mammary artery ligation and sham operation for angina pectoris. *American Journal of Cardiology, 5,* 484–6.

Dittes, JE (1957) Galvanic skin response as a measure of patient's reaction to therapist's permissiveness. *Journal of Abnormal Social Psychology, 55,* 295–303.

Donald, M (1991) *Origins of the Modern Mind.* Cambridge, MA: Harvard University Press.

Doob, LW (Ed)(1970) *Resolving Conflict in Africa: The Fermeda workshop.* New Haven, CT: Yale University Press.

Doob, LW & Foltz, WJ (1973) The Belfast workshop. *Journal of Conflict Resolution, 17,* 489–512.

Doob, LW, Foltz, WJ & Stevens, RB (1970) Appraisal by three Americans. In LW Doob (Ed) *Resolving Conflict in Africa: The Fermeda workshop.* New Haven, CT: Yale University Press.

Doxsey, J (1986) Simpósio: Vivência acadêmica. O enfoque centrado na pessoa. Instituto de Psicologia, Universidade de São Paulo.

Drinka, GF (1984) *The Birth Neurosis.* New York: Simon & Schuster.

Dubos, R (1981) *Celebrating Life.* New York: McGraw-Hill.

Duerr, HP (1985) *Dream Time.* Oxford: Blackwell.

Dunbar, RIM (1991) Co-evolution of cognitive capacity, group size and social grooming in primates: Implications for the evolution of language. Reported in Donald (1991).

Dutton, D & Aron, A (1974) Some evidence for heightened sexual attraction under conditions of high anxiety. *Journal of Personality and Social Psychology, 30,* 510–17.

Ehrlich, PR (1986) *The Machinery of Nature.* New York: Simon & Schuster.

Ellis, J & Zimring, F (1994) Two therapists and a client. *The Person-Centered Review, 1* (2), 79–92.

Emerson, RW (1929) *'Self-Reliance': The complete writings of Ralph Waldo Emerson.* New York: WH Wise & Co.

Engelhardt, DM & Margolis, R, (1967) Drug identity, doctor conviction and outcome. *Neuropsychopharmacology, 5,* 543–4.

Farson, R (1974) Carl Rogers, quiet revolutionary. *Education, 95* (2) 201.

Favazza, AR & Faheem, AD (1983) Indiginous healing groups. In HI Kaplan & BJ Sadock (Eds) *Comprehensive Group Psychotherapy*. London: Williams & Wilkins.
Ferenczi, S & Rank, O (1956) *The Development of Psychoanalysis*. New York: Dover (Original wwork published 1924).
Festinger, L (1957) *A Theory of Cognitive Dissonance*. Palo Alto, CA: Stanford University Press.
Fiedler, FE (1950) A comparison of therapeutic relationships in psychoanalytic, nondirective and Adlerian therapy. *Journal of Consulting Psychology, 14*, 436–45.
Field, MJ (1960) *Search for Security*. Evanston, IL: Northwestern University Press.
Frank, JD (1961) *Persuasion and Healing: A comparative study of psychotherapy*. Baltimore, MD: Johns Hopkins Press.
Frank, JD (1973) *Persuasion and Healing: A comparative study of psychotherapy* (revised edn). Baltimore, MD: Johns Hopkins University Press.
Frank, JD (1978) *Psychotherapy and the Human Predicament: A psycho-social approach*. New York: Scholken Books.
Freud, S (1959) *Group Psychology and the Analysis of the Ego*. New York: WW Norton.
Friedman, M (1984) *Contemporary Psychology: Revealing and obscuring the human*. Pittsburgh, PA: Duquesne University Press.
Fromm, E (1956) *The Art of Loving*. New York: Harper & Row.
Galeano, E (1985) *Memory of Fire: Genesis*. New York: Pantheon Books.
Gallagher, JJ (1953) The problem of escaping clients in non-directive counseling. In W Snyder (Ed) *Group Report of a Program of Research in Psychotherapy* (pp. 23–38). Psychotherapy Research Group, Pennsylvania State University.
Gardner, H (1985) *Frames of Mind: The theory of multiple intelligences*. New York: Basic Books.
Gazda, G (1982) Group psychotherapy and group counseling: Definition and heritage. In G Gazda (Ed) *Basic Approaches to Group Psychotherapy and Group Counseling* (pp. 5–36). Springfield, IL: Charles Thomas.
Gazzinaga, MS (1985) *The Social Brain*. New York: Basic Books.
Geertz, C (1983) *Local Knowledge: Further essays in interpretive anthropology*. New York: Basic Books.
Gendlin, ET (1961) Experiencing: A variable in the process of therapeutic change. *American Journal of Psychology, 15*, 233–45.
Gendlin, ET (1978) *Focusing*. New York: Everest House.
Gendlin, ET, Beebe, J, Cassens, J, Klien, M & Oberlander, M (1968) Focusing ability in psychotherapy, personality and creativity. In JM Shlien (Ed) *Research in Psychotherapy, 3*. Washington, DC: American Psychological Association.
Giesekus, U & Mente, A (1986) Client empathic understanding in client-centered therapy. *Person-Centered Review, 1* (2), 163–71.
Gladstein, GA (1983) Understanding empathy: Integrating counseling, developmental and social psychology perspectives. *Journal of Counseling Psychology, 30* (4), 467–82.
Goldstein, K (1939) *The Organism*. New York: American Book Co.
Gomes-Schwartz, B (1978) Effective ingredients in psychotherapy: Prediction of outcome from process variables. *Journal of Consulting and Clinical Psychology, 46* (5), 1023–35.
Goodman, FD, Henney, JH & Pressel, E (1974) *Trance, Healing and Hallucination*. New York: Wiley.

Gordon, T (1951) Group-centered leadership and administration. In CR Rogers *Client-Centered Therapy* (pp. 320–83). New York: Houghton Mifflin.

Gordon, T & Cartwright, D (1954) The effect of psychotherapy upon certain attitudes toward others. In CR Rogers & RF Dymond (Eds) *Psychotherapy and Personality Change* (pp. 167–95). Chicago, IL: University of Chicago Press.

Gransberg, G, Steinbring, J & Hamer, J (1977) New magic for old: TV in Cree culture. *Journal of Communication* (Autumn).

Greene, JT (1969) Altruistic behavior in the albino rat. *Psychonomic Medicine, 14* (1), 47–8.

Grotjahn, M (1978) A walk with Michael Foulkes. In LR Wolberg, ML Aronson & AR Wolberg (Eds) *Group Therapy 1978: An overview* (pp. 6–8). New York: Intercontinental Medical Book Corp.

Hall, ET (1959) *The Silent Language.* New York: Doubleday.

Hall, ET (1966) *The Hidden Dimension.* New York: Doubleday.

Hamilton, E (1930) *The Greek Way.* New York: WW Norton.

Haney, C, Banks, C & Zimbardo, PG (1973) Interpersonal dynamics in a simulated prison. *International Journal of Criminology and Penology, 1,* 69–97.

Hefferline, RF, Keenan, B & Harford, RA (1959) Escape and avoidance conditioning in human subjects without their observation of the response. *Science, 130,* 1338–9.

Heidegger, M (1962) *Being and Time.* New York: Harper & Row.

Heppner, PP, Rogers, ME & Lee, LA (1984) Carl Rogers: Reflection on his life. *Journal of Counseling and Development, 63,* 14–20.

Heron, W (1957) The pathology of boredom. *Scientific American, 196,* 52–6.

Hilgard, E (1977) *Divided Consciousness: Multiple controls in human thought and action.* New York: Wiley.

Hirst, W, Neisser, U & Spelke, E (1978) Divided attention. *Human Nature, 1,* 54–61.

James, W (1890) *The Principles of Psychology.* New York: Henry Holt.

James, W (1896) *Exceptional Mental States: The Lowell lectures.* E Taylor (Ed) Amherst, MA: University of Massachusetts Press.

James, W (1907) *Pragmatism.* Cambridge, MA: Harvard University Press.

James, W. (1929) *The Varieties of Religious Experience.* New York: Modern Library.

James, W (1948) *Essays on Pragmatism.* New York: Hasner.

Jankowiak, WR & Fischer, EF (1992) A cross-cultural perspective of romantic love. *Ethnology, 31,* 148–55.

Jaynes, J (1976) *The Origin of Consciousness in the Breakdown of the Bicameral Mind.* New York: Houghton Mifflin.

Jilek, WG (1974) *Salish Indian Mental Health and Culture Change.* Toronto: Holt, Rinehart & Winston.

Jones, EE, Cumming, JD & Horowitz, MJ (1988) Another look at the non-specific hypothesis of therapeutic effectiveness. *Journal of Consulting and Clinical Psychology, 56* (1) 48–55.

Jourard, S (1971) *The Transparent Self.* Princeton, NJ: Van Nostrand Reinhold.

Kakar, S (1978) *The Inner World: A psychoanalytic study of childhood and society in India.* Dehli: Oxford University Press.

Kamiya, J (1981) Symposium on healing. Los Angeles, March 21.

Karasu, T et al. (1984) *The Psychological Therapies.* Washington DC: American Psychiatric Press.

Katz, J (1968) *No Time for Youth.* San Francisco, CA: Jossey-Bass.

Keats, J (1899) *The Complete Poetical Works of Keats.* Boston, MA: Houghton Mifflin.

Kelley, HH & Thibaut, JW (1968) Group problem solving. In GR Lindzey & AE Aronsen (Eds) *The Handbook of Social Psychology* (2nd edn). Reading, MA: Addison Wesley.

Kilmann, PR, Albert, BM & Sotile, WM (1975) The relationship between locus of control, structure of therapy and outcome. *Journal of Consulting and Clinical Psychology, 43,* 588.

Kirschenbaum, H (1979) *On Becoming Carl Rogers.* New York: Delacorte Press.

Kirtner, WL (1955) Success and failure in client-centered therapy as a function of personality variables. Unpublished Masters thesis. University of Chicago.

Kirtner, WL & Cartwright, DS (1958) Success and failure in client-centered therapy as a function of client personality variables. *Journal of Consulting Psychology, 22* (4), 259–64.

Klein, RH (1983) Group treatment approaches. In M Hersen, AE Kazdin & AS Bellack (Eds) *The Clinical Psychology Handbook* (pp. 593–610). New York: Pergamon Press.

Kluckhohn, C (1949) *Mirror of Man.* New York: Whittlesay House. Reprinted 1963.

Knowles, JB & Lucas, CJ (1960) Experimental studies of the placebo response. *Journal of Mental Science, 106,* 231.

Koch, S (1959) *Psychology: A study of a science.* New York: McGraw-Hill.

Koch, S (1970) An implicit image of man. In LN Solomon & B Berzon (Eds) *New Perspectives on Encounter Groups.* San Francisco, CA: Jossey-Bass.

Koestler, A (1978) *Janus: A summing up.* New York: Random House.

Kohut, H (1978) *The Search for Self (Vols 1 & 2).* New York: International Universities Press.

Kohut, H (1985) *Self Psychology and the Humanities.* New York: WW Norton.

Konner, M (1985) Transcendental medication. *The Sciences,* May/June.

Korn, JH, Davis, R & Davis, SF (1991) Historians' and chairpersons' judgments of eminence among psychologists. *American Psychologist, 46,* (7), 789–92.

Kreuger, AP & Reed, EJ (1976) Biological impact of small air ions. *Science, 193,* 1209–13.

Lago, C (1994) Personal communication. 17 May.

Land, D (1987) Round table discussion. *Person-Centered Review, 1* (3), 340–1.

Langer, E, Blank, A & Chanowitz, B (1978) The mindlessness of ostensibly thoughtful action: The role of 'placebic' information in interpersonal interaction. *Journal of Personality and Social Psychology, 36,* 635–42.

Latané, B & Darley, JM (1968) *The Unresponsive Bystander: Why doesn't he help?* New York: Appleton-Crofts.

Lazarus, AA (1982) Multimodal group therapy. In G Gazda (Ed) *Basic Approaches to Group Psychotherapy and Group Counseling.* (pp. 213–34). Springfield, IL: Charles Thomas.

LeBon, G (1895) *The Crowd.* New York: Viking Press

Levi-Strauss, C (1967) The sorcerer and his magic. In *Structural Anthropology* (Ch 9). New York: Doubleday.

Levins, R & Lewontin, R (1985) *The Dialectical Biologist.* Cambridge, MA: Harvard University Press.

Lewin, K (1951) *Field Theory in Social Science.* New York: Harper & Bros.

Lieberman, EJ (1985) *Acts of Will: The life and work of Otto Rank.* New York: The Free Press.

Lieberman, MA (1975) Joyless facts? A response to Schutz, Smith and Rowan. *Journal of Humanistic Psychology, 15* (2), 49–54.

Lieberman, MA, Yalom, ID & Miles, MB (1973) *Encounter Groups: First facts.* New York: Basic Books.
Lifton, RJ (1961) *Thought Reform and the Psychology of Totalism.* New York: WW Norton.
Lifton, RJ (1983) *The Life of the Self.* NewYork: Harper Basic Books.
Lipkin, S (1954) Client feelings and attitudes in relation to the outcome of client-centered therapy. *Psychological Monographs, 68* (1), No. 372.
Luborsky, L, Crits-Christoph, P, McLellan, AT, Woody, G, Piper, W, Liberman, B, Imber, S & Pilkonis, P (1986) Do therapists vary much in their success? *American Journal of Orthopsychiatry, 56* (4), 501–12.
Ludwig, A (1964) An historical survey of the early roots of Mesmerism. *International Journal of Clinical Experimental Hypnosis, 12,* 205–17.
Ludwig, AM (1966) The formal characteristics of therapeutic insight. *American Journal of Psychotherapy, 20,* 305–18.
Ludwig, AM (1967) The trance. *Comprehensive Psychiatry, 8* (1), 13.
Ludwig, AM & Levine, J (1965) Alterations in consciousness produced by hypnosis. *The Journal of Nervous and Mental Disease, 140,* 146–53.
Lynch, JJ (1985) *The Language of the Heart.* New York: Basic Books.
MacMillan, M & Lago, C (1993) Large groups: Critical reflections and some concerns. *The Person-Centered Approach and Cross-Cultural Communication, 2.*
Mahrer, AR (1988) Discovery-oriented psychotherapy research: Rationale, aims and methods. *American Psychologist, 43* (9), 694–702.
Maliver, BL (1973) *The Encounter Game.* New York: Stein & Day.
Marin, P (1985) Body politic. *Harper's.* (December).
Maslow, A (1965) *Eupsychian Management.* Homewood, IL: Irwin Inc & Dorsey Press.
Masson, J (1990) *Against Therapy.* London: Fontana/HarperCollins.
May, R (1982) The problem of evil: An open letter to Carl Rogers. *Journal of Humanistic Psychology* (Summer, 1982).
McCardel, J & Murray, EJ (1974) Non-specific factors in weekend encounter groups. *Journal of Consulting and Clinical Psychology, 42,* 337–45.
McDougall, W (1928) *The Group Mind.* New York: Putnam.
McGaw, WH (producer) (1971) *Because That's My Way* (documentary film). WQED-TV Pittsburgh, PA.
McIlduff, E & Coghlan, D (1989) Process and facilitation in a cross-cultural communication workshop. *Person-Centered Review, 4* (1), 77–98.
McIlduff, E & Coghlan, D (1993) The cross-cultural communication workshops in Europe: Reflections and review. *The Person-Centered Approach and Cross-Cultural Communication, 2.*
McNair, DM, Lorr, M & Callahan, DM (1963) Patient and therapist influences on quitting psychotherapy. *Journal of Consulting Psychology, 27,* 10–17.
Meador, E (1971) Individual process in a basic encounter group. *Journal of Consulting Psychology, 18,* 70.
Meerlo, JAM (1956) *The Rape of the Mind.* NewYork: World Publishing Co.
Mente, A & Spittler, HD (1980) *Erlebnisorientierte Gruppen Psychotherapy.* Paderborn: Junfermann.
Merleau-Ponty, M (1964) *Sense and Non-sense.* Evanston, IL: Northwestern University Press.
Midgley, M (1978) *Beast and Man.* New York: Cornell University Press.

Midgley, M (1991) *Can't We Make Moral Judgements?* New York: St. Martin's Press.
Milgram, S (1974) *Obedience to Authority.* New York: Harper & Row.
Milosz, C (1985) *The Captive Mind.* New York: Penguin.
Mintz, I (1977) A note on the addictive personality: Addiction to placebos. *American Journal of Psychiatry, 134* (3), 327.
Mintz, NL (1956) Effects of esthetic surroundings: II. Prolonged and repeated experiences of a 'beautiful' and an 'ugly' room. *The Journal of Psychology, 41,* 459–66.
Mitchell, KM, Bozarth, JD & Krauft, CC (1977) A reappraisal of the therapeutic effectiveness of accurate empathy, non-possessive warmth, and genuineness. In A Gurman & A Razin (Eds) *The Therapist's Contribution to Effective Psychotherapy: An empirical assessment.* New York: Pergamon Press.
Monteiro dos Santos, A (1985) *Momentos Magicos: A natureza do processo energetico humano.* Brasilia.
Moos, RH & MacIntosh, S (1970) Multivariate study of the patient–therapist system: A replication and extension. *Journal of Consulting and Clinical Psychology, 35,* 298–307.
Moreno, JL(1966) *The International Handbook of Group Psychotherapy.* New York: Philosophical Library.
Morris, D (1994) *The Human Animal.* London: BBC Books.
Morris, D & Marsh, P (1988) *Tribes.* Salt Lake City, UT: Peregrine Smith.
Nesse, RM & Lloyd, AT (1992) The evolution of psychodynamic mechanisms. In JH Barkow, L Cosmides & J Tooby (Eds) *The Adapted Mind.* New York: Oxford University Press.
Newby, E (1986) *A Book of Traveller's Tales.* London: Picador.
Newton, JW & Mann, L (1980) Crowd size as a factor in the persuasion process. *Journal of Personality and Social Psychology, 39* (5), 874–83.
Nin, A (1966) *Diary (3 vols) 1931–1944.* G Stuhlmann (Ed). New York: Harcourt Brace Javonovich.
O'Conner, R (1982) The only problem in the universe. *The Atlantic Monthly,* May, 84–90.
Okumu, J (1970) A participant's comment. In LW Doob (Ed) *Resolving Conflict in Africa: The Fermeda experiment.* New Haven, CT: Yale University Press.
Orne, MT (1962) On the social psychology of the psychological experiment. *American Psychologist, 17,* 776–83.
Ornstein, R (1986) *Multimind.* New York: Houghton Mifflin.
Ornstein, R & Sobel, D (1987) *The Healing Brain.* New York: Simon & Schuster.
Park, LC & Covi, L (1965) Nonblind placebo trial. *Archives of General Psychiatry, 12,* April, 336–45.
Parloff, MB & Dies, RR (1977) Group psychotherapy outcome research 1966–1975. *International Journal of Group Psychotherapy, 27,* 281–319.
Peres, H (1947) An investigation of nondirective group therapy. *Journal of Consulting Psychology, 11* (4), 159–172.
Perry, JW (1976) *Roots of Renewal in Myth and Madness.* San Francisco, CA: Jossey-Bass.
Pinker, S (1994) *The Language Instinct.* New York: William Morrow.
Pinney, EL (1978) The beginning of group psychotherapy: Joseph Henry Pratt MD and the Reverend Dr. Elwood Worcester. *International Journal of Group Psychotherapy, 28,* 109–14.
Porter, L (1986) International tension-reduction through the person-centered approach: An interview with Larry Solomon. *OD Practitioner, 18* (3), 1–7.

Quadros, AM (1979) Um estudo teorico do conceito compreensão empatica nos obras de Carl Rogers. Unpublished Masters thesis. Pontifícia Universidade Católica de São Paulo.

Quinn, RD (1953) Psychotherapist's expressions as an index to the quality of early therapeutic relationships established by representatives of the non-directive, Adlerian, and psychoanalytic schools. In OH Mowrer (Ed) *Psychotherapy Theory and Research*. New York: Ronald Press.

Rank, O (1966) 'Yale lecture.' *Journal of the Otto Rank Association, 1,* 12–25.

Rank, O (1989) *Art and Artist: Creative urge and personality development.* New York: Norton. (Original work published 1932.)

Raskin, N (1986) Group psychotherapy II. *Person-Centered Review, 1* (4), 389–408.

Ravencroft, K (1965) Voodoo possession: A natural experiment in hypnosis. *The Journal of Clinical and Experimental Hypnosis, 13* (3), 157–82.

Razran, G (1938) Music, art and conditioned response. *Psychological Bulletin, 35,* 532.

Rennie, DL (1988) A model of the client's experience of psychotherapy. The International Conference on Client-Centered and Experiential Therapy. University of Leuven. September.

Ribeiro, R (1956) Possessão: Problema de etnospsicologia. *Boletim do Instituto Joaquim Nabuco, 5,* 5–44.

Rogers, CR (1937) The clinical psychologist's approach to personality problems. *The Family, 18,* 233–43.

Rogers, CR (1939) *The Clinical Treatment of the Problem Child.* Boston, MA: Houghton Mifflin.

Rogers, CR (1942) *Counseling and Psychotherapy: Newer concepts in practice.* Boston, MA: Houghton Mifflin.

Rogers, CR (1946) Significant aspects of client-centered therapy. *The American Psychologist, 1* (10), 415–22.

Rogers, CR (1947) Some observations on the organisation of personality. *The American Psychologist, 2* (9), 358–68.

Rogers, CR (1949) The attitude and orientation of the counselor in client-centered therapy. *Journal of Consulting Psychology, 13,* 82–94.

Rogers, CR (1951) *Client-Centered Therapy: Its current practice, implications, and theory.* Boston, MA: Houghton Mifflin.

Rogers, CR (1955) Persons or science? A philosophical question. *The American Psychologist, 10* (7), 267–78.

Rogers, CR (1957a) Dialogue between Martin Buber and Carl Rogers. Ann Arbor. University of Michigan. April 18.

Rogers, CR (1957b) The necessary and sufficient conditions for therapeutic personality change. *Journal of Consulting Psychology, 21* (2), 95–103.

Rogers, CR (1957c) A note on the 'nature of man.' *Journal of Counseling Psychology, 4* (3),199–203.

Rogers, CR (1959) A theory of therapy, personality, and interpersonal relationships, as developed in the client-centered framework. In S Koch (Ed) *Psychology: A study of a science. Vol 3: Formulations of the person and the social context* (pp. 184–256). New York: McGraw-Hill.

Rogers, CR (1961a) *On Becoming a Person: A therapist's view of psychotherapy.* Boston, MA: Houghton Mifflin.

Rogers, CR (1961b) The place of the person in the new world of the behavioral sciences. *Personnel and Guidance Journal, 39*, 442–51.

Rogers, CR (1961c) The process equation of psychotherapy. *American Journal of Psychotherapy, 15* (1), 27–45.

Rogers, CR (1963) The concept of the fully functioning person. *Psychotherapy: Theory, research and practice, 1* (1), 17–26.

Rogers, CR (1968) Interpersonal relationships: USA 2000. *Journal of Applied Behavioral Science, 4* (3), 265–80.

Rogers, CR (1969) *Freedom to Learn: A view of what education might become.* Columbus, OH: Charles E Merrill.

Rogers, CR (1970a) Foreword. In JT Hart & TM Tomlinson (Eds) *New Directions in Client-Centered Therapy* (pp. 3–22). Boston, MA: Houghton & Mifflin.

Rogers, CR (1970b) *On Encounter Groups.* New York: Harper & Row.

Rogers, CR (1972) Foreword. In LN Solomon & B Berzon (Eds) *New Perspectives on Encounter Groups.* San Francisco, CA: Jossey-Bass.

Rogers, CR (1973) My philosophy on interpersonal relationships and how it grew. Address to the Association for Humanistic Psychology, Honolulu, September.

Rogers, CR (1974) Remarks on the future of client-centered therapy. In DA Wexler & LN Rice (Eds) *Innovations in Client-Centered Therapy* (pp. 7–13). New York: Wiley.

Rogers, CR (1977) *On Personal Power: Inner strength and its revolutionary impact.* New York: Delacorte Press.

Rogers, CR (1980) *A Way of Being.* Boston, MA: Houghton Mifflin.

Rogers, CR (1981) Notes on Rollo May. *Perspectives, 2* (1), 16.

Rogers, CR (1983) *Freedom to Learn for the 80s.* Columbus, OH: Charles E Merrill.

Rogers, CR (1984) Building a person-centered approach to international disputes: A step in the practice of peace. Unpublished manuscript. (Proposal for what would become the Rust Workshop.) Center for Studies of the Person. La Jolla, California.

Rogers, CR (1986a) A comment from Carl Rogers. *Person-Centered Review, 1* (1), 3–5.

Rogers, CR (1986b) The dilemmas of a South African white. *Person-Centered Review, 1* (1), 15–35.

Rogers, CR (1986c) The Rust workshop: A personal overview. *The Journal of Humanistic Psychology, 26* (3), 23–45.

Rogers, CR (1986d) Journal of South African trip. Unpublished manuscript.

Rogers, CR (1986e) A client-centered/person-centered approach to therapy. In IL Kutush & A Wolf (Eds) *Psychotherapists' Casebook: Theory and technique in the practice of modern times.* San Francisco, CA: Jossey-Bass.

Rogers, CR (1987) Client-centered? Person-centered? *Person-Centered Review, 2* (1), 11–13.

Rogers, CR, Gendlin, ET, Kiesler, DJ, & Truax, C (1967) *The Therapeutic Relationship and its Impact: A study of psychotherapy with schizophrenics.* Madison, WI: University of Wisconsin Press.

Rogers, CR & Rosenberg, RL (1977) *A Pessoa como Centro.* São Paulo: Editora Pedagógica e Universitária.

Rogers, CR & Ryback, D (1984) One alternative to nuclear planetary suicide. *The Counseling Psychologist, 12* (2), 3–12. And in RF Levant & JM Shlien (Eds). *Client-Centered Therapy and the Person-Centered Approach: New directions in theory, research and practice* (pp. 400–22). New York: Praeger.

Rogers, CR, Wood, JK, Nelson, A, Fuchs, NR & Meador, BD (1986) An experiment in self-determined fees. *Estudos de psicologia, 3* (1 e 2), 5–22.

Rogers, CR, Wood, JK, O'Hara, MM & Lisboa da Fonseca, AH (1983) *Em Busca de Vida.* São Paulo: Summus Editorial.

Rose, AL (1986) *Reality on the Cutting Room Floor: Highlights of undocumented encounters from a prizewinning documentary.* Hermosa Beach, CA: Psychological Ecosystems.

Rosenberg, R (1977) Some notes on the intensive group in an evolutionary context. Unpublished paper. Instituto de Psicologia, Universidade de São Paulo.

Rosenthal, NE, Sack, DA, Gillin, JC et al (1984) Seasonal affective disorder: A description of the syndrome and preliminary findings with light therapy. *Archives of General Psychiatry, 41,* 72–80.

Rowan, J (1975) Encounter group research: No joy? *Journal of Humanistic Psychology, 15* (2), 19–28.

Russell, B (1917) Individual liberty and public control. *Atlantic Magazine.*

Russell, B (1950) *Unpopular Essays.* New York: Simon & Schuster.

Ryan, VL & Gizynski, MN (1971) Behavior therapy in retrospect: Patients' feelings about their behavior therapies. *Journal of Consulting and Clinical Psychology, 37* (1), 1–9.

Sabo, S (1975) Narcissism and social disorder. *The Yale Review, 44* (4), 527–43.

Sachs, JS (1983) Negative factors in brief psychotherapy: An empirical assessment. *Journal of Consulting and Clinical Psychology, 51* (4), 557–64.

Sargant, W (1957) *Battle for the Mind.* New York: Doubleday.

Schein, EH, Schneider, I & Baker, CH (1961) *Coercive Persuasion.* New York: WW Norton.

Schutz, W (1975) Not encounter and certainly not facts. *Journal of Humanistic Psychology, 15* (2), 7–18.

Sechrest, LB & Barger, B (1961) Verbal participation and perceived benefit from group psychotherapy. *International Journal of Group Psychotherapy, 11,* 49–59.

Seeman, J (1954) Counselor judgments of therapeutic process and outcome. In CR Rogers & RF Dymond (Eds) *Psychotherapy and Personality Change.* Chicago, IL: University of Chicago Press.

Sennett, AK (1980) *Authority.* New York: Vintage Books. [Citing Hegel (1827) *The Phenomenology of the Spirit* (p. 127).]

Shah, I (1987) *Darkest England.* London: The Octagon Press.

Shah, I (1988) *The Natives are Restless.* London: The Octagon Press.

Shapiro, AK (1971) Placebo effects in medicine, psychotherapy, and psychoanalysis. In AE Bergin & SL Garfield *Handbook of Psychotherapy and Behavior Change* (pp. 439–73). New York: Wiley.

Sheldrake, R (1981) *A New Science of Life: The hypothesis of formative causation.* Los Angeles, CA: JP Tarcher.

Sheldrake, R (1988) *The Presence of the Past.* New York: Times Books.

Sherif, M & Sherif, CW (1969) *Social Psychology.* New York: Harper & Row.

Shor, R (1959) Hypnosis and the concept of the generalized reality orientation. *American Journal of Psychotherapy, 13,* 582–602.

Singer, JL (1976) *The Inner World of Daydreaming.* New York: Harper & Row.

Slack, S (1985) Reflections on a workshop with Carl Rogers. *Journal of Humanistic Psychology, 25* (2), 35–42.

Sloane, RB, Staples, FR, Cristol, AH, Yorkston, NJ & Whipple, K (1975) *Psychotherapy versus Behavior Therapy.* Cambridge, MA: Harvard University Press.

Smith, A, Bassin, A & Froehlich, A (1960) Changes in attitudes and degree of verbal participation in group therapy with adult offenders. *Journal of Consulting Psychology, 3,* 247–9.
Smith, D (1982) Trends in counseling and psychotherapy. *American Psychologist, 37* (7), 802–9.
Smith, LP (1934) *All Trivia.* New York: Ticknor & Fields.
Smith, ML, Glass, GV & Miller, TI (1980) *The Benefits of Psychotherapy.* Baltimore, MD: The Johns Hopkins University Press.
Snyder, CR & Fromkin, HL (1980) *Uniqueness: The human pursuit of difference.* New York: Plenum Press. [Citing a study by Weir, 1971.]
Stainbrook, E (1952) Some characteristics of the psychopathology of schizophrenic behavior in Bahian society. *American Journal of Psychiatry, 109,* 330–4.
Steinhelber, J, Patterson, V, Cliffe, K & LeGoullon, M (1984) An investigation of some relationships between psychotherapy supervision and patient change. *Journal of Clinical Psychology, 40* (6), 1346.
Stoler, N (1963) Client likeability: A variable in the study of psychotherapy. *Journal of Consulting Psychology, 27* (2), 175–8.
Strupp, HH (1983) Psychoanalytic psychotherapy. In M Hersen, AE Kazdin & AS Bellack (Eds) *The Clinical Psychology Handbook* (pp. 471–87). New York: Pergamon Press.
Strupp, HH (1986) The non-specific hypothesis of therapeutic effectiveness: A current assessment. *American Journal of Orthopsychiatry, 56* (4), 513–20.
Stubbs, J (1992) Individual experiencing in person-centered community workshops: A cross-cultural study. Unpublished doctoral dissertation. University of Georgia.
Taft, J (1933) *The Dynamics of Therapy in a Controlled Relationship.* New York: MacMillan.
Taft, J (1958) *Otto Rank.* NewYork: The Julian Press.
Tart, CT (1969) *Altered States of Consciousness.* New York: Wiley.
Tausch, R (1983a) Empirical examination of the theory of helpful relationships and processes in person-centered therapies. In J Helm & AE Bergin (Eds) *Therapeutic Behavior Modifications.* Selected papers from the 12th International Congress of Psychology. Berlin: YEB Deutscher Verlag Wissenschaften.
Tausch, R (1983b) Corroboration from Germany. In CR Rogers (Ed) *Freedom to Learn for the 80s.* Columbus, OH: Charles E Merrill.
Thomas, L (1992) *Et Cetera, Et Cetera.* Boston, MA: Little Brown.
Thoreau, HD (1929) *Walden.* New York: Macmillan.
Tomlinson, TM & Hart, JT (1962) A validation study of the process scale. *Journal of Consulting Psychology, 26* (1), 74–8.
Trotter, W (1915) *Instincts of the Herd in Peace and War.* New York: Macmillan.
Truax, CB (1966) Therapist empathy, warmth and genuineness and patient personality change in group psychotherapy: A comparison between interaction unit measures, time sample measures, patient perception measures. *Journal of Clinical Psychology, 22,* 225–9.
Truax, CB, Carkhuff, RR & Kodman, F (1965) Relationships between therapist-offered conditions and patient change in group psychotherapy. *Journal of Clinical Psychology, 21,* 327–9.
Tyler, DB (1955) Psychological changes during experimental sleep deprivation. *Diseases of the Nervous System, 16* (10), 293.

Ulrich, RS (1984) View through a window may influence recovery from surgery. *Science, 224*, 420–1.

Van Belle, HA (1980) *Basic Intent and Therapeutic Approach of Carl R. Rogers.* Toronto: Wedge Publishing Foundation.

Verplanck, WS (1955) The control of the content of conversation: Reinforcement of statements of opinion. *Journal of Abnormal and Social Psychology, 51,* 668–76.

Walker, A, Rablen, RA & Rogers, CR (1960) Development of a scale to measure process change in psychotherapy. *Journal of Clinical Psychology, 1,* 79–85.

Wallach, MA, Kogan, N & Bem, DJ (1962) Group influence on individual risk taking. *Journal of Abnormal Social Psychology, 65,* 75–86.

Wallach, MS & Strupp, HH (1960) Psychotherapist's clinical judgements and attitudes towards patients. *Journal of Consulting Psychology, 24,* 316–23.

Watson, N (1984) The empirical status of Rogers' hypotheses of the necessary and sufficient conditions for effective psychotherapy. In RF Levant & JM Shlien (Eds) *Client-Centered Therapy and the Person-Centered Approach: New directions in theory, research and practice.* New York: Praeger.

Watson, D & Burlingame, AW (1960) *Therapy through Horticulture.* New York: Macmillan.

Watzlawick, P, Beavin, J & Jackson, D (1967) *Pragmatics of Human Communication: A study of interaction patterns, pathologies and paradoxes.* New York: WW Norton.

Weil, S (1951) *Waiting for God.* New York: Harper.

Weiss, E (1970) *Sigmund Freud as a Consultant.* New York: Intercontinental Medical Book Corp.

White, RW (1941) A preface to the theory of hypnotism. *Journal of Abnormal and Social Psychology, 36,* 477–505.

Whyte, MK (1974) *Small Groups and Political Rituals in China.* Berkeley, CA: University of California Press.

Williams, D (1971) The Sokodae: A West African dance. *Institute for Cultural Research Monograph.* Kent, England.

Wilson, DS & Sober, E (1994) Reintroducing group selection to the human behavioral sciences. *Behavioral and Brain Sciences, 17,* 585–654.

Wolf, S (1950) Effects of suggestion and conditioning on the action of chemical agents in human subjects: The pharmacology of placebo. *Journal of Clinical Investigation, 29,* 100–9.

Wood, CJ (1989) Challenging the assumptions underlying the use of participatory decision-making strategies: A longitudinal case study. *Small Group Behavior, 20* (4), 428–48.

Wood, JK (1984) Communities for learning: A person-centered approach to large groups. In R Levant & J Shlien (Eds) *Client-Centered Therapy and the Person-Centered Approach: New directions in theory, research and practice.* NewYork: Praeger.

Wood, JK (1985) Efeito do grupo. *Estudos de Psicologia, 2* (2 e 3), 5–19.

Wood, JK (1988) *Menschliches dasein als miteinandersein: Gruppenarbeit nach personenzentrierten ansatzen.* Koln: Edition Humanistische Psychologie.

Yalom, ID (1985) *The Theory and Practice of Group Psychotherapy.* New York: Basic Books.

Zimmerman, C & Bauer, RA (1956) The effect of audience upon what is remembered. *Public Opinion Quarterly, 20,* 238–48.

Index

Abascal, J 64, 262
Abramowitz, CV 64, 161, 261
Abramowitz, SI 64, 161, 261
acceptance see 'unconditional positive regard'
actualizing/actualization
    self- 13, 27, 227, 257
    tendency 41, 201, 225–6
Adler, A 24, 35
aggression 42, 96–7, 243
Albert, BM 161, 267
Allport, FH 92, 261
altruism 227
ambiance 72, 77
American Psychology Association 26
anonymity 96
Arias, O, President of Nicaragua vi
Aron, A 67, 264
Asch, SE 135, 171, 178, 261
Aspy, D 157, 261
Association of American Psychotherapists 26
autonomy 191, 193, 195
authenticity see 'congruence'

Bach flower remedies 15
Bandeira, E 21
Banks, C 178, 266
Barger, B 50, 272
Barker, RG 179, 242, 261
Barkow, JH 241, 261
Barrett-Lennard, GT 131, 261
Barton, A 200, 226, 233, 249, 261
Bassin, A 50, 272
Bateson, N 42, 261
Bauer, RA 171, 274
Bebout, J 49, 65, 261, 262
Becker, E 224, 262
Bednar, RL 39, 40, 262

Beecher, HK 199, 240, 262
behaviorism 24, 38
beliefs 209
Belo, J 181, 195, 262
Benson, HK 262
Bergin, AE 67, 202, 248, 262
Bettleheim, B 17, 262
Bion, WR 37, 67, 102, 262
Bixenstine, VE 64, 262
Blackwell, B 238, 262
Blake, W 174
Blank, A 175, 252, 267
Bloomfield, SS 238, 262
Boas, F 197
Borges, JL 79, 90, 262
Bortoft, H 75, 262
Botkin, JW 119, 163, 164, 165, 262
Bowen, M 70, 141, 262
Bowers, JW 120, 262
Bown, O 21
Bozarth, JD 15, 49, 131, 233, 246, 262, 269
Bradford, CP 37, 110, 262
Bramly, S 181, 182, 185, 262
Brandt, JM 179, 262
Braudel, F 205, 263
Brodeur, P 244, 263
Brodley, BT 18, 263
Brown, DE 221, 263
Brown, O 21
Buber, M ix, 35, 57, 67, 76, 137, 226, 258, 263
Burlingame, AW 244, 274
Burton, A 263

Caine, TM 64, 263
Camargo, C 181, 263
Campbell, DT 227, 263

275

capitalism 85
Caplan, G 138, 263
Carkhuff, RR 53, 273
Cartwright, DS 21, 40, 228, 232, 266, 267
Center for Cross-Cultural Communication 210, 217
Center for Studies of the Person 70, 86, 211
Central American Challenge 79
China, trip to 252
Chodorkhoff, B 43, 263
Cialdini, RB 67, 175, 252, 263
Cleveland, CC 156, 181, 263
client-centered
    approach 13
    framework 68
    therapy 14, 16, 18, 25, 27, 33, 53, 67, 93, 201
Cobb, LA 199, 263
coercion 129
Coghlan, D 38, 204, 206, 208, 209, 210, 211, 212, 213, 214, 216, 268
cognitive
    integration 145, 146
    psychology 76, 175
Cohen, R 227, 263
colonization 85
Colson, DB 59, 263
Combs, A 21, 244, 263
consciousness
    models of 32
    state of 243, 246, 256
        altered see 'trance state'
conditioning 24
confidentiality 215
conflict 80, 81, 84
    resolution 82, 84–7
conflicting values 119
confrontation 58
congruence 33, 53, 55, 68, 69, 195, 253
Corcoran, K 245, 263
Corey, G 49, 263
Cosmides, L 241, 256, 261, 263
Coulson, W 50, 66, 69, 129, 204, 263
Covi, L 239, 269
creative/creativity 153
    acts 153
    state 188

Crews, C 49, 264
Crick, F 252, 259, 264
crises 111, 114, 117
    surmounting 14
criticisms (of the PCA) ix
cross-cultural
    communication 130, 132, 204, 207
        workshops vi, 133, 204, 208, 211, 217
    culture 207
cultural
    context 202
    evolution 200
    setting 199
    values 85
culture 122, 148, 196, 200, 204, 224
    of PCA 204
    of the group 132
Cumming, JD 266

Darley, JM 175, 267
Davenport, FM 186, 264
Davis, R 34, 267
De Quincey, T ix, 196, 264
delusions 176
democracy 85, 107, 108, 211, 215
Deren, M 179, 181, 183, 185, 186, 192, 218, 264
Devonshire, Charles vi
Diekman, AJ 195, 264
Dies, RR 39, 54, 67, 264, 269
Dimond, EG 199, 264
Distinguished Professional Contribution Award 26
Distinguished Scientific Contribution Award 26, 31
Dittes, JE 231, 264
Donald, M 259, 264
Doob, LW 85, 88, 89, 171, 173, 190, 249, 264
Doxsey, J 56, 264
Drinka, GF 233, 264
Dubos, R 194, 264
Duerr, HP 175, 264
Dunbar, RIM 135, 264
Dutton, D 67, 264

economics 16
education 68, 79, 80, 157
Ehrlich, PR 227, 264
Einstein, A ix
Ellis, J 18, 264
Elmandjra, M 119, 163, 164, 165, 262
Emerson, RW 199, 257, 264
empathy 20, 33, 52, 63, 68–9, 93, 195, 220, 245–6, 248, 253
    idiosyncratic 49, 246
encounter iv, 40, 43, 61, 65
    Brazilian x
    groups 42, 46, 54, 79, 87, 92, 211
    total 42
Encuentro Latinoamericano de la Orientacion Centrada en la Persona (IV) 141
Engelhardt, DM 244, 264
environment 72, 148, 241
Estância Jatobá xii
evil 223, 224
evolutionary biology 76, 175, 256
expectations 143, 169
expression of personal feelings by the therapist 53

facilitator 48, 49, 51, 54, 60, 93, 207, 212, 215
    congruence 69
    overkill 82
    participant 48
    poor 65
Faheem, AD 182, 265
Farson, R 231, 264
Favazza, AR 182, 265
Ferenczi, S 24, 35, 265
Fermeda experiment 85, 88, 189
Festinger, L 176, 265
Fiedler, FE 198, 265
Field, MJ 177, 179, 185, 247, 265
Finn, Huckleberry 80
First International Forum of the Person-Centered Approach x
focusing 219–20
Foltz, WJ 89, 171, 249, 264
formative causation 138, 139
Frank, JD 65, 134, 179, 259, 265

free will 223
Freud, S ix, 34, 35, 36, 37, 68, 78, 255, 265
Friedman, M 41, 44, 265
Fromkin, HL 179, 262, 273
Fromm, E 40, 192, 265
fully functioning person 162

Galeano, E 94, 265
Gallagher, JJ 240, 265
Gardner, H 159, 265
Gazda, G 35, 36, 265
Gazzinaga, MS 159, 265
Geertz, C 245, 265
Gendlin, ET 14, 21, 219, 265, 271
genuineness 220
Gibb, JR 37, 91, 110, 262
Giesekus, U 63, 265
Gizynski, MN 230, 272
Gladstein, GA 245, 265
Glass, GV 233, 234, 273
Gloria 203
Goldstein, K 188, 257, 265
Gomes-Schwartz, B 232, 234, 265
Goodman, FD 179, 181, 195, 266
Gordon, B 65, 262
Gordon, T 21, 38, 40, 228, 266
Gransberg, G 184, 266
Greene, JT 204, 266
Grotjahn, M 37, 266
group/s viii, 42, 70, 141
    composition 64
    conductor 37
    culture 47
    dangerous 64
    dynamics 37
    facilitators 75
    family 39
    large v, vii, 90
        encounter 144
        workshops 90–1, 176, 211
    learning 122
    pressure 37
    process xi
    rules, implicit 47
    small 35, 39, 110, 145, 212
    structure 105
    tape recording of 99

therapy 38, 42, 65–6
wisdom 82
work xi

Hall, ET 215, 266
hallucinations 176
Hamilton, E 121, 266
Haney, C 178, 266
Hart, JT 232, 273
hazing 44
healing 184, 187
Hefferline, RF 179, 236, 266
Heidegger, M 254, 266
Henney, JH 195, 266
Heppner, PP 248, 266
Heron, W 179, 266
Hilgard, E 181, 237, 266
Hirst, W 195, 266
Hogan, R 21
Horwitz, L 59, 263
human
    nature 223, 256
        universal 256
    relationship 26
humility 192
Humphrey, G 23
Hungarian television 215
hypnosis 176, 181

individual/ism 100, 102, 226
innovation 21
innovative
    group learning 166
    learning 117, 163, 164
Institute for Child Guidance, New York 24
intercultural
    communication 205
    understanding 148
interpersonal
    fusion 192
    relations 146
intimacy 51
intuition 25, 107
    particpatory 107
'isness' 259

Jaguariúna group xi
James, W ix, 18, 35, 45, 56, 141, 182, 198, 237, 241, 247, 253, 255, 257, 266
jargon 209
Jaynes, J 177, 266
Jilek, WG 181, 266
job
    bank 73
    clinic 75
Jourard, S 41, 266
Jung, CG v, 78, 113

Kakar, S 137, 266
Kamiya, J 230, 266
Katz, J 267
Kaul, TJ 39, 40, 262
Keats, J 267
Keenan, B 179, 266
Kelley, HH 103, 267
Kierkegaard, S 137
Kilmann, PR 64, 161, 267
Kirschenbaum, H 80, 114, 197, 198, 224, 267
Kirtner, WL 232, 241, 267
Klein, RH 42, 267
Kluckhohn, C 199, 267
Koch, S 33, 44, 109, 195, 267
Koestler, A 195, 267
Kogan, N 42, 274
Kohut, H 245, 267
Korn, JH 34, 267
Khayyám, O 105, 169

La Jolla
    PCA Group ix
    Program 91, 211, 213
Lago, C 207, 212, 267, 268
Laing, RD iv
Land, D 14, 267
Langer, E 175, 252, 267
language 208
Lao Tse 258
Latané, B 175, 267
Lazarus, AA 37, 267
learning about learning 157
LeBon, G 101, 180, 195, 267

Levi-Strauss, C 197, 267
Levine, J 180, 268
Levins, R 225, 267
Lewin, K 37, 267
Lewontin, R 225, 267
Lieberman, EJ 24, 25, 34, 36, 78, 114, 267
Lieberman, MA 50, 57, 63, 64, 65, 267, 268
Lifton, RJ 15, 129, 179, 268
Lipkin, S 244, 268
Lloyd, AT 257, 269
locus of control 161
Lucas, CJ iii, x, xi, 267
Ludwig, AM 176, 177, 179, 180, 247, 268
Lynch, JJ 93, 230, 249, 268

Machado Assumpçao, Lucila iii, x, xi, 122, 156
Machado de Assis, JM 122
MacIntosh, S 63, 233, 269
MacMillan, M 207, 268
Mahrer, AR 142, 268
Maliver, BL 45, 268
manipulation 134
Mann, L 96, 269
Margolis, R 244, 264
Marin, P 43, 268
Marsh, P 218, 269
Maslow, A 21, 188, 268
Masson, J 259, 268
May, R 223, 224, 225, 252, 268
McCardel, J 50, 268
McDougall, W 101, 102, 139, 180, 268
McGaw, WH 54, 87, 268
McIlduff, E 38, 204, 206, 208, 209, 210, 211, 212, 213, 214, 216, 268
McNair, DM 235, 268
Meador, E 40, 268
meaning of life 154
Meerlo, JAM 97, 193, 268
Melnick, J 49, 264
Mente, A 51, 53, 63, 67, 265, 268
Merleau-Ponty, M 59, 268
metaphors 125
microphones 70

Midgley, M 124, 203, 222, 227, 268, 269
Milgram, S 170, 203, 269
Miller, M 141, 234, 262
Mintz, I 240, 269
Mintz, NL 179, 242, 269
Mitchell, KM 233, 269
modeling 38
Monteiro dos Santos, A 14, 246, 269
Moos, RH 63, 233, 269
morality 201, 214
Moreno, JL 36, 269
Morris, D 215, 218, 269
Murray, EJ 50, 268

National Council of Social Work 19
National Training Laboratories 88, 37
Neisser, U 195, 266
Nesse, RM 257, 269
neurology 76, 176
Newton, JW 96, 269
Nin, A 25, 269
non-directivity 27, 50
nudity 42

O'Conner, R 173, 269
O'Hara, M 70
Okumu, J 189, 269
opposing values 200
organismic experience 227
original sin 15
Orne, MT 135, 269
Ornstein, R 176, 195, 237, 245, 269
Osborn, MM 120, 262

Park, LC 239, 269
Parloff, MB 39, 67, 269
Patterson, V 242, 273
Pearsall Smith, L 36, 236
Peres, H 38, 269
Perls, F 233
Perry, JW 58, 269
personal
    choice 159
    development 184
    growth 187
personality change 196
Pinker, S 221, 269

Pinney, EL 35, 52, 269
pitfalls 79
place 242, 243
placebo 238–9, 245
political correctness 85
politics 16
Porter, L 85, 86, 89, 269
power 56
Pratt, JH 35, 52
presence 248
principles
    of client-centered therapy 22, 68, 69, 71
    of psychotherapy 160
prisoners and guards experiment 178
professional role 244
psychoanalysis 24
psychodrama 122
psychological contact 33
psychologist's fallacy 56
psychotherapy
    phenomenological 254
    process equation of 31–2
purists 16

Quadros, AM 248, 270
Quesalid 197, 198
Quinn, RD 229, 270

Rablen, RA 232, 274
Raimy, V 21
Rank, O 24, 35, 257, 265, 270
rape 42
Raskin, N 67, 270
Ravencroft, K 181, 270
Razran, G 179, 243, 270
Reed, EJ 243, 267
reflecting 52, 53, 69
religion 16
Rennie, DL 241, 270
respect for the client 229
Ribeiro, R 181, 270
ritual 174, 181, 214
Roebuck, F 157, 261
Rogers, CR 13, 14, 15, 16, 18, 19, 20, 21, 22, 24, 25, 27, 31, 33, 38, 40, 44, 57, 63, 68, 69, 70, 71, 79, 80, 82, 83, 84, 85, 87, 88, 91, 94, 128, 130, 131, 135, 141, 157, 160, 172, 196, 198, 201, 211, 213, 219, 223, 224, 225, 228, 229, 231, 243, 247, 248, 252, 253, 255, 256, 258, 270, 271, 272
Rogers N iv
Rogers, ME 248, 266
Rosenberg, RL x, 58, 141, 271, 272
Rosenthal, NE 243, 272
Rowan, J 64, 272
rules 47
Rumi iii
Russell, B 239, 272
Rust, Austria vi
    Workshop 79, 87, 88
Ryan, VL 230, 272
Ryback, D 80, 224, 271

Sabo, S 129, 272
Sachs, JS 246, 272
Sargant, W 128, 177, 179, 182, 272
Sartre, J-P 20
Schein, EH 193, 272
Schutz, W 64, 272
Sechrest, LB 50, 272
Seeman, J 21, 244, 272
self 224, 235
    -actualization 13, 27, 227, 257
    -centeredness 45
Sennett, AK 98, 272
sexual encounters 42, 147
Shah, I 218, 272
Shapiro, AK 196, 239, 272
Sheldrake, R 133, 218, 272
Sherif, CW 178, 272
Sherif, M 178, 272
Shor, R 176, 247, 272
Singer, JL 176, 272
Skinner, BF 38, 223
Slack, S 63, 172, 243, 272
Sloane, RB 234, 244, 272
Smith, A 50, 272
Smith, D 26, 34, 273
Smith, LP 36, 236, 273
Smith, ML 233, 234, 273
Snyder, CR 179, 273
Snygg, D 21

Sobel, D 245, 269
space 179
Spittler, HD 51, 53, 63, 67, 268
spontaneity 54
Standal, S 21
Steinbring, J 184, 266
Steinhelber, J 242, 273
Stoler, N 244, 273
Strupp, HH 37, 233, 234, 235, 273, 274
Stubbs, J 102, 213, 273
student-centered teaching 68

T-groups 37, 110, 190
Taft, J 24, 25, 119, 273
Tai Chi Chuan 14
Taoism 15
Tausch, R 157, 228, 273
Tavistock
    Clinic 87, 94, 171
    model 88
teddy bears 16
Temaner, B 15, 262
therapeutic relationship 25, 63, 93, 230
Thibaut, JW 103, 267
Thoreau, HD 242, 273
Tomlinson, TM 232, 273
Tooby, J 256, 263
trance state 176, 180, 182–3, 185, 187, 248
trans-individuality 149
transference 230
transpersonal 133
    awareness 40, 186
    reality 151
Trotter, W 194, 273
Truax, CB 53, 273
Tyler, DB 176, 179, 273

Ulrich, RS 243, 273
uncertainty 186
unconditional
    acceptance 195
    love 14
    positive regard 33, 53, 68, 219–20, 229, 253
unemployed 73, 75, 77
unemployment counseling 75

uniqueness 226
University for Peace, Costa Rica 86

values 148, 165, 185, 200
    conflict 165
Van Belle, HA 199, 274
Verplanck, WS 171, 274
victim-of-society myth 227
von Goethe, JW ix, 13, 75, 254

Walker, A 232, 274
Wallach, MA 42, 274
Wallach, MS 233, 274
Watson, D 244, 274
Watson, G 252
Watson, N 249, 274
Weil, S 193, 274
Weiss, E 34, 274
White, RW 193, 274
Whyte, MK 65, 274
Wijesinghe, B 64, 263
Wilde, O 84
Williams, D 186, 274
wisdom of the group 82
Wolf, S 239, 274
Wolpe, J 233
Wood, CJ 103, 274
Wood, JK 91, 141, 271, 272, 274
Worcester, E 35, 52

Yalom, ID 39, 63, 64, 268, 274
'yes-sense' 257

Zen Buddhism 15
Zimmerman, C 171, 274
Zimring, F 18, 264

THE LIFE AND WORK OF CARL ROGERS

Howard Kirschenbaum

ISBN 978 1 898059 93 6
(cased) £29.00 pp. 736
ISBN 978 1 898059 98 1
(with jacket) £50.00 pp. 736

Twenty years after his death, PCCS Books celebrates the life and work of Carl Rogers with the long-awaited second edition of his biography by Howard Kirschenbaum. This completely re-written and re-titled edition includes a more detailed personal and professional history, and a full account of the last decade of Rogers' life. That decade turned out to be one of the most important periods of his career in which he developed peace work all over the world including South Africa and Northern Ireland, culminating in a Nobel Peace Prize nomination just days before his death. Until now this work has not been widely known.

The new edition adds deeper understanding of Rogers' contributions to psychology, the helping professions and society. On a personal level, access to recently revealed private papers tells us much more about Carl Rogers the man than was known to many of his closest associates. Kirschenbaum's own understanding of Carl Rogers, psychotherapy, education, and the human condition has matured over the intervening years. This much-anticipated second edition reflects a wiser and more balanced perspective of his subject. Now fully referenced, this is the life and work of Carl Rogers.

I couldn't put it down. I kept jumping from one part of the book to another and getting absorbed in the close research and the wonderful detail. I know the book took years to research, and now I can see why. Even reading the footnotes is absorbing.
Professor Dave Mearns, ex University of Strathclyde

Buy direct for free shipping (in the UK) and permanent discounts from
www.pccs-books.co.uk